The Last Descendant of Aeneas

Yale
University
Press

New Haven
& London

The
Last
Descendant
of
Aeneas

Marie Tanner

The Hapsburgs

and the

Mythic Image

of the Emperor

Frontispiece. Jorg Breu the Younger, *Aeneas at the Site of Rome*. In *Historia del Origen y Sucesión de los Reinos e Imperios desde Noe hasta Carlos V*, vol. 1, fol. 32v. of *Origen de la Nobleza*, 1547–48. Escorial, MS 28. I. 11. Patrimonio Nacional, Madrid.

Designed by James J. Johnson.
Set in Joanna Roman type by The Composing Room
of Michigan, Inc.
Printed in the United States of America by
Thomson-Shore, Inc., Dexter, Michigan.

A catalogue record for this book is available from
the British Library.

The paper in this book meets the guidelines for
permanence and durability of the Committee on
Production Guidelines for Book Longevity of the
Council on Library Resources.

10   9   8   7   6   5   4   3   2   1

Library of Congress Cataloging-in-Publication Data

Tanner, Marie, 1937–
  The last descendant of Aeneas : the Hapsburgs and
the mythic image of the emperor / Marie Tanner.
    p.   cm.
  Includes bibliographical references and index.
  ISBN 0-300-05488-2

  1. Kings and rulers—Mythology.   2. Emperors—
History.   I. Title.
JC374.T36   1992
321'.14—dc20   92-20186

For my mother, and to the memory of my father

Contents

Acknowledgments   ix
Introduction   1
Prologue   5

I   The Trojan and Argonautic Legends   11

II   Byzantium and the Christianized Roman Myth   23

III   The Frankish Roman Empire   36

IV   The Revival of Epic Narrative in the Late Middle Ages
and the Renaissance   52

V   Mythic Genealogy   67

VI   The Legend of the Last World Emperor   119

VII   Philip II of Spain   131

VIII   The Order of the Golden Fleece   146

IX   The Escorial   162

X   Fidecrucem: The Hapsburg Veneration of the
Cross   183

XI   The Hapsburg Cult of the Eucharist   207

XII   The Regnum Apollonis   223

Epilogue   249
Postscript   251
Notes   253
Select Bibliography   313
Index   323

Acknowledgments

During the research and writing of this book and in preparing its foundations, I incurred many debts that I gratefully acknowledge here. I first came into intimate contact with the myth of Rome during 1978 when I traveled to the eternal city on a grant from the American Council of Learned Societies; it became my home for the next five years. During this time, and in subsequent summers, the Biblioteca Apostolica Vaticana's inestimable resources supplied most of the references I have used here; I thank especially its prefect, Father Leonard Boyle, for facilitating access to its collections. I also thank Matthias Winner, co-director of the Biblioteca Hertziana in Rome for similar privileges, and for conversations about related material. I am grateful to the founders, directors, and staff of the libraries of the Warburg Institute, the British Library, the Escorial, the Academia Belgica, the Institute of Fine Arts, Columbia University, and the New York Public Library. The Biblioteca Hertziana in Rome, Columbia University's Seminar on the Renaissance, and the College Art Association provided forums where I could present aspects of this research in progress. During the years 1984–86 my graduate students at Queens College of the City University of New York provided a sounding board for these ideas.

In acknowledging my teachers, the oldest debts have the deepest roots, and thus I thank first Leo Steinberg, the paradigm of the scholar-teacher, who with brilliance and eloquence transmitted the concept that the artist's vocabulary is the living language of past thought; and Leonard Albert, who in explicating Joyce's writing, showed that the puzzles of multivalent meaning can be solved. Many others shared their erudition and offered encouragement; of these I thank especially Staale Sinding Larsen, whose investigation of political ideas in their interaction with theological issues charted a new approach for the field and Eve Borsook who pioneered the study of political uses of ephemeral Renaissance art. I am grateful to Paul Oscar Kristeller, John Charles Nelson, and Maristella Lorsch for their penetrating research in philosophy and literature that helped broaden my approach to Renaissance studies. I thank David Rosand for sharpening my knowledge in related areas of study and for his always encouraging voice, and Colin Eisler for the sensitivity and wit with which he has shared his erudition and his time over the years.

I am grateful to Rene Taylor for his early insights into the enigma that was Philip II and for his encouragement of the direction I have taken; and to Jonathan Brown and John Elliott for their profound knowledge of Hapsburg art and history, and for their enthusiastic response to my labors in this area. And for those whom words of thanks must reach on the wings of an angel, I acknowledge the inspiration and encouragement of Frances Yates, Peter von Blanckenhagen, and Erwin Panofsky.

I owe a great debt to the understanding and affection of my devoted friends who suggested sources, engaged in dialogue, and aided with the structuring of my arguments. Of these I single out Godelieve Denhaene, who shared her knowledge of northern Renaissance art and literature and led me to several of the images I have chosen; Michael Koortbojian, whose genial sense for clarity influenced the present format of this book; and Jack Freiberg, who in many lively conversations showed deep interest in these studies and offered keen insights on relevant subjects. In matters of organization and presentation, this book owes much to his influence.With unstinting sympathy and support, these three scholars read the manuscript, provided invaluable criticism, and helped to crystallize many of the concepts presented here. I am grateful to Paul Gwynne for reviewing the Latin selections and improving the translation of several passages, to Jane Hedges of Yale University Press for her sensitive editing of my manuscript.

My mother, Geraldine Curto, my husband, Giuseppe D'Arcangelo, my sons, Adam and Lucas Tanner, and my daughter-in-law, Celia Graham Tanner, provided affection, inspiration, and encouragement, listening with enthusiasm as I unravelled new findings, offering helpful solutions to knotty problems, and assisting with many of the myriad small details involved in producing a manuscript.

As alive and present as all the others is my debt to Rome, site of my own ancestral moorings where, during a tumultuous moment in my personal life, old pains were eased, lasting relationships were formed, and the direction of this book took shape. Blessed with natural beauty and art and the heritage of the caesars, she continues to exert her tenacious grip on the human imagination.

The Last Descendant of Aeneas

Introduction

What is all history but the praise of Rome.
—PETRARCH, *Invectiva contra eum qui*
maledixit Italie

Despite the vast literature which considers one or another of its many relevant aspects, there is no comprehensive study of the emperor's mythic image. This book describes the creation and evolution of the imperial image in the West. It proposes that the image underwent a seamless development from its origins in antiquity to its consolidation by the Hapsburgs in the sixteenth century and that the Trojan legend was the consistent authority for determining that image. Thus this book begins with the fundamental myth of Rome as it was canonized in Vergil's *Aeneid*. Beyond simply glorifying the divine origins and mission of his patron, Augustus, Vergil deeded to the literary tradition a new amalgam of Roman history and Trojan myth that structured imperial ideology for the next two millennia. In the fourth century Vergil's epic and the concept of Rome's divine mission were Christianized. In this accommodation of cultures, biblical and pagan elements were amalgamated, narrative elements moralized, and Aeneas's role appropriated by the reigning Christian emperor. This assimilation was continued in the revival of narrative epic that reached its full flowering in the Renaissance.

To account for this development, I trace key themes in Vergil's epic from antiquity through the sixteenth century, linking transformations in content to historic milestones and to the migrations of the imperial seat, and showing that in each instance these entities meet to celebrate Rome's divine destiny. While the literary texts that substantiate this line of thought are well-known monuments of western culture, they have never before been investigated with this focus.

Historical chronicles, prophecy, and visual imagery all co-hered to create an internally consistent image of the universe and of the Roman emperor's central place in its structure. Of these, mythical genealogy—the core of historical chronicles in the past—was the most important. Successive emperors of Rome—whether ancient, medieval, or Renaissance—claimed kinship with their imperial predecessors in a genealogy that had its ultimate origin in the gods. Historical as well as legendary figures were coopted into this fictive ancestry; the Christian emperors expanded this tradition by gradually interpolating biblical figures into the pagan fold. The emperor's assimilation to the gods, his pretensions to divine roots, and the absorption of the imperial cult in the state religion—carefully guarded mysteries of the imperial court that were couched in Latin and thus hidden from profane sight—are all products of this process.

The uninterrupted continuity linking the first emperor of Rome to his sixteenth-century heirs through the Trojan ancestry has never been sufficiently appreciated in prior studies. The Christian emperor's syncretistic lineage and the practice of ancestor worship in the post-antique period has been similarly overlooked. In studying imperial genealogies, my intention has been to note the Roman roots of the tradition, to indicate how this was synthesized with Gentile and Jewish divine history, and to show that the encompassing unity yields a precise and cogent picture of theocratic imagery in the Christian era.

Prophecy was the handmaiden of genealogical mythmaking in its mixture of pagan and Hebraic elements and in its importance for imperial imagery; it differed in its eschatological focus. The unwavering insistence on the emperor's Trojan ancestry dovetailed with the prophecy that the dominion of the Roman empire was conceded by God in perpetuity to the successor of Aeneas. A discussion of the elements that made for a legend of the last descendent of Aeneas, who was to yield the terrestrial rule of Rome back to Christ, its true sovereign, places the battles for the faith, the crusades to the Holy Land, and the efforts to unify the eastern and western hemispheres in a millennial context. Thus history, prophecy, and legend meet in the crafting of the imperial persona.

A correlative to literary and historical concerns is the assessment of an underlying imperial and ancestral link in the visual monuments that carved a corridor of imperial veneration in the subject realms. An awareness of this conceptual substructure affords a new way to perceive familiar works of art; it also provides insight into the revival of classical and Hebrew subject matter and the portrayal of contemporary rulers as biblical patriarchs or ancient gods. The examples cited throughout the book give but a sampling of the much broader applicability that this context affords for understanding the use of Judeo-Christian and classical themes and images, and for appreciating in a new light such diverse phenomena as the collecting of antiquities and the shaping of religious dogma. It also fosters a revised view of the means of transmission by which artists, authors, and historians became acquainted with the storehouse of imperial motifs. For although artistic interchange affected the particular syntax, there can be no doubt that the vocabulary so central to the fashioning of a royal image was controlled by the imperial courts and emanated from them. In this tradition, its heirs were thoroughly schooled from their infancy. Readers will be familiar with the names of the eminent historians and artists who developed the ancestral canon. When seen in the present context, however, these individuals assume a new identity in a dramatic view of world history as a fraternity of savants who are indivisibly linked by the hermetic knowledge of Providence's intentions.

A measure of the authority of this system of beliefs was the wide acceptance of this very same vocabulary among the rulers and would-be rulers of Europe. Even the petty princes were engaged in this foray to attain Olympus. Although the imperial court is the catalyst for its development, the emperor's vassals and contenders self-referentially borrowed and elaborated the relevant imagery. For the vassals, genealogical claims were predicated on the dependent status they bore to the imperial scion. The commission of decorative programs exalting imperial, Trojan, and biblical heroes often bore a direct relationship to the bestowal of a hereditary title or to a planned imperial visit. A discussion of this subject in the light of feudal protocol reveals the double and sometimes contradictory function that imperial themes served at the vassal courts. A brief consideration is also given to the growing imperialization of the papal office that gained impetus when the famous forgery of the Donation of Constantine purported to transfer secular rights from Constantine to the church. As this developed, the imperial vocabulary was adopted by the papacy. Both emperor and pope benefited from this interchange: for as the papacy appropriated imperial ideas, the emperor made further forays into sacred privilege.

This study culminates with the Renaissance Hapsburgs, who imbued the holiest symbols of the faith with dynastic meaning as they attempted to consolidate all priestly and secular powers in their grip. In investigating this development, I draw attention to the unexpected mystical and dynastic significances attached to the Order of the Golden Fleece, the title to Jerusalem, Columbus's discovery of the Americas, and the monarch's solar identity. These meanings were brought to the fore during the reign of Philip II, whose development of the imperial myth relates to long-standing concerns that I have addressed in prior studies. In his drive to succeed to that title, which millennia of imperial propaganda had construed as a dynastic office, Philip was armed with an impressive list of titles and dominions and an iconographical storehouse whose contents had been amassed by the Hapsburg dynasty during five generations of imperial rule. By emphasizing the mystical dimension in this unparalleled iconic legacy, Philip created a new concept of absolute monarchy that determined the dominant form of government in Europe for the next two centuries.

For a topic as broad as the imperial image, the possible choices of material are vast. The materials I chose reflect my primary goals: to restructure the unbroken continuity in the making of the imperial myth and to draw out the unifying threads in what has often seemed a palimpsest of contradictory impulses. By examining how a related body of texts and images functioned in conjunction with historical factors, it has been possible to reassemble the past as it was expressed in the entire edifice of courtly self-definition. In underscoring the consistent elements in the symbolic image of sacred kingship, this study offers an essential key for understanding the vocabulary of those who aspire to world dominion. I hope that other scholars will fill out the lines of inquiry suggested here with knowledge from their special fields.

Prologue

In 1565 news of a Moslem threat to the safety of Malta sent a wave of feverish alarm throughout Christian Europe. Immediate danger was temporarily averted by a Venetian counteroffensive that routed the troops of Suleiman the Magnificent, but a dispatch that reached Madrid in November communicated the Sultan's intentions to pit his military strength against the Spanish king in the next year.[1] Philip II (1527–1598)—son of the Holy Roman Emperor Charles V, King of Spain, Portugal, and the Two Sicilies, Regent of the Netherlands, Duke of Burgundy and Milan, titular sovereign of Jerusalem, heir to the Eastern imperial title that was conceded to Spain by Byzantium, lord of the New World, unofficial Emperor of the Indies and the first monarch ever to rule all four continents—responded to this alert by issuing detailed instructions for the construction of a royal war galley. Philip dreamed of capturing Constantinople and delivering the Holy Land with this galley at the head of the fleet; he intended it for the captaincy of his half-brother, Don Juan of Austria.[2] Resplendent with images of the Hapsburg clan's mythic history, the ship was executed according to Philip's exacting specifications and christened "Argo."[3]

The name *Argo* derives from the ancient legend of the Golden Fleece: rescued from death by a ram on whose back he fled to Colchis, the Argolid Prince Phrixus sacrificed the ram and hung its golden pelt in the temple of Jove. The Fleece remained there until it was returned to its homeland by Jason and the

Argonauts, who sailed to Colchis on the *Argo*. In antiquity both the quest and the Fleece itself carried mystical meanings. For Pindar, who set the tone for later versions of the myth, the Fleece's rescue is a pious undertaking assigned to the Argonauts, the sons of gods, who initiate the navigation of the world's oceans on the first sailing vessel. They set out on the divinely crafted *Argo* whose painted sides depict divine members of the gens and their contests in the battle against evil. The successful repatriation of the Fleece, the guarantor of the Argonauts' invincibility, earned the ship *Argo* a place among the constellations of the Southern Hemisphere.

Equally fundamental to the legend's meaning is the subplot concerning the destruction of Troy. Stopping at the seat of ancient Eastern power on their way to Colchis, the Argonauts destroyed the Trojan citadel. This first destruction of Troy initiated the chain of retaliatory events that culminated in Troy's final destruction at the hands of the Greeks. In the *Aeneid*, where he reconstructed Rome's Trojan past, Vergil recalled this sequence of events; here the first fall of Troy forms the background to the ultimate conflagration of the Phrygian city and Aeneas's flight to found a better Troy in Rome. Vergil further developed the Argonautic theme in the *Fourth Eclogue*; there the Cumaean Sibyl prophesies that when the Argonauts shall once again set sail, then a new cosmic age of prelapsarian bliss shall follow under the rule of imperial Rome, the new Troy.

By the beginning of the first century A.D. this fusion of Trojan epic and Roman history established a mythic structure and a mystical rationale for viewing the subjugation of the East and the westward transfer of universal sovereignty. The foundations for the later Christological reading of these events were laid at the end of the first century when the Argonautic recapture of the Golden Fleece was identified with Titus's destruction of the Temple of Jerusalem and the transfer of its most sacred cult objects to Rome. These Argonautic themes and the eschatological meaning they were believed to convey, survived for more than a thousand years to resurface in the medieval Troy myths. Then the Argonautic expedition became a generic metaphor for a spiritual crusade to the Holy Land.

The Argonautic myth was specifically adapted to crusading objectives when, in 1429, Philip the Good of Burgundy, a direct ancestor of Philip II, formed the Order of the Golden Fleece. Philip the Good transformed the Argonauts into militant Christian chevaliers united under his leadership for a crusade to recapture Jerusalem and the Holy Land from the Turks.

The topos received a new impetus at the end of the fifteenth century with Columbus's journeys. Columbus's expeditions, which were intended to recover the Holy Sepulchre for the Spanish Ferdinand and Isabella—Philip II's great-grandparents—retraced the Argonaut's path and found the primeval Americas in the process. His ship, too, was identified with the *Argo*.

The symbolic resonances of these two significant fifteenth-century revivals of Argonautic imagery—the Crusades to the Holy Land and Columbus's journey—accrued to the Holy Roman Emperor Charles V, heir to both the Burgundian and Spanish thrones. Argonautic imagery thereafter became central to Hapsburg imperial ideology; the emblem of the Golden Fleece was a fixed attribute in their official portraits, and indeed Charles's personal device—the Columns of Hercules, which was to become Europe's most enduring symbol in the bid for universal theocratic monarchy—was created in conjunction with his elevation to the sovereignty of the Order of the Golden Fleece in 1516. The Fleece was regarded by the Burgundian-Hapsburgs as a unique dynastic heritage. Through the destruction of the Moslem Empire and the Christianization of the Americas, they claimed to restore the universal harmony that was prophecied in Vergil's *Fourth Eclogue*.

When Charles consigned the rule of the Low Countries to Philip II and transmitted the hereditary title to Burgundy to him on 10 June 1556, the sovereignty of the Order of the Golden Fleece passed from the emperor to his son. Of the many expressions of Argonautic imagery employed by Philip's predecessors, none was as elaborate, none more illuminating than the warship that Philip II sent out on the high seas to physically and spiritually meet the Turkish threat. The ship conformed to its ancient prototype not only by name but also by recalling its ideal form. So closely was the copy intended to imitate the original, that its design and dimensions were based on the star markings of the constellation Argo.[4] Painted as was its ancient namesake, the vessel bore scenes of the Argonautic journey on its stern.[5] Here, as in all expressions of the king's ideology, the confluence of Judeo-

Christian and pagan symbolism was the keynote of the imagery, and of the dynastic heritage it celebrated.

The contemporary crusading significance of the Argonautic imagery was established by a cityscape of Constantinople that stood for the ancient site of Colchis.[6] An image of Jason's recovery of the Fleece was interspersed with personifications of the Christian virtues in whose midst stood Philip II. A series of accompanying inscriptions identified Jason's Golden Fleece with that of his Old Testament counterpart Gideon; the Argonautic travels to the East with the journeys of Magellen and Christopher Columbus;[7] the Hapsburgs with the Argonauts, and their victories against the Turks and their defense of the faith with the capture of the Golden Fleece.[8]

Completed in 1569, the galley was inspected by Philip II in May of 1570. Well pleased with its execution, Philip straightway gave orders for the forming of the Holy League,[9] an alliance that was signed on 20 May 1571 by Spain, the Papacy, and Venice, who

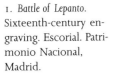

1. *Battle of Lepanto.* Sixteenth-century engraving. Escorial. Patrimonio Nacional, Madrid.

were to wage a united struggle against the Moslem threat. In the same year, the galley sailed at the head of the fleet of Christian warships into the Battle of Lepanto. The immediate impact of the Christian victory was breathtaking, for it broke the spell of Turkish supremacy in the Mediterranean. Celebrated in innumerable images throughout the Christian Empire, renderings of the Lepantian battle (fig. 1) made tangible not only the massive extent of the military forces that were pitted against each other, but the geographic importance of the battle site as the gateway to the eastern lands—Constantinople, Troy, and Jerusalem.

As an example of Philip's divine mission, and as the catalyst for a new phase in the unity of the Christian powers behind his leadership, the *Argo* symbolizes the ideology of the Hapsburgs, who distilled the imperial myth into its modern crystalline form. This book will provide an understanding of that myth, for which the painted *Argo* serves as introduction.

Chapter I *The Trojan and Argonautic Legends*

THE history of European literature begins with Homer's saga of the destruction of Troy. With the framing of the Eastern conquest, the capture of the Trojan gods, and the migration of world power westward to Greece in the *Iliad* and the *Odyssey*, Homer deeded to posterity the poetic matrix out of which Western imperial iconography was to be continuously recreated.[1] Homer charted the Italic landscape for Ulysses' return home in the *Odyssey*. This topography was re-adapted by Vergil in the *Aeneid*,[2] where he forged the canonic version of Rome's foundation myth and the enduring template for the emperors' mythic image.

In the *Aeneid* (26–19 B.C.), Vergil traced the adventures of Aeneas, the divinely descended scion of the Trojan kings. Pursuing his destiny in the aftermath of Troy's burning and the Greek subjugation of Asian sovereignty, Aeneas retraces his ancestors' steps to lead the Trojan race back to its native homeland in Italy. Led by Apollo who speaks to him through the Sibyl,[3] Aeneas is also guided by the Penates, the home gods of Priam's royal house. These gods reveal in a dream that "Italy is our abiding home; hence are Dardanus sprung and father Iasius, from whence first came our race."[4] The divine mandate to restore the ancestral *patria* is given visual emphasis in the late classical *Vatican Virgil*, where the gods approach Aeneas as he sleeps (fig. 2).[5]

Aeneas's role as city founder is only gradually revealed

2. *The Penates Appear to
Aeneas in a Dream.*
Biblioteca Apostolica
Vaticana, Rome. MS
Lat. 3225 (*Vatican Virgil*),
28r.

3. *Aeneas at Carthage.*
Biblioteca Apostolica
Vaticana, Rome. MS
Lat. 3225 (*Vatican Virgil*),
13r.

through a series of prophecies and tentative efforts (fig. 3),[6] and his mission is fully realized only when he draws the outlines of a new Trojan settlement in Latium.[7] His mother, Venus, is the first to learn of Rome's future greatness from Jove, who promises that her son will father a race of Caesars who will enjoy dominion without end and reign in perpetual peace through the conquest of impious Fury:

this thy son . . . shall wage a great war in Italy, shall crush proud nations, and for his people shall set up laws and city walls. . . . But the lad Ascanius, now surnamed Iulus . . . shall shift his throne [and] build the walls of Alba Longa . . . until Ilia . . . shall bear to Mars her twin offspring. . . . Then Romulus . . . shall take up the line, and found the walls of Mars, and call the people Romans after his own name. For these I set neither bounds nor periods of empire; dominion without end have I bestowed. . . . then shall come a day when the house of Assaracus shall bring into bondage . . . Argos. . . . From this noble line shall be born the Trojan Caesar, a Julius, name descended from great Iulus. . . . He, too, shall be invoked in vows. . . . Then shall wars cease. . . . The gates of war shall be closed; within impious Fury, sitting on savage arms, his hands fast bound behind . . . shall roar in the ghastliness of blood-stained lips.[8]

Aeneas first learns of his destiny when the ghost of Hector appears on the last night before Troy's fall, committing to Aeneas the household gods and sacred emblems to "take . . . to the mighty city, which . . . thou shalt at last establish."[9] Aeneas sets forth from Ilion carrying his father Anchises and the Penates.[10] In myriad monuments dispersed throughout the empire, the figure of Aeneas carrying an image of the gods was a continuous reminder of the pious foundations on which Rome was built (fig. 4).

Landing at Delos, where he pays homage at Apollo's temple, the god encourages Aeneas's pursuit: "Long suffering sons of Dardanus, the land which bore you first from your parent stock shall welcome you back to her fruitful bosom. Seek out your ancient mother. There the house of Aeneas shall lord it over all lands, even his children's children and their race that shall be born of them."[11] This fate is fleshed out for him when, led by the Sibyl to Apollo, Aeneas is granted the Golden Bough that permits his transport to the Elysian Fields. Here he views a pageant of his dead ancestors "Teucer's olden line, . . . Ilus and Assaracus and

Dardanus, Troy's founder."[12] These are followed by Aeneas's un-
born progeny who file before his eyes in a vision of Rome's future
greatness: "children of Italian stock . . . Silvius of Alban name, thy
last-born child . . . Romulus . . . the Kings of Rome and their
Republican progeny . . . Numa bearing the sacrifice . . . the Tar-
quin kings . . . the Gracchan race . . . Scipio's line, Caesar, and all
Iulus' seed . . . he, whom thou so oft hearest promised to thee,
Augustus Caesar, son of a god, who shall again set up the Golden
Age in Latium amid the fields where Saturn once reigned, and
spread his empire."[13] The vision ends with a directive for univer-
sal sovereignty as Aeneas is admonished with the immortal lines:
"parcere subiectis et debellare superbos" ("Remember thou, O
Roman, to rule the nations within thy sway . . . crown Peace with
Laws . . . spare the humbled, and tame in war the proud").[14]
Aeneas wears the badge of this destiny on his divinely fashioned
shield, which configures the battles, the peace, and the apotheosis of his Julian descendants. At its center is the image of
Augustus, bearing the Penates and ending civil war through his
triumph over Anthony at Actium: "In the center could be seen
brazen ships with Actium's battle. . . . Here Augustus Caesar, with
the great gods of the Penates, stands on the lofty stern; his joyous
brows pour forth a double flame and on his head dawns his
father's star. . . . Here Antonius with barbaric might . . . brings

4. *Aeneas with Anchises,
Ascanius, and the Palla-
dium.* Altar, late first
century A.D. Tunis,
Museo del Bardo.
Deutsches Archäo-
logisches Institut,
Rome. Neg. 61-653.

with him Egypt . . . and his Egyptian wife . . . turned to flee . . .
[and] Caesar [returned] . . . in triple triumph."[15]

Characterized by the piety ascribed to him by Homer[16]—
a trait expanded by Vergil to become the hero's standing epithet[17]—this virtue accounts for the glorious fate that the gods
assign to Aeneas. His devotion to them and to Rome's destiny
structures every substantive aspect of the narrative. In the ardent
displays of faith that are the epic's fugal counterpoint, Aeneas's
veneration of his ancestors plays a significant part. Stopping at
Actium before setting sail for Italy, Aeneas consecrates the site by
reenacting the Trojan games, an action that foreshadows the site's
importance for future Roman history.[18] In his first foray into Italy,
Aeneas stops at Sicily to initiate funeral games in honor of his
father. He sacrifices to the deceased Anchises in the presence of
the Penates and vows the dedication of a future temple to him in
Rome.[19] Allowed respite from his wanderings at last when he
reaches the banks of the Tiber and finds the omen that signals the
promised land,[20] Aeneas sacrifices to his ancestors and the gods.
This legendary history that culminates in a sacramental act was
commemorated on the Augustan *Ara Pacis*, where the veiled Aeneas performs these priestly rites in honor of the Penates, en-
shrined above in a marble temple (fig. 5).[21] Aeneas's piety towards
the gods, which he demonstrates at every step of his journey,
culminates in the promise he makes at Cumae to raise a marble
temple to Apollo.[22]

Inspired by his visions, protected by his goddess-mother,
Venus, guided by the Cumaean sibyl who prophesies for Apollo,
and armed with the ancestral gods of Priam's royal lineage, Aeneas battles to reclaim Latium, the land where the gods last ruled
on earth during the Golden Age.[23] For the ancients, the Golden
Age signified man's original state in which he lived a utopian
existence free from strife and innocent of vice.[24] Not only identified with a primordial time, the Golden Age was also located in an
ideal place, which Vergil placed under Saturn's rule in Latium.[25]
Lost in the Iron Age when the wicked love of gain corrupted
men's hearts,[26] the hope for the return of primeval bliss is restored with Aeneas's repatriation of the homeland.

Vergil ends his epic with a battle to the death for sovereignty
of Latium between Aeneas and the Greek Turnus.[27] Under the
spell of the hellish Allecto,[28] Turnus becomes the Frenzy of War

5. *Aeneas Sacrificing.*
Rome, Ara Pacis, first
century B.C. Deutsches
Archäologisches Insti-
tut, Rome. Neg. 72-648.

incarnate, but Aeneas triumphs over him in a victory preordained
by the gods. Jove weighs the destinies of the combatants on the
heavenly scales and as Turnus sinks down in death, so with him
falls the supremacy of Greece.[29] Appropriating the metaphor
with which Homer had proclaimed Achilles' victory over Hector,
Vergil readapted the scales as the instrument effecting the West's
triumph over the East to apply to Rome, the new Troy. From this
moment onward, Libra, the constellation of the scales, was
deemed the sign under which Rome was founded and the principal emblem of her imperial dominion.[30]

　　The decree issued and the death blow delivered, the gods
reward Aeneas's virtue with the promise of heavenly apotheosis.[31] The warring gods and their earthly counterparts unite
in concord;[32] East is submitted to West. Aeneas assumes the dual
roles of priest and king that every emperor will thenceforth claim
his prerogative.[33] Then, through his marriage to Lavinia, he sires a
new divine race destined to rule the universe in a new Golden
Age of peace and justice.[34]

The Argonautic Legend

In fashioning Rome's Trojan myth, Vergil interwove two Greek legends; as he had expanded on Homer so too did he expand on Pindar. This he accomplished by incorporating aspects of the Argonautic legend, a primordial account of the conquest of the East and of Troy's downfall. These events are interconnected with the quest for the Golden Fleece.[35] Unjustly condemned to death by a wicked stepmother, Prince Phrixus, the divine ancestor of the Argolids, was rescued from sacrifice by a ram on whose back he fled Thebes.[36] On arriving at Colchis, Phrixus sacrificed the ram and hung its skin, which had turned to gold, in the temple of Jove. At the moment of Phrixus's apotheosis, Jove created Aries, the heaven's first constellation, as his heavenly abode.[37] But the Fleece that was infused with Phrixus's spirit remained in captivity in Colchis until Jason and the Argonauts returned it to its homeland.[38] The deed was accomplished when Phrixus's kin Argos was divinely inspired to build the *Argo*, the world's first sailing vessel.[39]

Stopping at Troy on their way to Colchis, the Argonauts destroyed the Phrygian citadel in retaliation for King Laomedon's faithless refusal to reward Apollo and Neptune for building the city's walls.[40] Jove commemorates the Argonauts' compliance with divine will in accomplishing these deeds by creating the constellation Argo.

The capture of the Fleece and the destruction of Troy are the two Argonautic events which signal the toppling of Asia's power; thus the myth provides a preamble to the *Aeneid*. Indeed the Argonauts' return to Argos with the Fleece established the typology for Aeneas's journey to Rome with the Penates.[41] Part of an unalterable scheme for the rotation of empires that prepared the return of the gods to earth, the Argonautic destruction of Troy was providentially determined. Thus, since the razing of the Phrygian citadel distinguished the Argonauts as the first heroes to implement the supersession of empires decreed by Jove, their legend provided the prehistory to the second destruction of Troy, the exodus of Aeneas, and the founding of Rome. Vergil recalled this interaction in the *Aeneid* by referring to the city's two destructions. These references were expanded, and the rationale explained in Valerius Flaccus's Roman *Argonautica*. Here Jove reveals that both the capture of the Fleece and the rape of Helen formed part of his providential plan that Troy should be conquered by Greece, which must also fall to Rome.

> Then spake the Father [Jove]: "All these things have been established by us from of old and remain unalterable . . . for there was no stock of ours in any land when I was founding a line of kings to last throughout the ages. So then I will unfold the decrees that I made in my providence. [I myself cherished] the region that stretches down from the measureless East to the sea of virgin Helle. But now her last day is hastening on and we are leaving Asia tottering to her fall, while the Greeks now claim of me their time of prosperity. Therefore have my oak trees, the tripods and the spirits of their ancestors sent forth this band upon the sea.
>
> Nor is it the [Golden] fleece alone that is fated to rouse resentment . . . there shall soon come from Phrygian Ida a shepherd who shall bring lamentation and like rage and a rich requital to the Greeks. Thereafter am I resolved upon the end of the Danai, and shortly will take other nations into my care."[42]

The narrator informs the reader of the implicit meaning of Jove's last words:

> Twice must Troy fall victim. . . . But who now can change the destiny of Priam's kingdom? Fixed in the unstirred ages stands the night of the Dorians, the race of the Aeneadae and the glories of a better Troy.[43]

In the years immediately preceding 37 B.C.,[44] Vergil wrote the *Fourth Eclogue*, an allegorical poem that celebrates the birth of a divinely descended child whose destiny is intertwined with that of the Roman Empire.[45] The newborn "offspring of the gods, [the] mighty descendant of Jupiter"[46] sets into motion the realization of a spate of Utopian prophecies uttered by the Cumaean sibyl;[47] these will follow upon a repetition of history. Events from the Argonautic and Trojan legends serve as the necessary preliminaries to a return to prelapsarian bliss. The prophesied new Golden Age is preceded by a period of strife and the recurrence of the Trojan war; the recycling of bellicose events is set into motion by the Argonautic journey. Thus the Cumean prophesies: "A second Tiphys [the *Argo*'s helmsman] shall then arise, and a second *Argo* to carry chosen heroes; a second warfare too, shall there be, and again shall a great Achilles be sent to Troy."[48] In the new age of eternal spring that follows, Nature shall yield her produce without labor, Justice will triumph, the gods will return to earth, and Apollo will reign over a peaceful and abundant world.[49]

With Vergil's accommodation of the Trojan myth to contemporary Roman history in the *Aeneid* and the *Fourth Eclogue*, he forged an amalgam that shaped the structure of imperial ideology that would endure for the next two millennia. Thereafter the reenactment of the Argonautic quest for the Golden Fleece, the domination of the East, and the founding of a new Troy became stock portents of a divinely willed supersession of empires and a dawning of a new age of peace. At each decisive point in the transfer of sovereignty these topoi were called upon to validate the pretender's kinship in the royal blood brought to earth by Jove when he founded the line of kings to last throughout the ages.

Augustus

Augustus's victory at Actium in 31 B.C., which signalled the end of civil war and the unification of the Eastern and Western hemispheres of the empire under one sovereign, provided the catalyst for Vergil's *Aeneid*.[50] This historic battle is proleptically figured on the shield that Vulcan sculpts for Aeneas. There an image of Augustus bearing on his brow the Iulian *sidus*, the star symbolizing Caesar's deified soul, emulates his mythic ancestor by carrying the Penates which have been entrusted to him.[51] Augustus's role as custodian of the Trojan home gods was perpetuated in the coinage of the realm through juxtaposing the emperor's portrait with the image of Aeneas carrying out his sacred mission.[52] The Actian victory was celebrated at Rome by the closing of the doors of Janus, an event prophesied for Aeneas,[53] and by the dedication of a temple to Apollo on the Palatine in 28 B.C. in fulfillment of the vow made by Aeneas at Cumae.[54] In the following year he was granted the title "Augustus."

Throughout the *Aeneid*, Aeneas is the prototype for Augustus, who tracing his lineage through the Trojan bloodline to its ultimate origin in the supreme Jove,[55] assumes the divine filiation, exhibits the ancestral piety,[56] and extends the triumphs of his Trojan ancestor.[57] The epic marked the culmination of the poet's labors in praise of Augustus that had already begun in the *Fourth Eclogue*. In 20 B.C. the emperor's universal dominion was consoli-

dated with the reclamation of the Roman standards from the Parthians at the Peace of Brindisi. The symbolic importance of this reclamation is indicated on the statue of Augustus from Primaporta where, placed within a cosmic framework, it figures as the central scene of his historiated cuirass (fig. 6). At his feet a cupid astride a dolphin refers to his divine ancestry in Venus. History revealed Vergil's prescience with this event, for the *Pax Augusta* was deemed to mark the second founding of Rome and interpreted as the beginning of the new millennium of peace announced by the Cumaean sibyl in the *Fourth Eclogue*.[58] With the reclaiming of the standards, Augustus completed the chain of historic recurrences prophesied by this oracle that were to begin with the Argonautic recapture of the Golden Fleece.

A reclamation of a more personal nature occurred in 12 B.C. upon Augustus's appointment as Pontifex Maximus, chief high priest of the Roman state religion.[59] This dignity was celebrated in the *Res Gestae* and alluded to by the image of the veiled Augustus in the sacrificial procession on the Ara Pacis (fig. 7)[60] that flanks the scene of Aeneas sacrificing (fig. 5). Now officially granted the mantle of piety that was Aeneas's birthright, Augustus took the unprecedented measure of transferring the Penates to his own temple-palace on the Palatine.[61] Through these measures the emperor established a bond between his person and the state religion; at the same time he stimulated religious practices geared to ancestor worship. The constant references to Aeneas in his imagery provided Augustus with much more than the cachet of poetic metaphor, for they sustained his status as living kin of divine forbears.

The Trojan imprint was extended to the cosmic realm with the creation of the scales of Libra—a previously unknown constellation created to signal Augustus's apotheosis.[62] Thus the heavenly form by which Jove determined Rome's imperial destiny in the *Aeneid*[63] was fixed forever in the Empyrean as Augustus's deified soul.[64] As an eagle ascended from his funeral pyre to testify to his return to the gods, Augustus deeded to Rome this celestial pledge of Rome's universal jurisdiction.

While the prophecies of the *Fourth Eclogue* were deemed to have been realized by Augustus's achievements, the suggestive metaphors of a New *Argo*, a New Troy, and a New Golden Age provided future emperors with a mythic program that could be

6. *Augustus of Primaporta.* Rome, Vatican Museum, first century B.C. Musei Vaticani Archivo Fotografico, Vatican City.

personalized to assert their legitimate extension of this utopian rule. The legend that the gods returned to earth during the *Pax Augusta* took on considerable added nuance when Christ was born during the era of Augustus's rule. The bond that Vergil had established between history and myth was then given a new meaning that would be sustained throughout the long history of the Christian Empire.

7. *Augustus*, detail from imperial procession. Rome, Ara Pacis, first century B.C. Deutsches Archäologisches Institut, Rome. Neg. 57-883.

Chapter II Byzantium and the Christianized Roman Myth

ERGIL provided the empire with its inclusive myth by fusing an indissoluble bond between the Trojan legend and Roman imperial history. The reaction to pagan literature that accompanied the triumph of Christianity as the Roman state religion did not bring oblivion to Vergil, indeed his epic inspired Christian progeny. Yet from a need to codify the poem's underlying moral core there arose a fragmentation of content as narrative elements were sacrificed to the Trojan saga's mystical significance. In this transformation, the nobility, virtue, and divine election of the Vergilian ideal hero were retained as constants, as was the focus on his triumph in battle that brings justice to earth in an eternal peace. The slack in narrative diversity was taken up by the amplification of symbolic references as Judeo-Christian topoi were blended with their pagan counterparts.

Beginning in the late fourth century, Vergil's epic was subjected to a doctrinal interpretation. This development followed on the heels of the Christianization of Rome's divine mission, which held that Augustus had prepared for the coming of Christ by uniting the world in peace. Since the central event of history was seen to be the Incarnation and the Roman Empire was its setting, early Christian imperial apologists advanced the concept that the Roman Empire was founded to conform with God's purpose.[1] For the Greek Church Father Origen (b. ca. A.D. 180), who first expressed this contingency, it was "manifest that Jesus was born in the reign of Augustus . . . [because the Emperor] levelled together under His one kingship the many inhabitants of the earth. [For] it would have been a hindrance to the spread of the teaching of Jesus through the world if there had been many [warring] kingdoms."[2]

In the aftermath of Christ's Resurrection, Christians of the early church generally believed that Christ's Second Coming was imminent. Christian apocalyptic overtones were accommodated to the claim of Rome's perdurability through the application of Daniel's prophecy that the duration of the temporal world was calibrated to the reign of Four Monarchies. Through a vision, the prophet Daniel interpreted Nebuchadnezzar's dream of a man with a head of gold, back of silver, chest of copper, and feet of clay as an image of the world's Four Monarchies. After these will come the realm of God, which will be eternal.[3] In interpretations of the New Testament that were favorable to Rome's civic authority, it was expected that Christ's return would occur under the imperial rule of Rome—the Fourth Monarchy.[4] Thereafter Rome's role in uniting the world was seen as a step in the preparation of the coming spiritual empire when the far-off successor of Aeneas would bow down his knee to Christ.[5]

With the whole of the Trojan epic seen through a scrim of Revelation, Vergil's *Fourth Eclogue* was greeted as a Christian messianic prophecy. The biblical and the pagan paradises were fused, and Saturn's Golden Age became identified with the Eden of Holy Scripture. Its loss was associated with the Iron Age when Avarice emerged from hell and greed supplanted the love of God. The promise of the return of a new Golden Age was interpreted as the earthly paradise prophesied to descend with Christ at the end of time; it was thus made to accord with the Apocalyptic vision of the Lamb of God ruling in everlasting peace.

The Argonautic voyage that set into motion the Trojan epic pointed the path to this eschatological goal. A religious interpretation of the capture of the Golden Fleece was already inherent in the earliest versions of the story. The enterprise assumed new geographic specificity when Valerius Flaccus, a member of the exclusive college of priests with sole charge of the Sibylline books that contained the oracles of the gods, related the Fleece's retrieval to Titus's conquest of Jerusalem.[6] On the arch that was

erected on this occasion in Rome (fig. 8), the emperor returns in triumph bearing the Jewish Temple spoils and cult objects. These associations would gain Christian impetus in the Middle Ages as the repatriation of the Golden Fleece became identified with the conquest of Jerusalem and the recovery of the Holy Sepulchre.[7]

8. *Titus Returns to Rome in Triumph with the Jewish Temple Spoils.* Rome, Arch of Titus, first century A.D. Deutsches Archäologisches Institut, Rome. Neg. 89-2494.

Prudentius

Prudentius (A.D. 348–ca. 405), the greatest of the Christian Latin poets and an ardent supporter of the Byzantine emperor Theodosius,[8] numbered among the fourth-century apologists who adapted Vergil's texts to a Christian purpose. In the *Psychomachia*, considered the first Christian allegorical poem, Prudentius transposed the *Aeneid*'s battle for the sovereignty of Rome to a Christian metaphysical plane.[9] He effected a startling revision of the epic by assigning the breastplates of Aeneas and Turnus to personifications of Virtue and Vice, who replace their mythic counterparts in a struggle to the death.[10] Dependent on Vergil for the vivid

details that characterize the mortal struggle between the two pro-
tagonists, Prudentius consolidated this metamorphosis by giving
to the individual virtues and vices the characteristic moral quali-
ties of their epic prototypes. Thus Prudentius's Wrath, "showing
. . . teeth with rage and foaming at the mouth" is identifiable with
Turnus, in whom Vergil personifies impious rage, "roaring with
blood stained mouth, . . . [in whose] soul the fury swells."[11] In a
battle scene that demonstrates the uselessness of mortal arms
against Aeneas, "Turnus rises full height on his uplifted sword,
and strikes . . . but the traitorous sword snaps, and in mid stroke
fails its fiery lord . . . a hilt in his defenceless hand."[12] Recreated by
Prudentius as a struggle between Patience and Wrath, the scene is
vividly rendered in a ninth-century illumination of the *Psychomachia* (fig. 9). Here, protected by Roman armor, the Virtue
"braves the hail of weapons . . . [while] Wrath . . . putting all its
strength into a blow it rises high . . . the blade . . . breaks . . .
scatters away in rattling fragments . . . while her hand still grasps
the hilt."[13]

Out of Prudentius's martial conception of the virtues and
vices grew not only their characteristic mode of representation in
the Middle Ages,[14] but many of the commonplaces with which
we typify ethical states in modern times. Prudentius presents
Pride, an epithet for Turnus,[15] as a haughty figure felled from his
horse. The destruction of Pride by *Mens Humilis*, like Aeneas, "a
newcomer from unknown lands . . . trying to drive out the ancient princes"[16] is characterized first by hesitancy and finally by
resolution that is triggered with a pious memory: "seeing the vain
monster crushed and lying at the point of death . . . [the Virtue]
hesitates . . . [then, with] the sword of vengeance [in memory of
young David] severs the head."[17] The encounter is reminiscent of
the final scene of the *Aeneid*: "Fierce in his arms, Aeneas stood . . .
and stayed his hand . . . when high on the shoulder was seen the
luckless baldric, and there flashed the belt . . . of young Pallas, whom Turnus had smitten . . . so . . . [Aeneas] buries the
sword."[18]

Associating the contrasting moral states with the Gold and
Iron ages,[19] Prudentius pitted them against each other for possession of man's soul. Victory in the battle between these opposing
personifications of light and darkness is presented as divinely
revealed salvation history.

rauibi truncan mucronif fragmina uidit
Et paul inpartes ensem crepuisse minutas
Iamcapuli remenente manu sine pondere ferri
Mentas inopsf ebur infelix decorisq pudendi
Perfida signa abicit monimentaq tristia longe
Spernit &ad pprium succenditur effera letum
Missile demutus quae frustra sparserat unum
Puluere de campi neruensos f

Prudentius wrought yet another formidable transformation in the Roman imperial myth by introducing to it a new concept of divine legitimacy. This he accomplished by amalgamating biblical ancestry in the noble blood of the Trojan warriors.[20] Empowered to defeat evil and restore the Christian-Roman state through their sacred origins, these personified virtues are rallied to victory with a reminder of this pedigree: "Ye are the high-born children of Judah and have come of a long line of noble ancestors that stretches down to the mother of God. . . . Let the renowned David . . . awake your noble spirits."[21] The Virtue's blend of Christian and Roman heritages is suggested in an illustration to the passage that follows on this injunction (fig. 10). Against the seductive wiles of unbridled Luxuria, Sobriety, a Christian soldier garbed in Roman armor, "holds up the cross of the Lord in the face of the raging chariot horses."[22]

9. *Patientia and Ira.* In Prudentius, *Psychomachia.* Reichenau, ninth century. Burgerbibliothek, Bern, Cod. 264, fol. 4or.

L uxuriefmulto ftipata fatellice poenaf   Λ d
C umLegione fua xpo fubiudice pendat   C o
hic   ☩ SOBRIETAS CRUCE DNI OFFERT   ĸ u
    CVRTRVI LVXYRIF ·   S p
                                              C a
                                              E ,
                                              D e
                                              D ι
                                              L n
                                              C o

10. *Luxuria and Sobrietas.*
In Prudentius, *Psycho-
machia.* Reichenau,
ninth century. Biblio-
thèque Nationale,
Paris. MS Lat. 8085, fol.
62v.

The consolidation of Judeo-Christian and Roman cultural
heritages is amplified in narrative details drawn from the *Aeneid's*
final episodes, or from Augustus's Actian battle, which it glorified.
These associations are reinforced in typologies that adapt Roman
military triumphs to the language of the New Faith. Augustus's
victory at Actium brought the end of civil war and the beginning
of an age of concord, later to be identified with Christ's rule.[23]
This topos is evoked in the *Psychomachia* when cross-bearing Concord, whose identity with Christ is inferred by the blood-
dripping wound in her side,[24] deals the death blow to Discord-
Heresy, naming her the "upset of the common weal"[25] at home
and the cause of "faltering abroad."[26] Thus civil war is identified
with heresy, and Augustus's military victory is transposed to a
Christian mystical plane. When Concord gives the signal to take
the victorious standards back to camp,[27] the action imitates another Augustan achievement, the return of the Roman standards
at the Peace of Brindisi (fig. 6). This reference is underscored in an

ᴐᴇ CONCORDIA IVBET REDVCERE SIGNA INCASTRIS ·
D at fignum felix concordia · reddere caftrif
V ictricefaquilaf. atq; untentona cogi ;

illustration to Prudentius's passage where the standards are specifically those of the imperial legions (fig. 11). Into this blend of
pagan and Christian, Prudentius interpolated Old Testament references, as when Moses' crossing of the Red Sea provides the
prototype for Virtue's victory over Vice.[28] For the syncretistic
mentality that characterizes the Christianized Roman Empire, the
renewal of peace under Rome's universal sovereignty, the Isra-
elite homecoming, and Christ's restoration of Eden are equated.

In the ritual transfer of power with which the *Psychomachia*
ends, the bifurcated root of the Christian-imperial legacy con-
geals in a single symbol. When Aaron's flowering rod is given to
Christ-Sapientia,[29] the gesture subsumes the transfer of the scepter to the sires of Latium.[30] Like separate branches intertwined in
a mystical caduceus, the symbols of Jewish and pagan sovereignty are joined in the staff of Christ, priest and king of the New
Jerusalem.[31] As the melding of the heritages is effected through
the miracle of the god-man's birth, the tower of Babel crumbles,
the confusion of tongues is dissipated and the harmony of the
races revealed. Following the Vergilian saga whose typological
fulfillment it realized in Christ, the *Psychomachia* dissolves in the
vindication of Justice. In the reconsecrated city that is established
by context as Rome,[32] Faith assumes pious Aeneas's role as city

11. *Concordia Rejoices at
the Return of the Roman
Standards,* Prudentius,
Psychomachia. Reiche-
nau, ninth century.
Bibliothèque Munici-
pale, Lyon. MS 22 (Ly)
fol. 18v.

mmanes feruaue lupi· diferimina pdunt
ra· recenfq· cruor· quamuif decorpore fumo·
uidpoffic furuua manq· gemuuf dedit omif
uirtutum populuf· cafuconcuffufacerbo

Cum generofa fides hęc fubdidit· immofecur
noch· ceffeu ęmnu· concordia lefa eft

founder and traces out the foundation of Solomon's rebuilt temple (fig. 12).[33] Hewn from a single gem, the edifice rises, and in its
inner sanctum, Wisdom is enthroned.[34]

Here and throughout Prudentius's oeuvre, the Roman legend of Troy sustains Judeo-Christian mysticism; it makes of
Christ, the blood kin of David, a New Aeneas, and of Rome a
New Jerusalem.[35] By crystallizing the connections between the
priest kings of imperial and biblical literature Prudentius expressed the mystical amalgam through which the divine blood
that flowed to their veins from the Almighty is narrowed to a
single conduit that gushes forth from Christ's cardinal wounds.
The forces of darkness are eternally vanquished by this invincible
noble heir.

Theodosius and the Christian Empire

When Prudentius revised Vergil, he substituted Christ for Aeneas as the hero whose divine descent and perfect virtue designated him to triumph over the chthonic deities. This "Trojan" concept of the Savior was developed in tandem with the Christianization of the Roman state, which held that Christ's Incarnation and Second Coming were interdependent with Rome's historic destiny.[36]

The adaptation of the *Aeneid* to political realities was endemic to the myth, for Vergil had shaped his artistry to glorify Augustus. Prudentius adhered to this tradition for his poetic efforts supported Theodosius's (ca. A.D. 346–95) ambitions for supreme sovereignty of a unified Christian Empire.[37] Since Theodosius was the vicar of Christ, whom he was seen to mirror in nobility and virtue,[38] these efforts were envisioned in eschatological terms, and his battle against heresy was understood to mirror Jesus' victory over demonic Discord. In the newly formulated vision of the end of time, it is the Roman emperor's battles for the faith that restore the terrestrial paradise lost with man's fall from grace. With the emperor's pretensions to the regency of both Priam and David, the Vergilian topos of the emperor as the perfect god-man received its Christian formulation.

The way for Prudentius's adaptation of the Trojan myth to the new faith had already been paved at the beginning of the fourth century A.D. In 312 Constantine defeated Maxentius at the Battle of the Milvian Bridge, a victory that was attributed to the apparition of Christ's Cross on the battlefield. Shortly afterwards he became sole ruler of the Roman Empire and adopted Christianity as the state religion. In a medal of ca. 330, the hand of God reaches down to confirm his divine election (fig. 13).[39] In the works of Lactantius and Eusebius, the emperor's advisors, Vergil's words were reconciled with the Bible; the end of the Golden Age was identified with the loss of original Justice at the Fall, and its revival with the Advent of Christ.[40] In this assimilation of cultures, metaphors of Roman justice received particular emphasis. The Virgin Mary is hailed as the Virgo-Astraea, the goddess of Justice,[41] and the Scales of Libra—the emblem of Trojan destiny that emblazoned the heavens with Augustus's apotheosis—are assigned to Christ, the Sun of Justice.[42]

With his own lips, Constantine extracted these meanings

13. *Constantine*. Medal,
ca. 326. Kunsthisto-
risches Museum,
Vienna.

from the *Fourth Eclogue*. Quoting the phrases that announce the
return of the Argonauts and a new Trojan war,[43] the emperor
hailed Vergil: "Bravo, thou wisest of poets . . . [you] presented the
truth to those who could understand it: . . . [for Vergil] depicts the
Saviour as advancing to the war against Troy, and he means by
Troy the whole world for verily the Saviour waged war against the
opposing power of evil."[44] Quoting Vergil's words about the descent of a new savior from heaven who will bring the Golden
Age, Constantine identified Mary with the Virgin Astraea and the
return of Saturn's Golden Age with the Incarnation: "Who then is
the Virgin who returns? Is it not she who was filled and made with
child by the Holy Ghost? . . . He too [the beloved King Christ] will
return once more, and by his coming will lighten the burden of
the world."[45] In a later legend that developed Constantine's identification of Christ with the Savior of the *Fourth Eclogue*, the Virgin

14. *Augustus and the Tiburtine Sibyl.* In Hartmann Schedel, *Liber Chronicarum,* Nuremberg, 1493, p. xciii. Biblioteca Apostolica Vaticana, Rome.

and Christ Child appear on the Capitoline hill to Augustus and the Sibyl, and Rome is reconsecrated with the vision (fig. 14).[46]

In conforming religion to politics Eusebius followed Origen's precedent when he deemed the uniting in a single political body of the two divergent streams an expression of Divine Necessity: "Together, at the same critical moment, as if from a single divine will, two beneficial shoots were produced for mankind: the empire of the Romans and the teachings of true worship." But he went beyond earlier church fathers by identifying the *Pax Augusta* with the reign of peace prophesied in the Old Testament,[47] now brought to its full realization with Constantine, God's vice-regent.[48] Following this line of thought, Eusebius linked the disappearance of the Jewish state, the emergence of the Roman Empire, and the birth of Christ and produced a universal chronicle to show the contingency of these events.[49]

This synchronization of history was reinforced by applying

Judeo-Christian parallels for imperial actions, as when Constantine's crossing the Milvian Bridge and freeing the Christians from persecution was compared with Moses' crossing the Red Sea and liberating the Jews.[50] Constantine's transfer of the empire to the East, where the concept of the sovereign's divinity was an accepted premise,[51] facilitated the assimilation of the emperor to Christ,[52] and eternal,[53] cosmic,[54] and sacerdotal powers[55] were attributed equally to the emperor and to his heavenly model.[56] In this crossover of traditions, secular themes were given a biblical orientation and Christological dogma was cast in an imperial mode. Thus the divine archetype is defined as monarchy,[57] and God-Father, who elects Christ his "co-ruler," determines the dynastic pattern of ruler succession.[58] The imperial analogy is extended, as battle imagery is adopted for Christ and the term "Supreme Commander of the heavenly armies" applied to Him.[59] A parallel military mode is applied to the implements of the Passion, which are defined by the martial term *Arma Christi*. Above all Christ's Cross, "His own Saving Sign, by which He prevailed over death and fashioned a triumph over His enemies . . . [is His] victorious trophy, apotropaic of demons."[60] In a haunting vision of Christ in imperial armor from the end of the fifth century, the Cross is the symbol of conquest over demonic evil (fig. 15).[61]

The imperialization of Christ reached its zenith under Theodosius and his son Honorius (A.D. 380–420),[62] and Prudentius was the bard who sang the dithyramb. Scattered through the encomiastic literature of the empire though it was, a recapitulation of Vergil's vision of Rome's divine mission in a Christian key entered the mainstream of poetic literature only with the *Psychomachia*. With Prudentius's format for viewing the emperor's struggle for universal sovereignty as the preparation for the Heavenly Jerusalem, the edifice of imaginative political thought was forever transformed. The unification of the hemispheres in the True Faith portends the end of Rome's terrestrial rule, which is ceded back to Christ, its true sovereign. This last imperial obeisance signalled the end of time and the subjugation of temporal rule to the eternal sovereignty of the Savior. In the *Divinity of Christ* Prudentius envisioned Rome's final moment taking place when "the successor of Aeneas, in the imperial purple prostrates himself in prayer at the house of Christ, and the supreme lord adores the banner of the cross."[63]

15. *Christus Imperator.*
Mosaic, after 494. Ra-
venna, Chapel of the
Archbishop's Palace.
Deutsches Archäo-
logisches Institut,
Rome. Neg. 58-559.

Chapter III *The Frankish Roman Empire*

ETWEEN the deposition of Romulus Augustus in 475 and the election of Charlemagne, the phantom of empire remained quiescent in the West.[1] On Christmas Day in the year 800, Rome witnessed the coronation of Charlemagne and with it the transfer of the Roman Empire to the Franks.

The northern transfer of the empire was anticipated by a number of influential sixth-century historians. Cassiodorus (ca. 490–583), the chancellor and historian of Theoderic the Great, propagated an assimilation of Gothic and Roman empires when he presented the Gothic peoples as the worthy heirs of Rome in his lost *History of the Goths*. In his *Getia* of ca. 551, Cassiodorus's pupil Jordanes, who preserved a summary of his master's *History*, presented the Gothic kingdom of Italy as successor to the western empire.[2] While these scholarly accommodations of Roman to barbarian were to find their full realization in the suzerainty of Charlemagne, the doctrinal foundations of the new empire had long been established with Clovis, the first Christian king of all the Franks (481–511).

Clovis was introduced to Christianity through his marriage to Clothilde, daughter of the King of Burgundy. He made a compact with Christ when, losing a battle to the Alemanni, he saw a figure of the Savior and vowed that he would be baptized in the new faith if Christ would grant him victory. Upon pronouncing this

vow, the battle turned in his favor. In his account of Clovis's conversion, Gregory of Tours (b. 539) compared the incident to Constantine's vision and victory at the Milvian Bridge, and likening
Clovis's baptism to that of the first Christian emperor, he called
the Frankish king the New Constantine.[3]

Following his indoctrination in the new faith, Clovis converted his people. Although the Franks were already nominally
Christian, they were Arians; the epoch-making significance of
Clovis's conversion was to guide the Franks to Orthodox doctrine.[4] Since it signalled the decline of Arianism in the West, the
king's minister Avit regarded Clovis's conversion as an event that
reflected on all other kings; a dignity that gave him the right to
intervene in the affairs of other countries.[5] This position was
sustained by Gregory of Tours who recorded that the Byzantine
emperor Anastasius had conferred proconsular status on Clovis.[6]
As these imperializing pretensions were opposed by Pope Gregory, in Frankish quarters the king's sovereignty was declared not a
continuation of Constantine's,[7] but a new era of Christian royalty,
which found its legitimacy in the reign of Christ.

The transfer of authority that marked the new era of Christian royalty was consecrated by God, for at Clovis's baptism,
which took place on Christmas day in 506, a dove descended
from heaven with the holy oil of his anointment;[8] at that moment
he was endowed with the healing touch. Jesus' ritual inauguration
into his sacred ministry and his institution as King of the
Israelites, occurred at His Baptism through the descent of the
Holy Ghost.[9] At the same moment He began to exercise His
divine powers.[10] The replication of the baptismal miracle for
Clovis manifested the Frankish king's divine election to propagate the eternal rule of Jesus.[11] The parallel was suggested by
Hincmar of Reims in his Life of St. Remi (877). Hincmar specifically
noted the parallel appearance of the dove at the baptism of both
Christ and Clovis.[12]

The chrism that poured down from heaven to consecrate
Clovis was prefigured in the unction with which Samuel anointed
David into his sacred kingship,[13] and it signified the Merovingian
dynasty's divine election to succeed in perpetuity the Old Testament priest-kings.[14] The supersession of Jewish sacred authority
was effected first in Christ, whose own earthly parentage was
rooted in the Old Testament priest-kings.[15] In a thirteenth-

16. *Anointing of David, Presentation of Christ, Coronation of David, Baptism of Christ.* Illustration to Psalm 26. British Library, London, MS Add. 54179, fol. 18v.

century illuminated psalter this canonic typology is depicted through the juxtaposition of David's anointing and coronation with Christ's Presentation and Baptism (fig. 16).

Since Clovis's conversion effected the demise of Arianism in Gaul and the triumph of Orthodox Catholicism in the West, the holy oil also constituted a spiritual endorsement of his election to supersede the error-ridden Christian emperors of the East.[16] These traditions were perpetuated throughout the centuries, and in a sixteenth-century relief from the Church of Saint Remi (fig. 17), the baptisms of Christ, Constantine, and Clovis are aligned. The image suggests the legitimacy of Clovis's election, for while Constantine is anointed by Sylvester, Christ and Clovis are consecrated by the descent of the Holy Spirit.

As the *pugnator egregious*, the providential defender of the faith

17. *The Three Baptisms: Christ, Constantine, and Clovis. Ivory bas-relief, sixteenth century. Basilica of Saint Remi, Reims.*

on whom God bestowed a lily-patterned shield and a flaming lance, Clovis was rendered invincible against the foes of the Christian faith.[17] The sacred chrism—which transformed the Frankish king into God's anointed, the "christus of the Lord"—and with it the divine protection and the healing touch bestowed upon Clovis by God became the inalienable possession of his successors.[18] This highly enviable election, and the right to inherit it, would characterize all future claims to imperial legitimacy.[19]

Charlemagne, the Extension of the Roman Imperial Myth and Reflections of His Legacy in the Anticlaudian of Alain de Lille

The imperial powers that were merely implied for Clovis were legally assumed three hundred years later by Charlemagne on Christmas Day in the year 800. The acclamation of Charlemagne's imperial legitimacy, as well as the sanctity and supremacy of his rule is recorded in the annals of his biographer Einhard (770–840). In the Basilica of Saint Peter, when Pope Leo placed the crown of empire on Charlemagne's head, the whole of the Roman populus cried out "To the august Charles, crowned by god,

18. *Peter Gives the Vexillium to Charlemagne.* Sixteenth-century drawing after the lost Lateran mosaic. Biblioteca Apostolica Vaticana, Rome. MS. Barb. Lat. 2738, fol. 104r.

19. *Cross Base Reliquary* (detail). Seventeenth-century drawing after the lost ninth-century original. Bibliothèque Nationale, Paris. Fr. 10440.

the great and peaceful Emperor of the Romans, life and victory."[20] Coming to the aid of the blind and mutilated Pope Leo,
Charlemagne had conquered Lombardy and restored Italy to the
popes. It was asserted that the emperor at Constantinople lacked
similar piety and on these grounds the empire was taken away
from the Greeks and given to the Germans.[21] A contemporary
mosaic from the grand Triclinium that Leo constructed at the
Lateran publicly manifested this pivotal moment in imperial history to all who made the pilgrimage to Rome's Cathedral and the
papal residence. Here even as he bestows sacred powers on Pope
Leo, Saint Peter gives the Vexillium of secular power to Charlemagne (fig. 18).[22] With the accession of the title, Charlemagne
and his advisors developed an imperial vocabulary from classical
texts and imagery of the pre- and post-Christian era. One stun-
ning example of this appropriation is the cross base reliquary in
the form of a Roman triumphal arch (fig. 19) that Einhard gave to
the church of Maastricht.[23]

As Constantinople had been acclaimed the new Rome, so
now was that title conferred on Aachen, the seat of Charlemagne's power.[24] In a poem attributed to Einhard, who based
his *Life of Charlemagne*, the first secular biography since antiquity,
on the Suetonian portrait of Augustus,[25] the "caput mundi" is
transferred with Charlemagne to Aachen. When he paces out the
measure of the new Rome in Aachen, Charlemagne is compared
to the mythical founding fathers of the eternal city:

Lord too of the city where a second Rome flowers, Pious Charles
stands on the high palace, from afar pointing out each site, oversee-
ing the construction of the high walls of future Rome. In one place
he orders a forum to be built, in another a holy senate where the
people receive judgements and laws and God's commands. . . .
Elsewhere others strain with immense effort to build a church fitting
for the eternal king, the hallowed building with polished walls
mounts up to heaven.[26]

These lines recall Vergil's description of Aeneas as city founder;[27]
indeed, they evoke the scene as it was depicted in the late classical
Vatican Virgil (fig. 3). The similarities may not be coincidental since
the famed manuscript was one of the prized possessions of the
Carolingian rulers.[28] Portrayed by Einhard as the new Aeneas who
builds the sacred counterpart of Augustus's Rome in Aachen,[29]

Charlemagne's ambition to extend his domain beyond the Frankish realms was evoked by Alcuin's use of the Vergilian dictum "Parcere subiectis" in a letter to the emperor.[30] These famous words from the *Aeneid* were a directive from his ancestors that Aeneas must seek universal sovereignty.[31] The Carolingian court was thoroughly familiar with the phrase and the context from which it came, as evidenced when figures from the ninth-century *Vivian Bible* were traced to this scene in the *Vatican Virgil*.[32] Modelling himself in spirit as well as in practice on the ancient hero, Charlemagne assumed Aeneas's epithet "Pius."[33]

The sanctity of the Frankish Empire was shown by Charlemagne's divine coronation, God's call to him to win the Saxons to Christianity with a sword from heaven, and Pope Leo's transmission to Aachen of the Blood of Christ which appeared miraculously at Mantua. Moreover, tradition established that Charlemagne received the unction with the crowning.[34] His sacred and supreme powers were asserted by Paul the Deacon, who applied to Charlemagne the terms *Rex et Sacerdos*;[35] they were formally communicated in his titles *Decus Ecclesiae, Episcopus Episcoporum,* and Holy Roman Emperor.[36]

When he transferred the empire to the East where the concept of divine kingship had originated, Constantine found fertile ground for a Christological orientation of the Roman emperor's divinity. His Byzantine successors continued to proclaim these ideas to a public long habituated to theocracy. When the empire was transferred to the West because of the "impiety of the Byzantine emperor," the cult worship of the emperor was transferred with it.[37] The legends of Charlemagne's pilgrimage to the Holy Land, where the extent of his imitation and kinship with Christ was manifested at every turn, set the seal of Eastern emperor worship on the Frankish king.[38] In 1165, through the efforts of Emperor Frederick I, Charlemagne was canonized as a saint.[39]

The legends of Charlemagne focus on two principal crusades: first to the West where the Moor was entrenched; then to the East to recover the Cross and the Sepulchre of Christ. At the beginning of his voyage, Saint James appeared to the emperor. Identifying himself as the foster son of Mary and brother of John the Evangelist, the saint pointed out the starry road to Spain where the heathen stalked. As with Constantine, Charlemagne's victories in battle were seen as the repetition of Old Testament miracles: the fall of Pamplona was compared to the crumbling of Jericho's walls; the engulfing of a Saracen stronghold with the crossing of the Red Sea.[40] In the interpretations of his battles for the faith, in the Frankish creation of a lily-crowned image of the *Miles Christi* that is preserved in a ninth-century copy of the *Psychomachia* (fig. 20),[41] and in the appropriation of an imperial image of the militant Savior (fig. 21), the Carolingians were inspired by the Byzantine concept of Christ the warrior.[42]

20. *Miles Christi.* Ninth century. Bibliothèque Nationale, Paris. MS Lat. 8318, fol. 55r.

21. *Christ as Emperor.* In
The Stuttgart Psalter, A.D.
820–30. Würtem-
berger Landesbiblio-
thek, Cod. Bibl., fol.
23. Bildarchiv Foto,
Marburg.

Having destroyed the Moor in Spain, Charlemagne set off for
the East. When he reached Jerusalem and sat with his twelve
paladins in the Chapel of the Last Supper, at first glance he was
mistaken for the Savior. Then, acknowledged by the city's patriarch to be king over all earthly kings, he was granted the keys to
the Lord's Sepulchre and to Mount Calvary.[43] After routing the
besieging Turks from Constantinople, the Greek emperor bestowed upon him the most venerable relics of Christendom—
the Chalice from the Last Supper, wood and nails of the Cross,
and the Crown of Thorns. The emperor's election to succeed in
the royalty of Christ was confirmed when the Savior's Crown
bloomed with flowers and healed the sick in Charlemagne's presence. After witnessing this miracle, the populace cried out that
this was surely the day of the Resurrection for the aroma of the
flowers had filled the city and healed three thousand invalids.[44] A
chest bearing an image of the crown that flowered in the presence of Charlemagne is preserved and revered as a living memory of the miracle in the treasury of the Cathedral at Aachen.[45]

The Chivalric Riposte and the Northern Transfer of the Empire

The Vergilian literary topos we have been investigating continued notwithstanding the transfer of the empire to the north in the ninth century. Indeed the growth of the now-composite Trojan myth was stimulated by the intense East-West rivalry created in the wake of this event. With the flourishing of classicism in the later Middle Ages, additional aspects of pagan mysticism penetrated the nucleus of Christian thought. As they did, the hero of the Trojan epic became the embodiment of ever-more-comprehensive power. A turning point in this development was reached with Alain de Lille (1128–1202),[46] a poet referred to as "Vergilio melior and Homero certior."[47] In his allegorical poem, the *Anticlaudian*, Alain continued Prudentius's Christian interpretation of the Trojan battle,[48] reframing the elements into an epic of knightly adventure.[49] In this transformation he was inspired by the Third Crusade.[50] Whereas for Prudentius the divine Virtues are components of Christ, the God-Man, Alain created the mystical hero of his adventure by transforming Prudentius's Virtues into the spiritual forces of Christ's earthly counterpart, the microcosmic man.[51]

With the title of his poem, Alain reached back through history to invoke the work of Claudian, court poet under Emperor Honorius (396–408). Claudian had written In *Rufinum* in support of Honorius's efforts to establish a unified empire under western dominance, and to condemn Rufinus, the regent of Arcadius, the emperor in Byzantium.[52] The northern transfer of the empire in the ninth century had revived the issue of West-East imperial sovereignty; this controversy was settled by Canon Law in favor of the West in the year of Alain's death, when in the *Venerabilem* of 1202 Innocent III declared that the Apostolic See "transferred the Roman Empire from the Greeks to the Germans in the person of magnificent Charles."[53]

Claudian had characterized Rufinus as the embodiment of all evil.[54] Drawing inspiration from the conception of Adam before the Fall,[55] Alain brought together Prudentius's personified Virtues to form the deified counterpart to Claudian's antihero.

The poem is set in the royal reception hall of Nature's palace, where the amenities of the Golden Age flourish,[56] and murals of Trojan heroes figure prominently on the palace's painted walls.[57]

There the Goddess convenes a counsel of the Virtues and Liberal Arts. Drawing on the *Aeneid*'s account of man's disobedience,[58] Concord presents a capsule history of the impieties which brought about Troy's downfall and Rome's Civil War.[59] These events necessitate the creation of a New Man:

If my rights, my laws, my pacts the world had preserved, the globe would not be groaning with such great calamities. . . . The nobility of Troy, the honor of Troy, the illustrious fame of Troy would be flourishing still . . . the disturbances of war, the wrath of Fortune might easily have been avoided.[60]

The Virtues agree that the demon spirit can only be stopped when a creature, both man and God shall become the ruler of the earth: "A work in which all possible gifts may be infused, . . . a divine man shall inhabit the world by our endeavor. . . . In soul shall he adhere to the heavens, in body to the earth. . . . Thus a Man, thus a god will be made."[61]

While Nature can shape his body, only God can bestow his soul; thus Prudence is assigned the celestial mission of obtaining His consent. The Liberal Arts construct the chariot in which she travels to the region of the planets and constellations;[62] there she views the pagan gods who gained a place in the heavens through their Virtue.[63]

Led to the Empyrean by Theology, Prudence reaches the celestial court and views the realm of the angels and the Virgin Mary, who is addressed as the Virgo Astraea of the Christianized *Fourth Eclogue*,[64] at her "advent the golden age returned to the world."[65] At last, guided by Faith alone, Prudence beholds the "exceeding brilliance of Olympus."[66] In the figure-inscribed mirror that protects her sight from the celestial brilliance, the merits of the Trojan heroes are revealed to her as "she examines the celestial ideas. . . . Here she [learns why] Hector gleams in arms, Ulysses sparkles in the ray of genius, why . . . Typhis is the mariner."[67] After admiring these things for a long time, she ascends to the citadel of the King of Heaven and presents Nature's request for "a celestial godhood [to] visit the fleeting world and a heavenly spirit . . . [who] travels upon earth in body only . . . in order that he may by the very glories of his virtues harass the evil customs of others."[68]

Agreeing to create a new pilgrim for the earthly globe and to "bless the world with the divinity of a celestial man, who alone would possess as much wealth of virtue as possible,"[69] God fashions the perfect man's soul after the merits of Old Testament prototypes. He gives him "the beauty of Joseph, the wisdom of Judith, the fortitude of Job, the zeal of Phineas, the modesty of Moses, the simplicity of Jacob, the faith of Abraham, the piety of Tobias."[70]

On Prudence's return to earth, Nature fashions the New Man's body from a perfect balance of the Elements.[71] According to the Medieval doctrine of the humors, God had perfectly balanced the Four Elements in Adam. Following the Fall, the Elements were unequally distributed among men, an imbalance that accounted for the Choleric, Sanguine, Phlegmatic, and Melancholic temperaments and consequently man's predisposition to one or another group of Vices. Restored in Christ, elemental integrity is once again renewed in the New Man. Thus he, unlike ordinary mortals, is a perfect microcosm that reflects the harmony of the celestial spheres. Nature completes her work by adding the beauty of Narcissus and of Adonis, the gift of youth, and the severe morals of an old man.[72] The perfected creature is a composite of the merits and attributes of both pagan and biblical heroes.

The Liberal Arts add their contributions, which comprise the knowledge of all celestial and earthly wisdom: "The Instruction of Grammar . . . the penetrating power of Logic . . . the cultivations of Rhetoric . . . Mathematics exhibits her own secrets of Wisdom . . . Music yields her gifts . . . the teaching of Astronomy [finds a] lodging-place in him."[73] Following these gifts come the most important donations, those of the Theological Virtues; of these "Piety gives herself entirely, and commits so much to the man that he may be thought Piety [itself]."[74] In the abundance of this Virtue the New Man mirrors Aeneas, the great exemplar of piety.

The last to bestow her gifts is Fortune. In depicting her, Alain provides what would become the classic description of the Mutable Goddess and of her Dwelling Place.[75] Seducing all by her two-faced aspect, Fortune is found spinning the wheel upon which rulers representing the Four World Monarchies are perched; she manipulates their shifting destinies: "While Crosus holds the summit of the wheel, Codrus clings to the lowest part; Julius ascends, Magnus descends and Sulla lies low, Marius rises. . . . Thus the rotation ravages all in turn, and tumbling Fortune varies vicissitudes."[76] Recognizing her inability to affect the destiny of God's New Man, in this single instance she restrains her mutable ways: "I shall change customary deceits and lay aside the irksomeness of my error. I shall render myself steadfast. . . . I shall become stable who up to now have been fatuous, improvident deceitful and rash."[77] When the news of the New Man's creation reaches Alecto, the narrative turns to the battle between the Vices and the collective Virtues that are embodied in the New Man. Calling from hell a "whirlpool of sins, throng of vices, assembly of evils,"[78] Alecto rouses them to battle with her speech: "Against us . . . provident Nature has armed a boy. . . . let us wage combats and wars against him, who, alone . . . is armed against us."[79] "Now the mystic wars taste reality,"[80] as the New Man, rendered invulnerable by divine armor, prepares for battle: "Peace gives greaves, Probity confers spurs, Piety the cuirass, Prudence the helmet, True Faith the spear . . . Pious Reverence adds the reins, Concord performs the function of armor-bearer. . . . Nature . . . gives her own palm-wreath of combat."[81] Caparisoned as a crusading knight, the New Man goes off alone and defeats the enemy commander Discord and his ranks of Vices:[82] "True Faith destroys Hatred, Concord Strife, Peace Wrath. . . . Poverty is destroyed, Infamy is vanquished, Old Age withdraws, Malice grows listless . . . Lust is finished, Moderation makes war on Excess, sober Reason attacks Pride, Industry conquers Sloth, Impiety snatches up an axe. . . . But the youth stands secure. . . . at length overcome by her own exertion, Impiety grows feeble."[83]

Abandoned by the Vices, the purified realm is equated with Saturn's Golden Age and the Eden of prelapsarian bliss: "Now the earth vies with heaven, now the land endures ethereal brilliance, now Olympus ornaments the world. Now the field is not smoothed out with the rake nor injured by the ploughshare, nor does it lament the wound of the curved plow . . . the tree does not seek cultivation, nor the vineyard the pruning hook, but each gives of its own accord new fruits."[84]

The book ends with a repetition of the symbolic scenario that Prudentius had borrowed from Vergil: Avarice, the symbol of the Iron Age, is overcome, and Charity, which characterizes the Christian Golden Age, triumphs.[85] Once again the Scales—that metaphor of victory identified with the eternal city since Aeneas gained sovereignty of Rome—determines the outcome of the fray; the New Man crowns his achievements by establishing a kingdom on the basis of law: "Now crime's cohorts are defeated and flee to the Stygian shades. . . . Virtue rises . . . Vice sinks . . . the blessed man regulates the kingdom of the world with the reins of law. Now the Virtues locate their abodes upon the earth."[86]

The chivalric cast of Alain's work reflects a new northern gloss on the Trojan myth; other innovations show revived humanistic concerns. This is reflected in the praise of worldly achievement, and in the concept of Nature's perfectibility.[87] Her realm is idealized; although Fortune's chaotic activity is acknowledged a deterrent to harmony. The new humanism also colors the approach to pagan intellectual thought: philosophy is conceived of as the path to divine wisdom; towards this knowledge the Liberal Arts act as guide. In this schema, the sister arts astronomy and astrology are of paramount importance, for the planets and the stars are the domicile of the pagan gods. These ethereal creatures are immortalized in the heavens for their virtue as visible vehicles of God's will.[88] These same Virtues are carried to earth in the person of the perfect man, the microcosm in whom heaven and earth coincide. Alain's perfect man concurs with the image of the Roman emperor as it was formulated at the court of Charlemagne.

Praised as omniscient in divine wisdom,[89] unsurpassed in learning,[90] Davidic in battle, and Solomonic in judgment,[91] contemporary literature accorded to Charlemagne the dimensions of the microcosmic man. In the visual arts these accolades were compressed in the image of the emperor as the repository of all the Virtues who destroy Vice.[92] In a double portrait of Charlemagne and his son Louis destroying the Vices that is based on a Byzantine model (fig. 22),[93] the emperor is fit into the mold established for Theodosius in Prudentius's *Psychomachia*.[94] But as he defined the Trojan hero in his northern manifestation, Charlemagne provided the model for the perfect man as he would appear in the twelfth century in Alain de Lille's *Anticlaudian*.[95] A comparable transformation characterizes the crusading knight in a contemporary reinterpretation of the *Psychomachia* that is bound with another of Alain de Lille's works. A knight on horseback bearing a shield with a Trinitarian symbol is crowned by an angel

22. *Virtues Triumphant.* Ivory plaque, ninth century. Museo Nazionale, Florence.

(fig. 23). He is preceded into battle by the Virtues bestowed upon him by the Holy Spirit. These lead the assault against the Vices who confront him in the form of demons.[96] In the *chansons de geste* that constituted the most important genre of secular medieval literature, a feudal light was cast on the portrait of the Roman sovereign, now defined as a Christian pilgrim and a warrior knight, to whom his vassals owe absolute obedience. Sustained by the Christian emperor's biblical and pagan ancestors, to whom we shall soon turn our attention,[97] these northern glosses made a hybrid of the heir of Aeneas, transforming him into the Paladin of David, on whom are bestowed the blood relics of Christ.

Once fixed in this medieval chivalric mold, the image of the

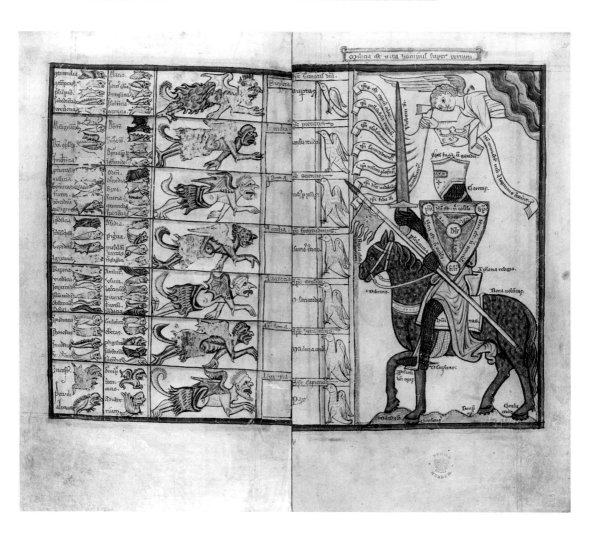

ideal sovereign affected the allegorical spin-offs of Vergil's epic. The individualization of the hero, the expansion of naturalistic incident, the revival of interest in astrology and the pagan gods, and the chivalric gloss—all of which occur in Alain's *Anticlaudian*—acted as stimulants that led to a contemporary revival of interest in a narrative retelling of the Troy legend. Into this revived genre were absorbed the Christian ideas whose poetic shape was formulated by Prudentius and Alain. In these, the new persona of the ideal hero-emperor, who was formed by and reflected the transfer of the empire to the north, leapt off the page to color the character and comportment of the pretenders to his throne.

23. *Knight Confronting Vices.* In Peraldus *Liber de Vitiis,* after 1235. British Library, London, MS Harley 3244, fol. 28.

Chapter IV *The Revival of Epic Narrative in the Late Middle Ages and the Renaissance*

AT the Treaty of Verdun in 843, Charlemagne's realms were apportioned among his heirs.[1] The largest portions of these divided lands configured eastern and western Francia, territories that assumed their final form in the nation states of Northern Europe. From that day forward, and intensifying with the death of Charlemagne's direct heirs and the Capetian elevation to the French throne in 987, a rivalry was established between the East and West Frankish ruling houses, and with it contending claims to the imperial title. The dissension was reflected everywhere, and nowhere more imaginatively than in the reshaping of the Trojan myth.

In the didactic variants of the Trojan legend—we have considered the *Psychomachia* and the *Anticlaudian*—Christian moral allegories were developed from motifs in Vergil's *Aeneid*. In these, the identity of the ideal hero was abandoned, leaving intact only the skeleton of his perfect moral virtue, which mirrored that of Christ. Beginning in the twelfth century interest was rekindled in the narrative elements of the legend.[2] When the narrative tradition was revived and the identity of the pagan heroes restored, the Christian elements that had been developed in the emblematic mode were carried over to form a hybrid genre. A spate of vernacular compilations followed, and these provided extraordinary early examples of cultural syncretism in which pagan and Christian history is amalgamated, a Christological gloss is applied, and the Trojan heroes are translated into knights of Christendom. From the thirteenth century onwards, these reworked legends invariably assumed a Roman imperial bias as the connecting link between past and present Trojan history. Prior scholarly discussions of these reworked narratives have paid little attention to their originality, to their mystical bias, or to their political motivations—all of which will concern us here.

A notable constant in the medieval legends of Troy was their dependence on two late antique texts—the *De Excidio Troiae Historia* of Dares the Phrygian, and the *Ephemerii Belli Troiani* of Dictys the Cretan—believed at the time to be eyewitness accounts of Troy's fall.[3] Dares, who is concerned with Troy's early history, begins his tale with the Argonauts' quest for the Golden Fleece and relates how they destroyed Troy the first time in retaliation for Laomedon's faithlessness. Rebuilt by Laomedon's son Priam, the city fell a second time in revenge for Paris's rape of Helen. Later Trojan history is the concern of Dictys.[4] By interpolating Dares and Dictys, the stories of Jason and Aeneas were bridged, and thus two destructions of Troy became a standard feature of the medieval accounts.

A number of important considerations accounted for the selection of Dares and Dictys as sources. Unlike Homer's poetic reconstruction of Troy's fall, Dictys and Dares claimed their accounts were a historical record, and they took a euhemeristic approach to the material. For the royal patrons who instigated this revival, the euhemeristic interpretation evoked their assimilation to the ancients, since these accounts portrayed the gods as free of human foibles, and as identical with the good princes of old.

The opportunity which this approach afforded for syncretic exegesis was even more important. In the hands of the medieval authors, the chronological scope of the Trojan narrative was extended and the whole legend was treated as a single development of revealed salvation history.[5] Thus supernatural events were given rational explanations, and mythological heroes, now treated as deified rulers, were ranked with figures from Holy Writ and assigned a place in human history.

Reworked in accordance with these principles, the vernacular legends trace the history of Troy's rulers and the vicissitudes of the city from its origins at the dawn of time, and they take into account the major heroes who figured in Trojan prehistory. Thus the Argonaut's quest for the Golden Fleece serves as a preamble to Aeneas's story. Some accounts continue the legacy beyond Aeneas's settlement of the new Troy in Latium to Pompey's destruction of Jerusalem, when war ended and all the civilized world was put under Roman rule. Others include the history of Augustus's reign;[6] some integrate the legend that the Sibyl revealed the advent of Jesus to Augustus. A few extend the legends to the present by tracing a Trojan genealogy for the Franks that includes the patron of the compilation. All reclassicize the Trojan epic by healing the rift that had developed after the fourth century between narrative and emblematic elements, thus they establish the Trojan legend's position as the thread that links all civilization in a linear pattern.

With the interpolation in the thirteenth century of the writings attributed to Berosus the Chaldean, the medieval Trojan legend assumed its definitive shape. Berosus provided the basis for the synthesis of pagan and Hebraic history which lent the compilations their unique quality.[7] Fragments of Berosus's Babylonian history, in which events from the Bible were aligned with pagan legend, had been preserved in the writings of Josephus and other venerable ancient authors. These fragments formed the rudiments for the Christian version of the Universal Chronicle, a genre of history that was developed in the fourth century in Eusebius's *Chronographia*.[8] In the twelfth century Berosus's schema was reconstructed to show that pagan gods descended from the same divine seed that sprouted in Christ's earthly parentage. Thus Berosus provided the blueprint for the medieval legends of Troy and for the Christian/pagan syncretism on which imperial claims to divinity were thereafter grounded.[9]

The adoption of Berosus in the medieval vernacular legends eliminated the problems which otherwise would have arisen when pagan history and idolatry were incorporated into a Christian context. More to the point, it postulated a single royal channel through which the divinity acceded to the earthly sphere. Once we reach the final flowering of this genre in the Renaissance, the recreated epics specify what had only been implied in Prudentius and Alain: the blood of both biblical and classical heroes is joined in the Christian heir of Aeneas.

Benoit de Sainte Maure's *Roman de Troie* (ca. 1160–65), created

at the Angevin court of Henry II Plantagenet and Eleanor of
Aquitaine, is the most important of the early French reworkings
of the Trojan myth.[10] Benoit began his tale with the Argonauts
and ended with Ulysses, with Troy as the conceptual link between the two stories. A thirteenth-century illustrated manuscript includes images of both the Argonauts' destruction of Troy
(fig. 24) and Jason's capture of the Golden Fleece (fig. 25). Benoit
gave the ancient figures contemporary relevance by transforming
the vestals into nuns and the warriors into cavaliers. By recounting the "secret" that the Palladium came down from heaven to
protect Troy and its ruling dynasty, Benoit prepared the foundation for the later development of its Christian identity.

A more erudite Latin version of the legend, the *Historia Destructionis Troiae* of Guido delle Colonne,[11] largely displaced Benoit's French poem and enjoyed widespread popularity throughout Europe up to the eighteenth century.[12] Like Benoit, Guido
began with the Argonauts' destruction of Troy, but, drawing on
Vergil, he expanded his legend to tell of Aeneas's divine ancestry
in Venus, his journey to found a new Troy in Latium, and the birth
of his son Iulus/Ascanius.[13] His work thus forms part of the

24. *The Argonauts Destroy
Troy.* In Benoit de Saint
Maure, *Roman de Troie.*
Biblioteca Apostolica
Vaticana, Rome. MS
Reg. Lat. 1505, fol. 21v.

25. *Jason Captures the Golden Fleece.* In Benoit de Saint Maure, *Roman de Troie.* Biblioteca Apostolica Vaticana, Rome. MS Reg. Lat. 1505, fol. 14r.

Vergilian literary tradition in which the Trojan legend is merged with the history of Rome and the Julian gens.

The potential for interpreting the Argonautic journey as a metaphor for a spiritual crusade had existed since the second century, when Valerius Flaccus linked the quest for the Fleece to Titus's capture of the Jewish temple spoils. Guido expressed the link between the Argonautic adventures and a Christian mystical purpose; thereafter the Argonautic expedition became a generic metaphor for a pilgrimage to the Holy Land.[14] Guido's poem was rooted in topical events. He was a poet and humanist at the Sicilian court of the Hohenstaufen Emperor Frederick II (1197–1250), who was titular sovereign of Jerusalem and planned a crusade to recapture the Holy Sepulchre.[15] Following ancient precedent, Guido updated the Argonautic quest to reflect contemporary history. It is this implicit meaning that colors the fourteenth-century illustration of his tale, where the Argonauts land at Troy wearing courtly dress (fig. 26).[16]

From both a literary and an ideological standpoint, Guido deserves significant credit for shaping the Trojan topos into a new mold. His contribution to cultural syncretism is even more note-

26. *Jason Arriving at Troy.*
In Guido delle Co-
lonne, *Historia Destruc-
tionis Troiae.* Biblio-
thèque Royale,
Brussels. MS 9240, fol.
2. Copyright A.C.L.
Bruxelles.

worthy. He appears to be the first author to refer in a vernacular
legend to Berosus the Chaldean, the fundamental source for the
syncretistic genealogies that pervade the contemporary imperial
chronicles and later Trojan legends. On the authority of Berosus,
Guido joined the pagan and Christian elements in the story and
attuned the fictional ancestry of the Trojan heroes to the mythic
genealogy that would become standard for aspirants to the imperial dignity.[17]

The challenge of bringing literature to life was seized by
Philip the Good of Burgundy, a direct descendant of Charlemagne and the most powerful ruler in Europe in 1429 when he
founded the Order of the Golden Fleece to undertake the task
accomplished by the Argonautic heroes in antiquity.[18] In so doing he forged the legendary into a martial tool. The Knights of the
Golden Fleece, self-proclaimed Argonauts, identified their crusading objectives of defeating the Turk and repossessing the Holy
Sepulchre with the capture of the Golden Fleece that had been
accomplished by their mythical prototypes.

The duke immersed himself in Trojan-Argonautic imagery, collecting manuscripts of the medieval Trojan tales for his library (see fig. 26) and tapestries of the Trojan adventures for his throne room and decorating the walls of his famous cosmic chamber at Hesdin with scenes from Argonautic history. With this imagery permeating the duke's court, the revival of scenes of Titus's conquest of Jerusalem, as in this fifteenth-century Flemish tapestry (fig. 27), must have evoked the Argonautic frame of reference that had accrued to the capture of the Jewish temple spoils in the first century with Valerius Flaccus's *Argonautica*. In its contemporary revival, the use of such imagery would therefore carry allusions to Philip's spiritual crusade to the Holy Land. At the Burgundian court the Christian implications of this topos were pronounced, for the Golden Fleece was identified as the Mystical Lamb by the knights who were named in its honor.[19]

Pursuing his interest ever further, Philip commissioned a history of Jason[20] and a Trojan epic from his chaplain, Raoul Lefèvre. Building on Guido's tale, Lefèvre announced in the Prologue of his *Recuyell of the Histories of Troye* that the theft of the Golden Fleece brought about Ilion's fall. He devoted the first book to Saturn and the Golden Age and drew from these mythic origins a constellation of heroes even more expansive than that of Vergil to prove both the mythic and sacred roots of the imperial family tree. While versions of the Trojan myth appear earlier

27. Attributed to Pasquier Grenier, *The Siege of Jerusalem by Titus.* Tapestry, French-Burgundian, ca. 1460. Metropolitan Museum of Art, New York. Rogers Fund, 1909 (09.172).

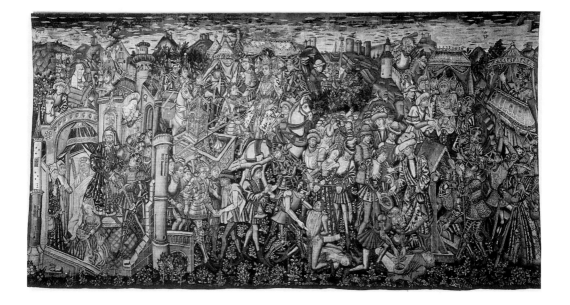

at the courts of France, Flanders, Germany, and Spain, the scope and narrative detail of Lefèvre's work is immediately distinguishing. Resorting to Berosus's authority, Lefèvre identified Noah and Janus, the respective fathers of the Hebrew and pagan peoples, as one and the same person. In this way the parent stem of the race was formed by merging Old Testament figures with their mythical counterparts.[21] This syncretistic approach cohered with the philosophy that all forms of culture were linked in a common network which served to reveal God's working in history.

In tune with the cast of the medieval legends, Lefèvre joined the Argonautic and Trojan tales. Time is collapsed between the past and the present for Lefèvre's transformed demigods are crusading knights who evoke the cavaliers of the Burgundian court. In an illumination to an edition of his tale, the rebuilding of Troy takes place in a medieval city of Flanders.

Lefèvre transposed the rich scenario of the Trojan epic into a Burgundian key, while the Knights of the Order of the Golden Fleece lifted into life from the pages of Christian moral allegory the psychomachian battle for the sovereignty of Rome. The narrative profusion and genealogical speculation of the *Recuyell* remained a constant that not only guaranteed authenticity to Burgundian versions of the legend, it also congealed the Trojan literary tradition into its most complete form to date.

In 1509 Jean Lemaire de Belges composed the *Illustrations de Gaul et Singularitez de Troye*.[22] In his self-styled Ur-version of the myth, Lemaire announced his intention to put forward the venerable antiquity of the princes of Gaul and to throw light on the arcane history of Troy. The work was dedicated to the future Hapsburg Emperor Charles V and to his aunt Margaret, regent of the Netherlands, on the occasion of the Peace of Cambrai between the Austro-Burgundian and French ruling houses.[23] Earlier versions of the myth had been consistent in their approach to primordial history, tracing the roots of the Trojans to the original race that descended from Saturn. But there was marked disagreement about more contemporary events; the disagreement was characterized by competing claims to Trojan heritage among eastern and western Franks. Replete with the adventures of the Trojan heroes, Lemaire did not neglect Frankish history. Asserting his as the authoritative version, after which no further account need be written, Lemaire showed that both branches descended from a common stem whose root he traced to Noah/Janus.[24] He brought this heritage forward through Priam and the emperors of Rome to culminate with Charles V.[25] In recreating his Trojan legend, Lemaire revealed the genealogy through which the Hapsburgs claimed to be legitimate imperial heirs who would realize a primal state of perfection in a new Christian Troy which stood as a civic metaphor for Eden before the fall.

Lemaire's genealogical pronouncement implied that the reigning Roman emperor was the living heir of Aeneas; the hero of the Christian spin-offs of Vergil's Trojan epic. For Charles, the scion of Austro-Burgundian and Spanish royal houses, this implication was given exhaustive visual treatment in the *Los Honores* tapestries.[26] In this cycloramic vision of Alain de Lille's *Anticlaudian*, which is enhanced with details from Lemaire's own work, myth and history are woven together to celebrate Charles's election as Holy Roman emperor in 1519.[27] The tapestries allude to Charles as the paradigm of Virtue, the New Man created to renew the earth, while the living presences of his ancestors converge to sustain him in the battle over Vice.

Following Alain's scenario, the Liberal Arts build a chariot for *Prudence* (bk. II, chap. 7), and she undertakes her celestial journey through the zodiac. The purpose of the journey is indicated in the *Divine Wisdom* tapestry (bk. V, chap. 1; fig. 28) by the figure of Prometheus in the zodiacal arc. He takes fire from the stars to kindle the human form, while below on earth a figure modelled on Adam awaits enlivenment. Old Testament, imperial, and mythic heroes stand at attention, witnessing the recreation of their merits in his person. A harbinger of the benefits that the New Man will bring appears in the tapestry's lower half, where evil is flagellated and the Virtues regain possession of the world (bk. IX, chaps. 1–7). The *Nobility* tapestry (fig. 29) depicts the celestial court of the Virgin Mary (bk. V, chaps. 8–9), and the throne room of God, where the New Man is formed from the composite merits of Joseph, Abraham, and other Old Testament prototypes (bk. VI, chaps. 1–8); we shall return to discuss this tapestry in another context.[28] The Virtues bestowed on the New Man by Nature (bk. VII, chaps. 4–7) are assembled on the *Seven Virtues* tapestry, while Alain's realm of Fortune (bk. VIII, chaps. 1–2) is brilliantly brought to life in the *Fortune* tapestry (fig. 30). Here Alain's account is enriched by the historical context in which the

28–32a–b. *Los Honores* tapestries, Brussels, ca. 1519. Palace of La Granja, San Ildefonso, Segovia. Patrimonio Nacional, Madrid.

28. *Divine Wisdom.*

29. Nobility.

30. Fortune.

31. Infamy.

32a. Fame.

Trojan legend thrived: Julius Caesar, Romulus and Remus, and Silvius Tullus are sheltered by Fortune's favor on the left, while Phrixus astride the Golden Fleece escapes the troubled waters on the right to join them. Following the promise of Alain's Fortune, who, though she previously shifted the destiny of the Four World Monarchies, vowed to become stable and steadfast abrogating her motion for the New Man, the wheel at the center of the tapestry is fixed in place by the imperial crown and insignia of the new Holy Roman emperor, Charles V.

The New Man's lone battle against the Vices (bk. IX, chaps. 1–7) is celebrated in the *Infamy* tapestry (fig. 31), where the triumphant hero enters at the left to drive out Cupidity, Malice, Libido, and the other Vices from the realm; below their exiting chariot heretics and miscreants are trampled under foot. An inscription celebrates Astraea's return to earth.[29] Other tapestries are devoted to the scenes of *Honor*, *Justice*, and *Fame* who, astride her elephant, blares forth tidings of victory. Here Hector and Priam appear, as does Jason; he acts as halberdier for Julius Caesar, who crushes Mohammed in this path (fig. 32a and b).

While the accretions to the Trojan tale have been treated elsewhere with the attitude that one good story attracts another, we have now seen that interest in the legend was guided by shifting pretensions to Roman imperial power. The dynastic issues that were allegorically addressed in the Trojan literature were much more concretely expressed in contemporary historical documents to which we now turn our attention.

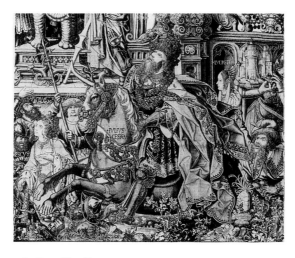

32b. *Fame* (detail).

Chapter V *Mythic Genealogy*

G ENEALOGICAL mythmaking, a now-extinct art form, held pride of place in determining the emperors' monolithic stature. Existing studies of this topos have been limited to local issues. The genealogies have not been discussed in relation to the continuously evolving tradition of Roman imperial ideology, nor to the singular role played by the Trojan myth in this development.[1] The focus here is the uninterrupted continuity that, over two millennia, linked the first emperor of Rome to the last through the Trojan ancestry.[2] In the case of the Christian emperor, the destiny that devolved on him from his divine roots has been obscured by a lack of attention to the importance of syncretistic ancestry. While scholars have been aware of the Old Testament and Olympian identities applied to the reigning monarch, they have disregarded the deeper resonances therein expressed. Attention to the significance implicit in the fusion of the emperor's Trojan and Hebraic forbears yields a precise and cogent picture of the meaning of theocratic rule in the Christian era.

What is at once the most provocative and ineffable aspect of the tradition as a whole has been virtually unheeded in the studies of the post-antique era. This is the inextricable bond the emperor established between his person and the state religion in order to yoke self-reverting veneration to religious practices that were geared to ancestor worship. Augustus, who imposed unity on the empire by restoring the most ancient religious traditions, defined the concept of piety along ancestral lines when he established an imperial cult for the worship of the Julio-Claudian gens.[3] In erecting a temple to the divine Julius Caesar, he followed the model of Aeneas, who makes a sacrifice and vows a temple to his father Anchises.[4] Linked by kinship to the Trojan Penates, to Vesta,[5] and even to Apollo,[6] all of whom he ministered to as Pontifex Maximus, Augustus sacrificed to the ancestral cult, while as emperor he basked in the worship that devolved from these associations. The priestly functions, cult worship, and even the apotheosis conceded to Augustus was continued in his Christian successors who shared in Augustus's divine ancestry.[7] This is particularly evident in the case of Constantine, Clovis, and Charlemagne, who were canonized as saints and venerated in the local liturgy.[8]

The manifestations of the emperor's divine ancestry are far more extensive than the limited number of examples investigated here. This sampling is indicative of the much broader applicability of an "ancestral" approach for appreciating in a new light phenomena that range in their diversity from the shaping of religious dogma to the collecting of antiquities whose subjects supported genealogical claims. Within these parameters fall the building of monuments and the commissioning of pictorial and literary works where biblical, historical, Trojan, and other mythological subjects—indeed a wide range of revived pagan and Old Testament themes and their New Testament counterparts—enforced genealogical pretensions. Although only developments at the imperial court are considered here, one must be aware that the emperor's vassals, as well as rival rulers and the Papacy itself, unhesitatingly invested their own pretensions to imperial prerogatives with a similar iconography. The claim to Trojan ancestry became common in all European cultures as they jockeyed for position in the global power structure.

Pagan Antiquity

The most potent aspect of imperial ideology lay in the creation of mythic genealogies. The tradition saw its origins in antiquity, and in tracing Augustus's descent from Aeneas, Vergil provided the Roman imperial prototype.[9] In Vergil's epic, the eternal city is designated by Providence as the arena for a metaphysical battle to the death between the forces of virtue and vice. To be won, the battle must be fought by a noble descendant of the Trojan race. Out of the poetic fiction of Aeneas's divine ancestry—which stretched forwards in time to Romulus, Augustus, and the Julio-Claudian emperors who succeeded him, and backwards through Dardanus, the founder of Troy, to Jupiter and Saturn—grew a symbolic heritage strong enough to situate the divinity in the imperial household and to unite the world under the emperor's universal monarchy.

Although the Aeneadae died out with Nero, the last of the Julio-Claudians who chanted a Trojan threnody as Rome burned,[10] his Flavian successors set the pattern for the future by appropriating the Trojan ancestry. Whatever form the genealogies took in the following centuries—and they were updated to accommodate Constantine, Theodosius, Charlemagne, and each subsequent emperor of Rome—one factor remained constant to the genre: the Trojan descent.

Byzantium

We have seen that the sacral charge implicit in the Trojan descent was given a Christian apocalyptic meaning in the fourth century. The Christian purpose of Troy's refounding in Latium was seen to be revealed when Christ sanctified imperial Rome through his birth. A *renovatio* of the empire implied the renewal of the peaceful reign of Roman rule in which Christ will reign again. In his poems written to glorify the reign of Theodosius, Prudentius extended Vergil's concept of Rome's divine mission. He defended the universality of Roman rule as a manifestation of God's plan;[11] he spoke for the predestined rule of "the seed of Aeneas [whose] successes were ordered by the governance of the God Christ,"[12] and he contended that Rome's role in uniting the world in good government was but a step in the preparation of the coming spiritual empire when the far-off successor of Aeneas would bow down his knee to Christ.[13]

For succeeding generations of Christian rulers, this awareness of the empire's sacred purpose spurred the search for ancestral forbears among the Aeneadae. Because Trojan descent was essential to the ambitious, indeed apocalyptic, ideology of rule that intended to bring about the return of those happy past times, the Trojan legend became an "ethnogenic" fable that traced the parent stem of the race in the cause of dynastic legitimacy. As one imperial dynasty was supplanted by another, ancestral claims were ever more insistently called upon to validate the new possessor of the realm. What began as a cry of continuity mushroomed into a principle of preemption when the physical seat of Roman power was at issue.

When Constantine consolidated the eastern and western hemispheres of the empire under his single rule, he revalidated the Augustan monarchical principle that had prevailed at the time of Christ's birth. An equally venerable precedent sustained his transfer of the imperial seat to Byzantium—indeed contemporary legends recount that he founded his new capital on what he believed to be the ancient site of Troy.[14] In returning to the native Phrygian soil, Constantine retraced the steps of Dardanus, the founder of Troy. He emulated Aeneas (his legendary ancestor according to contemporary sources)[15] by transporting the Palladium, guarantor of the empire's legitimate transfer, to Constantinople.[16] "There he placed it in the forum to which he had also transported a bronze statue of Apollo on which he had his features carved and his titles inserted; symbols of Christ's passion were inscribed on its base."[17] In this way, Constantine reconsecrated the New Rome and its gods to Christianity and established a formidable principle of preemption that would be adhered to by future claimants to the imperial throne.[18]

The Empire of the Franks

As the strength of the Greek Empire diminished with the spread of Islam, the Trojan ancestry became the battle cry of a new race of rulers. Frankish pretensions to be the sole valid heir of Rome with equal claim to world supremacy were guaranteed with the transfer of the empire to Charlemagne. More than any other mythic factor, the validity of the Roman Empire's transfer to the Franks depended upon Charlemagne's claim to Trojan ancestry. In a history of 784, Paul the Deacon traced Charlemagne's descent from the Frankish Anchises, the namesake of Aeneas's father.[19] Immediately following his coronation in the year 800 and the conferring of his imperial title, Charlemagne's Trojan origins were called upon to affirm his worthiness. On that occasion Dungal, successor to Alcuin, proclaimed that the empire of Romulus, descendant of Troy, was in the hands of Charles, descendant of Troy.[20]

Corroborating details were added as the legend of Charlemagne's Trojan ancestry became a standard set piece in the evolution of the imperial myth. The assertion that the Carolingian bloodline sprang from the union of the imperial scion Ansibert and Blichilde, a Merovingian princess, yoked together the ties to Clovis and the Roman roots of this heritage. These parents bore Saint Arnulf, bishop of Metz (ca. 580–655), who through his marriage to Doda begat the Frankish Anchises. When Anchises married Begga of Lotharingia and Brabant, the Trojan ancestry was communicated to their son Pippin the Younger and the Carolingians. These foundations provided future chroniclers with the basis for linking the dynasty through Clovis to Priam's royal house.

Based on this claim to Trojan ancestry, Vergilian topoi were assigned to Charlemagne in the poetry of the Carolingian court. In a poem by the emperor's minister Einhard that draws on imagery from the *Aeneid*, the "caput mundi" is transferred with Charlemagne, who is compared to Aeneas and to Romulus.[21] When Charlemagne renamed the months in the Germanic tongue, he emulated and superseded the ancestral Romulus, who had given the months their Latin names.[22] The Trojan ancestry conveyed with it the design for global rule, and Charlemagne's ambitions to extend his domain beyond the Frankish realms were transmitted in Alcuin's application to the emperor of Aeneas's dictum "Parcere subiectis."

The emperor's progeny made much of these pretensions. In a panegyric by the court poet Ermoldus Nigellus, Priam, Hector, and Aeneas cede their place to Charlemagne's grandson, Pippin of Aquitaine.[23] For another grandson, the future Emperor Charles the Bald, a poem on the exodus of the Franks proclaimed that Rome's Golden Age was now ruled by the Carolingians, the descendants of the royal line of Anchises.[24] On the occasion of Charles the Bald's imperial coronation, Hincmar of Reims—the same bishop who framed the legend of the Holy Spirit's epiphany at Clovis's baptism—drew on these foundations to support Charles's legitimacy.[25]

A notable ninth-century addition is the grafting of Greek ancestry onto Charlemagne's family tree; Alexander the Great is added to the ranks of his forbears,[26] and his right to the Byzantine Empire is said to derive from his mother's ancestor Heraclius;[27] a later chronicle traces Charlemagne's roots to Dardanus,[28] the founder of Troy. Refined and augmented for more than a millennia, the claim of Charlemagne's Trojan ancestry soon assumed the weight of dogma.

One offshoot of this credo was the authority it lent to the claim that the Frankish people as a whole were related to the Trojan race. A number of alternative interpretations were applied to this legacy; the most audacious claimed that Troy was a Frankish settlement. For the eastern Franks this claim was supported by Tacitus's assertion that the Germans were indigenous peoples who descended from the primordial earth god Tuisco.[29] In one formula for constructing this heritage that was later visu-

33. Peter Flotner, *Tuisco to Charlemagne*. Silver reliefs, German, 1537–43. Antwerp, Museum Mayer van der Bergh. Copyright A.C.L. Bruxelles.

alized in a series of silver reliefs (fig. 33),[30] the line of German kings was said to originate with Tuisco, the eponymous father of the Teutonic race, and to continue through to Charlemagne. Taken to its most extreme application, this indigenous approach fostered the belief that the Germans originated with the heirs of Noah, who left Babel before the confusion. While all other nations were derivative in language and culture, the Germans spoke "Alemanni," Adam's tongue and the language of all men.[31] Even though a pride in roots as well as a respect for the authority of Tacitus favored an autonomous origin for the race, the suggestion was palled by a negative flavor. Tacitus based his assertion on the belief that no one would choose to risk a perilous sea voyage to settle in a country that offered such poor weather and inhospitable terrain unless it was their native home. A more moderate approach asserted that an independent Frankish Empire was contemporary with Rome and stemmed from the same source— Troy—as did the Roman Empire.

On the whole, it appears likely that for the early history of the Frankish Empire, the pseudoclassical myths of origin dominated the indigenous folkloric ones because they were tailored to contemporary imperial needs. The most popular of these classical formulae postulated a twain settlement for the Trojan refugees, whereby Aeneas and Priam the Younger, both sons of Anchises and hence brothers, fled Troy together. Aeneas continued to Italy while Priam settled in Germany to become *Rex Alamannorum*.[32] The Frankish settlement was alternately attributed to Antenor, Sicamber, Franco; all direct kin of Priam and Aeneas. Franco, for whom the Franks were named, appears with Hector in the later chronicle of Hartmann Schedel that records the twain Trojan Exodus. The text defines the relationship: "Franco was Hector's son." (fig. 34).[33] Charlemagne's election as Holy Roman emperor was continuously interpreted as the act which reunited the two realms and the two branches of the family. In the twelfth-century *Speculum Regum* of Godfried of Viterbo, this reunification was hailed with metaphors of genetic determination: the seed of Troy gave off two sprouts; one grew into the diadem of Rome, the other into the Teutonic kingdom; in ancient times the Germans and Romans held their power communally and these two powers were united in Charlemagne who was *Romuleus matre, Teutonicus patre*.[34]

As the credo of Charlemagne's Trojan ancestry became a

Der zeheniarig troyanisch krieg ist (als Eusebius sagt) im erste iar Esebon des richters israhel entstanden. Zu
der selben zeit haben die hernachgeschriben gerechnet. dañ Troya (die der Jlon Troys des königs 8 troyer
sun fastweyt auffrichtet) was nur tausent vñnd fünfhundert schrit vorm meer gelegen. da dann auch noturft vñ
überflüssigkeit aller ding vorhanden was. vñnd als Troya ein zeheniarige belegerüg der kriechen erliden het do
wardt sie auch zuletst von ine abgetilgt.

hercules

Hercules mit Jasone hat Troyam (die doch pald vő Priamo herwider gepawt wardt) ver-
wüstet. vnnd den olimpiadischen
kampff aufgesetzt. vnd vil krieg ge-
übet. vnd sol (als sie sagen) zwolff
treffenlich vnd vnmenschlich that
begangen haben.

hector

Hector der erstgeporn sun Priami auß hecuba seinem weib
was ein man vngleichlicher stercke
vñ gestrengigkeit. vñ darüb vő wege des
übergroßen glätzs seiner ritterschafft bey
dě troyanern in grosser achtüg gehalten.
dañ er hat mit seiner vngleiplichen klüg-
heit vñ stercke. nit allein sein eltern sunder
auch sein vaterland in adel. ere vnd glori
erhebt vnd scheinper gemacht. Diser hat
auß Andromacha seinem weib vil sün geporn. der einer hieß Franco. von dem (als
Vincentius historialis burgundus spricht)
die frantzosen vrspung haben gehabt.

Menelaus   **Helena**

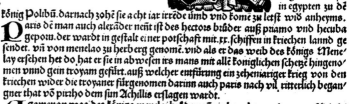

Paris

Helena wz
Menelay
des königs ee
weib vñ wardt
vő parıde dē sun
priami gerawbt
vñ gein troyã ge
fürt vñ darúmb
8 troianisch krieg
fürgenomē. vnd
nach der zerstő-
rüg troye wardt
helena dem me
nelao vő dē krie-
che wider geant
wurtet. der sty-
ge frölich mit ir
in ein schiff i wil
le anheyms zefa-
rē. aber auß ver-
hinderüng des
meers vngestü-
migkeit kome sie
in egypten zu dē

König Polibū. darnach zohe sie acht iar irrēde ümb vnd kome zu letst wid anheyms.
Paris dē man auch alexāder neñt ist des hectors brüder auß priamo vnd hecuba
geporn. der wardt in gestalt einer potschaft mit xx. schiffen in kriechen lannd ge-
sendet. vñ von menelao so herberg genomē. vnd als er das weib des königs Menelay ersehen het do hat er sie in abwesen irs mans mit alle königlichen schetze hingeno-
men vnnd gein troyam gefürt. auß welcher entfürung ein zeheniariger krieg von den
kriechen wider die troyaner fürgenomen darinn auch paris nach vil ritterlich began-
gner that vő pirrho dem sun Achillis erslagen wardt.

Agamenon

Agamenon was des königs menelai brüder vñ ein hawbtman des gantze kriechi-
schen heers wider troiam. die doch zeletst verretterlich vnd schetlich übergege-
ben wardt. vnd er was Atrei des königs sun. vnd von allem heer zu einē gepietter geordnet. der zohe hin in den krieg vnd verließe Clitemestram sein weib. auß der er vil
kinder geporn het. vnnd geduldet vil arbeit vnnd widerwillens der fürstē bey troya
vnd ward auch darúmb abgesetzt. vnd an sein stat Palamedes geordnet. do ine aber
Vlixes erslagen het do name er dē gewalt mit grössern ern widerüb an. do nw troya
gewūnē vñ zestöret wz. vñ er mit grosse kriegs rawb vñ mit cassandra 8 tochter priami widerúmb anhayms wolt. styge er in die schiff. aber auß verhinderüg des meers
vngewitters zohe er schier ein iar irr.

Turcus

Dise zwen Turcus vnd Franco fluhen von troya vnd
machten ywey königreich. aber lanng darnach.

Franco

Franco was hectoris sun vnd priami enicklein von dē
der name der frantzosen herkomt. der wardt vő troya veriagt. vnd als er vor das gantz asiam durchschwaift
het do kome er zu letst an die gestat der thonaw. als er sich aldo ettliche zeit enthalten het do suchet er ein vő gemei-
ner geselschafft 8 mēsche abgesünderte stat vñ kome an dē fluß thanai vñ meotitischen see. daselbst pawet er die
stat Sicambriam.

Turcus was ein sun Troili des suns des königs Priami. der wolt das man das volck das von ime her kome
nach ime turckos nennen solt. ettlich sprechen ir vrsprung sey auß der gegent Sathia.

constant of imperial rhetoric, the Roman legitimacy of future rulers required only that they trace their bloodline to this Frankish ancestor. Nonetheless, with a scope that will soon become apparent, the authors of the medieval chronicles that established the current ruler's descent from the Carolingians expanded this focus by documenting a Trojan ancestry for Charlemagne's Merovingian antecedents.

In the accommodation of Barbarian to Roman Empires, the credit for rerouting the footsteps of the Trojan exiles towards the north was placed with the ancestors of Clovis, the first Christian king of the Franks. The divine origins of the Merovingian house were implied by Clovis's own minister, Avit,[35] and fueled by the testimony that a theophany had attended Clovis's baptism. In a seventh-century chronicle attributed to Fredegarius, the first to record Merovingian history, this implication was broadened to an assertion of the divine birth of the eponym, Merowech.[36] These assertions were soon directed towards Roman roots for the Merovingians claimed to be the legatees of the Roman inheritance in Gaul. This position was supported by Gregory of Tours's (538–94) account that an envoy of the Byzantine basileus Anastasius delivered a crown to Clovis, who from that day forward wore a diadem, endorsed the Purple, and was addressed as Augustus.[37] In the poetry of the Bishop of Poitiers, Venantius Fortunatus (ca. 530–610), the most important contemporary source defining the self-idealized ruler portrait of the Merovingian kings, the grandsons of Clovis are depicted in the mold of the Roman emperors, and the eternal city's rebirth is celebrated under their rule.[38]

Since the sovereignty of the Roman Empire was destined for an heir of the house of Aeneas, the growth of Frankish hegemony soon witnessed the construction of a Trojan ancestry for Clovis. Although no written contemporary record attests this heritage, later sources claim that the knowledge derived from Hunibald, an authority purported to be contemporary with Clovis.[39] The grounds for this assertion were circumscribed by the parallel legacy of the Trojan ancestry of the Franks.

The earliest written tradition for the Merovingians' Trojan origins appeared in Fredegarius's mid–seventh-century chronicle, which adopted the format of the universal chronicle. This antique literary genre of aligned chronologies was expanded in

34. *Hector's Son, Franco, and His Trojan Kin, the Trojan Exodus*. In Hartmann Schedel, *Liber Chronicarum*, Nuremberg, 1493, p. 37. Biblioteca Apostolica Vaticana, Rome.

the fourth century to incorporate sacred and secular history.[40] Beginning with the creation of man and continuing through the priests, kings, and prophets of the Old Testament, biblical history terminates with the advent of Christ. These figures are chronologically aligned with pagan rulers following the division of history into four consecutive World Monarchies that culminate in the Roman Empire. Proceeding forward from this format, secular history is continued to the present ruling dynasty.

Fredegarius's Merovingian chronicle follows these conventions. He begins with Adam, the first priest-king, from whom is traced the genealogy of the rulers of Judea through the first-born who succeed him.[41] The pedigree is extended through Noah, Abraham, and Boz to David and Christ.[42] A parallel history chronicles the ancestry of the Roman emperors and the Frankish kings, retracing both origins to the Trojan exodus, and naming the younger Priam the first king of the Franks.[43]

Fredegarius based his history of the Franks' Trojan origins on Dares, the standard source for the imaginative Trojan literature of the later Middle Ages. Following Dares, Fredegarius begins his Trojan account with Jason's quest for the Golden Fleece, but he allows for no development of the Colchis story, placing emphasis on Jason's encounter with Laomedon and the ensuing first war waged against Troy. The account continues with the second Trojan war, Aeneas's founding of Rome, and the reign of the Julian gens.

A twain Trojan settlement accounts for the Franks' Phrygian origins, while a detour to Macedon in Priam the Younger's journey to the Rhine to found a new Troy provides the basis for the later inclusion of Alexander the Great among the ancestors of the Franks. From Priam descends Franco, their eponymous hero; his heirs are Clovis and Merowech, who gave his name to the Merovingians.[44] From Fredegarius's general history that tied the Franks to Trojan origins, Carolingian texts developed the concept of Clovis's direct descent from Aeneas.[45]

The Davidian Heritage

With the universal chronicle providing its historical foundation, the topos of the Christian sovereign as the Trojan heir was developed concurrently with his Davidian pedigree. Although the priest-kings of the Old Testament were not explicitly claimed as direct imperial ancestors before the Hohenstaufen so designated them in the twelfth century, they were nonetheless identified with Constantine and his Byzantine successors, with Clovis and

35. *King David. Psalter.* Biblioteca Apostolica Vaticana, Rome. MS Pal. Gr. 38, fol. 2r.

36. *The Battle of Jericho, Joshua Roll.* Biblioteca Apostolica Vaticana, Rome. MS Pal. Gr. 431, fol. 5r.

his Merovingian heirs, and with the Carolingians and Saxons in numerous well-known instances.[46] For the Byzantine emperor, literary allusions to this identity gained osmotic force through imagery, as when David is represented wearing the diadem and imperial robes (fig. 35). This interchangeability was reinforced for the Basileus when Byzantine battle victories were referred to their Hebrew prototypes. In the most famous visual example of this application, the campaigns to recover Jerusalem in the tenth century are alluded to by Joshua's reconquest of the Holy Land (fig. 36).[47] Mode and meaning are synthesized by the bipolar frames of reference, for in its continuous display of history, the Joshua Roll recalls the spiraling records of triumph on Roman imperial columns and on those erected in Constantinople by Theodosius and Arcadius.[48]

The Frankish appropriation of the Davidian topos reverts to the sixth century; one instance appears in a poem from the pen of Venantius Fortunatus, who was educated at the imperial school at Ravenna and drew inspiration for his argument from the Byzantine rulers' theocratic pretensions.[49] Celebrating the founding of the Church of Saint Vincent in Paris, on the walls of which the poem was designed to be inscribed, the edifice is associated with the Temple of Solomon, and Clovis's grandson Childebert is called "our Melchisedek, . . . king and priest."[50]

Such forms of apposite address were not just poetic license, for we have seen that the likening of the Merovingians to the priest-kings of the Old Testament was predicated on God's sacral anointment of Clovis's dynasty. Prefigured in the rites of inauguration that consecrated Saul and Jesus as king of the Israelites, the chrism that poured down from heaven to consecrate Clovis signified the Merovingian king's divine election to succeed as priest-king, following the model of the Old Testament patriarchs, and their blood kin, Jesus.[51] Since it was important to establish that both Jesus' kingly and priestly roles and those of his imperial successors were inherited, elaborate genealogies were created for Christ's earthly parents to show that although Joseph descended from the kingly line of Judah, Mary was descended from the priestly house of Levi. It was asserted that Elizabeth was descended from Aaron, and therefore belonged to the tribe of Levi, and Mary was her kinswoman.[52] Out of the New Testament tradition of Jesus' royal heritage grew the iconography of the Tree of

37. *Tree of Jesse*. British Library, London. MS Royal 2 B. VII, fol. 67v.

Jesse (fig. 37).[53] In this visual tradition the Old Testament patriarch is typically represented as though in prescient reverie, con-
templating the progeny that will be born from his line.

As the heir of the Merovingian blood royal,[54] Charlemagne
was the recipient of Clovis's Davidian heritage;[55] he was consistently addressed by the pseudonym David and he manifested this
legacy by modelling his throne and his palace at Aachen on Solomon's.[56] In its narrower sense, this sacred heritage evoked the
king's position as the legitimate *Rex et Sacerdos*; in the wider sense, it
established the link between the medieval kings and the holy
gens of Jesse.

Charlemagne's kinship in the seed of Jesse was indicated by
the miracle of his divine coronation and manifested when
Christ's Crown of Thorns flowered and healed the sick in his
presence.[57] Armed with a sword from heaven which was named
Monjoie for the wood of the cross it contained, and the ancestral
shield of David, which God had converted into Clovis's Christian
armor, Charlemagne's routing of the infidel evidenced his invincibility in the battle for the faith.[58] As it had for the Eastern rulers,
this assimilation could amount to an exchange of identities, as in
the frontispiece to the *Bible of Charles the Bald*, where Solomon
wears the mantle of a Roman ruler and the crown of the Carolingian king.[59] Like much of the imperial iconography of the
Carolingian court, this tradition had Byzantine roots. Undis-
turbed, and perhaps cross-fertilized by Carolingian rivalry, such
associations continued in the East.

The emperor's Trojan ancestry was not neglected in the development of his Davidian kinship,[60] and in the later Middle Ages
Charlemagne's genealogical tree was extended beyond secular
history to incorporate both Homer and Genesis.[61] For it was the
synthesis of these two divine heritages that constituted the
mythic image of the medieval king. By consolidating these traditions, the emperor's pagan forbears were joined in a single root to
the ancestors of Christ. In this way, wielding both Aaron's rod
and Latinus's scepter, the ruling emperor was confirmed as the
blood kin of Christ, the New Aeneas of the Christianized legend
of Troy.[62]

The amalgamation of these ancestral traditions received continuing emphasis and extension in both the historical chronicles
and the imaginative literature of the Carolingian court. In a poem

by Sedulius Scotus (ca. 844), which documents the Carolingian ties to the Romans and the Merovingians, a comparison between David's and Charlemagne's invincible armor is mentioned in the same breath with the emperor's ancestry in Anchises.[63] A much more elaborate celebration of this syncretistic heritage was visible in the pictures that adorned the imperial palace at Ingleheim painted for Charlemagne's son, Louis the Pious. The most complete historical record of this lost pictorial cycle is Ermoldus Nigellus's poem *In honorem Hludowici*.[64] Sprinkling his description of the members of the Carolingian household with frequent reference to the pagan gods, Ermoldus describes the palace and church at Ingelheim "where the wondrous deeds of God and generations of famous men are finely painted."[65] The "Picturae insignia" began with Old Testament scenes—from Adam's creation in Paradise, through the stories of Noah, Abraham, Moses, and David to the building of Solomon's temple. Sacred imagery is continued in images of the life and the miracles of Christ.

A complementary secular cycle depicted Cyrus, Ninus, and Alexander, following the schema of the Four World Monarchies that culminate with Rome;[66] this is represented by an image of "Romulus . . . [who] laid the foundations of Rome and . . . the might of Rome grew up to the very skies."[67] These scenes were apparently placed in Louis's reception hall, where he administered laws to his subjects. The Romans' achievements are linked to Louis by the phrase "Illi ergo pius Caesar dat iura subactis; more sub regni rite revoluit opus."[68] These words, which recall the *Aeneid*'s most famous motto, "parcere subiectis et debellare superbos," and which Alcuin had already applied to Charlemagne, are repeated for the dynasty's heir.[69] The Romans are also connected to the Carolingians by the sequence of images: "To the imperial conquests of [Caesar] are linked the Franks and their marvellous achievements: painted there is Constantine's dismissal of Rome from his affections and his building of Constantinople. . . . there the successful Theodosius . . . then there is a painting of Charles [Martel]; then . . . Pippin [and] . . . wise Charlemagne."[70]

In a recent reconstruction of these images, the Old and New Testament scenes are aligned in the nave of the imperial chapel; the famous men are placed on the long walls of the *Aula Regia*.[71] At the *Aula*'s apex, images of Charlemagne, his father, and grandfather trace the ancestral ranks of the Carolingians; these share the space with Constantine and Theodosius, to imply the transfer of empire and the acknowledgment of Charlemagne as the "New Constantine."[72] A new consideration of the series in the light of our knowledge of hereditary aspirations suggests the close relationships between the sacred and secular images. Such a consideration accords with the continuously developing imperial tradition of syncretistic genealogy, and it places the Carolingians in the conventional pietistic context that sustained ancient Roman claims to universal sovereignty. It also accords prototypical status to a cycle whose dual ancestral implications were developed in the most explicit way possible, in innumerable visual and literary progeny created for the Carolingian's imperial successors.

The German Empire

With the coronation of Otto I in the Roman basilica of Saint Peter's in 962, the Roman Empire was transferred to the Saxons. The Ottonian kings extended their reign beyond Germany eastward to parts of Bohemia, Moravia, Polonia, Hungary, and Russia, and southward to Burgundy and the Byzantine lands in Italy.[73] Fortified by the imperial title and a territorial domain that comprised almost the whole of Europe, the Ottonians placed a new emphasis on the German right to the imperium and revived the chimera of universal sovereignty that had evaporated with the division of Charlemagne's realms. Once again history witnessed the "relocation" of the eternal city. Now Trier, the first Roman settlement in Germany, received the designation "New Rome" and "Roma Belgica."[74]

Underlying these events was a conventional scheme of dynastic promotion. Through Otto I's marriage to Adelheid of Burgundy, he annexed the Merovingian and Carolingian bloodlines to his own. The continuous interweaving of politics and legend brought ever closer the usual dynastic goals. When Otto II married the Byzantine princess Teophane, he asserted his legitimate rule of the Byzantine Empire, a claim that was strengthened by Otto III through recall of Charlemagne's Heraclian ancestry.[75] These ambitions were publicly promulgated through the "Byzantinization" and deification of the emperor in Ottonian imagery.[76] Using the *Majestas Domini* formula that had been adopted for

38. *Apotheosis of Otto I.* In *Otto Gospels*, Reichenau, tenth century. Aachen, Cathedral Treasury, fol. 31. Bildarchiv Foto, Marburg.

Christ, the implications of this heritage are addressed in an extraordinary image that shows the emperor's apotheosis; he is raised to heaven in the presence of subject rulers (fig. 38).[77]

The Ottonian mythic genealogy maintained intact both the Trojan[78] and the Davidian heritages of their predecessors. Most significant is the fact that the election by divine unction was claimed a Saxon preserve.[79] The *Norman Anonymous*, a treatise that reflects the monarchical ideas of the Ottonian period, designated the king *Rex et Sacerdos*, by his anointing. The king's dual nature—at once king and priest—is referred to the divine model, Christ, in whose image he becomes "deified" at his consecration.[80] The anointing follows the consecration pattern of the Old Testament priest-kings,[81] and the right to succeed them was ceremonially announced by the imagery of the imperial crown of Otto II (fig. 39). It is inscribed with the title of the Roman emperor and em-

39. *Crown of the Holy Roman Emperor.* Second half of the tenth century with later additions. Treasury, Kunsthistorisches Museum, Vienna.

blazoned with portraits of the Jewish kings Hezekiah, David, and Solomon.[82]

The genealogical tradition continued without interruption for the emperors of the Salian dynasty, who descended from the Saxons through Liutgard, daughter of Otto I. Confirmed at his imperial election in 1014 by the descent of the Holy Spirit and surrounded by a mandorla that expresses his divine radiance, Henry II appears as the repository of the Virtues in a symbolic representation of his psychomachian victory over subjugated Vice (fig. 40).[83] Time lent its enhancements to his glories. In a later chronicle that includes a visual paean to legitimate marriage and to the progeny born of this pious blood, the three Ottonian emperors are grafted onto a common vine with Henry, who was venerated as a saint (fig. 41). For Emperor Conrad III (d. 1152), the last of this line, Ekkehard of Aura (d. 1125) composed a Universal

Chronicle that became a best-seller in the Middle Ages.[84] Here again the alignment of Old Testament and pagan history is appended to the Frankish Trojan myth of the dual settlement of Italy and Sicambria by Aeneas and his brother; this history is applied to the Germans at large. The biological chain that linked Anchises to the Merovingians and Carolingians is extended to Conrad, who appears in a version of this *Weltchronik* holding the globe of the Christian universe in one hand and roundels of his ancestors in the other. Before he died, Conrad designated his nephew, the Hohenstaufen Emperor Frederick I Barbarossa, as his successor.[85]

40. *Henry II. Evangelar of Henry II.* Biblioteca Apostolica Vaticana, Rome. MS. Lat. Ottobonian 74, fol. 193vo.

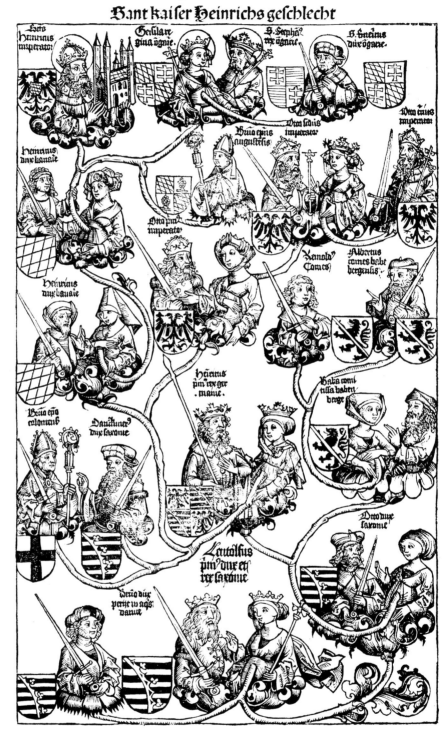

The Hohenstaufen, Berosus the Chaldean, and the Synchronization of Trojan and Biblical Genealogies

Following the death of the last direct male heir of the Carolingian dynasty, Hugh Capet ascended to the French throne in 979. Termed an usurpation by contenders, the event effected a never-ending rivalry between French and German Franks, with both claiming legitimate descent from Charlemagne. Generated by a twelfth-century intensification in the bid for the imperium between the French and German ruling houses,[86] the Hohenstaufen legitimized their tenure by mounting an impressive campaign to prove Charlemagne's German origins. Blows to the French position were leveled by Frederick Barbarossa's restoration of imperial Carolingian palaces at Aachen and Ingleheim, and by his successful efforts to have Charlemagne canonized (1165).[87] The German position was fortified by recall to Einhard's notation that Charlemagne had named the months in German, by the dissemination of Roman law throughout the empire,[88] and by an audacious manipulation of the Holy Roman emperors' mythic genealogy.

Beginning in the twelfth century under Hohenstaufen patronage, imperial chroniclers plumbed—or invented—the "rediscovered" Babylonian history of Berosus the Chaldean. Purported to have lived long before Alexander the Great, Berosus was summarily known in antiquity through citations in Josephus and other historians; these recorded Berosus's chronological alignment of Babylonian and Jewish history with pagan legend. This knowledge was transmitted to the court of Constantine, for Berosus is cited in the writings of Eusebius.[89] The recall of Berosus in the medieval historical chronicles effected a quantum leap in genealogical pretensions. For in twelfth-century references to Berosus's ancient history, knowledge of the past is amplified to reveal that at the origins of civilization, the priest-kings of the Old Testament and of Roman mythology were not only alike in functions but of a single identity. Although they were known by different names in the scattering of the races that followed the Deluge, Noah and Janus were in reality one and the same person. The impact of this revelation shattered the traditional concept that the deities of the Gentiles and the Jews were antagonistic; they were merely known by different names. To the enlightened mind, this knowledge of a "common root" dissolved the enigma

41. *The Ottonian Family Tree.* In Hartmann Schedel, *Liber Chronicarum,* Nuremberg, 1493. fol. 98v. Biblioteca Apostolica Vaticana, Rome.

of the uncanny coincidence of Christ's birth at the founding of the Roman empire. This seemingly irrational concatenation of pagan myth with biblical history established the line of transmission through which the sacred and secular powers of the priest-kings of Judea and Latium came together in the Christian emperor of Rome.

Critics have consistently treated the "rediscovery" of Berosus's history as the Renaissance fabrication of Annius of Viterbo,[90] but in truth this "rediscovery" reverts to at least the twelfth century. From that date forward and throughout the period under study, he is invariably cited as the source of the syncretistic genealogies that combine Homer and Genesis in the historical chronicles and in the vernacular Trojan legends that followed shortly with Guido of Colonna, who wrote under Hohenstaufen patronage. With the unveiling of Berosus's wisdom, the demarcation between history and legend was systematically eliminated, for the proofs of legitimacy which stood at the core of the "factual" imperial chronicles served as the coda to the vernacular legends of Troy we have already discussed. Both genres used Berosus for the syncretism by which they reconstructed the mystical chain of salvation that, stretching from Noah-Janus through Christ-Aeneas, culminated in the present imperial heir.

Hohenstaufen claims to universal sovereignty also found support in Berosus, since he identified Tuisco—the eponymous father of the German race, according to Tacitus[91]—as the son of Noah. The synchronism of Trojan and biblical genealogies in the German stock had two objectives: the more mundane aim was the suppression of rival claims to the imperium. Of more ephemeral and ambitious substance was the most important of the Hohenstaufen contributions to generic imperial lore: they merged the identities of the Hebraic and Olympian forefathers in their ancestry. Since the process of synchronization consisted in no less than the interweaving of Christ's Hebrew roots with those of the gods of Olympus, the emperor was revealed to be the sole repository of the divine blood on earth. The Hohenstaufen pretension to an all-encompassing divinity constituted the most significant expansion in theocratic ideology of the post-antique era. The new concept was immediately reflected in an increased emphasis on the eschatological character of the empire.

In the early development of these ideas, two historians were particularly important: Otto of Freising (1111–58) and Godfried of Viterbo (1125–92). The legend of the Trojan origin of the Franks is appended to the universal history of Otto of Freising, one of the most important authors of the mid–twelfth century.[92] Situated at the core of the imperial household as the uncle of Emperor Frederick I Barbarossa, Otto traced the empire's westward move from the Babylonians to the Romans and the Franks, following the rape of Helen and the destruction of Troy.[93] Beginning his chronicle with Adam's ejection from Paradise at the time of the Giants, Otto identified Janus as Noah's grandson,[94] thus paving the way for the audacious fusion of divine origins which the imperial heir claimed as his birthright.

The canonical form of the imperial pedigree was shaped by Godfried of Viterbo, notary and chaplain to Frederick I. In the *Speculum Regum* that he wrote for Frederick's son, Emperor Henry VI (1190–97), Godfried made important assertions regarding the Franks' Trojan origins and their right to universal sovereignty which, he declared, encompassed the Eastern Empire. Among his contributions are the assertion that Ninus's son Tribeta founded Trier and the claim that a layover in Macedonia accounted for the Saxons' descent from Alexander the Great. To Godfried is owed the construct that the seed of Troy gave off two sprouts— one grew into the diadem of Rome, the other into the Teutonic kingdom: "Romans and Germans are of one seed [descending] . . . from Priam, the Great, King of Troy . . . and Antenor and Aeneas were as if brothers . . . and the Romans and the Germans as if one populace."[95] The two powers were united in Charlemagne, who was *Romuleus matre, Teutonicus patre*.[96] This formula served as a continuous support of northern claims to the Eastern Empire since it expressed the unification of both Greek and Roman imperial heritages in Charlemagne.

For the future of imperial ideology, Godfried's most innovative contribution was the forging of a royal genealogy that traces its origins to the symbiotic relationship between the Hebraic priest-kings and the pagan gods. In this fusion, the royal blood is revealed to flow out from Noah-Janus; it wends its way to Saturn and his Trojan progeny to reach the Roman emperors. This noble lineage descends to Henry VI through his ancestors Clovis and Charlemagne.[97] In support of the German claim to Byzantium,

Godfried popularized Charlemagne's descent from Heraclius, an idea already developed in the tenth century. By establishing this encompassing vision of the emperor's divine pedigree, Godfried produced an invariable template for the Renaissance myth of the German Empire.

Godfried's vision extended to the empire's historical purpose. The sacred character of the empire was established by Christ when he chose Augustus's reign as the moment for the Incarnation. The empire's continuing sanctity under Augustus's Frankish successors had long been established by recalling both Clovis's divine anointment and Charlemagne's divine coronation. Godfried's proclamation that God bestowed the Roman Empire on the Germans to hold until the Second Coming formed part of an increased emphasis on the emperor's central role in salvation history.[98]

This messianic aspect was reinforced when Frederick I's grandson, Emperor Frederick II (reigned 1220–50), secured Jerusalem's hereditary title for his heirs in 1225 by marrying Isabelle, the future queen of Jerusalem. Since the Holy City was in the hands of the Turk, Frederick negotiated a treaty with Melek-el-Kamel, Sultan of Egypt, to receive Jerusalem in exchange for assistance in combating the Sultan's Syrian enemies.[99]

Notwithstanding Pope Gregory IX's attempt in 1227 to halt Frederick through excommunication—an event that precipitated the Great Interregnum (1255–73)—the emperor proceeded apace with his ambitions. Donning the auspicious crown of the king of Jerusalem in 1229, Frederick departed from his predecessors' more timid assertions and explicitly appropriated the Davidian ancestry to himself. In a text from his own hand he exalted in his joy that like himself "our Savior Jesus of Nazareth also sprang from David's royal stock."[100] Following the model of Adam, the first universal ruler, whose stainless nature was renewed in Christ, Frederick and his intimates coopted in styling him as the New Adam, the "stainless Prince," and the son of God, who would realize the return of Paradise to earth.[101] The messianic tone of Frederick's propaganda continued unabated as the future keynote of Germanic imperial rhetoric. Interweaving these pretensions with his dream of a *Renovatio Imperii*, Frederick revived Augustan triumphal ceremonies and assumed the mantle of justice, prophesied to return with Astraea in Vergil's *Fourth Eclogue*.[102]

The Burgundian Dukes and the Luxembourger Dynasty

During the vacancy in the imperial throne from 1254–73, the Papacy—in the throes of its own burgeoning imperial ambitions[103]—shifted its support from the powerful Germans to the French. Already in 1239 Gregory XI had offered the imperial crown to Saint Louis who, as an ally of Frederick II, refused it. Shortly afterwards, Innocent IV offered Charles of Anjou the crown of Sicily. The jolt of the papal defection had numerous consequences; it would eventually bring in its wake the transfer of the papacy to Avignon (1308–77) and the Great Schism (1378–1417) when Guelph popes and Ghibelline antipopes vied for Peter's chair. Imperial aspirants responded by stoking their ancestral fires.

With French and German contenders maneuvering for imperial position, the dukes of Lotharingia and Brabant came forward to present their valid credentials. Although they held neither the imperial title nor the throne of France, the most direct line to the Carolingian stock was intact in their bloodline. The Saxon, the Salian, and the Hohenstaufen emperors had at best a marginal kinship to Charlemagne; little better was Hugh Capet's, who had usurped the French throne upon the death of his cousin Charles, duke of Lotharingia and Brabant.[104] But Charles had a daughter, Gerberga, whose offspring preserved the dukedom and the precious link to the Carolingians. Gerberga married Lambert, count of Hainaut and Louvain, and the couple had offspring. With the growth of political power and the imperial vacancy to prod him, John I, duke of Brabant and a ninth-generation descendant of Gerberga, had this heritage described in a chronicle of 1268.[105] Continuously connected to the Trojans through Clovis, who was "descended from Priam . . . [and] consecrated by an oil from heaven,"[106] and the Carolingians, John is shown to be the heir of Charlemagne by primogeniture and as such, legitimate ruler of the Frankish Empire.[107] A later chronicle brings the heritage of the clan to life in juxtaposed scenes of the Trojan war, Aeneas's flight from Troy, the foundation of Paris, and Clovis's baptism (fig. 42).[108] The duke's daughter, Margaret, conveyed this birthright to her husband, Henry of Luxembourger, and it became a crucial component in Henry's successful bid for the imperium.[109]

42. *The Trojan War, the Flight of Aeneas, the Foundation of Paris, the Baptism of Clovis: Les Grandes Chroniques de France.* Bibliothèque Royale, Brussels. MS B.R. 2, fol. 2. Copyright A.C.L. Bruxelles.

Dante lent his inestimable prestige in support of the Roman imperial myth and of Henry's right to inherit it.[110] For Dante, universal harmony was possible only under one monarch who would restore peace and bring back the Golden Age predicted by Vergil. He insisted that global leadership belonged solely to the Roman emperor, who held his position providentially. Advocating the God-given pattern of universal rule, Dante suggested that the human race should imitate the heavens, which are governed by a single motion and a single mover.[111] He envisaged this rule for Henry VII.

In *De Monarchia*, as well as in other theoretical writings, Dante brought out the by-now-millennial Trojan topos, using Vergilian rhetoric to support his position. In reviewing the tradition of the Four World Empires, and the grounds for the permanent transfer of global sovereignty to Rome, he lent support to the imperial myth of synchronic history when he proclaimed that the coming of Aeneas to Italy coincided with the birth of David, and the founding of Jerusalem with that of the Roman *patria*.[112] He extended the analogy by relating the Tablets of Moses to the sacred precepts of Roman law.[113] Quoting the whole of the relevant passage from the *Aeneid*, he set out to prove by rational argument the divine purpose underlying the mandate "Parcere Subiectis,"[114] in which Aeneas was instructed to extend the laws of Rome to the whole world. Noting that Christ submitted Himself to its tenets,[115] Dante attributed to Rome's jurisdiction the universal peace that prepared for His Advent.[116]

Pointing to the perfection of Augustus's rule—the "fullness of time" in Paul's words—in which peace was attained, Dante pleaded for the restoration of that blessed era.[117] He repeated the claim that the empire belonged to the Roman people, in whom was blended the noble Trojan blood, and whose rule Christ had consecrated by his presence on earth. Accepting the legendary imperial descent from Dardanus and Aeneas as a fact,[118] he saluted Henry VII as the legitimate Trojan heir and hailed him as the prophetic savior of Vergil's *Fourth Eclogue* who will bring about the return of Saturn's Golden Age and the rule of Astraea.[119] In the *Paradiso*, Dante sustained Henry's mystical stature by placing his throne in the Rose that encircles the beatific Vision.[120]

The implications of so exalted a heritage were drawn out with audacity and imagination in the following decades by Charles IV (1316–78), Henry VII's grandson and his successor in the imperial dignity. Charles's father had married Elisabeth, daughter of the Premyslide. With Elizabeth's wedding dowry extending the empire to Bohemia, Poland, and Slovenia, the now immensely powerful Charles transferred the imperial capitol and established Prague as the New Rome. On the reverse of Charles's seal bearing his portrait appears an image of Rome with the words *Caput Mundi*.[121]

In his exaltation of Charles's divinity, Lupold of Babenberg (1297–1363), archbishop of Bamberg, reflects the burgeoning scholarly consciousness that would guide Renaissance historiography. Lupold reached back through history to sustain his conjectures with impeccable sources; he credited Eusebius as a source for the Franks' Trojan origins and for predicting the German possession of the Roman Empire.[122] Noting that history confirmed the German status through the transfer of the empire

43–54. *Ancestors*. In Johan Marignola, Chronicon. Sixteenth century.
Bildarchiv der Österreichische Nationalbibliothek, Vienna. MS N.8330.

43. Noah, fol. 6.

44. Saturn, fol. 12.

45. Jupiter, fol. 13.

46. Dardanus, fol. 14.

47. Priam, fol. 17.

48. Clovis (called Louis at his baptism), fol. 23.

49. Blichilde and Ansibert, fol. 27.

50. Anchises, fol. 31.

51. Begga, fol. 32.

52. Gerberga and Lambert, fol. 42.

53. Charlemagne, fol. 36.

54. Charles IV, fol. 58.

to the Ottonians, Lupold cited Einhard's notation that Charlemagne named the months in the mother tongue.[123] Lupold also looked to Einhard for the mystical definition of the unction by which Charles IV was consecrated in his eternal powers.

Leaning on this historical background for support, Lupold traced a pedigree for Charles in which no caesura interrupts his descent from the priest-kings of Olympus and Judea. Passing from Noah directly to Saturn and Jupiter, then via Dardanus, founder of Troy, the tendrils of sacred pedigree reach to Charles through the Roman emperors, Clovis, and the Carolingians. The blood of the brothers Aeneas and Antenor, who established Trojan realms in Italy and Germany, meets in Charlemagne, who was born of a Roman mother and a German father; the union is sanctified by God who reaches down from heaven to bestow the imperial crown.[124] This royal bloodline, perpetuated through millennia according to God's Divine Plan, culminates in Charles IV.

Charles's claim to sacred and secular powers was developed with care at the Bohemian court. In a chronicle by John Marignola, composed immediately following the imperial coronation, Charles's inherited right to the prerogatives of priest and king was established by reconstructing the heritage of Adam, Noah, and Christ.[125] Noting that Adam was the first priest, after which the unification of the powers of priest and king was a natural law that endured until Jacob, Marignola traced Christ's seed to both the priests and the kings of the Old Testament by linking Jesus to the house of Levi through Mary, and to the house of Judah through Joseph.[126]

Turning to secular history, Marignola delineated the lines of Charles's Gentile ancestry. While convention had conditioned much of Marignola's "ancient history," there is no precedent for the astonishing direct statement that "through the uninterrupted kinship in the Trojan blood of Aeneas, Charles descended from the pagan gods Saturn and Jove."[127] For the next 150 years, no proclamation of the emperor's status as the sole repository of the divine blood *ex judaeos* and *ex gentibus* would exceed that of Charles IV. By this proclamation, Charles IV provided the model for all future possessors of the imperial dignity.[128]

In his castle at Karlstein, near Prague, Charles celebrated his genealogy by lining the walls of the royal reception hall with his ancestor's portraits.[129] Now lost, this striking visualization of his pedigree is preserved in a sixteenth-century manuscript copy for the Hapsburg Emperor Maximilian II.[130] Here appear in succession not only Charles's Jewish and pagan ancestors, Noah (fig. 43), Saturn (fig. 44), Jupiter (fig. 45), Dardanus (fig. 46), and Priam (fig. 47), but also the Merovingian dynasty that proceeds from this lineage: Pharamund and Meroveus are here; followed by Clovis (fig. 48). A "marriage album" illustrates the further links securing the emperor's uninterrupted succession from the Merovingians, the Carolingians, and the dukes of Brabant. Thus are included the wedding portraits of Blichilde and Ansibert (fig. 49),[131] the Frankish Anchises (fig. 50), and Begga (fig. 51),[132] Gerberga and Lambert (fig. 52).[133] These lead directly to Charlemagne (fig. 53). Followed by Charles, duke of Lotharingia and Brabant, from whom the Burgundian dukes could trace their pristine ancestry through Gerberga and Lambert to the Luxembourger Henry VII, who appears with his wife Margaret of Brabant, the heritage culminates in the reigning ruler, the Emperor Charles IV (fig. 54).

Although not yet embellished with the exotic flourishes that would be added in the Renaissance, Charles IV had established the template for future developments. With the Holy Roman emperor's mythic genealogy set in this form, genealogical investigation remained sporadic for more than a century. Following the reign of his sons Wenceslaus (d. 1419) and Sigismund (d. 1437), an unsuccessful bid for the imperial title was made by Philip the Good, duke of Burgundy and Brabant, who had the most valid claim to be Charlemagne's direct heir.[134] Through the marriage of Mary of Burgundy to Emperor Maximilian I, Philip's credentials became the preserve of the Hapsburg family.

The Hapsburgs

55. Gerard de Roo, *Annales Rerum Belli Domique ab Austriacis Habsburgicae Gentis*, frontispiece, Innsbruck, 1592. Biblioteca Apostolica Vaticana, Rome.

The Trojan ancestry may have seemed a stale premise by the end of the Middle Ages, so traditional was the posture to imperial claims. Yet its unfaltering importance led each successive dynasty to invigorate its candidacy by these means. The Hapsburg dynasty's own tentative claim to Roman roots was already in place by the end of the reign of Rudolf I (d. 1291), first of the Hapsburg emperors.[135] Those roots proliferate in a later history of the House of Austria that shows him generating imperial heirs (fig.

RVDOLPHVS PRIMVS ROMANORVM IMPERATOR.

55). That Hebrew and Roman heritages are bred in Rudolf is here communicated by the brilliant synthesis of two visual formulae: the imagery of Jesse's Tree (see fig. 37) is assigned to the emperor, who appropriates the pose of a Roman river god. In the text by Gerald de Roo that accompanies this image, the Hapsburg tree is rooted in Troy,[136] and the etymology of the cognomen is deciphered: Hapsburg=Aventine.[137] Named for Aventinus, a descendant of Aeneas, Mount Aventine in Rome was the dwelling place of the city's last kings.[138]

The basic mythic apparatus was ripe for amplification as Maximilian I prepared to succeed his father, Frederick III, who had ruled the empire for nearly half a century. Maximilian laid the cornerstone for the most comprehensive genealogical restructuring to date when he secured a clear title to the Trojan ancestry through his marriage in 1477 to Mary of Burgundy, granddaughter and only living kin of Philip the Good.[139] Since French pretensions still remained a threat to German imperial sovereignty, Maximilian repeated the time-honored legend that the Germanity of the empire had been preempted in Constantine, who was born of a German mother, and realized in Charlemagne.[140] In a portrait Maximilian commissioned from Dürer, Charlemagne's Teutonic origins are asserted by the imperial regalia that the house of Austria now possessed (fig. 56). Still the papacy did not waver in its support of the French king. This endorsement reached a climax when Pope Alexander VI called Louis XII to Italy to receive the imperial crown. Maximilian responded to the affront in two extraordinary ways: he made a bid for the Byzantine title;[141] and he contemplated taking the papal tiara. A letter from the emperor's own hand to the bishop of Trent (10 June 1507) reveals that Maximilian planned to go to Rome and become both pope and emperor. His correspondence with Cardinale Hadrian of Castello, his advisor in this plan, underscores the profound secrecy that cloaked these aspirations.[142] An idealized portrait of 1498 that illustrates a poem written in anticipation of Maximilian's planned Roman coronation affords a glimpse of the young emperor's awesome stature. He has been removed from approach to a surreal inner sanctum. When the cloths of revelation are drawn back on the baldachin we behold an iconic image of Maximilian enthroned within a sacred enclosure that was habitually reserved for the Almighty (fig. 57; see fig. 118). Maxi-

56. Albrecht Dürer,
Charlemagne. 1512–13.
Treasury, Kunsthisto-
risches Museum,
Vienna.

milian continued to hold papal ambitions, and a letter from the
Venetian historian Sanuto that was written on 21 February 1513,
when he had not yet learned of Pope Julius II's death the day
before records: "Prospero Colona has learned that the Pope is
very ill; he does not want to remain in Milan and he will leave for
Rome. It is said that he is going to Rome for the bestowal of the
papacy on Emperor Maximilian."[143]

To support him in his global ambitions to rule as priest and
king, Maximilian burst the boundaries of traditional ancestral
stalking.[144] In construing his mythical past, Maximilian concentrated on a single idea: the widening of the net of races that
converged in his pedigree. Cultural borders offered no barrier to
the medley of figures that were swept into the common genealogical root; the uninterrupted flow of the divine blood and

not the rivalry of the races impelled the vision here. The archeological intensity with which he pursued this ancestral quest set Maximilian apart from his predecessors, as historians were sent throughout Europe to document his legendary past. The most renowned humanists of the Northern Renaissance, including Johann Aventinus, Heinrich Bebel,[145] Conrad Celtis,[146] Hieronymous Gebwiler,[147] Wolfgang Lazius,[148] Jacob Mennel,[149] Johannes Naucler,[150] Conrad Peutinger,[151] Johann Stabius,[152] and Franciscus Irenicus give some indication of the prodigious talent devoted to these endeavors. The elaborate architecture constructed by Providence to provide the empire's legitimate ruler is shown in a diagram illustrating Irenicus's chronicle: here Maximilian and his grandson, the future Emperor Charles V, are joined in consanguinity to the Carolingians, the Ottonians, the Hohenstaufen, and the Burgundians (fig. 58). Among the peculiar results of this scholarly speculation was Irenicus's assertion that the Argonauts sojourned in Germany; he also claimed to draw on Hunibald's lost history for knowledge of Clovis's Trojan ancestry.[153] Gebwiler, too, contributed arcana. He revealed that the hidden meaning informing the familiar bifrontal image of Janus (fig. 59) was his dual nature as Noah-Janus.[154] All of these humanists lent their authority to reconciling indigenous, classical, and biblical myths of origin in Maximilian's pedigree.[155] Among his ancestors were Jewish kings and prophets, Greek and Egyptian demigods, Roman divinities and Christian saints, Trojan heroes and their historical progeny among the Frankish emperors; thus Saturn and Osiris, Hector and Priam, Noah and Christ, Clovis and Charlemagne sprout from various branches of the Hapsburg family tree. This remote group of ancestors was augmented with others drawn from the ranks of church history. By the end of his life, Maximilian would claim more than a hundred martyrs, popes, and saints as his direct kin.

As random as the medley may appear, this crisscrossing of heritages was no haphazard proposition, for an iron-clad logic underlay the construction of Maximilian's ancestral cult. These ancestries are linked in Jacob Mennel's *Fürstliche Chronik*, the fruit of more than a decade's efforts—a first version was finished in 1507, the final version in 1518.[156] Maximilian's legitimacy to rule the Roman imperium was made evident by the Trojan ancestry that descended to him from Priam and Hector (fig. 60)[157] through his progenitors among the kings and the caesars of ancient and

57. Flemish Master, *Maximilian I.* In Michael Nagonius, *Huldigungsgedichte an Maximilian*, Netherlands, 1498. Bildarchiv der Österreichische Nationalbibliothek, Vienna. Cod. 12750, fol. 4v.

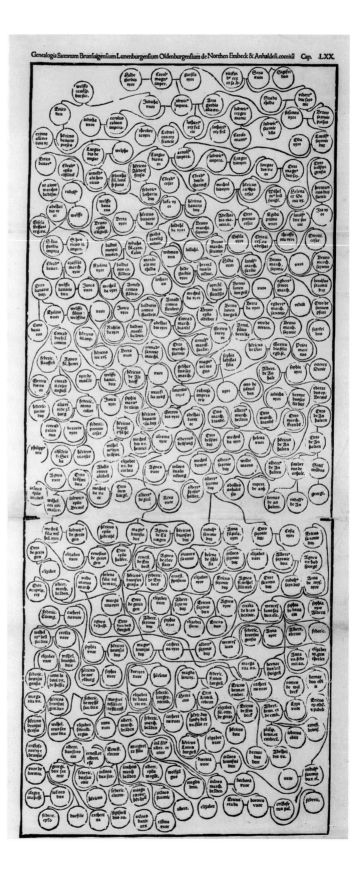

58. *Charlemagne to the Hapsburgs*. In F. Irenicus, *Germaniae*, Basel, 1520, genealogical diagram, preceding p. lxxxi. Biblioteca Apostolica Vaticana, Rome.

NOA, qui & Ianus,

59. *Noah/Janus*. In H.
Gebwiler, *Epitome Regii,
Hapsburgi*, Hannover,
1530, opposite p. B.
Biblioteca Apostolica
Vaticana, Rome.

‹HECTOR PRIAMI MAGNI
REGIS TROIANORVM FIL ‹

60. Hans Burgkmaier,
Hector. Engraving. Uni-
versity of London,
Warburg Institute,
London.

medieval Rome. A parallel Greek ancestry sustained Maximilian's right to the Eastern Empire.[158] The tracing of his parentage to Noah—successfully defended by the theological faculty in Vienna—sustained his right to succeed as the king of Jerusalem.[159] Thus, the commingled blood of prelates and kings, gods and saints, supported Maximilian's ambition to consolidate all priestly and secular powers in the Hapsburg grip. The most striking visual manifestation of Maximilian's ancestral cult is the Triumphal Arch designed by Dürer (fig. 61).[160] Here the Hapsburg family tree is rooted in the Judaic priest-kings, the Roman emperors, the Greek and Trojan heroes, and their Frankish progeny. Members of this retinue reappear as daunting sentinels in the final statement of the emperor's efforts to glorify his past and salute his survivors, the monument at Innsbruck that was intended for his tomb.[161] The most concise statement attesting to Maximilian's sacred roots is an illustration to Jacob Mennel's *Fürstliche Chronik*. Here Maximilian's pagan and Judeo-Christian ancestors are drawn together in a symbolic colloquium that transcends time and the constraints of orthodox history (fig. 62)[162] On the right, a figure wearing the Lily crown and identified as Aeneas by an inscribed cartouche is linked by a silver chain through the emperors of Rome to Clovis. He peers across the ages to engage in a dialogue with his biblical counterpart, Boaz. Boaz, the grandfather of Jesse, is linked by a gold chain that terminates in his descendant Jesus. These two frame the central image of Juno's peacock—symbol of the Austrian house's Greek ancestry[163]—which leads from Hector and Turnus to Maximilian's grandson, Charles V. In the accompanying text, Mennel explains the significance of the network of chains: gold symbolizes the highest sacred office, silver the highest secular office. When the two heritages are united in a single ruler, the powers of priest and king are consolidated in him.[164] Already by the first decade of the sixteenth century, with the rumor of Julius II's impending death to spur his hopes, Maximilian conceived of passing the imperial crown to his grandson as soon as he would be made pope.[165]

The fantasy of his mythic past consoled Maximilian to the end of his life. On his deathbed in 1519, he summoned Jacob Mennel to recite aloud the litany of his ancestral moorings.[166] Vitalized by the artistry of Leonhard Beck, the ghosts of his

61. Albrecht Dürer, *Triumphal Arch of Maximilian I.* Woodcut, 1515. New York Public Library.

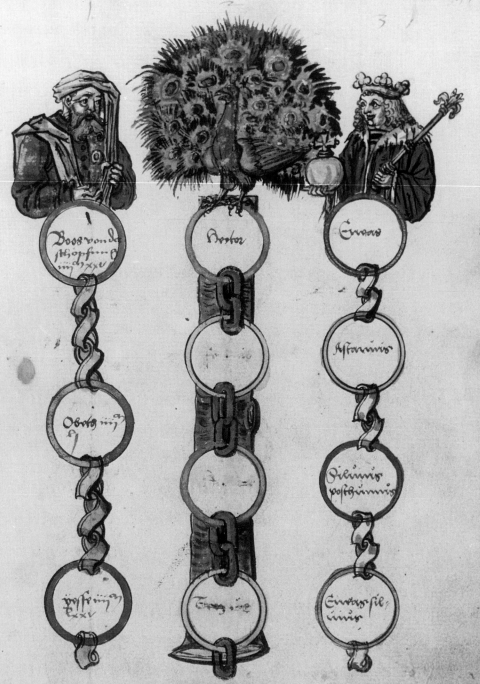

Boos von der
schopfung
in dxxv

Hector

Eneas

Obot in iij

Astanius

Siluius
postumus

post in ??
txxv

Troya in?

Enearsil
uuis

linea hebreorum

linea grecorum

linea latinorum

saintly ancestors paraded to the music of their names, displaying family crests and sacred attributes before his ailing eyes. Like a personalized version of Aeneas's ancestral vision—lately figured for the emperor in the first illustrated edition of Vergil[167]—came Clovis with the shield from heaven (fig. 63); Begga, yoke of the Merovingian and Carolingian dynasties; Charlemagne with the implements of the Passion (fig. 64), and countless more in saintly guises, who reached down a long chain of fate and history to find their ultimate flowering in the Hapsburg dynasty.

Once firmly established in this sacred mode by Maximilian's devotion to the genre, the Hapsburg ancestors assumed the role of paradigmatic piety that they would have for successive generations. Although future scions need only add their own name to Maximilian's unparalleled list of worthy forbears, even this was not required of Charles V. Since he conceived of the imperium as a hereditary office, Maximilian thoughtfully annexed Charles's name alongside his own. This foresight on his grandfather's part did not prevent Charles from indulging in what had now become a family art.

Scion of the Austro-Burgundian and Spanish royal houses and the first direct heir of the Burgundian dukes to attain the imperial title, Charles V brought an extraordinary heritage to bear on his claims to mythic genealogy. The accident of his birth conceded to him domains of unprecedented proportions: among them a united Spain; the newly discovered continent of the Americas; the two Sicilies; the Burgundian Low Countries; Austria; and the Hapsburg lands within Germany. The Spanish inheritance included as well the honorary title king of Jerusalem and the title to the Byzantium Empire that Andreas Paleologus bequeathed to Ferdinand and Isabella in 1502.[168] These great holdings and dignities provided Charles with the basis on which he presented his claim to the imperial title. He had to overcome rival pretensions, for the French king, Francis I, was vying for the same title by declaring himself Charlemagne's true heir. The material reality of Charles's wealth and territorial strength insured his election as Holy Roman emperor in 1519, and that title sustained the mystique of his inherited divinity.

Boosted by the sacred aura of his titles and by his possessions in Italy, northern Europe, and the New World, Charles contrived to become universal monarch.[169] He was graced with advisors of great vision who shaped the rhetoric that validated these

62. Jacob Mennel, *Linea Hebreorum/Linea Grecorum/Linea Latinorum.* In Jacob Mennel, *Fürstliche Chronik*, 1518. Österreichische Nationalbibliothek, Vienna. Cod. Vind. Palat. 3072, vol. 1, fol. 44.

63. After Hans Burgk-
maier, *Saint Clovis*.
1516–18. Graphische
Sammlung, Albertina,
Vienna.

64. After Hans Burgk-
maier, *Saint Charlemagne*.
1516–18. Graphische
Sammlung, Albertina,
Vienna.

pretensions. Luigi Marliano, the royal physician, created Charles's personal emblem, the *Columns of Hercules*.[170] The emblem's motto "Plus Ultra" emphasized Charles's extension of empire into the east and west, beyond the boundaries achieved by the ancients. The ancestral chronicles of the medieval past were published in new editions to include his name. Venerable treatises were also revised on his behalf: Mercurino Gattinara proposed that Dante's *De Monarchia*, a treatise advocating universal monarchy for Emperor Henry VII, be republished to apply to Charles,[171] and a contemporary translation of Orosius's scheme of history as four divinely decreed World Monarchies was amended to name Charles its present glory.[172]

Not only rhetoric but also the resources of antiquarian research were exploited by Charles's apologists to perpetuate his extension of Augustus's reign. His ceremonial entries evoked such parallels, and, entering Rome following his victory at Tunis, "he celebrated a Capitoline triumph according to the custom of the ancient Roman Emperors."[173] He adopted Augustus's emblem of Capricorn, and Vergilian rhetoric was applied to the "one Lord of the World who has induced Astraea to return to earth."[174] He was assimilated to Aeneas crushing blind Fury in Leone Leoni's colossal bronze statue (fig. 65),[175] and to Marcus Aurelius in Titian's equestrian portrait (fig. 66) that, following the victory at Muhlberg, celebrated what seemed to be his infallible power to unite the empire.[176]

In delineating his mythic genealogy, Charles followed the traditional idiosyncratic format, now enhanced by the addition of Spanish genealogical lore. Thus, for example, in the *Catálogo real de Castilla*, Charles V's bloodline is traced for millennia to culminate in Noah-Janus, revealed to be one and the same person according to the testimony of the venerable Berosus. Elsewhere Charles's Trojan heritage is traced to the Roman emperors and Aeneas; his Jewish ancestry is traced to the patriarchs and Noah and culminates in Adam.[177]

The lineal pattern of Charles V's divine ancestry was maintained in Pietro Mareno's *Compendio della Stirpe di Carlo Magno et Carlo V*. The dedication and the proemium of this work provide an opportunity to discuss a related issue of no little importance for the Renaissance application of the dynastic topos we have been discussing. The proemium acknowledges the rule of Tuscany by

65. Leone Leoni, *Charles V Dominating Fury*. Sixteenth century. Museo del Prado, Madrid.

66. Titian, *Charles V at Muhlberg*. 1548. Museo del Prado, Madrid.

Charlemagne and now Charles V; an examination of this sovereignty leads the author to their original ancestor Tuisco, from whom Dardanus and the rulers of Troy are descended.[178] The dedication to Cosimo de Medici and his wife, the Spanish Eleanora of Gonzaga, acknowledges the vassalage of the duke and duchess to the Holy Roman emperor. Not only had Charles elevated the Medici to ducal status, thus establishing the Medici principate in 1532, but the Gonzaga were related to the imperial house.[179] A statue of Charles was erected as part of the festival decorations for Cosimo's marriage to Eleanora in 1539; its inscription saluted the emperor as the offspring of the gods and the founder of the Golden Age. A sustained manipulation of imperial iconography ensued in the many artistic commissions with which Cosimo adorned the city of Florence.

What is explicit here is implicit for the claims to mythical ancestry that became common among the petty princes of Europe—the Medici, Gonzaga, and Este dukes provide notable Italian Renaissance examples. Predicated on the dependent status they bore to the imperial scion, these provincial rulers could claim such a venerable ancestry for themselves when they formed part of the imperial phalanx, a status perpetuated when Charles named members of these families to the Burgundian order of the Golden Fleece.[180] It is far from coincidental that literary works or decorative programs exalting imperial, Trojan, and biblical heroes were often commissioned when a noble title was granted or an imperial visit planned. Intended to flatter and confirm the legitimacy of the emperor, such imagery also conveyed more personal reverberations to the vassal's own subjects. According to imperial theory, as the emperor's liege, the feudal lord stood in Caesar's place as the representative of these directives in his own province. On an international scale, however, these subject-rulers could only claim to be mirrors for the undisputed prerogatives of the emperor and his direct heir. Thus with an eye to confirming the emperor's legitimacy, and by reflection their own, no energy was spared in preparing a public display of imperial iconography.

At the imperial palace in Genoa—which became an imperial protectorate during Charles's reign—scenes from the history of Jason were painted on the building's southern facade and a series of Aeneas tapestries designed by Perino del Vaga (fig. 67) was

67. Giulio Bonasone after Perino del Vaga, *Neptune Calming the Tempest.* Engraving. University of London, Warburg Institute, London.

woven in time for Charles's visit there in 1536.[181] Raised to the title of duke of Mantua by Charles in 1530, Federigo Gonzaga similarly decorated his Palazzo del Té for Charles's impending visit. Scenes from biblical history adorned the Loggia di Davide, while Trojan history was reserved for the Sala di Troia. The Sala del Imperator was painted with scenes from the lives of Scipio, Caesar, and Alexander—Charles's ancestors all. A reference to the emperor, inherent in the use of the topos that Horace had established for Augustus,[182] was implicit in Giulio Romano's cycloramic mural of Jove crushing the giants (fig. 68).[183] At the court of the Este dukes in Ferrara, where Ariosto was commissioned to write the *Orlando Furioso,* Charles V's ancestry is traced to Hector and the emperor is cast as the living Charlemagne.[184] By assimilation or evocation, both at home and at the vassal courts, in countless examples throughout his life and in the funerary monuments that followed his death,[185] Charles was the object of a cult veneration not equalled since antiquity. In the light of our knowledge of the Roman emperor's continuously evolving mythic image, there can be no doubt that the stimulus for these artistic visions emanated from the inner circle of the imperial court.

    This "vassal" interest in propagating the mythic history of the

elected emperor took on rival reverberations in the case of the
Florentines, as it did for others with similar shifting allegiance.
Traditionally allied with the Guelph cause, in support of French
and papal as well as their own ambitions, the Florentine use of
canonic imperial imagery served the dual purpose of obeisance
to Caesar on the international front, and aspirant yearnings for his
title at home.

The artistic projects that carved a corridor of imperial veneration through the realms of Charles's empire were all aspects
of a larger idea which was most succinctly stated in the *Los Honores*
tapestries. For like his grandfather before him, Charles V was an
avid patron of the arts, and he did not leave his dynastic legacy to
languish in the outposts of the empire or in the dusty pages of
the chronicles. In the tapestries, which were exhibited at the
moment of his imperial election and at every official ceremony
thereafter, a larger-than-life consort of Trojan, Greek, imperial,

68. Giulio Romano,
Fall of the Giants. Section
of fresco, Sala dei Gi-
ganti, Palazzo del Té,
Mantua. Alinari/Art Re-
source, N.Y. (Al.
18754).

and Judeo-Christian ancestors appear like visionary presences to proclaim Charles's noble heritage and his messianic destiny.[186] On the left lateral of the *Nobility* tapestry (see fig. 29), Noah, Trajan, and Apollo are grouped; beneath Joseph's chariot on the right, Augustus beknights the duke of Brabant—a title now held by Charles V—as Charlemagne extends his blessings. Charles's divine election to rule is referred to an eternal model by the Coronation of the Virgin in Heaven that appears at the apex of the composition. Directly below, Samuel anoints David, who kneels on the coat of arms of the Holy Roman Empire. The ritual is witnessed by Melchizedek, Moses, and Abraham, who are accompanied by Constantine's mother, Helena. The divine heritage so carefully construed by millennia of imperial antecedents provided the Hapsburgs with more than a legitimate right to the sovereignty of Rome. The mystical significance that inhered in this ancestry is visualized as *Infamy* (see fig. 31) is routed and the Golden Age of Edenic peace is restored to the world.

In *Italia Liberata dai Goti*,[187] Giangiorgio Trissino, likening Charles to Justinian for many of his accomplishments, counted among his achievements that Charles had pacified Italy and liberated it from war (the Battle of Pavia); taken Africa from the Turks (the battles of Tunis and Goleta); united France in friendship (the Peace of Cambrai); corrected the errors of the German princes and brought them back to the true Catholic church (the victory at Muhlberg). He would soon, Trissino prophesied, liberate Asia from the Ottomans and reconquer Constantinople. The oracular element expressed here was symptomatic of a much broader tradition, and it is to prophecy's role in designating the Last Descendant of Aeneas that we now turn our attention.

Chapter VI The Legend of the Last World Emperor

ENEALOGICAL mythmaking and prophecy, two disciplines so remote from twentieth-century rational thought as to be disregarded in modern historical studies, went hand in hand to sustain the emperors' mythic image. Prophecy's fundamental difference was its eschatological focus. Throughout the period under study, the unwavering insistence on the emperor's mythic ancestry dovetailed with the prophecy that God conceded the rule of the Roman Empire to Aeneas's successor in perpetuity. So universal was interest in apocalyptic doctrine that the printing of the *Sibyllenbuch*, a book of prophecies concerning the fate of the Holy Roman Empire, is believed by some scholars to have preceded Gutenberg's Bible and therefore to be the earliest known printed document.[1] Recent studies have illustrated the importance of prophetic writings, in which the prospect of universal peace was interpreted as a return to the primal state of man's perfection.[2] In the admittedly mystical context of the prophetic texts, imperial aims were declared to be one with the history of salvation, the two illustrating complementary modes of a changeless revelation of eternal truth. Rome's universal sovereignty was understood to satisfy a millenarian prophecy that had been applied to the Christian state since the fourth century. According to imperial rhetoric, the restoration of the empire of the ancient Romans was the precursor to the return of the Golden Age in Rome, the new Troy, which stood as a civic metaphor for Eden before the Fall.

As in the reconstructed myths of imperial descent, the syncretization of pagan and Hebraic traditions was endemic to imperial prophecy from the fourth century onwards. Just as rule over the Roman Empire was the preserve of the royal descendant who could trace his lineage both to Noah and to Aeneas, so attainment of universal peace was the fated destiny decreed for this heir. Indeed the millenarian message and the apocalyptic role assigned to the emperor reveals the real purpose underlying the concept of the last descendant of Aeneas.

The Legend of the Last World Emperor

The Christian communities of the first century were pervaded by apocalyptic ideas, for they believed that Christ's return would follow soon after the Resurrection. Apocalyptic rhetoric ascribed to Jesus was expanded upon in the Gospels and, above all, in Revelation. Influenced by Daniel's interpretation of the Four World Monarchies, the last of which would be followed by the realm of God,[3] Saint John prophesied a thousand-year reign of Christ and the saints on earth after the Second Coming but before the end of the world.[4] Reiterating Saint John's revelation that this cataclysm is to be preceded by the arrival of the Antichrist, Saint Paul spoke of an obstacle that will hold off this menace.[5] Tertullian (160–225) provided an interpretation of Paul's words that was favorable to the imperium. According to Tertullian, Paul's "obstacle" was the Roman Empire, which would hold off the cataclysm of the world's end: "We know that the great danger which hangs over all the globe—I mean the end of the world and the fearful sufferings with which it threatens us—is postponed by virtue of the respite brought by the Roman Empire."[6]

Lactantius was an influential advocate of apocalyptical thought at the courts of Diocletian and Constantine. He applied a syncretistic view to these beliefs by integrating the *Sibylline Oracles* and Christian rhetoric; in this way he showed that all religious systems supported the concept of the imminent end.[7] During the reign of Theodosius in the fourth century, this millennial framework was tailored to imperial aims with the development of the legend of the Last World Emperor.

The legend of a Last World Emperor revived for Christian Rome the prophecy revealed at the Fall of Troy by the Cumaean

Sibyl.[8] To the prediction of the rise of Augustus from the Trojan race and the subjugation of the entire inhabited world to him was annexed the name of "Constans . . . the king of the Romans and the Greeks [who] will claim the whole Christian Empire for himself."[9] Other addenda provided that the Kingdom of God, which was foreshadowed in Revelation, will come when the Last World Emperor has defeated the heretic. After this, the emperor will go to Jerusalem and recover the Holy Sepulchre. When this is accomplished, he will put off his diadem, lay aside his whole imperial garb, and render the empire to Christ. This event will usher in the thousand years in which Satan is bound. At the end of this time, divine forces shall defeat the Antichrist in a final battle; then will occur the *Parousia*.[10]

The text known as the *Tiburtine Sibyl* is acknowledged to be the earliest proof of this tradition in the Christian Roman Empire.[11] Yet Prudentius must be credited for framing a critical element of the legend. He defined the image of the emperor's abdication to Christ, when in the *Apotheosis*, he envisioned Rome's final moment to take place when "the successor of Aeneas, in the imperial purple, prostrates himself in prayer at the house of Christ, and the supreme lord adores the banner of the cross."[12]

Once set into place, the legend—though it was updated to refer to the current reigning emperor and to changing identities for the Antichrist—remained unvaried in its substance with a few notable additions.[13] The legend was revised by the Pseudo-Methodius in the seventh century when Islam appeared to provide an enemy with the proper weight to be identified with the forces of evil; this definition remained constant through the sixteenth century and beyond.[14] This same author identified Byzantium as the New Rome which restrains the Antichrist, before whose advent a Cross would appear in the heavens to announce the moment.

Methodius's treatise was translated into Latin and disseminated at the court of Charlemagne in the eighth century.[15] The first surviving account that transferred the destiny of the last emperor to the Franks is Adso's *Letter on the Antichrist* of circa 950. Composed by a noted hagiographer and confidant of the West Frankish royal family, the *Letter* was dedicated to the sister of Emperor Otto I.[16] Adso quoted the prophecy that the Antichrist will not come until the end of the Roman Empire but corrected the identity of the emperor to reflect the reign of the Saxon kings.[17]

The period of the Crusades to the Holy Land, which were arguably undertaken to realize the apocryphal portents of the millennial year 1000,[18] saw an increase in apocalyptic literature. During the years in which Jerusalem was recaptured from the Turks (1095–99), the legend of a Last World Emperor was applied to the Salian Emperor Henry IV (1084–1106) by Benzo of Alba, who drew on the prophecy of the Cumaean Sibyl. The transfer of this destiny to the Hohenstaufen in the next century was attested by another revival of Sibylline literature that appeared with the *Vaticinium Sibillae Erithraeae*, a sketch of world history, that was purportedly written during the reign of Priam to reveal Troy's final destiny. The Sibyl prophecies a "horrible beast [with seven heads] coming from the East . . . to oppose the Lamb [and] . . . blaspheme his covenant." She foretells that "a most mighty lion," an apparent reference to the Last World Emperor, "will make an attack on the beast and crush his power, but [the beast] will live . . . until the Abomination comes. After the Abomination, the Truth will be revealed and the Lamb will be known. . . . The Last Judgment will follow the Abomination."[19] The names and glorious deeds of Frederick II and his sons were appended to the text.

Imaginative prophetic flourishes were continually added to the Western accounts. An important variable concerned the identity of the northern emperor, which was disputed between the French and German ruling houses.[20] When the world was still found to be intact after Charlemagne's death, a most influential French coda provided that a second Charles would arise to bring the prophecy to completion. The specifics of this prophecy included the information that he would arise "from the nation of the Lily" and be called "King of the Greeks." It also defined the prophesied ruler's physiognomy: "a lofty forehead, high eyebrows, wide eyes and an aquiline nose."[21] This was countered by the German prophecy of the rise of a third Frederick.[22] Notwithstanding the elective rather than hereditary nature of the imperial office, these "revivals," like the continuous delineation of a mythic genealogy, attempted to place a dynastic stamp on the right of succession to the role of Last World Emperor.

Although the Christian emperor assumed an early role in the

drama of the Last Days, it was not until the Interregnum and the great reform movement that accompanied it that the pope assumed a similar apocalyptic status. This application and the most innovative of the medieval additions to the legend are the contributions of Joachim of Fiore (1135–1202). Considered the most influential apocalyptic author of the Middle Ages and one of the most significant theorists of history in the Western tradition, his importance for imperial ideology lies in assigning the battle against the Antichrist to a historic personage.[23]

Before he entered monastic life, Joachim was an official at the Sicilian court at Palermo, then under Hohenstaufen rule; there he undoubtedly came in contact with the imperial myth. Following a series of visions, Joachim transferred the role of the Last World Emperor to the evangelical rule of an "Angelic Pope,"[24] and in this way he transformed the course of Christian apocalyptical thought. Joachim amplified the pope's messianic destiny when he assigned to him the defeat of the Antichrist and the restoration of God's rule to earth within historical time. In this development, Antichrist rhetoric was directed against the emperor,[25] charges which quickly ricocheted back from imperial quarters.[26]

The historic role that Joachim had conceived for the Angelic Pope was first appropriated to an imperial context with Emperor Frederick II (1194–1250).[27] In the new schema, the emperor replaces the divine forces in the final battle against the Antichrist. Thus his role in universal salvation history takes on a more direct messianic tone.[28] The significance of this alteration was to designate the emperor as divinely elected to bring about the End of Time, the Second Coming, and the descent of the Heavenly Jerusalem. Speculation became focused as Joachimite prophecy was fused with Arabic astrology in order to determine the date of the apocalyptic appointment.[29]

The legend was augmented to include Saint Brigid of Sweden's (1303–73) vision of the emperor's chastisement of the church. Saint Brigid linked this prophecy of destruction to Ezekiel 17:3 with her claim that "beneath the great eagle . . . the Church shall be trampled down."[30] This concept was soon reflected, for example, in a text ascribed to the fictitious "Gamaléon," who was apparently invented by German polemicists. Gamaléon speaks of a future German emperor who will overthrow the French monarchy and the papacy, and a German patriarch "of the race of eagles" who will rule a church renovated and subordinated to the emperor. Then will come the Last Days, the Second Coming, and the Last Judgment.[31]

With the Joachimite, astrological, and Brigittine elements in place by the end of the fourteenth century, the legend of the Last World Emperor assumed its definitive shape. Despite the Interregnum the tradition had already survived intact to pass to the Hapsburg dynasty with the election of Rudolf I in 1273.[32] Symbolic as well as historic events, including the fall of Constantinople (1453), the increase in Guelph prerogatives, and the approach of the prophetically charged year 1500, contributed to the revival of the "Frederick" prophecies for the Hapsburg Emperor Frederick III (1452–93). These were augmented for his son, Maximilian I, around whom prophetic expectations gathered from the time of his youth.[33] The name Constantine was bestowed on him[34] and in both text and image he was recognized as the prophesied emperor. Maximilian's historiographer, Joseph Grunpeck, dedicated a *Prognosticum* to him in 1496. The front of Sebastian Brandt's popular illustrated version of this work shows Maximilian standing before Jerusalem, and its text exhorted the emperor to take up his proper apocalyptic role.[35]

In another *Prognosticatio*, of which there are more than fifty known editions, the court astrologer Johann Lichtenberger again looked to astrology in an attempt to determine the course of history through cosmic announcements.[36] These led him to conclude that the Hapsburgs were destined to destroy the Turks, to be identified with the Antichrist, and to satisfy the Brigittine prophecy of chastising the church. Perceiving that the consummation of history would be achieved through the union of German and French aspirations—the Eagle and the Lily—Lichtenberger expected a Burgundian emperor to rise as the second Charlemagne. This status was ascribed to Maximilian through his marriage to Mary of Burgundy, and the prophet applied to him the legend of the Last World Emperor. Tradition had determined that the second Charlemagne's most characteristic feature was his "eagle's nose."[37] It is tempting to speculate whether Dürer's portrait of the "Divine" Maximilian (fig. 69), the most famous of the many images of the emperor that give prominence to his aquiline profile,[38] was influenced by this physiognomic prophecy.

The papacy stimulated Maximilian's apocalyptic promulgations, for it had shifted its support to French claims to the Imperium and had amplified its own secular ambitions. With the end

POTENTISSIMVS · MAXIMVS · ET · INVICTISSIMVS · CÆSAR · MAXIMILIANVS
QVI · CVNCTOS · SVI · TEMPORIS · REGES · ET · PRINCIPES · IVSTICIA · PRVDENCIA
MAGNANIMITATE · LIBERALITATE · PRÆCIPVE · VERO · BELLICA · LAVDE · ET
ANIMI · FORTITVDINE · SVPERAVIT · NATVS · EST · ANNO · SALVTIS · HVMANÆ
M · CCCC · LIX · DIE · MARCII · IX · VIXIT · ANNOS · LIX · MENSES · IX · DIES · XXV
DECESSIT · VERO · ANNO · M · D · XIX · MENSIS · IANVARII · DIE · XII · QVEM · DEVS
OPT · MAX · IN · NVMERVM · VIVENCIVM · REFERRE · VELIT ·

69. Albrecht Dürer,
Maximilian I. 1519.
Kunsthistorisches Mu-
seum, Vienna.

of the Great Schism and the reestablishment of Rome as the
papal seat under Pope Martin V (1417–31), the centuries-long
restoration of the ancient imperial city to its ancient splendor
began. This renewal was continued under Martin's successors
and the intention single-minded: the installation of the pope
as the legitimate heir to the Christian Empire of Rome. The
methods adapted to endorse this mythic status were not unfamil-
iar to Maximilian, for the language of persuasion was most often
drawn from the imperial sphere. Borrowings from visual rhetoric
pervade the architectural and decorative renovation of the Vatican Palace during Maximilian's reign. The appearance of Aeneas
and Anchises in Raphael's *Fire in the Borgo* is one salient example of
this appropriation. To combat so formidable a foe as the pope,
Maximilian encouraged a messianic view of his monarchy and he
talked of taking the tiara.[39] In his *Commentary on Methodius,* Wolfgang Aytinger predicted Maximilian's chastisement of the church
on the authority of Saint Brigid: "The papacy will be vacant and
the German emperor with a multinational army will invade Rome
and persecute the clergy." A reference to Julius II's cognomen,
della Rovere, was encased in the phrase, "the acorn tree of propaganda shall be overturned."[40] Although a profusion of written
texts sustained this interpretation of Maximilian's monarchy, a
more gripping vision of its chiliastic realization was achieved in
Dürer's *Apocalypse.*[41]

Maximilian's son Philip the Fair was heir to this apocryphal
status, and favorable portents were strikingly manifest in his magical name: "It says in the Book of the Frankish Kings that it will be
from the Carolingians, that . . . an Emperor named P. will arise in
the last days. He will be a prince and a monarch and will reform
the Churches of Europe. After him there shall be no ruler."[42]

With the early death of Philip, his son Charles V fell heir to
these pretensions; indeed, the prophetic issue was significant in
determining Charles's election as emperor in 1519.[43] Possessed
of the title Holy Roman emperor, of a domain which exceeded
that of ancient Rome, surrounded by imperial rhetoric and at-
tired in imperial regalia, Charles V was perceived as the individual
towards whom the history of Revelation had been pointing for
more than a millennium. Through his Spanish heritage Charles
was able to enhance his stature in several significant ways. The

preconditions to the emperor's deposition of his crown and the rendering of the Roman Empire back to God on Mount Olivet were the lordship of Jerusalem and the acquisition of the Byzantine title.[44] As we have seen, Charles's Spanish heritage conceded to him both the titles emperor of Byzantium and king of Jerusalem. With the latter title came a particularly auspicious insignia to support his status as the Last World Emperor. Godfrey of Bouillon, a direct ancestor of Charles V, who was elected the first Christian king of Jerusalem in 1099, had made a rule that he himself followed. The rule established that no king of Jerusalem should ever wear a golden crown but should wear instead a crown of thorns in deference to Christ.[45]

Charles's Spanish heritage brought him yet more, for Spain's conquests in the New World revealed lands to be conquered for Christ. A mystical intention had guided Columbus's journeys, whose course he professed to chart from the pages of Isaiah.[46] In a letter of 1501, which accompanied a book of prophecies prepared for Ferdinand and Isabella, Columbus revealed that the royal intention for his voyages lay in no less an objective than the recovery of the Holy Sepulchre.[47] When this undertaking revealed a primeval land that had until then remained hidden from sight, it is not surprising that the previously unknown territories and the constellations of the Southern Hemisphere were hailed as the "new heaven and new earth" signalled by John to descend as the Heavenly Jerusalem.[48]

Columbus interpreted the Spanish discovery of the New World as only part of a larger providential plan; such a plan was first indicated when Saint James led Charlemagne to Spain to indicate the site on which Jerusalem and Mount Sion were to be rebuilt.[49] He expressed this belief in a letter to Ferdinand and Isabella: "Not unworthily nor without reason, Most Splendid Rulers, do I assert that even greater things are reserved for you, when we read that Joachim the Calabrian abbot predicted that the future ruler 'who would rebuild the Temple of Jerusalem must rise from Spain.'"[50] These portents were sustained by Columbus's professed discovery in the Americas of the treasure that Solomon had sent to Ophir.[51] In his *Lettera Rarissima* (1502–4), an account of his final voyage to the New World, Columbus rejoiced in his belief that the Spanish ruler's conquest of Jerusalem, as well as his own divinely inspired mission to find a path to Asia, were events that would herald the universal peace and the end of the world.[52]

With all the necessary portents in place, Charles V—in whom the blood of both French and German ruling houses was blended—was heralded as both the Great Eagle prophesied by Saint Brigid, and the second Charlemagne.[53] He was identified with Charlemagne in the chivalric sagas which constituted one of the most important genres of Renaissance literature,[54] and in both historic and imaginative imperial literature, the apocalyptic prophecies were revised to apply to his person. As early as 1511, Jean Lemaire de Belges, whose Trojan legend for Charles we have already discussed, predicted a chiliastic destiny for the future emperor: "And before Antichrist comes, there will be a great and extraordinary schism in the church, by which the secular princes will be forced to set their hands to the reformation of churchmen as has been foreseen by . . . many prophets [and] sibyls . . . the blessed king of whom Methodius writes will enter the promised land and lay waste Turkey. . . . Caesar shall reign everywhere and under him the vainglory of the clergy shall cease."[55] Lemaire proclaimed that through his fulfillment of the prophecy of universal peace, Charles would satisfy the gospel prediction of one sheepfold guided by one shepherd.[56]

For Charles V history seemed at last to truly bear out the designation "Last World Emperor." The chastisement of the church was seen to be accomplished by Charles's Sack of Rome in 1527,[57] and the defeat of the Antichrist of Revelation by his victories over the Turks, while with the victory at Muhlberg, Charles stemmed the rise of Protestant hereticism. Charles V's predestined accomplishments were sustained by a body of literature which employed Sybilline texts, astrological calculations, and cosmic imagery as proofs. Using the science of astrology to determine its exact moment, one of the many prophecies in favor of Charles predicted the consummation of history and the end of prophecy: "Within the year 1548 the whole world will be gathered in one flock with one shepherd."[58] Perhaps Titian's portrait of *Charles V at Muhlberg* of 1548 (fig. 66)—where Charles appears as the *Miles Christianus*, bearing Charlemagne's Holy Lance with the nail from the Cross, as well as the spear that embodied the ancient Roman emperor's supreme power[59]—and Philip II's triumphal parade through the empire that began in 1548 to present him as

70. Titian, *Gloria.*
Museo del Prado,
Madrid.

Charles's co-ruler were planned to coincide and celebrate this date. Charles's profound belief in his apocalyptic destiny is suggested by Titian's contemporaneous *Gloria* (fig. 70). This picture accompanied Charles to his monastic retirement at Yuste and a copy in relief was ordered to decorate his tomb. The *Gloria* evokes the topos of the Last World Emperor, for it shows David and Moses with the Erythrean Sibyl and Ezekiel,[60] who appears with the eagle that had been identified with the German emperor in the legend of the Last World Emperor. In the presence of these respective pagan and biblical prophets of the end of the world, Charles V yields his crown to God and Christ in a cloud of glory.

Chapter VII *Philip II of Spain*

I N the Renaissance the emperor's mystic image was brilliantly brought to life by the charismatic Charles V. From the moment of his own coronation in 1530, Charles was possessed with the idea of passing to his son Philip II (1527–98; fig. 71) that title which millennia of imperial propaganda had construed as a dynastic office.[1]

Drawing on the imperial court's accrued treasury of cultural expertise, Philip II manipulated the traditional vocabulary to emerge as the master coordinator of the traditions we have been exploring. Although embellishments to the "icon" of the world ruler would be made after his demise, Philip II's place in the development was definitive. Assimilating the entire preceding history of the sacred imperial system of beliefs, Philip formulated the concept of absolute monarchy on which the dominant political systems of the seventeenth and eighteenth century would be structured.

In contrast to the acclaim and scholarly attention accorded to his father's achievements, Philip's brilliant contributions to imperial ideology suffered from neglect both at home and abroad. Tarnished by the Protestant "Black legend" that pursued him as the scourge of the Inquisition, Philip II's regency was denigrated by his rivals.[2] Within his own domains, the peculiarly secretive Philip shrouded his ambitions under a hermetic cloak. But it was precisely his isolation that enhanced his mystical aura, for, adapt-

71. Pompeo Leoni,
Philip II. Museo del
Prado, Madrid.

ing the rigorous court protocol of his Burgundian and Castilian ancestors, Philip concentrated on shaping his monarchy in the mold of the unapproachable god-king.[3] The concluding chapters of this book focus on establishing Philip as the most significant theocratic ideologist of the modern era.

Plans for Philip's accession to the imperial throne were initiated by his father. By the middle of the 1540s Charles began preparations to concede his realms to Philip. At the height of his power, following the victory at Muhlberg, the ailing and battle-weary Charles directed his primary attention to these goals. It proved to be an onerous task. Notwithstanding the rebellious acts of his own subjects in Germany, which Charles managed to hold together by a system of carefully plotted alliances, the largest threat to the division of empire revolved around claims to the imperial title advanced by his brother Ferdinand, with the support of German electors.[4] In a letter to his sister Mary, Charles confessed that not even his battles with the king of France had caused him as much heartache as these struggles with Ferdinand.[5]

In 1548, Charles and his brother Ferdinand agreed that neither of them would negotiate with the German electors for the imperial title for their respective sons until the two brothers had met again to discuss the issue. In the meantime, Charles conceived of an ingenious plan to sway the electors. He sent Philip on his great debut through the empire, which was to culminate in Augsburg, where he would be introduced to his non-Spanish subjects. Then Charles sent Ferdinand's son Maximilian to Spain to act as regent in Philip's absence, thereby cleverly eliminating him from the political arena where negotiations were proceeding.

In an event heralded by contemporaries as the most elaborate triumphal entry in history, Philip II was introduced to the imperial realms as the heir apparent to the title of Holy Roman emperor. Following the antique tradition, triumphal monuments were erected along the prince's processional path; beneath these passed a courtly pageant en route to the imperial seat. The journey culminated at Augsburg in 1549, where Charles had convened a diet of the German electors to settle the question of the imperial election.

The imagery for the prince's *Adventus* was designed to serve

these ends, and its iconography explicitly referred to the genealogical traditions we have been tracing. Drawn from legend,
prophecy, and astrology and chronicled in the official royal account by Calvete de Estrella, the compendia of Philippian themes
stressed the divine right of kings, the conquest of vice through
his innate virtue, and the presentation of Philip as the incarnation
of justice.[6] All of these celebrated the prince as the legitimate
heir of the empire who was to bring about the return of eternal
peace. Images of consanguinity and co-sovereignty were the keynote mode for exhibiting the uninterrupted progression of divine election that passed to the Hapsburgs from the Old Testament priest-kings, the gods of pagan myth, and the emperors of
Rome. These included Priam yielding his realm to Hector; Philip
of Macedon conferring the imperium on Alexander the Great;
Vespasian conducted in triumph with Titus, already his co-
sovereign; and Charlemagne donating his realm to Louis the
Pious. Accompanying these, in effigies "so real that they appeared
to the spectators to be the emperor and his son instead of
statues,"[7] were nearly identical figures of Charles V and Philip II
holding royal scepters and jointly supporting the globe of the
earth (fig. 72). An accompanying inscription explains the juxtaposition: "As King Philip gave the realm to Alexander, so the
Emperor Charles . . . desires that in his lifetime his son Philip will
be elected Caesar."[8]

Judaic prototypes of dynastic co-rule complemented their
imperial counterparts. The Old Testament references were subsumed for Philip under the rubric "New Solomon"; an epithet,
which, as we shall see, would become the cornerstone of his
imagery at the Escorial. At Louvain—as well as at Brussels and
Antwerp—David crowns Solomon king of Israel. The image was
juxtaposed with a lifelike statue of Charles crowning Philip, and
the parallel clarified by inscription: "As David, a true prophet
before his death made Solomon king, so Caesar has his son
crowned."[9]

While the Solomonic model depicted Philip's divine calling
to rule being transmitted through the seed of Jesse, the pattern
also drew upon the eternal authority of the heavenly prototype.
At the Council of Nicaea in 325—whose deliberations were depicted on one of the lunettes in Philip II's library at the Escorial—
the Son of God had been declared consubstantial with the Fa-

De hooch
tr.l.voetē.
De biepte
rrviij.voe.
De diepte
rr.voeten.

72. Pieter Coecke van
Aelst, *Philip II and Charles
V.* In Cornelius Grapheus. *Le Triomphe d'Anvers*,
Antwerp, 1550. Biblioteca Apostolica Vaticana, Rome.

ther. At the same time it was established that: "The only Begotten Logos of God endures with his Father as co-ruler from ages that have no beginning to ages that have no end."[10] In the public arena of Philip's triumphal entry, legendary antetypes of hereditary rule were presented in serial progression; in the already mentioned *Gloria*, that was ordered from Titian upon Philip's arrival at Augsburg (fig. 70), the formula was contracted to reveal the divine model. Appearing to the emperor and the prince are two nearly identical, symmetrically placed figures of Christ and God the Father ruling in tandem.[11]

Through the effigies of millennia of ancestors who lined Philip's triumphal path, the Hapsburgs proclaimed that the source of their sacral and temporal powers was divine and hereditary. This concept was condensed in an image at Antwerp where God Himself crowns Philip and invests him with the imperial regalia.

Along the triumphal route, these genealogical monuments with their dry didactic message were interspersed with more

De figure des triumphalen Boogs der Geneuopsen.

De geliele hoochte C. voeten.
De breyd- de. lrr.
De diepte rr. voet.

73. Pieter Coecke van Aelst, *Philip and the Olympian Gods* (detail). In Cornelius Grapheus, *Le Triomphe d'Anvers*, Antwerp, 1550. Biblioteca Apostolica Vaticana, Rome.

De gehecle hoochte.lrr. voeten.
De brepde rrvij. voet.

74. Pieter Coecke van Aelst, *Philip between Ascanius and Servius Tullius* (detail). In Cornelius Grapheus, *Le Triomphe d'Anvers*, Antwerp, 1550. Biblioteca Apostolica Vaticana, Rome.

spirited mythical pageantry. Now identified with Jason retrieving the Golden Fleece, now with Hector defending the port of Troy,[12] now as the heir of Aeneas, whose armor is bestowed by the gods (fig. 73) and frequently addressed as Ascanius, Philip is presented as the hero of the Trojan epic and the savior of the *Fourth Eclogue*; his pacific rule induces Astraea-Justice to return to earth.[13] In a telling example of this Vergilian imagery, Philip stands in the center between Ascanius and Servius Tullius, who bear the flames of divine election on their heads. Below Philip's feet are personifications of the three parts of the world: Asia, Africa, and Europe (fig. 74). The inscription is addressed to Philip: "By the apparition of flames, Ascanius and Servius received a presage of their future reign of the Roman imperium, but your eagle is the certain sign of your imperium of the whole world."[14] The imagery is congealed in the dialogue entitled *Philippino* that was prepared for the young prince; there is recounted the Trojan settlement of Rome, and God's intention that this realm should devolve on Philip.[15] In a tapestry in Philip's collection where the players are transported to the timeless present by their contem-

75. *History of Aeneas.* Sixteenth-century tapestry. Madrid, Royal Palace. Patrimonio Nacional, Madrid.

porary dress, Aeneas's wedding to Lavinia establishes the congenital foundations of this destiny (fig. 75).[16]

Phrases drawn from the literature of the Last World Emperor confirm Philip's destiny. At Antwerp statues of all the famous Philips (Philippus Arabus, Philip of Macedonia, Philip the Fair, Philip the Good, and so forth) were followed by one of Philip II, as most victorious of all these illustrious men. A prophetic tone is attached to this grouping in the recall of the Nomine "P."[17] These implications were enhanced by the image of Philippus Arabus, first of all the Christian emperors. Orosius, whom the inscription identifies as the authority on Philippus Arabus, had perceived the coincidence between his rule and the millennial anniversary of Rome's founding.[18] At Douay, the young prince's prophetic calling was summed up in the inscription that announces: "A new light is born and peace will reign and the Golden Age will return. For Philip will liberate Africa and Asia from darkness and fulfill the prophecy of a sole king and pastor on earth."[19]

At the end of Philip's journey, he joined his father who had him recognized as heir apparent of the Netherlands and invoked a diet to consider the imperial succession. Unable to secure the imperial title for Philip, Charles proposed that his son be elected his co-ruler, succeeding him at his death as king of the Romans, while Ferdinand would succeed to the imperium. Ferdinand flatly rejected this too.

Even if his brother had acceded to Charles's demands, which Ferdinand had no intention of doing, the electors were not disposed to accept a Spanish head of state. An ambassadorial report of 15 February 1551 records that in the light of these negotiations, the electors openly declared that many of their princes would sooner come to an accord with the Turks than elect a Spaniard emperor. Charles was not to be denied and he continued to exert pressure on the electors. When all attempts at conciliation had been exhausted, Charles decided to impose his will by the Diktat of 9 March 1551. According to the terms of this document, the imperial title was held in reserve for Philip to assume it at a future date; in the interim, it was to go to Ferdinand.[20] Although Charles's plan for Philip's imperial accession was never to take effect, the lifelong struggle and the bitter defeat left Philip with an unbending resolve to acquire the title. In a medal struck to commemorate Charles's abdication, these intentions are expressed through an image of Philip-Hercules assuming the burden of global rule from his father, Charles-Atlas. Philip left Flanders for Spain, where he proceeded apace to construe his own vision of the emperor's mythic image in the expectation that he would soon become emperor himself.

The Formation of Philip's Empire

In his quest for European hegemony, Charles V had undertaken an ambitious plan of conquests, alliances, and marriages; in the last of these strategies the young Philip played the principal part. As early as 1543, the sixteen-year-old prince was betrothed to Mary of Portugal, a union that was perceived to have joined the East to the West. The marriage enhanced Spanish claims on the Portuguese territories; these were consolidated in 1580 when Philip gained sovereignty over Portugal. The importance of these possessions was immense both in tangible and ideological terms. The acquired territories in the New World and in the Far East gave the king of Spain a vast empire which was greater than that of any past age. In this unification of the hemispheres, Philip exceeded the ancients, for the Portuguese holdings brought him the distinction of being the only monarch ever to rule all four continents. These possessions stimulated his identification with Jove, and an emblem created in his honor by the marquis of Pescara, displays Philip's dominion over all the lands and the seas of the earthly globe (fig. 76). The explanatory text relates that the emblem's motto "Cum Jove" is drawn from Vergil, and it is to be applied to Philip whom God elected so the world would be under one pastor and one flock.[21]

Mary of Portugal died in 1545 giving birth to Philip's son, Don Carlos. Following her death, world events assisted Charles in realizing an earlier plan. As early as the mid-1530s Charles had contemplated Philip's marriage to his cousin Mary Tudor. Mary had supported the Catholic faith throughout her brother's reign, and her policy was encouraged by the Hapsburg emperor. Her marriage to Philip was celebrated in 1554, following on Mary's accession to the English throne in the previous year. This union renewed the hope of worldwide Catholic dominion with England ruled by Mary as a Catholic province of Spain, and with the Hapsburgs uniting the world under Catholic sovereignty. Mary

took the motto "Veritas Filia Temporis"—referring to the liberation of Christian Truth under Hapsburg auspices[22]—as her personal emblem and the state seal of her realm. The popularization
of this motto in the Renaissance lent its weight to Charles's and
Philip's quest for dominion over Europe. It continued to serve as
a family dictum long after the Spanish-English alliance had been
dissolved; for example, the motif prominently appears in
Tiepolo's eighteenth-century fresco that decorated the throne
room of the Royal Palace in Madrid.[23]

In October 1555, Charles took an unprecedented action for a
living monarch by ceding to Philip the sovereignty of Flanders.
The following June he ceded the hereditary title to Burgundy and
the sovereignty of the Order of the Golden Fleece, a dignity long
intermingled with the Trojan heritage. Most significant for
Philip's budding pretensions to the sacred and secular powers of
the Old Testament priest-kings, the title conveyed the mystical
kinship with the Merovingian and Carolingian kings.[24]

In 1556, on the eve of his imperial abdication, Charles conceded to Philip the sovereignty of Spain. With Spain came the
New World, the realms of Naples, Sicily, and Lombardy, the titular sovereignty of Jerusalem and the Byzantine imperial title.
Philip's Spanish heritage provided a strong basis on which he
could continue the Hapsburg claim to unite the world in Christianity. Philip's great-grandparents Ferdinand and Isabella had
been extremely instrumental in advancing Spanish ambitions for
leadership of a united Church. Isabella had already conceived of
a universal Christianity with Spain as its center and Spanish as its
international language.[25] Spain's role in expelling the Turks had
been given primary emphasis in this scheme for Iberian dominion of the faith. Ferdinand had conquered Granada and expelled
the Turks from Western Europe. Spain had also taken a principal
role in suppressing the Turk in the Mediterranean, and Ferdinand
stood at the head of the Crusades to recover the Holy Land.[26]
Spanish discoveries in the New World under these same ancestors had opened new lands to be conquered for Christ; these
territories became a symbol of the reviving strength of the Catholic faith. In a contemporary history the import of the prodigious
discovery of the New World is ranked with Christ's advent: "The
greatest thing after the creation of the world apart from the Incarnation and the death of He who created it, is the discovery of the

76. *Philip II Rules the Four
Continents.* In Luca Con-
tile, *Ragionamento sopra la
proprietà delle imprese,*
Pavia, 1574, figure fol-
lowing p. 43. Biblioteca
Apostolica Vaticana,
Rome.

Indies."[27] All of these conquests revived the centuries-old prophecy that a world ruler would emerge from the Spanish race who would destroy the Turks, restore the Church, and reestablish Christ's reign from Jerusalem.[28] An auspicious corollary to these claims was the Spanish crown's titular sovereignty of the Holy Land.

An aggregate of historical events occurring in the years 1557–58 brought an end to the vision of an Anglo-Flemish state and conceded in its place the Hapsburg domination of the European continent. In 1557, on the feast day of the Spanish Saint Lawrence, Philip defeated Henry II of France at the Battle of Saint Quentin. The death of Mary Tudor in 1558, which put an end to the alliance between England and Spain, liberated Philip to form a new marital union. In the same year, the peace with France was secured by Philip's betrothal to Henry's daughter Isabel de Valois. Since the Treaty of Chateau-Cambrensis marked the end of long-standing enmity between contending French and Austrian claimants to imperial legitimacy, Philip's marriage to Isabel was perceived to have ended civil war.

Philip's new peace treaty restored the lost concord that, with the Treaty of Cambrai of 1508, had for a few years ended hostilities between the Valois Louis XII and the House of Austria. That earlier peace was celebrated in Jean Lemaire de Belges's *Concord of the Human Race* which was commissioned by Maximilian's daughter Margaret to celebrate the alliance. In this work, in which biblical and imperial events and their contemporary counterparts are fully synchronized, the peace is compared to Augustus's closing of the Temple of Janus, and Maximilian's daughter Mary, who negotiated the peace, is compared to the Annunciate Virgin.[29] It was following this alliance that Lemaire prepared the *Illustrations de Gaule & Singularitez de Troy* in which he asserted that the Ur-Trojan heritage descended from Noah-Janus by two lines to these royal houses. Philip's renewal of that harmony was enveloped in a similar sacro-imperial aura.

French kings as well as Austrian and German emperors claimed descent from Clovis and Charlemagne, and hence the directives of Sacred Imperium. A later genealogy that Philip II commanded from Esteban de Garibay celebrates Philip's kinship with all the past rulers of France and celebrates the consummate amalgamation of these heritages in Philip's marriage to Isabel.

Garibay also affirms Philip's sole legitimacy as ruler of the imperium.[30] When Henry III Valois died without issue and the Valois line became extinct, Philip attempted to have Isabella Clara Eugenia, his first daughter born of this marriage, crowned queen of France.[31]

By 1558, the year of Charles V's death, the configurations of a new political order were in place. The imperial title had passed to Ferdinand, and Philip's empire had detached itself from the German block. Philip permanently returned to Spain in 1559 and established there the seat from which he governed an empire—comprising the Netherlands, parts of Italy, the Iberian peninsula, and most of the New World—that was vaster, richer and more coherent than that of Charles V.

At the dawn of the new decade, Philip prepared to assume the imperial office in accordance with the agreement between Charles and Ferdinand that the empire would revert to Philip at Ferdinand's death. But when Ferdinand I died in 1564, the German electors granted the imperial title to his son, Maximilian II. Philip may have foreseen this turn of events and planned to deflect its impact, for by 1563 rumors were already circulating in ambassadorial reports that he would seek a new imperial crown as emperor of the Indies.[32]

Philip took as the chief tenet of his monarchy his right to restore the universal rule of the Roman Empire from East to West. He employed an increasingly sophisticated syncretism of classical and Judeo-Christian traditions to achieve this goal, and he shaped his kingship in the mold of the priest-kings of antiquity. Drawing all of his possessions together to bear on this status, he immersed his being in the legendary personae of his ancestors and brought to the forefront the mystical associations inherent in these heritages. Grounding his family tree in the divine and saintly progeny of the emperors of Rome, the kings of France, and the emperors of Constantinople, Philip established himself as the heir to Adam's Edenic rule. With this foundation to sustain him, he solidified the concept of piety as a Hapsburg virtue, and the Cross and Eucharist as dynastic preserves.[33] As a corollary to his messianic destiny, he identified himself with Solomon and established a Christianized version of all'antica ancestor worship in the Temple of Jerusalem at the Escorial.[34] This expression in stone was implemented by more ephemeral imagery. He or-

77. Jorg Breu the
Younger, *The Prophecy of
Daniel.* In *Historia del Origen y Sucesión de los Reinos
e Imperios desde Noe hasta
Carlos V*, vol. 1, fol. 27v.
of *Origen de la Nobleza*,
1547–48. Escorial MS
28. I. 11. Patrimonio
Nacional, Madrid.

dered from Titian a series of mythic paintings that extolled Hapsburg destiny in the manner of the ancient Caesars,[35] a painted
Argo for use in his "divinely ordained" victories against the Turks,
and a solar identity in the tradition assigned to Apollo in Troy's
millennial destiny.[36] Holding his identities with Solomon and
Apollo in perfect equilibrium, he extended that identity to the
Articles of the Faith. And this, the foundation of the theocratic
state, he accomplished when he distilled the essence of both
Judeo-Christian and Gentile religious sentiment in an icon that
was indistinguishable from the royal presence.[37]

As the visionary whose absolute monarchy established the
model for the dominant form of rule in Europe for the next two
centuries, Philip deeded to posterity living proof that the Hapsburg heir was decreed by God to be the Last Descendant of
Aeneas. The epithet refers to the advent of millennial peace
when, having defeated the heretic and unified the hemispheres
in the Christian faith under his rule, the successor of Aeneas
yields the terrestrial rule back to Christ, its true sovereign. In the
Monarchy of Spain which he dedicated to Philip at the end of the
century, Tommaso Campanella proclaimed that Philip had realized the plan that God had prognosticated through his prophets:
Spain had become the Last World Monarchy.[38] These words expressed a long-held conviction at the Hapsburg court, one that
was visually expressed in a treatise dedicated to Philip, where the
prophet Daniel reveals his dream of the Four Monarchies directly to Charles V (fig. 77).[39]

Chapter VIII *The Order of the Golden Fleece*

THOUGH the Hapsburgs maintained dynastic solidarity and a dominating grip on Europe and the Americas, Charles's abdication split the empire between the family's Austrian and Spanish branches. With this rift, there developed a new rivalry for legitimate rule of the universe and the prophetic title of Last World Emperor. The Austrian branch held the imperial dignity, but it was little more than a symbol, for Philip II had the geopolitical strength and material wealth required of a world ruler. Armed with a daunting list of titles, Philip continued to conceive of himself as the legitimate emperor of Rome, a guise in which he had already been immortalized (see fig. 71). More than just his fantasy that was indulged in by followers at the court, his pretensions were sustained by the Salic principle of primogeniture that northern rulers had endorsed for a thousand years.

As the first-born heir of the Burgundian-Hapsburg clan, Philip II had title to Flanders and the sovereignty of the Order of the Golden Fleece. Through the symbolic meaning for the Golden Fleece that Philip the Good appropriated to the Burgundians when he founded the Order in its name, that sovereignty communicated the direct kinship with Clovis on which legitimate succession to the Old Testament priest-kings was grounded in the north. This heritage is alluded to in an anachronistic image of the duke that is embedded in a history of the Trojan origins of

78. *Philip the Good Attends the Baptism of Clovis. Les Grandes Chroniques de France.* Fifteenth century. Bibliothèque National, Paris. MS. Fr. 2605, fol. 13.

Clovis and the Franks and juxtaposed with a scene of the Trojan war. Wearing the collar of the Order and bearing the sacred regalia of rule, Philip the Good witnesses Clovis's baptism and the bestowal of the heavenly shield that proved his divine election (fig. 78). Before discussing the Fleece's meaning for the duke, we should stop to consider the impressive symbolic identity that had long invested Aries, the constellation that immortalized the Golden Fleece in the heavens. For although the affinities have never been observed, the Order's evangelical and imperial meanings were contained *in nuce* in this cosmic insignia.

Formed of a cluster of stars that configure the shape of a ram, the constellation Aries commemorated the apotheosis of the demigod Phrixus, whom the Golden Fleece had safely carried to the shores of Asia.[1] Possessed with Phrixus's "incorruptible" spirit,[2] the ram's fleecy pelt that remained in the Temple of Colchis was the earthly counterpart to this heavenly icon. Both the relic and its quest carried mystical meanings. The return of the ram's fleece to Argos was an act of ancestral homage undertaken by Phrixus's kin Jason: "For Phrixus biddeth us go to the halls of Aeetes, and bring his spirit home, and recover the fleecy fell of the ram, on which he was erstwhile rescued from the sea."[3] It was in the midst of accomplishing this quest that the Argonauts destroyed Troy and toppled Asia's power.[4]

Since antiquity Aries had occupied a unique first place in the cosmic calendar. According to ancient astronomical theory, the signs of the zodiac were established in the heavens in direct correspondence to the historical epoch over which they held sway. Aries represented the first zodiacal epoch, for the earth was created when the sun was in its boundaries.[5] This primacy is commemorated in Aries' position as the sign in which all astronomical calendars begin the year. Legend identified this cosmic Arian Age with Saturn's rule of Latium in the proverbial earthly paradise of the Golden Age. The ram's appearance in the heavens each spring heralded the cyclical renewal of the earth and promised the return of man's state of innocence. Platonic theories of the universe gave added dimension to this idea. According to these theories, at some point in time all the heavenly bodies would return to the same position they occupied at the creation of the world.[6]

Vergil may have been the first to connect these cosmic concepts to Roman mythic history. In the *Fourth Eclogue*, the sibyl prophesies that the imminent rebirth of the cosmos in a new Apollonian age of prelapsarian bliss will begin with the return of the heroes who conquered the Golden Fleece.[7] This will be followed by a recurrence of the Trojan war: "A second Tiphys [the *Argo*'s helmsman] shall then arise, and a second *Argo* to carry chosen heroes; a second warfare too, shall there be, and again shall a great Achilles be sent to Troy."[8] This period of strife is followed by an age of harmony under a new savior king who reigns over Rome, the new Troy, then "Every land shall bear all fruits . . . of himself the ram . . . [who] shall change his fleece, now to sweetly blushing purple, now to a saffron yellow."[9] This description of the ram's chromatic splendor implies that the New Age will begin with the sun's reentry into the sign of Aries, a reference expanded in Apollonius Rhodius's *Argonautica* where the Golden Fleece is described as "blushing red with the fiery beams of the rising sun."[10]

Through a serial development that spanned more than a millennium, a framework was fixed for associating the rebirth of the world with a new Argonautic expedition. Aries' cosmic influence over the rebirth of Rome was expressed by the Augustan poet Manilius, who associated the constellation with the Argonautic and Trojan legends and with Augustus's victory at Actium.[11] And, as we have seen, the topos of the Fleece's safe passage home was applied to Aeneas's repatriation of the ancestral gods of Priam's royal lineage to Latium, and by association to Augustus's translation of the Penates to his own temple-palace on the Palatine hill.[12] Following its application to Titus's destruction of the temple of Jerusalem and the transfer of the most sacred Jewish cult objects from Solomon's temple to Rome, the Fleece and its recapture assumed a Christian meaning.[13]

In this transition the Fleece's cosmic significance was retained, for Aries' symbolism was well suited to Christian exegesis. The constellation marks the vernal equinox, the moment when "day gained the victory" over night.[14] Thus Aries' return to the heavens each year was viewed by the ancients as a psychomachian triumph in cosmic terms. To the medieval Christian mind, this cosmic triumph of light, together with the constellation's ovine configuration, served to establish Aries as a stellar emblem for Christ. Since Carolingian times, the ram in the heavens that immortalized the Golden Fleece was identified with the Apocalyptic Lamb of Saint John's vision.[15] Through that form of syncretistic Christian thought which sought to amalgamate the sacred and the profane, the ram's celestial reappearance that heralded the returning Golden Age was identified with Christ's restoration of the state of innocence that existed in Eden before the Fall. What is more, the beginning and the end of Christian time are accorded in this sign. Announced in the heavens since the creation, Aries marks the seasonal moment of the Incarnation. Each year at Eastertide Aries returns to announce its eucharistic message and to reiterate Saint John's apocalyptic promise. Thus in Christian thought the whole cycle of Redemption—the beginning of Christ's life on earth and the sign of His sacrifice and return— cohere in this cosmic icon. This cluster of ideas remained a perennially valid construct of pagan-Christian symbolism.[16]

Aries takes on the meaning of Christ's apocalyptic emblem in Guido delle Colonne's *Historia Destructionis Troiae*: "The fleets of allys of [Jason and] Hercules meet at Thessaly, and at the season of the year when the sun enters Aries, they set sail for Troy. . . . Thus kynges with knightes in companies grete . . . sailed [to]

Troy."[17] Here the constellation's return in the spring is the clarion call for a new Argonautic expedition, which is intended as a generic metaphor for a spiritual pilgrimage to the Holy Land. We have seen that Guido's poem was an allegorical counterpart to his patron Frederick II's crusade to recapture the Holy Sepulchre.

This implicit symbolism was made explicit when Philip the Good of Burgundy founded the Order of the Golden Fleece on 10 January 1429 to unite the flower of knighthood under his leadership for a crusade to Jerusalem to defeat the Turks and recapture the Holy Sepulchre.[18] The duke identified his crusading objectives with the capture of the Golden Fleece that had been accomplished by his mythic ancestors.[19] An extensive treatise on the Order written by its chancellor Guillaume Fillastre revealed the interconnection between the Trojan legacy and the knighthood's crusading objectives. The Burgundians are further identified as God's elect, chosen to prepare for the Second Coming. Although it has escaped scholarly attention, Fillastre's treatise reveals that the Golden Fleece signifies Jesus Christ, Lamb of God, sent to redeem the world and prophesied to return at the end of time to rule an earthly paradise from Jerusalem:

When Juno, our first mother, chased her children from heaven for their sin, they embarked on this world of tribulations. Some fall; others, fixed on the ram like Phrixius, arrive at Colchis to the Temple of Jupiter that is the Church Triumphant. . . . Jupiter sent us the ram . . . of His Grace Jesus, the Lamb of God, who offered His sacrifice to the world . . . covered in the golden fleece of our humanity.[20]

Following this declaration, Fillastre announced the messianic purpose of Philip's divinely ordained Knighthood: "[The] conquest of the Golden Fleece refers to the deliverance of humanity . . . because of these dignified mysteries, God ordained this Order for Philip."[21]

An imperial prerogative formed the crux of the promise that the Burgundians were to accomplish this redemption. Recalling the biblical story of Nebuchadnezzar's dream of the Four Monarchies, Fillastre linked that dream to the proclamation that Christ's Second Coming would occur under the imperial rule of Rome: "In the Fifth Monarchy the world will end. Then one shepherd will reign [over] one fold, which is the Church, of which Christ is the shepherd. And all will begin and end with the Romans whose rule was consecrated by Christ on earth."[22] Following Daniel's interpretation of the dream, in which the human body stands as a cryptogram for the Four Ages of the world, Fillastre identified Philip with the head of the microscosmic body, representing the first and renewed Golden Age. "As gold surmounts all other metals," he declares, "so Philip is the King of Kings on earth."[23] He concluded the treatise by venerating his patron's imperial and biblical forbears. These statements reinforced the Burgundian claim to the sovereignty of the unified Eastern and Western Empires that had long been symbolized in the cross of Saint Andrew, the patron saint of Burgundy and of the Order of the Golden Fleece. Andrew's X-shaped cross symbolized Eastern and Western unity in Christ. The Eastern Empire was long deemed the property of the Burgundians, deriving from Charlemagne's Greek mother, and descending through Baldwin, king of Jerusalem and emperor of Constantinople.[24]

Philip the Good selected the Golden Fleece as the symbol, ornament, and namesake of the Order. Since it communicated such subtly spun comprehensive meanings, it is not surprising that this stellar beacon, which enfolded pagan and imperial as well as Christian concepts of the earth's first light and the perennial promise of the conquest over darkness should represent the objectives of the Order. He created a visible tribute to these mystical goals by adopting the Golden Fleece as the hereditary garment of the dynasty. Dangling proudly from a collar, the Golden Fleece became the ever-present attribute displayed in official portraits of its sovereigns. The emblem announced to the world that by divine election Burgundian Rule would make manifest on earth the promise of salvation which had been encoded in the heavens since the beginning of time. Philip the Good announced these mystical intentions by naming the Annunciate Virgin as the Order's patron and the realization of Saint John's vision as its goal.[25] The association between the Fleece and the Incarnation was visualized in a painting of the *Annunciation* by Philip the Good's court painter Jan van Eyck; where the Annunciate stands on the sign of Aries.[26]

With Philip the Good's formation of the Order of the Golden Fleece, the myth's Christian meaning was adapted to the Burgundian cause: the Order's treatise identified the Golden Fleece as Christ, the Lamb of God; its recapture as the deliverance of humanity; and the Burgundians as God's elect to prepare for the Second Coming by defeating Islam and recapturing Jerusalem. Then would come about the mystical time of Saint John's vision of one Shepherd ruling one flock. Since the Burgundians traced their ancestry to the seed of Jessé through Clovis, the appropriation of the Golden Fleece as the insignia of their stirps alluded to Christ as an ancestral divinity and the Sacrificial Lamb as their apotropaic shield. In reserving the sovereignty of the Order to his heirs by decree, Philip safeguarded both the singularity of the Burgundian prerogative and the subjugation of other nobles to its tenets. Like a minion of warring angels designated by the creator to prepare for a future time, these self-proclaimed Argonauts gathered behind Philip's leadership in a common mystical goal.[27] In duplicating the accomplishments of their mythical ancestors, the knights of the Golden Fleece intended to realize in Christian terms Vergil's prophecy for the restoration of a timeless Golden Age under the auspices of the legitimate imperial heir.[28]

79. Jan van Eyck, *Ghent Altarpiece*, lower section without far right panel. Ghent, Saint Bavo. Copyright A.C.L. Bruxelles.

These apocalyptic objectives may enhance our understanding of the dynastic significance attached to the *Ghent Altarpiece* that was unveiled two years after the formation of the Order. Commissioned from Jan van Eyck, by Jodocus Vijd, a wealthy official in Philip's government, the altarpiece was reconstructed as a hundred-foot-long, three-storied tableau vivant bearing emblems of the Order for Philip's Triumphal Entry into Ghent in 1458.[29] As Philip approached the tableau, the curtains were drawn back as though to reveal a vision. Through our knowledge of the meaning Philip the Good attached to the Golden Fleece, we have an insight into the personal reverberations that the painting's central image carried at his court. Here, in the presence of Philip the Good, his storied ancestors, and past and present members of the Burgundian ruling clan, the descent of the heavenly Jerusalem ruled by the Lamb of God is presented as a visionary fait accompli (fig. 79).

The Hapsburgs

The concept that Aries' pious influence dominated the Golden Age was reiterated for the Renaissance in the *Urania*, an astronomical poem dedicated to Emperor Maximilian I by the Neapolitan poet Giovanni Pontano. Beginning his catalogue of the zodiac with Aries, which he identified with the traditional fable of the Golden Fleece, Pontano commented on the "moral" quality of the epoch: under Aries, the new star which dominated the earth at the beginning of time, men practiced faith, and peace and love abided. This, the poet tells us, was the happiest of times, when mankind, singing hymns to the rebirth of the sun, lived in a state of innocence.[30] Maximilian could bask in the application of this imagery to his person. Since no direct male offspring of the Burgundian dukes survived after the death of Charles the Bold in 1477, Maximilian appropriated the Fleece as the sign of the Burgundian-Hapsburg clan following his marriage to Mary of Burgundy (see fig. 69).[31]

An extraordinary chain of events that occurred around the potentially apocalyptic year 1500 confirmed that this marital union had been determined by Providence. Since the Argonauts sailed towards the east on the world's maiden voyage, they were proclaimed the first to open the way to the treasures of the Indies. When Columbus's eastward-bound journeys to recover the Holy Sepulchre revealed a primeval land previously hidden from sight, his ship was identified with the *Argo* and the West Indies with the lost Eden.

In the aftermath of their incredible discovery of the New World, Ferdinand and Isabella succeeded in 1496 in marrying their unstable daughter Juana to Philip the Fair of Burgundy, the emperor's son. The mystical goals of the knighthood seemed miraculously close at hand once the Spanish "New Eden" was in the possession of the sovereign of the Order of the Golden Fleece. With this unparalleled mirror of ancient events to sustain them, the royal rhetoricians attuned the Spanish monarchs' achievements to the Burgundian pretensions. This union of historical and mythical circumstance guaranteed a perpetual place of honor to Golden Fleece imagery among the actual and would-be Roman emperors for the next four hundred years. Eventually Austrian and Spanish branches of the Order developed; Napoléon formed a third independent French branch in the nineteenth century.[32]

Charles V and the Order of the Golden Fleece

Charles V adapted the *Columns of Hercules* (fig. 80) as his personal device to mark his accession to the sovereignty of the Order of the Golden Fleece in 1516.[33] This emblem expressed his ambition to extend his sovereignty east to the Holy Land and west to the New World, beyond the boundaries Hercules had once marked at Gibraltar to indicate the farthest reaches of Europe in antiquity.[34] The columns themselves evoked imperial,[35] Spanish,[36] and Solomonic references to which Charles was uniquely entitled.[37] Despite its personal reverberations, Charles's emblem was to become Europe's most enduring symbol in the bid for universal theocratic monarchy.[38]

On the *Potence* of the Order (fig. 81), and in myriad places where Charles was publicly celebrated, these columns were juxtaposed with the firestone and flints—Burgundian emblems as-

80. Luigi Marliano, *Columns of Hercules*, emblem of Charles V. In Girolamo Ruscelli, *Le Imprese illustri*, Venice, 1566. Biblioteca Apostolica Vaticana, Rome.

sociated since Philip the Good's establishment of the Order of the Golden Fleece with the defeat of the Turks and the conquest of the Holy Land.[39] For the oration delivered at Charles's inauguration as grand master of the Order in 1516, Luigi Marliano, who created the device, confirmed the propriety of the rule of a single monarch over the entire world, emulating the rule of God in heaven.[40] Thus, the earliest form of Charles's device linked his ambition for a global Christianity under the rule of Spain to the knighthood's mystical intentions. To aid him in these goals, Charles augmented the Order's strength by increasing the number of knights for the first time since its organization.[41] Among the international rulers he elected was Francis I of France, Andrea Doria of Genoa, and members of the Medici, Gonzaga, Este, and Farnese clans.

Charles's use of Argonautic imagery increased following his imperial election. On a triumphal arch erected for his entry into Milan in 1541, he was identified as Jason retrieving the Golden Fleece. Preserving the established relationship between the Argonautic story and the Order's eschatological goals, the battle against the Turks which took place at Goleta was represented above Jason's image. The inscription read "I will capture a fleece which will bring back the Golden Age."[42]

81. *Potence of the Order of the Golden Fleece.* Netherlands, after 1517. Treasury, Kunsthistorisches Museum, Vienna.

Charles's sovereignty of the New World underscored the legitimacy of these claims. In Ariosto's *Orlando Furioso*, the chivalric counterpart in structure, scope, and mimetic power of its model, the *Aeneid*,[43] Charles V and the "New Argonauts" of imperial Rome realize in Christian terms the *Fourth Eclogue*'s eschatological prophecy:

> New Argonauts I see and Tiphys new
> Opening, till now an undiscovered way . . .
> To the fifth Charles' triumphant captains bend
> That this way should be hidden was God's will . . . Of old . . .
> Nor will he suffer its discovery till
> The sixth and seventh century be done
> And he delays his purpose to fulfill
> In that he would subject the world to one
> The justest and most fraught with prudent lore
> Of emperors, since Augustus, or before . . .
> Of Arragon and Austria's blood I see a monarch bred. . . .
> Astraea rethroned by him will be
> For such . . . Heaven . . . designs . . .
> And wills that in his time Christ's scattered sheep
> Should be one flock, beneath one Shepherd's keep
> And that this be accomplished with more ease
> Writ in the skies from all eternity.[44]

In Ariosto's poetic terminology, the phrase "Heaven[s] . . . design . . . writ in the skies from all eternity" connotes at once the vision of the Apocalyptic Lamb and the cosmic symbol of Aries that heralds the return of the Argonauts; these are construed as interchangeable icons eternally announcing Charles's destiny to rule as sole monarch of the universe.

Philip II

In 1529 at the Treaty of Cambrai, when Charles V ceded the duchy of Burgundy to Francis I, he maintained the honorific title of duke of Burgundy. Philip II assumed that title on 25 October 1555. In the same year Philip adopted a personal emblem with the suggestive motto "Iam Illustrabit Omnia" (Now He Will Illuminate Everything). He assumed the office of sixth chief and sovereign of the Order of the Golden Fleece together with the title king of Spain on 16 January 1556. At a meeting of the knighthood on 19 January of that year, he increased the Order by the election of nineteen new knights. In 1573 he declared himself its sole chief and sovereign with absolute power to elect new knights; these rights were confirmed by Gregory XIII's papal dispensation in the same year.[45] Philip made Argonautic imagery an integral part of his ideological and political ambitions, as we have seen, when his commission for a painted *Argo* to lead the Christian fleet against the Turk at Lepanto was intimately connected to his formation of the Holy League.

Although other courts might borrow Argonautic imagery, Philip occupied a unique position in regard to the Golden Fleece. He presented his credentials as the sole legitimate heir to this mystical prize when he demonstrated his right to Clovis's anointing. A treatise dedicated to Philip II by the Carmelite Monk Francisco Sixto in 1573—one of many that would reaffirm this special status—describes the heavenly anointing and proves Philip's right to this sine qua non of sacral kingship: "When Saint Remi baptized Clovis . . . the skies opened and an angel appeared with a lily and a vase with oil . . . [and Clovis was consecrated] and the angel pronounced the holy oil and the lily that promised his reign over the Franks the possession of Clovis and his successors. . . . [These trophies of his divine election and of God's covenant with Clovis] descended by way of primogeniture to Sicamber who possessed the rule of Austria, and hence to Charlemagne and his successors . . . and to the Emperor Rudolf . . . and to Philip, the Christian Jupiter." Following this explication, Sixto named the ancestors that led from Adam through Priam and Clovis directly to Philip.[46] In innumerable documents published under royal imprimatur during and after Philip's rule, the consecration by unction was declared the inalienable right of the Spanish kings.

As the sacrificial image of Christ and thus eucharistic, and as the hereditary emblem of the Order's sovereign, the Fleece served Philip II as the mark of divine election, the tropaeum of his victory in battle and the ultimate symbol of his right to hold the office of Holy Roman emperor as a dynastic birthright. Philip never relinquished his Burgundian title and the benefices it bestowed. When he ceded sovereignty of the Low Countries to his daughter Isabella in 1598, Philip expressly reserved to himself the title of duke of Burgundy and the sovereignty of the Order.[47] His actions affected the Spanish Hapsburgs' enduring claim to the prerogatives of the Order of the Golden Fleece and his contributions continued to affect international politics into the twentieth century. This effect was demonstrated in claims to ownership of the Order's treasury. Indeed, the dispute over this property has been called "a first alert to the War of the Austrian succession."[48] As victors in the First World War, the Belgians presented the Austrians with their demand for the return of what they deemed their national treasury. Philip II's action in maintaining the sovereignty of the Order when he ceded the Lowlands in 1598 was cited as the precedent for the Austrian refusal. It stood as proof that the sovereignty of the Order was a dynastic and not a geographic prerogative.[49]

The Golden Fleece remained the most significant symbol of the Burgundian-Hapsburg dynasty, and Philip's heirs continued to convey their sacred powers with this imagery. One instance of the many that could be cited occurred when the Cardinal-Infant Ferdinand of Spain made his triumphal entry into Ghent in 1636. Ferdinand indicated his proprietary right to this Flemish city by arriving dressed as a Roman emperor aboard a ship named *Argo*.[50]

In relation to both the Holy Land and the New World, the Argonautic topos remained a symbol of the Spanish Hapsburg's fulfillment of the *Fourth Eclogue*'s eschatological prophecy. For the founding of an unexplored hemisphere that would be dedicated to Christ lent tangible reality to the *Eclogue*'s promise of a "cosmic rebirth." While the Spanish kings continued to evoke this topos through Argonautic imagery, they nonetheless paid homage to Philip II's unique contributions to consolidating the iconography. In funerary celebrations held at Naples for his grandson, Philip IV, each member of the dynasty was accorded a stellar apotheosis. The elder Philip was addressed as the "emperor of the Indies" and awarded the constellation "Indus." The iconographer's account explained that this constellation was first observed by the Argonauts who opened the way to the treasures of the Indies and the triumph of the faith. This constellation belongs to Philip II, he declares, who extended his domain to the previous unknown part of the world, amplified and conserved an empire greater than that of any past age.[51] At the end of the seventeenth century, the fulfillment of the *Fourth Eclogue*'s apocalyptic oracle was celebrated in the elaborate visionary ceiling that Luca Giordano executed at the Casón del Buen Retiro for Charles II, the last of the

Hapsburgs to succeed to the Spanish throne (fig. 82).[52] Beneath a stellar globe that is spun to reveal the entering figure of Aries, Apollo bestows the Golden Fleece on the King (fig. 83), Fury is chained, the Giants are cast out of heaven, and the Golden Age returns under the auspices of the glorified Spanish monarchy. It was in prophetic conformity with that vision that Philip II construed his own mythic image.

83. Luca Giordano, *Allegory of the Golden Fleece*, detail. Seventeenth century. Madrid, Casón del Buen Retiro, main staircase. Museo del Prado, Madrid.

82. Luca Giordano, *Allegory of the Golden Fleece*. Seventeenth century. Madrid, Casón del Buen Retiro, main staircase. Museo del Prado, Madrid.

Chapter IX *The Escorial*

Al Rè del ciel sacro elevato Empio
A santo colle sopra
D'alto lavoro opra stupenda eresse
Il nepote elettissimo di Giesse;
Il qual forse di questo altero essempio
Il buon Filippo elesse.
      —BIAGIO RITI, *Poemi scritti in Lode de
          la sacra Real Fabrica de lo Escuriale.*

ON 10 August 1557, Philip defeated Henry II of France at the Battle of Saint-Quentin. To commemorate this achievement, Philip commissioned the building of the Escorial, to be dedicated to Saint Lawrence on whose feast day he secured the victory. As the conquest brought peace to the eastern and western limits of Catholic Europe, it stirred Philip's dreams of universal rule, such as had prevailed at the inception of the Christian state. The Laurentian sanction underscored these ambitions, for it seemed a prescient announcement that ancient history was about to be repeated. In the Escorial's official chronicle, Father José Sigüenza (1544–1606) noted the historical importance of Philip's victory and his resolve to dedicate a temple to Lawrence. In the following sentence he recorded that Lawrence was "the first martyr to receive a public temple . . . which was erected by the Emperor Constantine . . . for the God-given victory over Maxentius, from which began the peace and the Christianization of the Roman Empire."[1]

The reference to Constantine suggests that in court circles the new monument to Lawrence was seen as the material bridge linking the achievements and ambitions of the first and last legitimate universal Christian sovereigns. On the Escorial's foundation medal, which bears the motto, "Sic Erat in Fatis" (fig. 84), appears a tripartite globe with Jerusalem at its center—an intelligible symbol of universal Christian monarchy since the early Middle Ages.[2]

84. Jacopo da Trezzo, *Sic Erat in Fatis*. Foundation medal, Escorial. Patrimonio Nacional, Madrid.

Perpetuated in the building's complexity and comprehensiveness, and reinforced through its variegated architectural and decorative motifs, all of the Escorial's elements reflect the king's ideological intentions, for the monument was close to Philip's heart.[3] He selected its architects, surveyed its construction, lived there in monastic seclusion, and died there in 1598. His heirs rendered visual homage to Philip's monumental achievement; one seventeenth-century engraving records him glancing down from the height of Mount Escorial to survey the edifice by which he hallowed the holy battle site; another shows Philip as he directs the building of the temple.[4]

At its completion in 1582, the Escorial comprised a royal palace and church, pantheon and family crypt, library, Jeronomite monastery, hospital, and alms house (fig. 85). Foremost among these were the pantheon and crypt, for at the onset of the project, Philip announced that his principal intention was "to provide a proper burial place for my father and mother."[5] In this imposing and severe structure, the architectural language is as diverse as its functions. Here Christian and imperial architectural vocabularies overlap; contemporaries compared the building simultaneously to the pagan Olympus, the seven Wonders of the World, and the Temple of Jerusalem;[6] its patron was addressed not only as David, Moses, and Solomon but also as Jupiter, Alexander, and Augustus.[7] In the fusion of religious and royal imagery that is incorporated in the Escorial's fabric lies the key signifier of Philip's concept of kingship. For biblical-pagan syncretism, as a hereditary construct, is the defining constant of its iconography.

ORIENS

85. After Pedro Perret, *View of the Escorial*. Madrid, Royal Palace. Patrimonio Nacional, Madrid.

Rectangular in plan, except for a narrow handlelike extension at the eastern end to conform the building to the shape of the grill on which Saint Lawrence was martyred (fig. 86),[8] the Escorial is comprised of a fortresslike facade enclosing a series of alternating courtyards and interior spaces. The surrounding walls are punctuated by four corner towers, a motif evocative of the global extent of Philip's domain. These towers and the connecting corridors are covered by pitched slate roofs, a hallmark of Flemish architecture style,[9] and therefore a tacit but persistent reminder of this ancestral heritage. The gravity of the exterior is relieved by a pedimented central portal, a usage adopted— as we are informed by the Bishop of Vigevano, Juan Caramuel Lobkowitz (1602–82)—from the model established by Julius Caesar when he appropriated the temple fastigium for his private palace.[10]

Beyond the central portal lies the Courtyard of the Kings, named for the colossal statues of the six builders of the Temple of Jerusalem. These kings, to whom the Hapsburgs traced their ancestry in the seed of Jesse,[11] appear on the porch of the Basilica that houses the royal pantheon (fig. 87 and 88).[12] The kings are

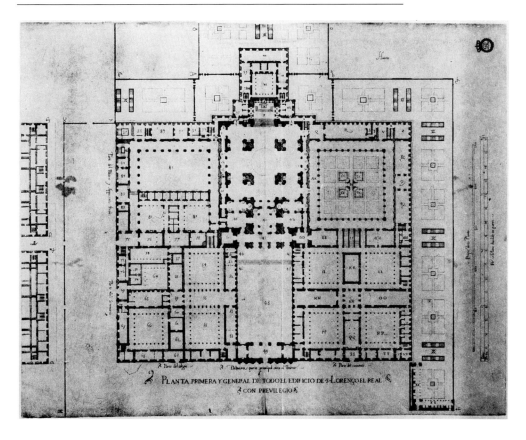

flanked by domed twin towers, a Byzantine architectural motif
that, as we shall see, resonates with familial significance.[13] Protected by these masonry sentinels, the king's and queen's private
quarters fan out on either side of the royal chapel, within which
lies the Hapsburg family crypt and pantheon. A monumental
correlative to the dynasty's genealogical fabrications, the Escorial
may be seen as a physical vestige of Hapsburg imperial ideology
as it was consolidated under Philip's rule. That these references
were self-conscious is clear from contemporary records that discuss the iconography of the edifice.

86. Pedro Perret after
Juan de Herrera, *Ground
Plan of the Escorial*. Mad-
rid, Royal Palace. Patri-
monio Nacional,
Madrid.

The Escorial as Solomon's Temple

Father Sigüenza, who chronicled its construction and took credit
for the library's iconographical program, hailed the Escorial as
Solomon's rebuilt temple: "Here as in Noah's ark, many souls will
be saved. . . . Here, as in the tabernaculum of Moses, God is

87. Juan Bautista Monegro and Sebastian Fernandez, *Courtyard of the Kings*. Facade of the Basilica of San Lorenzo with statues of the Jewish Temple Builders, Escorial. Patrimonio Nacional, Madrid.

88. Juan Bautista Monegro and Sebastian Fernandez, *Solomon*, detail. Facade of the Basilica of San Lorenzo, Escorial. Patrimonio Nacional, Madrid.

present. . . . Here as in that other Temple of Solomon which . . . Philip II was imitating . . . the divine psalms are sung day and night, sacrifice is continuously offered, incense always burns, and the flame is never extinguished, . . . before the divine presence, and below the altars rest the ashes and bones of those who were sacrificed for Christ."[14] Past recreations of the Solomonic edifice had been but figurative copies of the prototype.[15] Philip directed his attention to recreating a more literal copy of the model. An indication of this intention is provided in the imaginative reconstructions of Solomon's temple which Philip commissioned from the humanists at his court.

In the reconstruction of the earthly temple by Benito Arias Montano, the Escorial's librarian, editor of the *Polyglot Bible*, and a specialist in biblical archaeology, the temple precinct rises on a hill above the city (fig. 89).[16] Within a rectilinear walled enclosure, successive courtyards, whose access is determined by rank, rise up to the sacred space that houses the Holy of Holies. Here stand the two crowned columns, Jachim and Boaz. Sigüenza so identifies the columns in front of the Sancta Sanctorum and acknowledges but declines to explain their mystical meaning.[17] These heraldic icons were familiar to contemporary viewers in the form adapted by Charles V for his personal emblem.[18] Although the Escorial's building plan predates the engraving, its hillside setting and the fortresslike surrounding walls that enclose a network of inner courtyards link it to Montano's reconstruction; these elements reinforce the Escorial's references to Solomon's earthly edifice.[19]

The Escorial's conformity to Solomon's temple extends to the combination of royal palace and center of worship in a mortuary context that was intrinsic to the model. This intention is expressed in a chronicle of the building prepared for Philip's heirs by the Escorial's prior Fray Francisco de los Santos (1618–99): "As [Philip] had gained the appellation of the Second Solomon, it was his royal intention likewise to imitate the Jewish monarchs in building an august sepulchre for his father."[20]

Philip communicated his identity as the Second Solomon to his domains by appropriating the Hebrew king's iconography. In a picture by Lucas de Heere inscribed "Philippus . . . alter Salomon," he is depicted on Solomon's lion-flanked throne receiving Sheba (fig. 90).[21] The subject underscores Philip's eastern

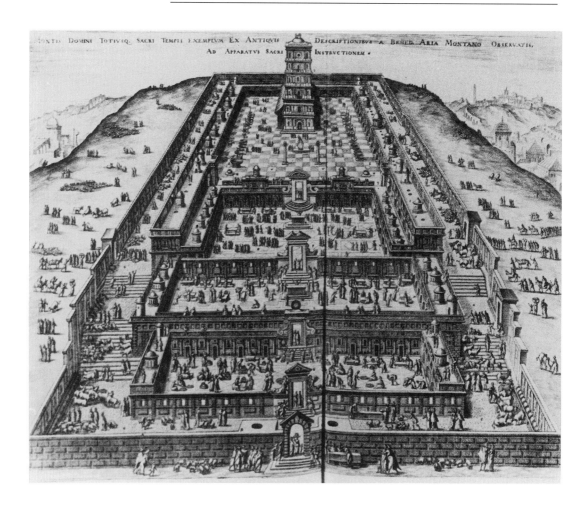

89. Pieter Huys or Ian Wierix, *Reconstruction of Solomon's Temple*. In Benito Arias Montano, *Biblia Poliglota*, V.VIII, Antwerp (Plantin), 1572. Biblioteca Apostolica Vaticana, Rome.

political ambitions, for Sheba's homage to Solomon had long been used as an analogue for the East's subjugation to the West. Philip also adopted Solomon's epithet "Prudent" (II Kings 10:18) as his own. His domination of the Americas reinforced this identity, for Columbus believed he had rediscovered there the fabled treasure of Solomon's Ophir.[22] Others followed suit in perpetuating Philip's Solomonic identity, which became canonic through frequent literary repetition. So tenacious did it become that future Hapsburg rulers paid homage to Philip's precedence over them in the Solomonic succession, while frequent architectural reminiscences of the model lent a similar authority to the Escorial's prestigious temple status.[23]

90. Lucas de Heere,
Philip II as Solomon.
Ghent, Saint Bavo.
Copyright A.C.L.
Bruxelles.

The Escorial as the Heavenly Jerusalem

Forse Gierusalemme
Si come ornata sposa
Al suo consorte scender giù dal cielo
Tal vide gloriosa
L'altissimo scrittor de l'Evangelo[24]

As consistent as the suggestion that the Escorial was Solomon's rebuilt temple was the insistence that it superseded the ancient model. Father Sigüenza made much of this distinction, expanding the Escorial's biblical references to include the divinely constructed temple that an angel revealed to Ezekiel. He clarified the distinction between the two Judaic temples by contrasting Solomon's man-made edifice to the perfect Ezekelian temple that was fabricated by Christ.[25] As long ago as the fourth century, Origen postulated the transformation of Solomon's temple into the apocalyptic temple of the New Testament.[26] Sigüenza suggested that transformation was effected at the Escorial, where the sacrifice of Christ's body substituted for the Solomonic slaughter of animals, and the temple veil was raised through the substitution of Manna by the Eucharist.[27] From this layering of biblical references emerged an image of the Escorial that, with its monks in perpetual prayer and contemplation, appeared to adherents much like that Jerusalem that John saw descend from heaven.[28]

Indeed, the building's granite mass evokes the gemstone from which was hewn the heavenly Jerusalem in John's poetic description.[29] But it is above all in the royal chapel that the Escorial seems to conform to the spiritual temple; in the process the heavenly vision is refigured in a dynastic mode. In Ezekiel's dream, an elaborate vision of the Holy of Holies revealed angelic presences in perpetual veneration of the Ark of the Covenant. A reconstruction of the heavenly temple by the Jesuit Juan Bautista Villalpando that was published with funds provided by Philip II provides a graphic illustration of that vision (fig. 91).[30] In Philip's new temple, the Sancta Sanctorum is transformed into its Christian mode, and the angels who adore the Ark are replaced by their Hapsburg counterparts. Within a cordon of the Golden Fleece, monumental escutcheons delineate their pedigrees,[31] as below, life-size bronze effigies of Charles V and Philip kneel with their families in perpetual devotion to the Sacrament (figs. 92a–d).[32] As he attended mass from the elevated position of his bedchamber, it was this holy site that Philip peered down upon from the window that opened directly on the royal chapel. By his command two supplicants kneeled in the Chapel in perpetual veneration of the Eucharist, praying day and night for the soul of Philip's ancestors, who were buried below in the crypt.[33]

The Escorial's Roman Imperial Legacy

We have seen that in 1563, the year in which the foundation stone was laid, Philip sought to be crowned emperor of the Indies. More ambitious rumors circled in the year following its completion, when on 6 June 1583, the French Ambassador de Maisse wrote from Venice to King Henry II: "Sire, I have learnt from these lords that Cardinal Granvelle is coming to Rome this year to have the title of Emperor conferred on his master [Philip II]."[34] In the light of these pretensions, the impetus of Roman imperial imagery must be considered in determining the Escorial's ultimate significance.

From the fourth century onwards, no break had occurred in the imperial position that Christ's Incarnation and Second Coming were interdependent with Rome's historic destiny. In the literature of the early Christian court these paired destinies were brought together in the metaphysical paradise of the New Faith. The new temple of Jerusalem was the name of this utopia, its attainment a quasi-eschatological goal.

In the *Psychomachia*, Prudentius had poetically transformed Solomon's temple into the heavenly Jerusalem.[35] He established Rome, the "purgati corporis urbs," as the temple's setting,[36] and the Virtues, in whose veins flow Trojan and Judaic blood, as its masons (fig. 12).[37] Here dwells the Apocalyptic Christ, whose powers as priest and king of the Gentiles and the Jews are confirmed by the scepter in which the regencies of Aaron and Latinus are intertwined.[38]

The pattern was set with the Roman model, and geographic realities aside, no city ever dislodged Rome's status as the New Jerusalem, the divinely decreed site of Solomon's rebuilt temple to which Christ would return at the *Parousia*. With Charlemagne at Aachen, with Otto at Treves, with Charles IV at Prague, a new geographic stratification came into being: the New Temple of Jerusalem was rebuilt in transalpine Rome. Whatever its actual physical location, the identification of the imperial palace-church complex with Solomon's rebuilt temple—like its assimilation to Roman fora prototypes and with the same implication of transfer and supersession—was geared to these presumptions.

With its pervasive blend of imperial and sacred architecture that occasioned comparisons to the Christian Olympus,[39] the Escorial conformed to these ideological conventions. A similar hybrid vocabulary was used in the building's decorative program; the pagan gods share space with Judaic and Christian images in the library and in the royal reception hall where the enthroned king sat.[40] While the metaphors differed, the message was consistent, for the all-inclusive divinity of the king made a protean interchangeability of modes a rational artistic alternative. The twin concepts of sacred and Roman justice were encoded in the Escorial's foundation emblem (fig. 84). Here the yoke evokes the scales of Justice[41]—a celestial symbol assigned to Augustus's

91. Anonymous, *Interior of the Holy of Holies with the Arc of the Covenant.* In Hieronymi Pradi et Ioannes Baptista Villalpando, *In Ezechielis prophetae visione*, Rome, 1596–1604, II, among plates following p. 88. Rare Books and Manuscripts Division, New York Public Library. Astor, Lenox and Tilden Foundations.

PROSPECTVS TESTVDINIS MVRORVM ET PAVIMENTI SANCTI SANCTORVM ATQVE ARCÆ TESTAMENTI CVM CHERVBINIS

92a–d. View of the High Altar (opposite). Pompeo Leoni, Hapsburg effigies: Charles V and Family on the gospel side; Philip II and Family on the epistle side; and detail of Philip II and Family (right). Gilded bronze statues. Basilica of San Lorenzo, Escorial. Patrimonio Nacional, Madrid.

apotheosis—and appears above a globe of the earth that is marked with the cross of Jerusalem. In a poem in praise of the edifice by Giovanni Strasoldo, this emblem's relationship to Philip is poetically expressed, and the beholder is informed that if he no longer observes the scales in the heavens it is because these are now on earth with the Spanish Augustus.[42]

A more specific reference to imperial prototypes may have been intended for the complex as a whole.[43] Built to celebrate a parallel extension of peace, and accessed by a pedimental portal that recalls its Julian origins, the Escorial can be compared to Augustus's temple-palace on the Palatine. The disposition of this ancient edifice was known from Suetonius's description.[44] Like it, the Escorial combines the ruler's residence with a library, an administrative center, and a place of worship. The Escorial conforms most closely in this last element. When Augustus transferred the Penates to an altar within his own palace, where they

93. Juan Bautista Monegro, *Saint Lawrence*. Facade of the Escorial. Patrimonio Nacional, Madrid.

were flanked by ancestral portraits and attended by a domestic priestly community, he assigned a familial identity to the most sacred icons of Roman state religion. Philip mimicked these actions by his dynastic enshrinement of the Eucharist, which was later referred to in Spanish court circles as the "true Palladium of the Hapsburg gens and the emblem of the dynasty."[45]

In attributing an imperial significance to Philip's temple-palace we can turn for collaboration to the patron saint, Lawrence, whose iron grill was monumentalized in the Escorial's ground plan and whose statue—placed above Philip's coat of arms over the main portal—is the only figure on the facade (fig. 93). Lawrence's legend was shaped into its Roman political configuration by Prudentius in the *Crowns of Martyrdom*.[46] Although the analogy has not previously been suggested, it seems that Prudentius equated the saint with Ezekiel, for both martyr and prophet bore their slow punishment on the iron grill, now suffering on the right side, now turning to suffer on the left.[47] And following this punishment, both were rewarded by a place in the heavenly Jerusalem. By comparing Lawrence's trial and tribulation to that of Ezekiel, Prudentius recast the image of heaven into its Christian-Roman mode. The echo of these stratified Judeo-Christian references in the ground plan of the Escorial accords with the imperial conviction that Rome had a divine mission in God's unfolding plan for the universe.

The narrative of Prudentius's poem is set in third-century Rome, where Lawrence, the highest-ranking Levite priest,[48] is condemned to a slow death on the gridiron[49] for defying the pagan Prefect of Rome.[50] In the agony of his death, Lawrence becomes the spokesman for the Christian purpose propelling Rome's universal sovereignty:[51]

[Looking] up to heaven [Lawrence] . . . prays in pity for the city of Romulus: "O Christ, . . . who hast set the scepter of the world on Rome's high citadel . . . that thou might'st bring under one system of laws the customs and observance, the speech and character and worship of nations which differed among themselves; lo, the whole race of men has passed under the sovereignty of Remus, and usages formerly discordant are now alike in speech and thought. This was appointed that the authority of the Christian name might bind with one tie all lands everywhere. Grant, O Christ, to thy Romans that the city may itself be Christian . . . and may Romulus become one of the faithful, and Numa himself be now a believer."[52]

In this poem, where Prudentius was creating a prospective vision for his patron, the Spanish-born Theodosius, the dying saint prays for the conversion of the Trojan home gods, and prophecies of a future emperor who will fulfill Rome's sacred destiny:[53]

"The superstition which came from Troy still confounds . . . [those] doing homage at secret altars to the Phrygians' exiled Penates. . . . Wipe away this shame, O Christ that the straying blindness of Julus may recognize the true God. . . . I foresee that one day there will be an emperor who will be a servant of God and will not suffer Rome to be in the service of vile . . . rites. . . . Then at last will her marble shine bright . . . and the statues . . . which now she thinks of as idols, will be guiltless." So ended his prayer, and with it ended his imprisonment in the flesh; the spirit broke forth eagerly after his words . . .[54]

The conversion of the city of Romulus into the earthly counterpart of the heavenly Jerusalem is accomplished when the saint effects the Christian transformation of the Palladium:

From that day the worship of those base gods flagged, . . . and there was a rush to the sanctuary of Christ. . . . The death the holy martyr died was in truth the death of the temples. That day Vesta saw her Palladian house-spirits deserted. . . . The priest who once wore the head bands is admitted to receive the sign of the cross and a vestal Claudia, enters thy Church.[55]

The poem ends with a vision, where Lawrence himself is equated with Augustus and awarded the civic crown.[56] In this guise he assumes his perpetual role as Roman consul in the heavenly Jerusalem's everlasting senate:

Lawrence, . . . thou hast two seats, that of thy body here on earth, that of thy soul in heaven. Admitted there as a freeman of the ineffable city, thou wearest the civic crown in that Capitol where sits the everlasting senate. . . . I see the hero flashing with brilliant jewels, whom the heavenly Rome has chosen to be her perpetual consul.[57]

Simultaneous with his planning of the Escorial, Philip ordered from Titian a picture of Lawrence's martyrdom that was destined for the royal chapel (fig. 94). Titian based the picture on Prudentius's account of the legend, and he focused on the climactic moment when the saint utters his dying prayer and

94. Titian, *Saint Lawrence*. Escorial. Patrimonio Nacional, Madrid.

paganism yields to Christianity. This transformation is symbolically represented by a statue of Claudia that substitutes for one of Vesta.[58] Claudia carries a replica of the Palladium to symbolize the rededication of the Trojan home gods to Christianity. In the engraving after Titian's picture by Cornelius Cort, the statue base is inscribed: "invictiss. Philippo Hispanorum Regi D." Staged in contemporary costume, Prudentius's ancient legend was projected into the present to evoke the substitution of Prudentius's patron, Theodosius, for Titian's patron, Philip—the prophesied ruler who will bring Rome's Christian destiny to its ultimate fulfillment.

As the prophet who proclaims Rome's eternal destiny, as the priest who transforms her Trojan piety into the worship of Christ, as perpetual Augustus in the heavenly Jerusalem, Lawrence was an ideal persona to represent Philip at the Escorial. In the component elements of Lawrence's legend, including the Christian sanction of Rome's Trojan origins, the prophecy of a universal empire ruled by Aeneas's Christian heir, the rededication of the Penates to Christ,[59] and the transposition of the heavenly Jerusalem into its Roman mode, we find an uncanny template for Philip's mythic image. As we shall see, Philip's conformity to Lawrence extended to the saint's Apollonian identity, and this was writ clear in the Escorial's commemorative emblem.[60]

Campanella and the Monarchy of Spain

In the *Monarchy of Spain*, written in 1598, Tommaso Campanella gave theoretical sanction to the ideology that was immortalized in the Escorial's "indestructible" fabric. He assigned a definitive Iberian orientation to the theory of the Four World Monarchies when he concluded that "the universal monarchy migrated from East to West, from the Assyrians, Medes, Persians, Greeks and Romans, to finally come into the hands of the Spaniards."[61] Campanella announced that the great discovery of the New World and the extension of the Spanish domain to the east and west with the consequent diffusion of Christianity were signs of the political and religious union of all men. This unity constituted a return to the original blessed state that had prevailed in Eden. By pointing to Adam, king and priest of all mankind and ancestor of all the firstborn monarchs of Scriptures who succeeded him,

Campanella showed that kingship and priesthood properly belonged in the hands of one ruler, to be passed to his kin by
primogeniture. He supported this theocratic concept by divulg-
ing the providential design: "And I want to reveal another secret,
that all the Imperiums come from the sons of Japhet via Sem,
according to Noah's prophecy."[62] He traced Sem's seed through
Isaac to Christ and the rulers of Christian Rome. Philip represented the culmination of this hereditary scheme in God's plan
for the universe.[63] Thus Campanella pleaded for the election of
the Spanish king as emperor.[64] He advocated as well the election
of a Spanish pope, preferably of the house of Austria.[65]

This visionary conception was contingent on the destruction
of the Turks. Campanella related this destiny to prophetic and
astrological predictions that Charles V's world dominion and his
conquest of the Crescent prepared this time. With the defeat of
Islam would come the end of the Babylonian captivity and the
election of the Spanish king to rebuild the Temple of Jerusalem.
Just as the Lord's anointed Cyrus had been charged by God to
build a house at Jerusalem and to bring to it the vessels of the
house of the Lord which Nebuchadnezzar had carried away to
Babylon, so the Spanish king was charged with this mission.[66] A
cycle of tapestries of circa 1550 depicting the history of Cyrus in
the Spanish royal collections served as visual reminder of that
precedent.[67] Parallel references were also present: in a tapestry
Philip personally ordered from William Pannemaker in 1553 and
on which appears his armorial shield, Noah orders the building
of the Ark (fig. 95).[68] In another, Moses directs the building of the
Ark of the Covenant (fig. 96).[69] In these and in tapestries of related subjects that lined the walls of Philip's palace, the images of
biblical architects engaged in housing the deity served more than
devotional purposes. These haunting ancestral presences lent
mnemonic testimony to Philip's sacred charge.

Like Columbus before him, Campanella attributed the
prophecy that Spain should inherit the Roman Empire to the
prophets.[70] Joachim of Fiore had generated the concept that
the battle against the Antichrist would be fought by a historic
personage, and that it would be followed by the kingdom of God
in the here and now. The imminence of this moment had already
been declared by the Abbot Hortolà, Philip's representative at the
Council of Trent. Challenging the view that the prophetic Age of

95. Willem Panne-
maker after Michael
Coxie, *Noah Constructs
the Ark*. Tapestry, 1553–
56. Madrid, Royal Pal-
ace. Patrimonio Nacio-
nal, Madrid.

96. *Moses Directs the Con-
struction of the Arc of the
Covenant*. Tapestry,
Brussels, ca. 1530.
Madrid, Royal Palace.
Patrimonio Nacional,
Madrid.

Beatitude belonged to eternity, Hortolà asserted that the descent of the New Jerusalem would occur within history and that the time was now at hand.[71] Campanella resurrected these ideas and assigned the apocalyptic moment to the year 1600. Since Rome is the successor to the kingdom of the Jews and the king of Spain its ultimate ruler, he predicted by that date the end of the Four Monarchies, the destruction of the Antichrist,[72] and the advent of Christ's Final Judgment.[73] Since the Spanish Christianization of the New World had satisfied the apocalyptic prophecy of the translation of light to that part of the world which had theretofore been steeped in darkness, Campanella declared in them the realization of Saint John's prophecy of the universal rule of one shepherd over one flock.[74]

There were many voices that predicted this destiny for the ruler with the magical Nomine "P." In contemporary documents that speculated upon his future and reflected upon his death, we find the application to Philip II of the Last World Emperor theme with "the destruction of the Turk . . . the recapture of Jerusalem . . . the rebuilding of the Temple of Solomon . . . the rule of one shepherd over one flock . . . the end of the world and the Second Coming."[75] Philip gave tangible evidence of his belief in this credo by building the Escorial, where he assumed a monastic way of life and where he was perceived as the hereditary successor to the priest-kings Solomon and Christ, reigning in the New Jerusalem that John saw and Philip built. According to this interpretation, Philip's universal historic mission is fulfilled and the kingdom of God on earth has become visible in Philip's palace-church. We may speculate that such a concept influenced Philip's commission for a haunting series of Apocalyptic tapestries as plans for the Escorial got under way.[76] In the culminating image of the end of time (Revelation 7:9–12), throngs gather to adore the ram-horned figure of the Lamb who claims his throne in the New Jerusalem (fig. 97).

Philip's assimilation to Christ, implicit in his fabrication and inhabitation of the New Jerusalem, was sustained beyond his lifetime. A funerary catafalque that was erected for this earthly king of Jerusalem was designed to duplicate the Holy Sepulchre, the site of Christ's burial and of his resurrection, and his tomb resounded with eucharistic motifs.[77] Since the Latin kings of Jerusalem, from whom Philip descended through his Burgun-

97. Workshop of
Willem Pannemaker,
Adoration of the Lamb
(detail). Tapestry, 1560–
61. Segovia, Museo de
Tapices, Palacio de San
Ildefonso. Patrimonio
Nacional, Madrid.

dian ancestors, had all been buried in Adam's Chapel in the Holy
Sepulchre, the adaptation of Christ's tomb for the Spanish king
could be symbolically understood as the culminating act in the
transfer of the Holy Site to Spain, the New Jerusalem. By drawing
on and augmenting legends of Hapsburg ancestral piety, Philip
disseminated the concept of sacred kingship that was embedded
in the Escorial to the world at large.

Chapter X Fidecrucem: The Hapsburg Veneration of the Cross

THE Hapsburgs' revival of the dream of universal sovereignty under the Roman emperor's rule was similar to the ancients both in conception and premise. Seen as a mission, to which they had been elected by God, the claim to world dominion was based not on geopolitical strength, but on virtue, and above all on piety.[1] As had the ancients, the Hapsburgs conceived of that piety as an ancestral virtue, the inalienable birthright of the clan.[2] A pervasive tenet of their theocratic ideology, this piety was emphatically expressed in their devotion to the Eucharist and their faith in the Holy Cross.

The legends of Hapsburg pietistic devotion originated with Rudolf I; the contributions of each successive generation reinforced the congenital nature of that trait. But the quintessential definition of the family's political ambitions along these sacred lines was masterminded by Philip II. When he sustained the Hapsburg connection to the most sacred symbols of Christ's Passion with new genealogical evidence, Philip established the foundations of the theocratic state in an unbroken tie to the Holy Blood. A preliminary discussion of the traditions that inspired him puts Philip's actions in their proper imperial context.

The Origins of the Veneration of the Cross

In the year 312, as Constantine marched on Rome against Maxentius, a vision appeared in the heavens and a voice from above proclaimed "In Hoc Signo Vinces" announcing his invincibility in battle. Interchangeably interpreted as the sign of the Cross and as Jesus' monogram, the vision was perceived as the revelation of Christian truth to the emperor of Rome. These symbols took on an added martial aspect as Constantine substituted a staff inscribed with Christ's monogram for the eagle-bearing pagan battle standard.[3] As orthodox thought put the accent on Jesus expiring on the Cross and triumphing over death through His Resurrection, a transcendent meaning was applied to the Milvian battle.[4] In this way an identity was established between Roman military victory and the cosmic battle between good and evil, won by Christ in his triumph over death. This heightened meaning is expressed on a contemporary coin where, with the monogrammed Labarum as his staff, the Roman emperor tramples the serpent of symbolic evil (fig. 98). The Cross legend was perpetuated by Constantine's heirs. In Prudentius's *Contra Orationem Symmachi* where Theodosius admonished Rome to abandon idolatry, he announced that he would "trample under foot . . . the usurpers . . . with this standard that made Constantine invincible . . . [against] Maxentius."[5] On an ivory diptych of 406, Theodosius's son, the Emperor Honorius, is twice represented: on the right he prepares for combat; on the left he receives the Palm of Victory that was perennially conceded by the vision of the Cross: "In Nomine XPI vincas semper" (fig. 99). With its manifold meanings intact, the Labarum was soon appropriated by rival courts. With this adoption, and in the related development of a special cult of the Cross, Constantinian echoes were always present.

98. *The Labarum, the Imperial Standard Bearing the Cross and Monogram of Christ.* In Matthaei Jacuti, *Historia Visionis Constantini Magni*, Rome, 1755, p. lxxxiii. Drawing after coin of 325 A.D. Biblioteca Apostolica Vaticana, Rome.

99. *Honorius.* Imperial diptych. Ivory, Roman, ca. 406 A.D. Aosta, Cathedral Treasury. Bildarchiv Foto, Marburg.

In the early Middle Ages, when the growth of Frankish hegemony spawned yearnings for imperial status, Constantinian imagery was adopted in the legends surrounding Clovis. As early as the sixth century, Gregory of Tours, the most authoritative source for Merovingian history, assigned quasi-imperial status to Clovis and proclaimed him the "New Constantine." Constantine's baptismal conversion, which effectively yoked Christ's ministry to the Roman imperium, was the prototype for the baptism of Clovis. As Gregory recalled the details of Constantine's baptism and the cleansing of his leprosy by Saint Sylvester, he adopted the scenario for Clovis and Saint Remi.[6] These associations were soon perpetuated throughout the Frankish kingdom by the adaptation of the chi-rho and Cross imagery on Merovingian coinage.[7] The fleur-de-lis that appeared on a shield brought from heaven guaranteed Clovis's invincibility in his battles against the infidel (fig. 63);[8] it was interpreted as the counterpart of Constantine's vision of the Cross. Since Clovis led the Franks away from the Arian doctrine to the teachings of the orthodox faith, the appellation "New Constantine" implied supersession. A sixteenth-century relief from the Church of Saint Remi in Rheims, where the aligned images of Christ's, Constantine's, and Clovis's baptism trace the tripartite steps of imperial succession, attests to the perpetual validity of this construct (fig. 17).

Charlemagne followed in Clovis's footsteps, appropriating the Constantinian name to himself. Anxious to deflate the position of the Eastern emperor, the papacy was instrumental in promoting this identity. Already in a letter of 778, Pope Hadrian I addressed the Carolingian king as the "New Constantine." We have seen that this identity was alluded to at the Lateran, where Charlemagne is represented as the recipient of the Vexillium (fig. 18).[9] Thereafter the Constantinian epithet was continually applied to Charlemagne in the literature of the Carolingian court.[10] Charlemagne's association with the Cross was reinforced by the legend that he received a lance from heaven containing a relic of the Cross to deliver the realm from the Saracens; later the lance was revered as the one with which Longinus pierced Christ's chest.[11] Another of his heavenly gifts, the Oriflamme, was associated both with the Constantinian and the Clovian standards.[12] These oblique associations with Constantine were solidified by more concrete assertions in the later Middle Ages, when a popular legend attested that Charlemagne received a vision of the Cross that bode victory against the heathens at the battle of Regensburg.[13]

In Alcuin's ninth-century acrostic poem—a format derived from the Constantinian court poet Porfyrius that was subsequently used to glorify the Merovingians—the name Flavius Anicius Carlus is the title given three times to Charlemagne. Anicio was Constantine's family name, and while scholars have puzzled over the meaning of this inscription, we can assume an ancestral intention in the light of sixteenth-century developments that we shall soon investigate.[14] This format and more direct Constantinian implications were adopted in the dedicatory image to *Laudibus Sanctae Crucis*, a series of acrostic poems written by Alcuin's student Hrabanus Maurus, archbishop of Mainz (b. ca. 780). The poem is intersected by an image of Charlemagne's son, Louis the Pious (fig. 100). Adopting the Byzantine prototype (fig. 99), Louis wears Roman armor and bears the cross staff.[15] A

100. *Louis the Pious.* In Hrabanus Maurus, *De Laudibus S. Crucis.* Biblioteca Apostolica Vaticana, Rome. Reg. Lat. 124, fol. 4v.

101. *Louis the Pious.* In Hrabanus Maurus, *De Laudibus S. Crucis.* Bayerische Staatsbibliothek, Munich. Clm. 8201, fol. 38v.

102. *Frederick I.* In Robert von Saint Remi, *Historia Hierosolmitana,* South German, 1189. Biblioteca Apostolica Vaticana, Rome. MS. Vat. Lat. 2001, fol. 1r.

northern transformation of the model appears in a later illustration of this same text. Here the format remains intact while Louis's cloak and crown are worn over the distinctive armor of a crusading knight (fig. 101). In the poem that describes a painted cycle of Carolingian ancestral portraits at Ingelheim, to which we have already referred, the transfer of Constantine's crown to Louis confirms him as the legitimate ruler of Rome.

By the middle of the ninth century, the application of the Constantinian name to the reigning emperor had become a convention, and legends of the Cross were updated for the Ottonian and Hohenstaufen emperors. The visual model we have been exploring was appropriated for Emperor Frederick I in the frontispiece for an account of the First Crusade in 1099 (fig. 102). As it had since the fourth century, the Cross retained its meaning as the symbol of the emperor's invincibility. This meaning is applied to Frederick by the inscription that hallows his menacing glance: "The magnificent, pius, augustus Caesar Frederick drove the Saracens from the Holy Land."[16]

With his elevation to the imperial dignity, Rudolf of Hapsburg fell heir to these traditions. A recall of Constantinian imagery had traditionally served as evidence of the Christian empire's uninterrupted succession from Byzantium to Aachen. But the repetition of the miracle for Rudolf lent fresh impulse to the

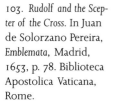

103. *Rudolf and the Scepter of the Cross.* In Juan de Solorzano Pereira, *Emblemata*, Madrid, 1653, p. 78. Biblioteca Apostolica Vaticana, Rome.

104. Bernard Strigel, *Calvary Panel*. Part of the Calvary Altarpiece, Prague, National Gallery. Krajske Stredisco (Statni pamatkove pece). Pamatkovy ustav (Institute for the Protection of Historical Monuments).

topos. On the eve of his imperial coronation in 1273, while
Rudolf passed the night in prayerful vigil, a cloud appeared to
him in the form of the Cross. As he observed it, the Cross dissolved in streams of blood.[17] Accepting this vision as God's ap-
probation of his election, Rudolf vowed an oath upon the Cross,
announcing that the sign in which the whole world was re-
deemed would replace the scepter as the insignia of his sovereignty. In a later emblem, in which Rudolf relinquishes earthly
symbols of power for the implement of Christ's passion, he declares: "This is my scepter" (fig. 103).[18] The confirmation of
Rudolf's invincibility was manifest when, marching in battle under the Cross, he triumphed over the Bohemian infidel Ottocar.
Prefigured in the Dream of Constantine, Rudolf's vision was seen
as an augury that the Hapsburgs would once again achieve the
unification of the Eastern and Western empires in Christ first
realized by Constantine.[19]

Maximilian I, to whom the epithet "New Constantine" was
also applied, appropriated these associations to his person. In an

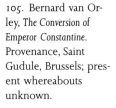

105. Bernard van Or-
ley, *The Conversion of
Emperor Constantine.*
Provenance, Saint
Gudule, Brussels; pres-
ent whereabouts
unknown.

unconventional *Calvary* painting by the emperor's court painter, Bernard Strigel, scenes of Constantine with the Cross appear in four separate panels.[20] In the one which lends its name to the polyptych, Constantine appears as Simon of Cyrene carrying the Cross, while Maximilian walks behind him leading the way to Calvary. The two emperors are physically likened to each other by the prominent nose that was the hallmark of the Last World Emperor and of the Hapsburg clan (fig. 104).

The veneration of the Cross increased significantly under Charles V. He personally propagated the Constantinian legacy and attributed his victories against both Protestants and Turks to an image of Christ's Cross that was affixed to his arms.[21] Constantine's vision was evoked for a mise-en-scène mounted to celebrate his victories at La Goletta and Tunis. A mock battle was staged in front of a model of Constantinople; when the imperial eagle swept down and the Turks were vanquished, a Cross suddenly appeared in the sky.[22] In Brussels, where Charles established an imperial seat, the dynasty's invincibility is presaged in Bernard van Orley's *Vision of Constantine* for the Burgundian family church of Saint Gudule (fig. 105). Constantine kneels on the battlefield before the vision of the Cross. Seen from the rear, the emperor's fluttering cloak reveals the double-headed eagle adopted by the Hapsburgs to symbolize their right to universal rule.[23]

Based on the similarity of their supernatural apparitions, Rudolf's Constantinian legacy became a set piece in the litany of Hapsburg pious legends. The blueprint for this dynastic cult was altered when Philip II conceived of vital fluids as a substitute for the fleeting phantasms which were held in such high esteem in the Middle Ages. He rationalized the family's special relation to the Cross by establishing his kinship with the Byzantine emperors, and he made the Hapsburg consanguinity in the Holy Blood the fulcrum of his ideological pretensions. A topical event provided the impetus for this focus.

Lost for over a millennium, the bodies of thirty-seven martyred early Christian saints were miraculously rediscovered in the early decades of the sixteenth century through the efforts of Charles V.[24] Among these were saints Vittorino, Placido, Flavia, and Eutichio; the last of these was the patriarch of Constantinople and all were descendants of the imperial Anicio gens. Correggio (d. 1534), whom Charles V patronized, painted this martyr-

106. Correggio, *The
Martyrdom of the Four
Saints*. Ca. 1520. Galleria
Nazionale, Parma.

dom for a private chapel in the imperial city of Parma.[25] The saints' piety is evoked by the transcendent ecstasy of their private visions at the moment of their brutal deaths (fig. 106).

The discovery of their bodies inspired a torrent of research devoted to untangling the noble descendants of these Anicio saints. The results of those investigations first appear in the literature dedicated to Philip II. In the *Lignum Vitae* by the Benedictine monk, Arnoldo Wion, the glory of the Anicio family, and with it that of the Hapsburgs, is exalted by the martyrdom of the rediscovered saints: "In 536, Placido, Eutichio, and Vittorino, nephews of the Emperor Justinian, were martyred for the Christian cause. Your Highness and the whole of his dynasty, is related to these warriors of Christ, because their blood is from the same Anicio root as that from which the House of Austria draws its origins."[26] Wion recalled the Trojan origins of the Anicio clan according to Vergil;[27] and he looked to Prudentius for the testimony of their Christian piety.[28] First to acknowledge the divinity of Christ, this precipitous piety is bred in the bone, for saints Helen and Constantine stem from the same Anicio root.[29] In culling this illustrious ancestry for the Hapsburgs, the monk gathered in other noble Roman kin—the Olybria, Perleoni, and Frangipani families and the Symmachi, Bassus, and Probus gens (fig. 107); names familiar to the present age from their patronage of early Christian art. Notable among these is the diptych honoring Honorius on which his kin, the Consul Probus, twice inscribed his name (fig. 99). With Claudian as the authority for the transfer of a branch of the Anicio family to Germany, Wion recorded the formation of the Hapsburg cognomen from the family's original Roman home on the Aventine, where an eagle had landed in antiquity to indicate to Aeneas the seat of his universal realm: Aventine=Avemburgum=Hapsburg. Passing through Merovingian, Carolingian, and Burgundian stock, the Anicio strain reached its present glory in Philip II.[30]

In the *Arbor Aniciana* dedicated to the young prince Philip III, the Cistercian monk Ioanne Seifried recapitulated the whole familial infrastructure on which these claims were based.[31] He lent color to Wion's research with narrative digressions and visual emblems. Constantine, he notes, "the greatest zealot for things Trojan, and most keen about Aeneas, whose descendent he declared himself to be, wanted a new Rome to be built in Troy, but

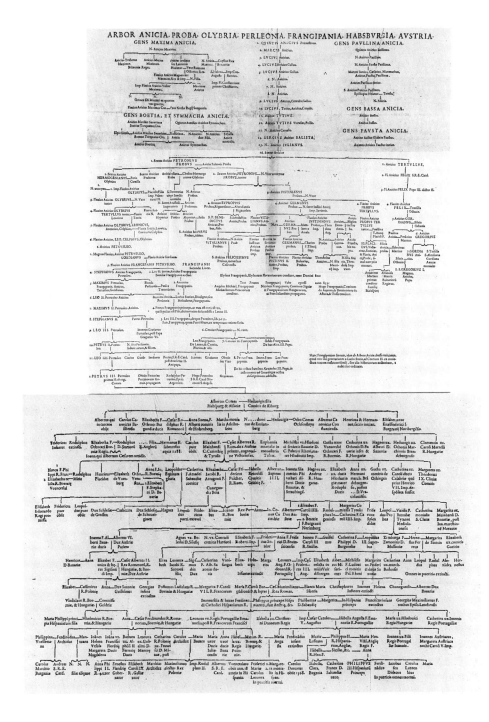

107. Arnoldo Wion,
Lignum Vitae. Venice,
1595. Biblioteca Apos-
tolica Vaticana, Rome.

then, the omens being ominous, he ordered it to be built in Byzantium. To that city he transferred the Palladium which had been brought from Troy by Aeneas."[32] He revived interest in the imperial Bassus gens by describing Junius Bassus's successful efforts to defeat heresy, and for which, he notes, his sarcophagus in Saint Peter's stands as testimony (fig. 108).[33] He was referring to the orthodox representation of the Savior's dual nature—the suffering Jesus of the Passion and the ruling cosmocrator of the universe—that appears on this, the most famous of the early visual monuments to represent Christ as King. The monument lent support to imperial pretensions for, enthroned above the vault of heaven, Christ's role as vice-regent of the earth is indicated by the figure of Tellus below him. Wion also clarified the enigma of the imperial family heritage by explaining that the strands had been unraveled by Dares and Dictys, and he traced the family's pious origins to Adam and Noah.[34]

108. *Sarcophagus of Junius Bassus.* 359 A.D. Vatican grottos. Fabbrica di San Pietro, Vatican City.

Heady with the results of these investigations, Philip II commissioned a more extensive genealogy from Estevan de Garibay in 1572, an undertaking that engaged its author for twenty-four years. At the end of that period, Garibay's results showed that Philip descended from an even more extensive list of Roman and Byzantine emperors. Prominent among these is the "Emperor Heraclius, who recovered the Holy Cross from the Persians and restored it to Jerusalem in 627 . . . Your Highness descends from this same line. Later came the Comneni in 1058, and Your Highness descends from this royal blood. The Greek rule of the empire ended in 1200, when it passed to Balduin, count of Flanders,

109. *Heraclius.* In Justus Lipsius *De Cruce*, Antwerp, 1594, drawing after the medal. Biblioteca Apostolica Vaticana, Rome.

whom we have always shown Your Highness descends from through the dukes of Flanders. Thus Your Highness descends from the Eastern emperors by four Greek lineages and two Latin lineages . . . so that you descend not only from Western but also from Greek imperial lineages up to the Paleologans."[35]

This establishment of a continuous dynastic relationship to the Eastern emperors constitutes Philip II's most significant contribution to Hapsburg genealogical lore. The new genealogy was created with the intention of stressing Philip's hereditary right to the empire of the Greeks, whose title had been conceded in 1502 to the Spanish kings.[36] This foundation reinforced the Burgundian claim to the sovereignty of the unified Eastern and Western empires that was presaged by the transfer of Jesus' monogram to the Franks and prophesied for Charlemagne's heir.[37] The Eastern Empire was long deemed the property of his Burgundian ancestors, deriving from Charlemagne's Greek mother and descending through Baldwin, king of Jerusalem and emperor of Constantinople. Recall of this heritage may well have been intended by the "discovery" in the fifteenth century of an "antique" medal—most likely a contemporary Flemish forgery—representing Heraclius arriving at the gates of Jerusalem with the Cross. This image appeared in a learned treatise on the Cross written in the 1590s by Philip II's historiographer Justus Lipsius, who also wrote a syncretistic genealogy for the king (fig. 109). It was again reproduced in a later genealogy of the Austrian clan.[38] In Lipsius's treatise the Roman and Judeo-Christian religious symbols are amalgamated. Noting that the Cross was prefigured in the Tau, the Hebrew sign of salvation, Lipsius also revealed that the rudimentary form of the Palladium was a cross.[39] A similar train of thought pervades Jacobus Valdesius's *Prerogative Hispaniae* that was written for Philip III. Here, Constantine's, Clovis's, and Charlemagne's visions and insignia are treated as interchangeable manifestations of divinity: "singular benefices are bestowed by God in the *vexillium*, which is called *auriflamma* in Latin . . . and other authors affirm it is the Labarum conceded to Constantine, who saw the sign of the cross in victory; others affirm that it is the lily which the angel brought to Clovis, and which Charlemagne used against the infidel."[40] All are claimed for the Spanish kings as ancestral prerogatives derived through their Burgundian forefathers.

With the Greek ancestry firmly established, Philip II made his bid for universal sovereignty of a domain that extended beyond the Eastern and Western empires to the ends of the earth. Throughout this expansion of heritages, the family's dually derived ancestral piety was never forgotten; and twin-spirited Noah-Janus remained the source of those origins. This is demonstrated in a treatise of 1573 by Francisco Sixto that preserved the syncretistic genealogy that had been viable since the Middle Ages: "There are two opinions regarding the Hapsburg descent from Noah. One is that they descend from Cam by the Trojans; another from Sem through the Greeks. Cam begat Osiris, otherwise called Apis, who begat Hercules Libicus, [from this line was begotten] Dardanus . . . Priam . . . Hector . . . and from them proceeds Clovis."[41] At the head of this ancestral rank he placed Adam. This cultural crisscrossing substantiated how deeply anchored in ancestral pilings were the roots of Hapsburg piety. As the individual who brought together the various strands of the divine inheritance, Philip was said to personify the concord of the whole world, a prophetic title for Christ.[42] In the following century these diverse heritages were assembled by Didaco di Lequile, court historiographer at Innsbruck, in a comprehensive monument of Hapsburg genealogical imagination composed for Emperor Ferdinand III (fig. 110).[43] Here, where the whole is centered on Dardanus, and each contributing clan's particular virtue is glorified, Aeneas is the epitome of Piety, and the house of Austria that of faith in the Cross.

Once these comprehensive roots of the Hapsburg family were established, practitioners of genealogical detective work could devote their efforts to subsidiary pursuits; considerable imagination produced a cachet of Hapsburg inherited symbols. The emblems of Ioanne Seifried that are contemporary with Philip II and the later ones of Didaco di Lequile reveal the transformation and perpetuation of genealogical constructs in visual counterparts. The heraldic insignia of the Domus Anicia is the twin-towered facade, which derives from a Constantinian coin (fig. 111). The towers symbolize "Invictus," the Latin interpretation of the Anicio name. Arnoldo Wion, who dedicated his labors to Philip II, is the source for the information that the twinning of the towers signifies the clan's invincibility in both flesh and spirit.[44] Myriad symbolic references were applied to the lion that appears in the Spanish royal arms as a sign of their defense of the Faith. To its significance as the insignia of Judah, and therefore of Christ, who was of the tribe of Judah,[45] was added its meaning

110. *Prospectus Genea-
logicus.* In Didaco di Lequile, *Piisima . . . Domus
Austriaca,* Innsbruck,
1660. Biblioteca Apos-
tolica Vaticana, Rome.

111. *Twin Towered Domus Anicia.* In Didaco di Lequile, *Piisima . . . Domus Austriaca,* Innsbruck, 1660. Biblioteca Apostolica Vaticana, Rome.

112. *Austriacae Gentis Stemma ex Stirpe Aenae Trojani. In Didaco di Lequile, Piisima . . . Domus Austriaca*, Innsbruck, 1660. Biblioteca Apostolica Vaticana, Rome.

as the insignia of the Trojan royal house. In an emblem that displays the lion of the shield of Aeneas, the Hapsburgs carry the evidence of Aeneas's ancestral piety (fig. 112).[46] Stimulated by the later contest between the Austrian and Spanish branches of the family, other treatises were geared to preemption. A presage that the Spanish Hapsburgs would establish their empire on the Cross is derived from the use of a cross-labarum among the Cantabrians of Spain prior to the birth of Christ.[47]

Ever demonstrative of his ancestral piety, Philip II lived and battled with the Cross, and deeded its burden to his son upon his death. This devotion is acknowledged in court panegyrics that praise him for imitating Rudolf in "accepting the Cross of Christ as the Scepter of his reign."[48] Following the direction to which Philip lent such impetus, Hapsburg devotion to the Cross culminated in the taking as a family motto "In Hoc Signo Vinces," which at one time belonged to Constantine the Great and with which he triumphed over his enemies.[49]

Through his support of the arts, Philip communicated the Hapsburg-Constantinian relationship beyond court circles, and in this way stimulated popular devotion to the Cross. Through literature and pamphlets, and most dramatically through the medium of Jesuit theater, the message of Hapsburg piety was spread throughout the dynasty's realms.[50] The influential literary topos of the *Triumph of the Church Militans* that was based on the model of Constantine and associated with Hapsburg "Pietas" originated with Justus Lipsius.[51] It was spread in the seventeenth century through the writings of Lipsius's students Vernulaus and Avancini, among others. When the *Triumph* was staged as a theatrical production, it took the form of a military battle waged by martyrs and saints. The scenario was grounded in Constantine's triumph over Maxentius, which served as the prototype for the Hapsburg victory over the Turks. In Nicholas Avancini's play *The Triumph of Piety, or Constantine's Victory over Maxentius*, the cosmic battle won by Christ in his victory over death and the devil was enacted as the prelude. This struggle was replayed in the triumph of Constantine over Maxentius; at the play's finale Saint Helena reveals the battle as a harbinger of Hapsburg universal empire. The work was staged in Vienna under a proscenium arch exhibiting the Imperial Eagle and flanked by portraits of the Hapsburg clan.[52]

Philip anticipated these public promulgations through a pri-

113. El Greco, *The Dream of Philip II*. Escorial. Patrimonio Nacional, Madrid.

vate commission. In his triumphal tour of the empire of 1549, an image of Constantine's dream had already appeared on the English arch. The inscription applied the motto "In Hoc Signo Vinces" to Philip, as the heralded possessor of the empire.[53] Following his great victory at Lepanto in 1571, considered to be the final blow to Turkish power in the Mediterranean and symbolically represented by the capture of the Turkish standard, Philip deemed this ancient portent fulfilled and appropriated the Constantinian vision of the Cross to himself. In the *Dream of Philip II* that he commissioned from El Greco to commemorate the victory (fig. 113), saints and martyrs, the warriors of the Church Triumphant, perch on clouds in adoration of a vision in which the Cross appears with Jesus' monogram "IHS." The Jesuits had adopted this icon as the emblem of their Order. To it they added three nails from the crucifixion—which were read as a "V."[54] This addition yielded IHSV, a tidy acronym for the Constantinian motto "In Hoc Signo Vinces"; this motto also appeared on the banner of the Holy League. In what appears to be the first application of this symbolic construct to a narrative context, the Cross and the name of the Savior that appeared to Constantine to signal the unification of the Roman Empire in Christ and to herald victory in battle are joined to form Philip's personal vision. Directly below, amidst members of the Church Militant, Philip II kneels in veneration of this celestial apparition, while behind him lies the slain demon of hell.[55] The picture compresses eternal and historic battles into a single victorious image. Through this chronological synthesis, Philip's vanquishing of the Turk is equated with the triumph achieved by his sainted ancestors and, indeed, with Christ's victory over death. It has been suggested that the picture may have been intended to hang over Philip's tomb.[56] This suggestion gains impetus from our knowledge that the Labarum inscribed "His Vincimus Armis" appeared on Philip's funerary catafalque at Seville. We are informed by the ceremony's chronicler that the inscription relates to Constantine's motto "In Hoc Signo Vinces" and to Philip's imitation of Constantine. It was accompanied by another inscription "Imperium Sine Fine Dedi," that was drawn from the phrase in the *Aeneid* where Jupiter promises Aeneas universal empire.[57]

According to Hapsburg apologetics, Rudolf's vision of the Cross was equated with a Christian compass, binding his descen-

114. Bartolomé Esteban Murillo, *Fray Julian's Vision of the Ascension of the Soul of King Philip II.* 1645–48. Sterling and Francine Clark Art Institute, Williamstown, Massachusetts.

dants to carry the Cross to the ends of the Earth, "and not only to the East and the West but to the Arctic and Antarctic, where the Constellation of the Cross is an auspicious sign (of their universal rule)."[58] Perceiving himself as a new Rudolf,[59] it was Philip II who fulfilled this destiny by extending his rule to the Four Quarters of the globe. Contemporaries disseminated the idea that Philip received a heavenly apotheosis at his death; this was given testimony by the religious community, as in the picture of *Fray Julian de Alcala's Vision of the Ascension of the Soul of King Philip II* (fig. 114). The poet Giovanni Strasoldo assigned the king's apotheosis to the constellation of the Cross that appears in the Southern Hemisphere.[60] From the mount of Eden, the four stars that formed the Cross had been visible to Adam and Eve, but after the Fall they vanished from the sight of man.[61] When the equator was crossed by Iberian navigators, the Southern Cross miraculously appeared again on the horizon.[62] This established an eternal resting place for the ruler of the New World that communicated a subtle apocalyptic message, for the heavenly reappearance of the Cross was held to signal the *Parousia*.[63]

Chapter XI *The Hapsburg Cult of the Eucharist*

Eucharistia = Hic Austria—Pius nome et omen habet.
—DIDACO DI LEQUILE, *Rebus*

AS the place where He shed His blood, Jesus' Cross had been identified since the fourth century as the "signum . . . veri et divini sanguinis."[1] Thus eucharistic connotations were attributed to the chief implement of Christ's Passion. With the appropriation of the Cross for the Roman emperor's Labarum, death in the battle for the faith became equated with Christ's own Sacrifice. Indeed Jesus' monogram that was revealed at the Milvian battle was stamped on the Host beginning in the fifth century.[2] At the court of the Spanish Hapsburgs such connotations were intensified through the proclamation that "the Spanish *Vexillium* . . . is the consecrated *Corpus Domini*."[3] The consanguinous relationship to Christ that underlay Hapsburg veneration of the Cross similarly sustained Hapsburg devotion to the Eucharist.

The orthodox belief that Christ is present in flesh and blood in the consecrated Eucharist was challenged during the Reformation by the Protestant position that the Sacrament was a symbol.[4] The Tridentine Council reaffirmed the orthodox position; thereafter acts of sacramental veneration increased in response to the Protestant heresy. In contrast to the late-medieval practice of exhibiting the Eucharist only on the Feast of Corpus Christi, the Eucharist was periodically exposed, and both laity and clergy were encouraged to frequently partake of communion. Within the imperial realms, Hapsburg devotion to the Eucharist played

an important part in this development. Underpinning these de-
votions lay the House of Austria's claim to the Eucharist as a
dynastic preserve, a position based on a miracle involving the
paterfamilias.

According to a legend that was recorded as early as 1340,
Rudolf I experienced an apparition of the Eucharist in 1264
when he lent his horse to a priest who was transporting the
Sacrament through the woods.[5] Out of veneration for its sacred
burden, Rudolf refused to remount the horse, a deed which
elicited the priest's prophecy of Hapsburg world dominion.[6] The
prophecy was satisfied when Rudolf was elected emperor in
1273. The legend is commemorated in a seventeenth-century
emblem that reproduces the event (fig. 115). The legend of
Rudolf's eucharistic epiphany prompted his identification as the
"Second Asser." The name derives from the Old Testament, and it
occurs in the context of Jacob's proclamation that his house has
the hereditary right to rule over God's people until the coming of
the Messiah.[7] Blessing his son Asser and elevating him over his
brothers, Jacob pronounced Asser's bread—an archetype for the
Eucharist—a delicacy fit for kings. Since Asser was seen to prefig-
ure Rudolf, the analogy stamped a priestly character on Rudolf's
kingship.[8] Following the Jacobian principle of hereditary privilege, this status was deemed the birthright of his stirps,[9] and the
Eucharist was adapted as the hereditary insignia of the gens.[10]
Crowned with an aureole of light and identified as a saint, Rudolf
stands before a shield with the family coat of arms and bears this
insignia in an engraving by Leonhard Beck for the Emperor Maximilian I (fig. 116). Rudolf's candidacy for such sublime status was
later said to derive "from his Anicio ancestors, at whose breast he
drank the sweet milk of piety."[11]

During the course of the legend's dissemination which continued to the current era, new eucharistic miracles involving
members of the Hapsburg family were added to those of the
founding father.[12] These additions underscored the validity of
the interpretation that had been applied to Rudolf's theophany.
As they confirmed the clan's pervasive piety, the Hapsburgs proclaimed the Eucharist their perpetual preserve.

Rudolf's legend was significantly enhanced by Maximilian I's
marriage to Mary of Burgundy, for sanctioned by their descent
from God's anointed Clovis, Mary's forbears had long proclaimed

115. *Rudolf Leads the Priest Bearing the Eucharist.* In Juan de Solorzano Pereira, *Emblemata*, Madrid, 1653, p. 70. Biblioteca Apostolica Vaticana, Rome.

116. *After Hans Burgkmaier, Saint Rudolf.* Graphische Sammlung Albertina, Vienna.

a special status in regard to the Holy Sacrament.[13] We have seen that Clovis's baptism was prefigured in Christ's own baptism, which carried eucharistic connotations.[14] The anointing transformed Clovis into the "cristus of the Lord," signifying his divine election to propagate the eternal rule of Jesus in the office of priest and king. This dignity, which was commuted through the heavenly liquor, remained the inalienable possession of Clovis's heirs; it devolved on Charlemagne, who was similarly acclaimed *Rex et Sacerdos*.[15] This status and his ties to the Holy Blood were reinforced by the legend that he possessed the Holy Grail. The legend was recapitulated in a painting of ca. 1515 by Bernard van Orley, court painter to Maximilian's daughter, Marguerite, who was regent of the Netherlands. Here Charlemagne consigns the chalice and the silver dish from the Last Supper to the Cathedral of Aachen (fig. 117).[16] These eucharistic traditions were bolstered by the acquistion of a relic of the Precious Blood caught from Christ's wounds in a vessel by Joseph of Arimathea and sent by Baldwin to his family in Bruges following the sack of Constantinople in 1204.[17]

Philip the Good of Burgundy, the most direct descendant of

117. Bernard van Orley, *Charlemagne Depositing the Holy Grail*. Part of a triptych, between 1515 and 1520. Galleria Sabauda, Torino. Archivio Fotografico della Soprintendenza per i Beni Artistici e Storici.

118. *Gnadenstuhl* (*Throne of Grace*). Ivory, Burgundian-Netherlandish, 1453–67. Treasury, Kunsthistorisches Museum, Vienna.

the Merovingian and Carolingian stock, evoked the dynasty's sacramental powers and underscored his status as the paterfamilias of this priestly caste by founding the Order of the Golden Fleece. Bearing the Fleece on a collar, the duke gave perpetual visibility to the dynasty's sacral pretensions. These rights may well be alluded to in works of art commissioned by the court; for example, the Order's Flint and Steel are embedded in a relief that he possessed of the *Throne of Grace*, an image symbolic of the eucharistic Sacrifice (fig. 118). Contemporary with founding the Order, Philip confirmed Burgundian piety by erecting a Sacrament Chapel to commemorate a eucharistic miracle associated with his royal house. In Brussels in 1369, consecrated hosts were stolen from the Church of Saint Gudule, a Burgundian ancestral saint.[18] When the hosts miraculously bled and revealed the sacrilege, the offenders were persecuted. By building a chapel at Saint Gudule and thus rendering monumental homage to this miracle, Philip established a model precept for conveying Burgundian dynastic piety towards the Divine Sacrifice.

While Maximilian I perpetuated the veneration of Philip the Good's holy relic, he secured his own sacramental aura though a miracle that earned him the epithet "New Elijah." Injured while

119. Flabius Aristo, *Agate Bowl*. Trier, fourth century A.D., believed to be the Holy Grail. Treasury, Kunsthistorisches Museum, Vienna.

hunting at Martinswand, Maximilian lay at the point of death. As he prostrated himself in prayer, resigning his soul to Christ, an angel appeared to him bearing the Eucharist.[19] The emperor was restored by the bread from heaven, and the miracle was interpreted as confirmation that the Eucharist was indeed the "Palladium" and protective amulet of the House of Austria.[20] Maximilian's interest in genealogical fabrication had provided a basis for such exalted claims, for he joined the Hapsburg blood to Christ's in the common seed of Jesse. This connection was reinforced by the Hapsburg possession of the chalice of salvation, the Holy Grail in which Christ had inscribed his name (fig. 119). The Grail was declared "the inalienable heirloom of the House of Austria."[21]

Charles V paid homage to his dynasty's mystical aura in myriad ways. At the Church of Saint Catherine in Hoogstraten (fig. 120) he commissioned a stained glass window depicting the Last Supper; below ruling members of the Burgundian-Hapsburg families, including Philip the Good, Maximilian, and Charles, exhibit dynastic solidarity in their devotion to the Sacrament. At another window, in the Church of Saint Michael in Brussels, Charles kneels before a vision of the Throne of Grace; he is presented to God by his patron, Saint Charlemagne (fig. 121). A more elaborate series of stained glass windows was ordered for

120. *Last Supper*, and portraits of Philip the Good, Philip the Fair, Charles V, and other members of the Burgundian-Hapsburg dynasty. Hoogstraten, Saint Catherine. Copyright A.C.L. Bruxelles.

121. After Bernard van Orley, *Charles V Accompanied by His Patron, Saint Charlemagne Kneeling before God.* Stained glass, 1537. Brussels, Church of Saint Michael, north transept. Copyright A.C.L. Bruxelles.

Philip the Good's Sacrament Chapel at Saint Gudule. In the chapel's north transept, portraits of Charles V and his wife, Isabella, kneel before a reliquary of the miraculous bleeding hosts which are held by God. In the south transept, Charles's sister Mary and her husband, Louis of Hungary, venerate the Trinity in the form of the Throne of Grace. Other family members represented in poses of sacramental adoration include Maximilian with Mary of Burgundy, Philip the Fair with Joan of Castille, and Philip II with Mary of Portugal.[22] Even in a relocated site, these testimonies to Hapsburg eucharistic veneration were to be preserved, for the windows were the source for the bronze effigies of the Hapsburgs kneeling in adoration of the Eucharist at the Escorial.[23]

Charles also solemnized his inheritance through new forms of eucharistic devotion. Considered by contemporary sources one of the greatest champions of the Sacrament, the emperor was personally responsible for the increase of the eucharistic cult among his subjects.[24] Vowing on the Eucharist in battles against the Turks and the Protestants, Charles made the public privy to this devotion—by imperial edict Charles established that in processions celebrating his military triumphs, the Eucharist would be displayed in a monstrance carried by the archbishop.[25] As participants in the cortege, "Caesar and the princes of the royal house [bowed in pious ardor], and love of the Eucharist grew in the hearts of the people [following the imperial example]."[26]

The coincidence of another miracle that occurred within his provinces provided an additional venue for Charles's veneration of the Eucharist. In the early thirteenth century, Saint Giuliana of Liege received a vision in which she saw the moon marked with a black spot. The moon was interpreted as an image of the militant church, with the spot indicating the absence of a feast to honor the Holy Sacrament. Giuliana's vision aroused zeal for the worship of the Host, which was celebrated with ritual and ceremony in Liege as early as 1230. Pope Urban IV, a native of the region and ex-deacon of Liege, established the Feast of Corpus Christi as a universal feast of the church in the Bull of 1264.[27] During these celebrations the Host was exhibited in a monstrance for the first time.[28] As the cult grew in popularity in the following centuries, the monstrance—commonly referred to as a throne—was protected by a baldachin and publicly paraded in the company of celebrants costumed as characters from biblical and church history.[29] Thus the trappings of triumphal procession were accorded to the Host. From these processions, which were to become the stateliest ceremony in the Catholic liturgy, there gradually evolved the Auto Sacramentales[30]—dramatic enactments of sacramental worship, in which productions the Spanish excelled.

Peering back over time, Rudolf's heirs observed the chronological coincidence of Rudolf's encounter with the Eucharist and the universal celebration of Giuliana's miracle—both of which occurred in 1264. This coincidence bolstered Hapsburg dedication to the cult of Corpus Christi.[31] A memorable show of this devotion occurred when, on entering Vienna in 1530 and encountering the procession of Corpus Christi, Charles removed all his imperial regalia and followed humbly in the train of the Sacrament.[32] He later transformed the feast into the centerpiece for the public manifestation of Hapsburg eucharistic devotion—a position it retained in church festivals with the emperor's approval into the nineteenth century.[33]

By continuing his father's devotional practices and through his sponsorship of sacramental literature and drama, Philip II continued to reinforce public awareness of the family's inherited piety. In this, the new religious orders were instrumental, and in celebrations of the Feast of Corpus Christi, the Forty-Hours Veneration of the Eucharist, and the Auto Sacramentales, the Eucharist was associated with the royal house.[34] This awareness reached global proportions when the royal pretensions were yoked to the good news of the Redemption that reached the New World, for under Philip's sovereignty the mass was said in all four parts of the world for the first time.[35]

With the imperial title as the prize, Philip made much of his mystical heritage; in expressing eucharistic devotion he exceeded his ancestors both in concept and in presentation. His Solomonic identity, reinforced when he built the Escorial on the model of Solomon's temple, offered a forum for these expressions. We are reminded by Father Sigüenza that the access to the Holy of Holies was a privilege accorded only to the high priest and to Solomon,[36] who on the dedication of the temple, and perennially on the holiest of feast days, "offered the burnt offering and the fat pieces of the peace offerings."[37]

Genealogy sustained this privilege. At Philip's court a special

122. Titian, *Allegory of Lepanto*. Museo del Prado, Madrid.

emphasis was placed on the lineage that bequeathed to him the dual powers of the Old Testament priest-kings. Both sacred and secular powers were accorded by God to Adam at the Creation; from him they passed by the principle of primogeniture to all the firstborn monarchs of Scriptures who succeeded him.[38] Inherent possessions of the Davidic Messiah, these powers were confirmed for Christ by His descent from both the tribe of Judah and Levi, expounded in His two names Jesus and Christ, and manifested to the world at His anointing.[39] Francisco Sixto documented Jesus' human genealogy and his right to the scepter of David as a complement to his proofs of Philip's continuity of that lineage.[40] These assertions were aimed at demonstrating that the Hapsburgs had preserved the heritage through Clovis by observing the rules of Salic law that the French had disregarded.[41] According to this same law, it was the legacy of the Spanish and not the Austrian branch of the family.[42] In the office of priest and king, Philip embodied the union of "two sticks" that must be joined by God's command as a prelude to the arrival of the messianic kingdom.[43]

Through his establishment of a dynastic link to the Byzantine emperors, Philip evoked for himself the quasi-sacerdotal powers inherent from the beginning in the Christian imperial office.[44] His interest in the cult of relics underscored his relationship to his medieval ancestors who had held priestly and kingly powers before the Investiture Controversy. A list of the Escorial's relics that is recorded by Father Sigüenza includes the body of an innocent young boy who descended from the tribe of Judah, a priest of Clovis's time, and pieces of Christ's Cross, eleven thorns from His crown, a part of the vinegar-soaked sponge and some of His vestments[45]—relics related to Christ's kingship and priesthood. A picture of this same period provides a visible record of the sacramental imprint that Philip imposed on his monarchy. In the *Allegory of Lepanto* (fig. 122) that he commissioned from Titian following the defeat of the Turks in the Mediterranean in 1571, Philip elevates his son to God, a gesture derived from the priest's consecration of the Host during the offering of the mass.[46] Especially when compared with *Charles V at Muhlberg* (fig. 66), for the pictures were hung as pendants in the royal palace at Madrid, the *Allegory of Lepanto* reveals the new tenor of Philip's monarchy.

In the culminating monument of Philip's theocratic ideology, the royal chapel of the Escorial, the Sancta Sanctorum of the Heavenly Jerusalem was transformed into its Christian mode, and the angels replaced by larger-than-life Hapsburg effigies kneeling in perpetual devotion to the Sacrament.[47] Their number is augmented by the presence of the holy ancestors who were consecrated by prefigurations of the eucharistic miracle. In frescoes behind the altar, invisible from public view in a narrow chamber, Elijah is fed by Angels, Moses receives the Manna, Abraham accepts the offering of Melchizedek, the Passover meal is celebrated.[48] There, before the assembled genii of his holy gens, Philip paid homage to the ancestral cult in his capacity as priest, while as the living king he received the worship attendant on his divine presence.

In perpetuating this system of beliefs, Philip's kin deferred to his exemplary piety. A series of tapestries commissioned from Rubens by Philip's daughter, the Infanta Isabella Clara Eugenia, for celebrations of the feast of Corpus Christi at the Monastery of the Descalzas in Madrid, provides a Baroque counterpart to the dynastic piety venerated in her father's Royal Chapel.[49] Here, companion depictions of Triumph revive ever-valid imperial themes. *The Triumph of the Eucharist over Pagan Sacrifice* (fig. 123) recalls Theodosius's defeat of the pagan usurpers,[50] while *The Victory of Eucharistic Truth over Heresy* (fig. 124) effects a psychomachian victory over personified evil. In the midst of this symbolic assembly one recognizable portrait stands out. As Time lifts Truth heavenwards—*Veritas filia Temporis*, a canonic Hapsburg motif—Time's outstretched wings frame a portrait of the aged Philip. The king turns his back on the fray of tumbling Vices as the rescue of eucharistic Truth unfolds in a private vision before Philip's upward gaze. The lion embracing the lamb in the lower foreground enhances the image's eschatological context. Philip appears again in the lower left of the group of tapestries designed to form the monastery's monumental altarpiece. Here he is at last accorded the imperial status he so ardently desired. Dressed in imperial robes that are adorned with the Hapsburg eagle, his crown at his side, Philip is surrounded by past and present members of his clan in adoration of the Sacrament.[51] Among these is Rudolf, whose eucharistic miracle set the tradition of Hapsburg piety into motion.[52] In another image from the series, Isabella Clara Eugenia, who carries the eucharistic monstrance, perpetuates this

123. After Peter Paul Rubens, *The Triumph of the Eucharist over Pagan Sacrifice.* Tapestry model, 1625–28. Madrid, Descalzas Reales. Patrimonio Nacional, Madrid.

124. After Rubens, *The Victory of Eucharistic Truth over Heresy.* Tapestry, 1625–28. Madrid, Descalzas Reales. Patrimonio Nacional, Madrid.

125. Rubens and assistants, *Eucharistic Saints, in Their Midst Is Isabella Clara Eugenia*. The John and Mable Ringling Museum of Art, Sarasota, Florida.

126. Claudio Coello, *The Adoration of the Sagrada Forma*. Escorial. Patrimonio Nacional, Madrid.

piety into the present (fig. 125). Other tapestries in the cycle depict those Old Testament ancestral prototypes whose prefigurations of the eucharistic miracle appeared earlier behind the main altar at the Escorial.

Nearly a century after his death, Philip II's eucharistic devotion was recalled in a painting of the *Sagrada Forma* that Charles II, the last of the Spanish Hapsburgs, commissioned from Claudio Coello. It shows Charles II worshipping a miraculous host that bled when Protestants desecrated it during the religious wars in Holland; the host was given to Philip II as a symbol of his intransigence in defending Catholic orthodoxy.[53] The picture, which served as the frontispiece for the great monstrance that held the holy relic, is inscribed "Regalis Mensa Praebebit Delicias Regibus" (fig. 126). In its recall of the words with which Jacob pronounced Asser's bread a delicacy fit for kings, the inscription evokes Rudolf's identification with Asser, and by association, Philip II as the new Rudolf-Asser. By associating himself with Philip, Charles II underscored the Hapsburg relationship to the Sacrament that bound members of the dynasty in a pietistic continuum.

By the middle of the seventeenth century, a series of verbal similitudes were developed to blur forever the distinction between the Eucharist and the House of Austria. In one variant a complex anagram is unscrambled to reveal that the House of Austria derives its name from the Eucharist: Eucharistia = Hic Austria. The anagram is directly related to Rudolph's eucharistic miracle, and his role as the New Asser is reiterated.[54] Onomastic synonyms that proclaimed identities between Austria = Ostica and Osterreich = Hostyreich yielded proof that the Eucharist was at once the dynasty's genetrix and protective amulet. The congenital nature of this relationship is communicated in a panegyric that uses lactation imagery to convey its message: "From its first infancy, the House of Austria drew sustenance from the Eucharist; this heavenly mother's milk which nourished Rudolf thrives in the Hapsburg family tree. By this antidote against heresy, they continue to live, and flourish. This true Palladium of the Hapsburgs . . . this manna . . . this miraculous bread . . . is the emblem of the gens."[55] The mystical relationship that was expressed verbally by these formulae was given material form through the theatrical magic of an Auto Sacramental created for the King's participation by Calderon. Here during the eucharistic miracle of transubstantiation, Philip IV, who had temporarily "re-tired into the Host" emerged bearing a cross to reveal his true divine nature.[56]

The Hapsburg cult of the Eucharist was at once the most visible and enduring manifestation of the clan's sanctity. Towards the end of the seventeenth century, the Villa Troy was built out-side Prague to pay tribute to the sovereigns of the Hapsburg dynasty. Here an illusionistic environment that encompasses the upper walls and the ceiling wraps the Grand Hall in a vision of Hapsburg piety. Rudolf's eucharistic miracle is the catalyst for the ensuing victories of his progeny; these culminate with the defeat of the Ottoman's by Emperor Leopold I (d. 1705).[57] Begun as a dynastic convention, the House of Austria's link to the Holy Blood so deeply penetrated public consciousness that it gradually grew from a familial to a national prerogative. As late as the eve of World War I, these concepts were kept alive by the repetition of the old miracles. At the eucharistic congress held in Vienna in 1912, the litany began with Rudolf's forest apparition and ended with a paean to the Hapsburg emperor, Charles Francis Joseph (d. 1922), surnamed "the Eucharistic Emperor."[58] At that same con-ference, mention was made of the immense monstrance that dominated the altar for the marriage of Empress Maria Theresa (d. 1780). The monstrance bore the anagram: "Eucharistia = Hic Austriae vita."[59] These miracles were still viable in 1957, when their recitation stood as contemporary proof of the piety of the Austrian nation.[60]

While other members of the Hapsburg clan contributed to establishing this sacramental concept of their kingship, it was Philip II who fused both his own and the Eucharist's identity with the sun. Future and past came together in this single symbolic construct, for both the foundations of the theocratic state and the realization of the *Fourth Eclogue's* messianic prophecy exuded from its genial design.

Chapter XII *The Regnum Apollonis*

Now is come the last age of the song of Cumae; the great line
of the centuries begins anew. Now the Virgin returns, the rein
of Saturn returns, now a new generation descends from heaven
on high. . . . Thine own Apollo now is king.

—VIRGIL, vol. 1, *Eclogue* IV.4–10

I
N 1555, as he was preparing to assume sovereignty of Spain
and of the Order of the Golden Fleece, Philip II adopted a
personal emblem with the motto "Iam Illustrabit Omnia"
(Now He Will Illuminate Everything) (fig. 127).[1] Framing
the emblem are personifications of the Christian Virtues Justice
and Temperance. At the center, the nude Apollo—an unprecedented subject for a Christian monarch's personal device—rides
his quadriga through the heavens. Below the sun god, a rolling
ocean flows onto a globe; on it appears an early map of the New
World that would now be dominated by Philip. The stars of the
Southern Hemisphere appear above.

Philip's emblem marks a turning point in the evolving tradition of ruler iconography, for in a contemporary treatise dedicated to the king, Girolamo Ruscelli revealed Philip's intention to
establish his own solar identity with this emblem:

The King who is the author of the Impresa [intends] to illuminate
this shadowy world with the holy light of God; this is communicated
by the motto. . . . We know that frequently not only Philosophers
but also Theologians often identify God with the sun . . . this applies
also to the king in whom resides God's intentions. In order that the
King . . . may illuminate every heresy with his own splendid light,
God has imbued his mind with the sun's rays . . . and inspired this
emblem which is an oracle or a prophecy that the whole world will
soon be illumined with divine light through the universal conversion of the infidel to the true Catholic faith.[2]

Ruscelli underscored the augury's messianic significance, for he related Philip's light-bringing powers to Isaiah's prophecy that the Messiah would one day rise to illuminate Jerusalem.[3] By associating himself with the illumination of the earthly and the heavenly realms of the New World, Philip suggested through his emblem that the revelation of a new hemisphere was timed to coincide with the one who would be the lux mundi.

A parallel messianic message infused Vergil's Fourth Eclogue, where Apollo is the prophesied king of a reborn universe. In the Eclogue's first stanza the Sibyl predicts that the time is at hand when a new progeny will descend from heaven to begin anew the circuit of the ages; in this new Golden Age, Apollo will reign. We have seen that the Christian interpretation of the Eclogue had transformed the Isaian and the Cumaean prophecies into interchangeable revelations of Christ's Advent. This interpretation was reinforced by the legend that the Virgin and Child had appeared in a solar aureole to Augustus.[4] Christ's continuing identity as the "New Sun" is underscored in a seventeenth-century emblem of the legend created for the Spanish Hapsburgs. The inscription refers to Jesus "who shines more brightly than Apollo" (fig. 128).[5]

The Eclogue's prophecy was perennially revived as part of the rhetoric of praise devoted to each reigning emperor. Sweeping away the generalized allusions that characterized past pretensions, Philip secured his claim to this destiny though his direct identification with Apollo. By personifying himself as the cosmic divinity who brings light to the unknown half of the globe that had languished in darkness before his advent, Philip inferred that the reign of Christ-Apollo had arrived in his person. The myth of the redeemer king now found its historical application in the geography of the New World.

Philip's Apollonian iconography deserves attention for its preeminent place in his imagery; it is no less important for determining the dominant precept of seventeenth-century monarchical theory. The significance of his achievement becomes clear as we consider the role assigned to Apollo in Troy's millennial destiny.

127. Iam Illustrabit Omnia, emblem of Philip II. In Girolamo Ruscelli, Le Imprese illustri, Venice, 1566. Biblioteca Apostolica Vaticana, Rome.

Deus solus Dominus.

EMBLEMA II.

Aspice splendentem Puerum, radijsq́; coruscum,
  Qui Phœbi nitidas lumine vincit opes.
Quem Dominŭ mõstrat Tyburis manus almâ Sybilla,
  Nam soli, & solus Rex tonat ille Poli.
Principis æterni reverentes cernite numen,
  Qui geritis multis sceptra caduca modis.

Solar Kingship and the Trojan Legend in Antiquity

With the Hellenization of the West, the Alexandrian concept of the sun king permeated Roman ruler imagery. Since Apollo was the most active defender of the Phrygians in the *Iliad*, the Trojan legend contributed greatly to defining his stature.[6] Champion of the migration of sovereignty that—like his own diurnal course—moved from east to west, Apollo figured prominently in both the Argonautic and Trojan sagas. He enjoins Jason to undertake the recapture of the Golden Fleece and he guides the Argonauts in fulfilling the task.[7] The image of the Fleece's recovery on the doors of Apollo's temple indicates that this accomplishment was predestined.[8] Praised for proposing a sanctified site for Troy's founding and for building the city's walls, some ancient sources suggested that disobedience to Apollo's oracle brought about the city's destruction and the Trojans' forced exodus.[9] The solar god's prestige migrated to Rome with the myth. His importance attained new heights when Pompey's advocate, the Praetor Nigidius Figulus, identified Apollo with the Penates that Aeneas had carried from Ilion to protect the New Troy in Rome.[10] Nigidius anticipated Vergil in assigning to Apollo the rule of a reborn universe.[11] In popular worship, as well in the imaginative literature that defined the idea of the state, Apollo's stature grew apace with Rome's imperial status.

In Vergil's poetry for Augustus, Apollo is accorded ever greater prominence. In the *Fourth Eclogue* the Sibyl prophesied that the rebirth of the world would be distinguished by Apollo's reign from the old Golden Age under Saturn.[12] This new pietistic age, in which the Vices are expunged and the gods return to earth, was predicted to begin with the birth of the redeemer king.[13] Throughout the *Aeneid*, the Sibyl is inspired by Apollo who guides Aeneas through the perils of the underworld, the glories of Elysium, and the safe-conduct of the Penates to the long-lost patria in Latium.[14] The god's importance for Roman history is evident from the illustration in the *Vatican Virgil* (fig. 129), which depicts Aeneas seeking Apollo's oracle.[15] Through both Aeneas's and Lavinia's kinship with Apollo, his offspring are, in fact, the sun god's direct kin.[16]

Myth became history as Apollo determined Augustus's victory at Actium in 31 B.C. In a proleptic vision of the battle that appeared on Aeneas's shield, Apollo was seen launching his ar-

128. *Augustus and the Sibyl, with the Legend* "Puerum . . . Qui Phoebi . . . lumine vincit opes / Quem Dominum monstrat . . . Sybillae, Nam soli, & Solus Rex tonat ille Poli." *In Juan de Solorzano Pereira, Emblemata, Madrid, 1653, p. 9. Biblioteca Apostolica Vaticana, Rome.*

TEMPLVM APOLLINIS

ACHATES   AENEAS   SIBYLLA

129. *Aeneas Approaches the Sibyl before the Temple of Apollo.* Biblioteca Apostolica Vaticana, Rome. MS Lat. 3225 (*Vatican Virgil*), 45v.

rows against Antony from Octavian's ship. Thus the Actian victory was attributed to the god's intervention, and Augustus erected a temple in Apollo's honor on the spot.[17] On hand again in the Parthian battle, Phoebus's participation insured the ejection of the Vices from earth.[18] These victories resulted in the unification of the East and West, the birth of the imperial state and the extension of peace *terramaremque* under the auspices of Rome. They signalled as well the triumph of justice that would allow the gods to return to that land where they had last dwelled on earth.[19]

Following the victory at Actium, Augustus claimed Apollo as his special patron and made his association with the sun a central motif of his iconography.[20] He even inferred a familial relationship to the god, adopting him as a tutelary deity who vouchsafed his protective companionship.[21] Ovid expressed this relationship when he referred to *Phoebus domesticus* as one of Augustus's household gods.[22] As an act of piety that fulfilled a vow made by his ancestor Aeneas,[23] Augustus erected a temple to Apollo on the Palatine alongside his own palace.[24] Then, in a consummate act of veneration, he transferred the Sibylline books that had pronounced the coming of Apollo's reign from the temple of Jupiter Optimum Maximus to Apollo's own sanctuary on the

Palatine. He completed the domestication of Rome's protective divinities when he moved the Penates from the Roman Forum to an altar within his own palace and adorned the altar with Apollo's laurel insignia.[25] Thereafter, Apollo was frequently identified with Augustus—now as the genius of the Julians,[26] now as the emperor's father,[27] now as the emperor himself.[28] Coins of Octavian inscribed "Imperator Caesar divi filius" depicted Apollo in his quadriga on the reverse. These and contemporary gems (fig. 130) disseminated the imagery throughout the realms. All of these elements combined to confer divine status on Augustus, and to mark his reign as the absolute consummation of the Sibylline prophecy of a *Regnum Apollonis*.[29] Indeed, in his commentary, Servius affirmed that the *Fourth Eclogue*'s reference to Apollo was meant to signify the Emperor Augustus.[30]

By identifying with the cosmic properties of the sun, Augustus guaranteed the perpetuation of his solar image into posterity. He chose Capricorn, the sign in which the sun is reborn after the winter solstice as his emblem, and he renamed Sextilis, the month in which the sun reaches its greatest strength, August in his own honor. According to poetic fiction, Augustus's interchangeability with Apollo was reflected in his apotheosis and in his continuing influence on earth. For the scales of justice that were created in the heavens as his final resting place had been associated with Apollo in the Homeric hymns.[31] The connection between the emperor's cosmic identity and the rotation of the

130. *Apollonion Quadriga.* Augustan gem (cast in reverse). Naples, Museo Nazionale. Deutsches Archäologisches Institut, Rome. Neg. 83-1914.

seasons that he engenders was given poetic posterity both in
Vergil's *Georgics* and in Ovid's calendar poem, the *Fasti*.

Since Apollo had become affiliated with the gens Giulia, an
association with the god became—for Octavian's blood heirs and
aspiring pretenders alike—a proof of divine ancestry and imperial legitimacy. Not only did Nero have himself represented as
Apollo-Helios, he resided in a House of the Sun, and he flaunted
his pivotal role in maintaining the harmony of the spheres. Thus,
attributing to Nero the same cosmic position as the sun, Lucan
exhorted the emperor to choose his seat exactly in the middle of
the universe lest the cosmic system lose its equilibrium.[32] The
cult of Apollo increased in the second century. It reached a zenith
under Aurelian, who, convinced that absolute monarchy was
the means of saving the imperium, adapted *Deus Sol Invictus* as
the official deity of the Roman Empire. He identified himself as
Apollo's direct descendant, wore all the external attributes of his
divine ancestor, and was the first to take in his lifetime the title
Deus—the official god on earth.[33] The sun god's invincibility was
figured on coins of the era by the image of Apollo as charioteer;[34]
the reverse showed the emperor's portrait.

Apollo's sponsorship of the imperial office continued un-
diminished into the fourth century, when it figured prominently
in Constantine's pre-Christian imagery. In 310, when he stopped
at the Sanctuary of Apollo in Trier, the god appeared to him in a
vision to present him with a laurel crown of victory.[35] Constantine interpreted this as a presage of the *Regnum Apollonis* that would
initiate his own thirty-year reign.[36] The recreation of Apollo's
realm gave mythical stature to Constantine's claim to be Augustus's legitimate heir. Declaring that he had seen his own features on the face of Apollo,[37] the emperor—whom Eusebius
called "one with Apollo, rising together with the sun"[38]—
followed Aurelian in disseminating the many guises of his solar
identity on prominent public monuments as well as on the coinage of the realm. Prominent among these was the colossal statue
of Apollo in the forum at Constantinople that bore his features.[39]

On the eve of Christianity, solar worship had become so
widespread in patrician circles that it promoted a tendency towards monotheism. This is suggested in Macrobius's *Saturnalia*,
where, stripped of individual identity, the gods are reduced to a
homogenized aggregate of the sun god's unlimited powers.[40] In
the same author's *Dream of Scipio*, the sun assumes a heliocentric

function in the ordering of the universe. The prince becomes a microcosm of the sun, the center of the four points of the compass which are his virtues.[41] This monotheistic tendency in pagan religion prepared for the parallel that was to be drawn between Apollo and Jesus.

The New Sun: Christ Helios

With the conversion of Constantine and the Christianization of the Roman state, it became generally accepted that the Cumaean prophecy foretold the advent of Christ. Accordingly, the early Christian exegetes of Vergil's *Fourth Eclogue* followed Constantine in interpreting the prophesied rule of Apollo as a veiled reference to the Incarnation. This development was anticipated by the Christian Emperor Philippus Arabus, who in 248 had already appropriated the topos of the *Regnum Apollonis* for the Christian religion and celebrated a *saeculum novum* in that year.[42] As the hagiographers of the fourth century attempted to reconcile the Roman Empire's mission with Christianity, solar metaphors became standard for the Savior. The Christian liturgical celebration was transferred to Sunday, and the Savior's birthday was moved to 25 December, the morrow of the winter solstice.[43] Attempts were made to preserve Christ from the taint of idolatry by distinguishing his solar status; he was hailed as the new spiritual sun that eclipses the natural sun in its plenitude—a "sun without setting" and a "light without evening." Yet such distinctions did not prohibit the continuing transfer of Apollonian imagery to Jesus. Eusebius and Clement of Alexandria, for example, cast Him in the image of the Apollonian charioteer,[44] and He is represented in this guise in an early Christian mosaic from the Vatican necropolis (fig. 131).[45] Christ's solar identity congealed in the epithet "Sol Iustitiae," which both recalled an Old Testament designation (Malachi 4:2) and enveloped Christ in a judicial metaphor that evoked Roman imperial sovereignty.[46] The framers of the legend of the Last World Emperor applied a millennial interpretation to this designation, and Christian imperial apologists adapted the newly enhanced solar metaphors to Jesus' earthly counterpart.[47] As the recognized *Christomimetes*, the emperor was identified as the Sun of Monarchy shining in his palace as the parallel of Christ, the Sun of Justice.[48]

In Byzantium, the solar iconography that was adopted for

131. *Christ as the Solar Charioteer*. Mosaic. Vatican Grottoes. Fabbrica di San Pietro, Vatican City.

Jesus continued to serve imperial pretensions, and the metaphors coined for the King of Kings applied to his earthly surrogate.[49] The emperor physically manifested his solar nature to his public on Christmas and Epiphany, ecclesiastical celebrations of Christ's humanity and His divinity.[50] During these feasts, the emperor appeared on a raised tribune draped with golden curtains. Throughout these ceremonies the court poets recited poems which alluded to the emperor rising on his tribune as the sun rises in the heavens.[51] This solar veneration of the Eastern emperor continued throughout the Middle Ages, reaching a climax when—in anticipation of the future findings that would support Renaissance monarchical theory—the Paleologan court revived the ancient hypothesis that the earth circles the sun.[52]

The Solar Imagery of the Northern Emperor

With the accession of Clovis, who borrowed the relevant metaphors from the reigning Byzantine emperor, the ruler's solar
identity was appropriated by the Merovingians.[53] Thereafter it
became the legacy of the Frankish Roman emperor. Panegyrics in
honor of Charlemagne, whose imperial coronation took place
on Christmas Day, are filled with solar metaphors. A poem by
Einhard puns on the etymology Karolus–Cara Lux, casts the emperor as the Apollonian leader of the Muses, and ascribes to him
a Christ-like transcendence, calling him a sun without setting,
who surpasses the pagan sun in brightness and perdurability.[54]
These solar associations were propagated in the sun-burst image
assigned to the Oriflamme that God conferred on Charlemagne
as a sign of divine election. The triple association emperor-
Apollo-Christ continued in the Middle Ages, growing to new
prominence with the Hohenstaufen emperors.

Frederick II was hailed as the *Sol Novus*, the *Sol Mundi*, and even
Sol Iustitiae, Christ's prophetic title.[55] The *Romanitas* of the German
Empire was also recalled in the latter appellation; for Frederick II
founded his royal absolutism in his right to administer Roman
law.[56] The ruler's association with the sun gained an authoritative
voice when Dante restored the title of *Sol Mundi* to Emperor
Henry VII.[57] Thereafter solar imagery became a significant component in the revived dream of universal empire.

The mystique of imperial-solar worship, a tradition by now
more than a thousand years old, was not lost on the Hapsburgs.
They significantly expanded the range of Apollonian iconography as they propagated their solar identity through artistic patronage. In Dürer's *Triumphal Car*, Maximilian parades beneath an
image of the sun; the inscription "Quod in celis sol, Hoc in Terra
Caesar Est" defines the emperor as the sun's earthly counterpart
(fig. 132).[58] Following in his grandfather's footsteps, Charles V
parades beneath an image of the sun in an engraving that records
his imperial election (fig. 133). As heir to the Spanish discovery of
the New World, Charles V was able to inject a powerful new
element into imperial solar pretensions; he was acclaimed for
bringing the light of the sun to the dark hemisphere. A panegyric
that attached messianic significance to these claims assigned an
eternally decreed universal monarchy to Charles: "God wanted

these lands concealed until this time—Charles shall rule every land that sees the sun, for his rule has been written in heaven from all time."[59]

Philip II—Iam Illustrabit Omnia

In 1555, on the eve of his imperial abdication, Charles V ceded Flanders to Philip, a donation which comprehended sovereignty of the Order of the Golden Fleece. The Fleece's inherent solar iconography was made explicit when blazing suns were added to the Order's collar. Charles ceded Spain to Philip the following year, effectively bestowing his solar status with the two domains. With his personal emblem "Iam Illustrabit Omnia," Philip enveloped his political ambitions in a symbolic identity with Apollo.

In his triumphal debut through the empire in 1549 Philip had already been identified with Apollo; in one example he appeared as Apollo in his chariot accompanied by the Hours. In another, Apollo's arrows are described as the faith by which Philip destroys the dragon of impiety. In the year following the establishment of his Apollonian emblem, a very elaborate celestial testimony to Philip's solar nature was prepared by the king's official astrologer, Mattheus Hacus Samburgensis. Philip was born on 21 May, under the sign of Gemini. Presided over by Apollo, this constellation was traditionally considered the "domicile" of the sun.[60] Mattheus affirmed that the appearance of Philip's "own" sun in the "house" of the sun, resulted in a doubling of solar influence on the king. This was confirmed through a "corrected" horoscope in which each significant radius on his horoscope was aligned with a cardinal point in solar procession.

Astronomy acted as handmaiden to her sister art astrology in support of these phenomena. While his forefathers' resources had been limited to imperial rhetoric and historical circumstance, the triumph of heliocentricity in the sixteenth century afforded precipitous advances for Philip's cosmic ideology. The placement of the sun in the center of the universe follows the Chaldean Order. This system was already pertinent to imperial ideology from Macrobius's Dream of Scipio, the classic treatise on the apotheosis of a prince. Through commissions of stellar spheres from Dürer and Peter Apianus, where the movement of the heavens was recharted with scientific accuracy and peopled

132. Albrecht Dürer, Maximilian I's Triumphal Car with the legend "Quod in celis sol / Hoc in Terra Caesar Est" (detail). University of London, Warburg Institute, London.

133. Hans Schaufelein, Triumphal Chariot of Charles V (detail). University of London, Warburg Institute, London.

with the gods of Roman mythology, Maximilian and Charles V had insinuated a connection between their rule and the inexorable order of the cosmos. With the publication of Copernicus's *De Revolutionibus Orbium Caelestium* in 1543, the sun's central placement in the ordering of the heavens provided irrefutable confirmation of the ruler's long-standing claim to be the nexus of that order on earth.[61] Philip II, who brought the light of the Spanish sun to the four quarters of the globe, could claim credit for the ultimate fulfillment of this mystical destiny.

A constant iconography throughout his lifetime, all other mythic references to Philip were subsumed—in the Macrobian sense—under the rubric of his solar identity. In an engraving of 1558 that was dedicated to Philip by Francisco Terzi, the chariot of the sun is set above an image of the king to symbolize his invincible powers against the Protestant and the Turk. His battles against these enemies of the faith are communicated by the images of Hercules, whose twelve labors were, according to Macrobius, a metaphor for the sun's movement through the twelve signs of the zodiac (fig. 134).[62]

134. *Philip II.* In Francisco Terzi, *Austricae Gentis Imaginum*, Innsbruck, 1569. Biblioteca Apostolica Vaticana, Rome.

Philip's identification with Apollo was so prominent and well known that it could be used by his enemies as the basis for malicious parody. His arch-rival Elizabeth I, who consistently raided the Hapsburg storehouse of political imagery for her own self-glorification, did not hesitate to adopt Philip's most comprehensive and arrogant myth. When Spenser wrote an allegory of the triumphs of Elizabethan Protestantism in the *Faerie Queene*, he applied an ironic view of Philip's impresa to characterize the defeat of the Spanish Armada in 1588. Reassigning the dominating light-symbol to Prince Arthur, who was closely identified with Elizabeth and English claims of imperium, Spenser turned Philip's Apollo into a Phaeton, the false sun.[63] It is tempting to speculate that Philip may have been similarly parodied by the papacy under Gregory XIII, who was equally interested in deflating Philip's image. In fact, a similar cosmic pun appears in visual form in the map of the constellations that Gregory commissioned from Giovanni Varosino for the Vatican Palace. Here Ursa Major, the Great Bear that was and is the symbol of Madrid, is moved off its normal position on the central axis to make room among the standard repertoire of stellar configurations for Phaeton's crashing fall.[64]

At the Spanish court, on the other hand, solar references to the king characteristically were phrased in sacred terms. In an epithalamium celebrating his marriage to Isabel de Valois in 1562, Philip's solar emblem is acclaimed an augury of his conquest of the Holy Land, his conversion of the infidel, and the perpetual peace of the world. The royal couple is addressed according to a Byzantine cosmic formula in which the king is identified with the sun and his spouse with the moon (fig. 135).[65] Through her union with the solar hero, Isabel is promised the vision of perpetual light that is granted to the blessed in heaven, and the marriage song ends with the bride's invitation to "come to the golden house of the sun, your consort, and receive that joy which the heavens yield to the earth."[66]

Philip's funerary monuments provide further examples of his solar symbolism. In the obsequies that he planned for his father, Philip II had already adapted ancient Roman funerary rites and implicit solar imagery to convey the concept of Charles's apotheosis. In a funerary catafalque at San Giacomo dei Spagnoli in Rome, a step pyramid was surmounted by the sun god's quadriga of four white horses. According to Juan de Montemoya, who published the account, this denoted the apotheosis of the emperor's soul.[67] In Bologna, a crowned imperial eagle was released to fly heavenwards from the top of yet another catafalque, following the model of ancient rituals denoting apotheosis.[68]

Upon Philip's own death, the use of solar imagery and the references to apotheosis were made much more explicit. On a funerary catafalque at Seville, the four parts of the world were surmounted with an image of the solar chariot inscribed "Iam Illustrabit Omnia." The image is referred to "Philip II, our Lord, who is like the sun, prince of the planets rising in the East and traveling through the zodiac illuminating all."[69] Similar iconography was used for Philip's catafalques at Saragossa. There these mythic references were complemented and indeed sustained by sacred ones befitting this earthly king of Jerusalem. Philip was also saluted as the rising sun, *Sol Oriens*, a prophetic title for Christ.[70] The parallels with Christ were reinforced through the adaptation of the form of Christ's sepulchre for the Saragossa catafalque. The monument was surmounted by an imperial crown and an image of Apollo in his quadriga.[71]

This exalted imagery was not limited to the celebrations held in Spain; it also prevailed in the festivities throughout the realm

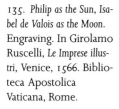

135. Philip as the Sun, Isabel de Valois as the Moon. Engraving. In Girolamo Ruscelli, Le Imprese illustri, Venice, 1566. Biblioteca Apostolica Vaticana, Rome.

by which the Hapsburg vassals honored his passing and saluted his heirs. We know, for instance, that in the funerary catafalque erected for Philip by Ferdinando de' Medici, grand duke of Tuscany, at the Medici Church of San Lorenzo, the light of 1200 torches appeared "like a most luminous sun."[72] The allusion was intended as more than a literary cliche. Philip's emblem, the chariot of the sun, appeared on the catafalque's main facade and on the altar wall. The solar quadriga was identified with the four Christian virtues which aided Philip in the battle of the faith, and the emblem was read as a cipher for the extent of Philip's power which, like the sun, reached every corner of the world. Below the quadriga, a combat with the moon suggested a psychomachian victory in which Philip triumphed over the powers of darkness, heresy, and death. Here, as in his Spanish obsequies, personifications of the four quarters of the globe indicated the universal extent of the empire over which he shed his solar light. As it had for his Roman imperial predecessors, the solar metaphor sustained the concept of Philip's divine apotheosis. An image of the setting sun was accompanied by the motto "Nec Occidet Ultra," to indicate that this monarch, like the sun, does not lose his light at sunset, but transports it to another hemisphere.[73] As an assurance of the sun's continuing illumination, Philip's son is heralded as the *Futurus Alter Sol*.[74]

In the continuing reign of the Spanish Hapsburgs the sun never goes down. Philip's solar imagery, which reflected such fundamental ideas of theocratic rule and which was born from the cumulative layering of ancient imperial prerogatives, could not be expected to die with its creator. These potent symbols of absolute power were translated intact to his legitimate heirs and were celebrated in the art executed to glorify the Hapsburgs' most ceremonious occasions. Thus Philip IV's birth was celebrated as the rebirth of Apollo in human form, his advent attended by a triumphal chariot on which the four continents that were subject to the sun god's rule proclaimed his absolute domain.[75] Taking the solar metaphor yet a step further than did his grandfather, Philip IV identified himself with the sun, the fourth planet, and took the title "The Planet King." His personal motto "Illuminat et Foret" echoed that of Philip II, and his death was similarly announced by a solar eclipse.[76] The metaphor lived on for the Spanish kings. In 1764 Tiepolo painted a vision of the

136. After Luca Giordano, *Indus*. Engraving. In Marcello Marciano, *Pompe Funebri dell' Universo nella morte di Filippo IV*, Naples, 1666, p. 117. Biblioteca Apostolica Vaticana, Rome.

137. Flemish school, *Philip II in Armour as the Rising Sun*. Sixteenth-century engraving. Biblioteca Nacional, Madrid.

Triumph of Spain on the ceiling of the throne room in the Royal Palace in Madrid. The icons of Spanish theocratic rule are gathered here: the personified church with the chalice and cross, the pillars of Hercules, the defeated Vices, the conquest of the Moors, the four continents. As tutelary spirit of the Spanish monarchy, Apollo stands behind the throne.

Throughout, Philip II's role in the establishment of the monarchy's solar iconography continued to be commemorated. In funeral celebrations for Philip IV that were held in Naples in 1666, where the cosmic identity of each member of the Hapsburg dynasty was revealed, that of Apollo was reserved to Philip II, who is referred to as the emperor of the Indies (fig. 136).[77] In another commemorative image, he appears in armor, the imperial crown at his side, while the chariot of the invincible sun rides over the battlefield to denote his victory in combat (fig. 137). This invincibility is recapitulated in Juan Caramuel de Lobkowitz's seventeenth-century treatise entitled *Philippus Prudens*, where Philip is credited with the conquest of Islam. The victory is assim-

DOMINVS MIHI ADIVTOR

PHILIPPVS IIII. DVX BRAB. HISP. II. REX.

Saepè reuersurus fugit Draco signa Leonis. / Saepeque restituit colla superba pedi:

Nec fugiet.Capitur iuste; defendere PRVDENS / Armatis manibus scit sua iura LEO.

PHILIPPVS
PRVDENS
CAROLI V. IMP. FILIVS
LVSITANIAE
ALGARBIAE, INDIAE, BRASILIAE
LEGITIMVS REX
DEMONSTRATVS
A D. Ioanne Caramuel Lobkowitz
Religioso Dunensi Ord. Cister.
S.T. Doctore Louaniensi
et Melrosensi Abbate.

ANTVERPIAE,
EX OFFICINA PLANTINIANA
BALTHASARIS MORETI.
M.DC.XXXIX.

ilated to a cosmic battle, and the frontispiece of a lion destroying a dragon is identified in the commentary as Philip-Apollo who destroyed the lunar dragon that symbolizes the Moor (fig. 138).[78] Thus in human, in astral, and in symbolic terms, his heirs continued to commemorate Philip II's solar identity.

The greatest testimonial to the significance and the pervasiveness of Philip's Apollonian imagery was Tommaso Campanella's *City of the Sun*. We have seen that in the *Monarchy of Spain*, Campanella had turned to world events to prove that the Spanish monarchy realized the Sibylline prophecy of a rebirth of the blessed original state of man; the Golden Age of which the poets sang.[79] The Spanish king had vanquished the Turks and brought the light of the sun to a part of the world that had been damned to eternal darkness. Though these achievements, Philip II had satisfied God's wish, voiced by the prophets, that Spanish rule succeed the Four World Empires. For the Spanish monarchy, which had realized God's eternal scheme, Campanella composed the *City of the Sun* in 1602, a treatise on the theocratic state. Based on the new physics of Telesio, Campanella envisaged a utopia, in the midst of which rose a temple to the sun, the most concrete image of God.[80] The edifice was to be bounded by seven concentric walls and four radial divisions, corresponding to the planetary system and the divisions of the year. Within its walls there was to be an altar decorated with the globes of heaven and earth. At the head of the hierarchy governing this state sat the philosopher king called Sol, himself a metaphysician who had most profoundly studied the secret causes of things. The ruler would exercise the duties of both priest and king, following the pattern established by Adam, Noah, Sem, and Melchizedek, and the papacy itself would have to be absorbed in this higher and more universal religion which was consonant with nature. This kingdom of the universe was designated for the Spanish king because the Spaniards discovered the rest of the world in order to unite them all under a single law; the philosophers testify to their mission, for which they were elected by God.[81]

The question of solar symbolism in the architecture of the Escorial bears examination in the reflected light of Campanella's mystical edifice. In Herrera's design for the building all the proportions of the Escorial rise from a single principle, so as to express in the building the unity, proportion, and harmony of the universe.[82] We are aware that a cosmic scheme was referred to

138. After a lost painting by Erasmus Quellinus, *Philip-Apollo*. Title page to Caramuel de Lobkowitz, *Philippus Prudens*, Antwerp, 1639. Rare Books and Manuscripts Division, New York Public Library. Astor, Lenox, and Tilden Foundations.

Solomon's temple, for Proverbs 9:1 relates that Wisdom built her
house on seven columns. A cosmic plan for the Escorial would
accord with Philip's desire to give the edifice the form of an *imago
mundi*, and in this way to provide a parallel with Solomon's temple. Such a plan may be reflected on an engraving of the Escorial
that was executed under its architect Herrera's personal supervision; here the ground plan is marked by the signs of the planets
and the zodiac.[83]

The solar metaphors applied to the Escorial in contemporary descriptions testify to the successful communication of this
abstract visual rhetoric. The Escorial is referred to as "Better than
the house of the sun,"[84] and again as the terrestrial paradise in
which the "Sun never sets."[85] When Philip IV built his new Palace
of the Buen Retiro, a monument of equal architectural stature to
the Escorial, these metaphors seem to have been very much in
mind, for the palace was called the "House of the Sun."[86]

Solar imagery is present in the narrative scenes decorating
the Escorial library. One image shows Dionysius the Areopagite
observing the sun's eclipse at Christ's Passion. The philosopher

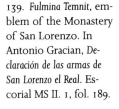

139. *Fulmina Temnit*, emblem of the Monastery
of San Lorenzo. In
Antonio Gracian, *De-
claración de las armas de
San Lorenzo el Real*. Es-
corial MS II. 1, fol. 189.

had acknowledged the divinity of the king because he resembled the king of the heavens. Given our knowledge of Hapsburg genealogical speculations, the most pointed in its reference to Philip is the image of King Hezekiah. Hezekiah watches the retrogression of the sun's shadow that delays his death. Father Sigüenza, who takes credit for the iconographic program captures the essence of the imagery's applicability to Philip with the phrase: "For the heir of Jesse, the sun stands still."[87]

The most allusive solar symbol at the Escorial relates to the patron saint himself. Named for the laurel that was sacred to the sun god, Lawrence's namesake is evoked on the Escorial's emblem that was intended for the building's main facade. In his *Declaración de las armas de San Lorenzo el Real*, Philip's secretary Antonio Gracian describes its suggestive imagery: "The emblem of this exalted monastery is a green laurel tree on a golden field above a flaming grill. . . . Above the laurel is a crown inscribed 'F' (Filippo)" (fig. 139).[88] Both the emblem and the building's orientation paid homage to Apollo, for the Escorial was aligned to the sunset on 10 August—the date of the sun's annual zenith and of Saint Lawrence's feast.[89]

In 1623 Campanella rewrote the *City of the Sun*. The new version was dedicated to the king of France, to whom he transferred the utopian dream he had conceptualized for Spain and subsequently offered to the papacy. Philip's granddaughter Anne of Austria was the mother of Louis XIV; his great-granddaughter Maria Teresa was Louis's wife. Campanella's writings served as the theoretical basis for the ideology and imagery of this *Roi Soleil*. This aspect of Campanella's influence is well known, for it helped to shape the imagery by which France was catapulted into a primary position in world history. Our interest in the theorist ends here, while first acknowledging that Philip's solar ideology must have played a crucial role in shaping Campanella's concept of monarchy.

By creating a comprehensive solar identity, Philip defined the image of the absolute monarch that was to dominate European politics for the next two centuries. In the development of this monolithic figure, one contribution stands out above the rest. Philip intuited the essence of theocratic rule when, through his perpetuation of a solar identity, he drew himself into the orb of eucharistic iconography.

A solar motif for the Eucharist was propogated in celebrations for the Feast of Corpus Christi which was established in 1264—a date coincident with Rudolf's acclamation as the destined ruler of the empire.[90] Through his endorsement of the Corpus Christi celebrations, Charles V perpetuated this iconography, and by association, the link to the House of Austria. In a later panegyric, it is observed that the Laurentians, Rome's early settlers, first exhibited their piety in venerating the laurel in honor of Apollo. This laurel germinated, it notes, in the Hapsburg family tree, and Charles perpetuated the piety of the ancients by spreading the adoration of the eucharistic sun throughout the world.[91]

Philip went beyond his father's measures when he publicly proclaimed the Eucharist's solar identity with his own lips: Fearing for the king's health in the intense heat that pursued Philip as he followed the Eucharist during one of these feasts, his courtiers warned him to take cover from the scorching summer sun. With his characteristic instinct for nuance, Philip shaped a symbiotic relationship to the Eucharist with his reply: "Set aside your fear. The sun in the sky can cause no harm to he who adores the Divine Sun."[92] The incident became part of the standing litany of Hapsburg eucharistic legends.

Towards the end of Philip's reign, the Eucharist—which frequently bore the image of a crown[93]—was exhibited within the Hapsburg realms in a monstrance that had the form of a radiating sun.[94] Thereafter in myriad representations of the solar-monstrance that adorned palaces and churches within the empire, veneration of the Divine Sacrifice was inextricably linked with the supreme symbol of Hapsburg monarchy.

In a fanciful reconstruction of a Corpus Christi procession that was created for his grandson Philip IV, laurel-crowned Gentiles and Jews march alongside the chariot of personified Hapsburg Piety to celebrate "a triple Capitoline triumph after the manner of the ancient Romans" (fig. 140).[95] In the heavens above them, a eucharistic monstrance is surrounded by a solar aureole; it signifies the Hapsburg "extension of sacramental devotion throughout all the realms of the earth."[96] Only in such a bizarre visual image as this could formal expression be given to Philip II's sublime construct through which the sun became the indistinguishable symbol of the Eucharist and of his dynasty.

With the adoption of a personal icon that simultaneously

140. *Eucharistic Chariot.* In Didaco di Lequile, *Colossus Angelicus,* Innsbruck, 1659. Biblioteca Apostolica Vaticana, Rome.

Super hanc Petram

Hic Pietatis honos fulgēs sculptura triumphans
Avstriaca, ingēuos pandit in Orbe Toros.

Quæ Laqueos Fortvna pares fecundior vnquam
Attulit, Europæ splendida iuga trahens?

evoked both the Host and the Hapsburg ruler, Philip II secured the Hapsburgs' mystical bond to the elixir of Christian salvation. Moreover, this solar imagery helped to fix his irrevocable primacy in the family annals of sacramental devotion. For, once the profound affinities that bound their separate natures had been illuminated, Philip succeeded in transferring to the king that adulation previously accorded only to the holiest expression of Christian religious sentiment.

Just as the identification of the Eucharist as the Genetrix of the Hapsburgs converted Christ's body and blood into a palpable ancestral icon, so did its assimilation to the sun confer sacramental status on Christ's heir and kin, Philip-Apollo. With this consummate "alchemical" transmutation, Philip completed the centuries-long process of amalgamating in a single cosmic emblem the universal ruler and the most venerated symbol of divinity *ex-gentibus* and *ex-judaeos*. Denied his legitimate right to rule the universe by the capriciousness of Fortune, it was nonetheless this emperor-manqué who placed the finishing brushstroke on the Roman emperor's mythic image.

Epilogue

LEGENDARY, historical, and prophetic traditions converged with ritual practices in the making of the Roman emperor's mythic image. Remodeled by a thousand alterations, the image's original and its final form are barely distinguishable, for its ultimate substance is reducible to the cult of the imperial gens. With this perspective it is easier to see that the identification of the Host as the Palladium of the Hapsburgs conferred upon the Christian sacrament an explicit interchangeability with the most venerated icons of imperial ancestor worship[1]—the sacrificial Fleece that was the soul of Phrixus and the Penates that were the ancestral kin of Priam's royal lineage. Since the Eucharist was identified with the Manna of the Old Testament, the effect of this synthesis was to consolidate all the divine effluvia in the one true heir of the Gentiles and the Jews.[2]

Alike in function, the Fleece for Argos, the Penates for Troy, and the Eucharist for the Holy Roman Empire were presences that invested the ruler with a mystical aura and guaranteed the perdurability of the state. Irenic bliss was restored to the universe when, through the pious devotion of their living kin, these spiritual presences were conveyed to their ancient patria—now Argos, now Troy, now Jerusalem—all subsumed under the rubric "New Rome" and all connoting the true terrestrial paradise. Venerated in the palace temple of the ruling monarch, these celestial icons were paraded as implicit ancestral symbols in the train of the ruling priest-king and publicly perceived as the *praesens numens* with which he governed the world.

If reduced to a concentric "memory image" this cluster of ideas could provide a hermetic formula for the emperor's mythic powers in the consummate form to which they were brought by the sixteenth-century Hapsburgs. And so it was in a seventeenth-century heraldic emblem (fig. 141), whose explanatory text recalls the *Fourth Eclogue*'s promise of global sovereignty in a new age of universal peace that was prophesied to begin with "a second *Argo*, [and that has now been realized] by our kings, New Jasons, who discovered the New World."[3] Here a crowned lion is surrounded by the collar of the Order of the Golden Fleece, from which hangs the sacrificial ram framed by replicas of the blazing sun. The equivocal Christian and pagan meanings of these motifs are transformed into an internally consistent image of universal theocratic rule by the cross-orbed crown of the Holy Roman emperor. The ancestral context that sustains this abstract symbol is revealed by the injunction to Aeneas with which it is inscribed: "Parcere Subiectis."[4]

Though imperial rituals and cult worship differ in details, the traditions that shape them into eternally valid constructs conform in substance. This book has been concerned with the consistency of those elements in the makeup of the emperor's mythic image. Towards this end it has shown that the allusive imagery which we are accustomed to encountering in ruler iconography is not haphazard but dependent on a rigorously programmatic system of ideas, whose foundations are venerable with age, whose language is abstract and secret, and whose aim is the transferal of spiritual yearnings from a remote to a proximate deity. By inculcating a symbiotic relationship between a people's ruler and the most venerable religious symbols of its culture, kingship is rendered sacrosanct. In the West, these traditions are invariably centered on Rome and on the Trojan myth.

141. *Parcere Subiectis.* In Juan de Solorzano Pereira, *Emblemata*, Madrid, 1653, p. 786. Biblioteca Apostolica Vaticana, Rome.

Postscript

A T once remote and exotic, the concept of the emperor's mythic image is yet a palpable reality for our time. The renewal of apocalyptic rhetoric that is the predictable concomitant of the approaching new millennium is accompanied by a revival of monarchical worship that has swept across the borders of the Old World. Although not immediately apparent, this veneration is sustained by mythic traditions that have remained intact since the beginning of Western civilization. In some instances those traditions are recalled and referred to the reigning ruler.[1] In cultures with a continuing imperial heritage, divine genealogy is directly asserted as the root of the legacy.[2]

The Vatican is studying a petition from the Spanish archdiocese to raise to sainthood Queen Isabella of Spain, who commissioned Columbus's voyage to the New World;[3] in Greece, there is a movement to restore former King Constantine II, whose name resonates with implication for his people.[4] More dramatic scenarios resound behind the parted Iron Curtain, where the breakup of the Communist world has witnessed a wave of nostalgia for the "good old days" that prevailed before 1918.[5] Accompanying this nostalgia for the cultural and commercial activity that characterized the previous era, is the long-suppressed but still-flourishing adulation of the monarchical status.

In Russia, the cult of the Romanov czars has risen from the underground to be embraced by church and state. A church is planned to replace a popular shrine on the site where Nicholas II was executed by the Bolsheviks, and plans are under way for the canonization of this czar who "died for his faith and for orthodoxy." Descendants of Russian nobility and small groups of monarchists have rallied to the Romanov revival, and exhibitions that glorify the reign are being mounted in Moscow.[6] This emphasis on the clan's piety is a typical preliminary to a more ambitious strategy that may soon follow. The late czar's cousin and the pretender to the Romanov throne, Grand Duke Vladimir Kirillovich Romanov, who recently advocated monarchy as "a good solution" to the country's problems,"[7] died this spring. Hundreds of tapers were burned during the royal funeral service accorded him in the Cathedral of St. Petersburg, and his coffin bore the double-headed eagle of the czarist crest.[8] Rome's mythic history enframes this tradition. Russian pretensions to the Eastern imperial title that was formerly held by the Byzantines grew following the fall of Constantinople and crown prince Ivan III's marriage in 1472 to Sofia, niece of Constantine, the last Byzantine ruler. These pretensions were realized in 1547 when Ivan IV became his country's first czar, and Rome was once again transplanted, now to Russian soil.

Perhaps a new stage in East-West imperialist rivalry is to follow. A revival of imperial prestige is also occurring in the old Austro-Hungarian empire that was ruled by the Hapsburg emperors before the end of World War I brought a realignment of national boundaries—among these peoples are the Czechs, Slovaks, Hungarians, Slovenes, Croatians, and Transylvanians. The luster of the past is publicly evoked by the Austrian tourist board's campaign that uses a picture of the Hapsburg crown with the words *Austria Imperialis*.[9] The imperial hearse—last used for the funeral of Emperor Franz Josef—must have stirred images of that glory when it was brought back into service in 1989 at the death of Empress Zita.[10] In the spring of 1992, when five hundred people gathered in Vienna to hear Franz Joseph's great grandnephew, Archduke Otto von Hapsburg, affirm his historical duty to shepherd the peoples of the old monarchy back into the West,[11] the acclamation "Your Imperial Highness" was heard in the thunderous applause that followed his speech.[12]

Notes

PROLOGUE

1. See Braudel, *Mediterranean*, 1014ff., 1021, and 1088ff.

2. Mal Lara, *Descripción*, 14–15: "Don Philippe nuestro señor . . . Tuvo per bien emplearlo en un tan alto cargo, come es de Capitan General de la Mar . . . le dió [a Don Juan] instrucion . . . con que govierne las riendas del imperio sobre la mar, y juntamente en 1568 se mandó se . . . hiziesse una Galera Real . . . y fuese adornada de la escultura y pintura . . . acompañdola de historias fábulas, figuras, empresas, letras . . . y que la misma galera serva de libro de memoria . . . al Sen. Don Juan en todos sus partes lo que deve hazer." Widely acclaimed for his erudition, Mal Lara numbered among his disciples the most celebrated members of the Academy of Seville. Among his major works are a *Filosofía vulgar*, a compilation of proverbs based on Erasmus's *Adagia*, which he dedicated to Philip II. He composed a number of other works on classical themes and an illustrated edition of Alciati's emblem book. He was also the chronicler of Philip's triumphal entry into Seville in 1570. On his life and works, see Sanchez y Escribano, *Juan de Mal Lara*. For a general description of the galley, see Beer, "Die Galeere," 1f.

3. Mal Lara, *Descripción*, 7ff. The description of this sailing vessel, a compendia of painted and sculptural motifs, begins on page 17. Nearly a hundred pages of text are devoted to explaining these images and the relevant ancient sources—on one page alone (p. 76), the author mentions Varro, Valerius Flaccus, Apollonius Rhodius, Euripides, Seneca—elsewhere (p. 84ff.) several pages are devoted to translating Pindar's verses on the Argonauts, the morals they convey and the meaning they carry for the royal family.

4. Mal Lara, *Descripción*, 83–84. For the *Argo's* astronomical imagery, Mal Lara draws upon the descriptions of the ancient authors Hyginus and Aratus and upon the fifteenth-century poet Giovanni Pontano. The *Argo* appears on Dürer's map of the southern constellations that was created for Philip's great-grandfather, Emperor Maximilian I.

5. Mal Lara, *Descripción*, 20–21: "Bien es que comience la obra con la nao Argo. Colchis está en el rincon del Ponto Euxino . . . y que la órden del Tuson venga de Jason."

6. Mal Lara, *Descripción*, 20; on 79, in relating the story of Phrixus, Mal Lara says that Phrixus arrived first in Constantinople and, after traversing the Euxine Bridge, reached Colchis.

7. Ibid., 82–83.

8. Ibid., 489ff.

9. "rey Don Phelippe nuestro señor, en la mesma galera, en el rio desta ciudad, el mesmo dia de Pascua del Espiritu Sancto, en Mayo, año de M.D. LXX . . . y viendo esta galera y mostrandole todo lo que en ella avia, . . . quedó con-

tento de lo que en ella se ordenava; y tambien ordenandose el mesmo año la liga entra el Sumo Pontifice y Papa Pio Quinto, el Rey Don Phelippe y venecianos" (ibid., 502).

CHAPTER 1

1. For the *Odyssey* as the primary model for the *Aeneid*, and for the influence of the *Iliad*, see the discussion in Cairns, *Augustan Epic*, 194ff.

2. In Homer's *Iliad* (20.307), Poseidon prophecies that Aeneas and his descendants will rule over the Trojans. In other books of the *Iliad*, Aeneas fights against the Greeks, exhibits marked piety towards the gods (20.298 and 20.347), and is himself honored like a god (11.58). Out of this tradition developed the legend of Aeneas's flight from Troy. By Vergil's time, Aeneas's founding of Rome had become a national legend. His journey to Latium appears first in Hellanicus (active 406 B.C.) and became popular as a Roman foundation myth with Naevius and Fabius Pictor (both active mid–third century B.C.) and Ennius (239–169 B.C.). For Vergil's sources in this and other early Roman literature see Knight, *Vergil's Troy*, 74ff. For other sources, see Georgius Regel, *De Vergilio Poetarum*, 9ff.

3. Virgil, *Aeneid* III.79f.

4. Ibid., III.166f. Dardanus, who descends from Jupiter via Electra, is the founder of Troy. Again, in VII.240f. Latinus reveals to Aeneas Dardanus's descent from Saturn and the Italic origins of the Trojans: "the Latins are Saturn's race . . . in this land sprang Dardanus and hence passed to the towns of Phrygian Ida. . . . From Jove is the origin of our race; in Jove, as ancestor, [rose] the sons of Dardanus; of Jove's supreme race is our king himself, Trojan Aeneas. Hence was Dardanus sprung, and hither he returns." These Italic origins remain a constant of the tradition. In some medieval versions, Dardanus founds Troy after he exchanges inherited Italic lands for territory in Asia Minor.

5. This famous manuscript is commonly agreed to have been written in Rome within a generation of the year A.D. 400. See Wright, ed., *Vergilius Vaticanus*, 11f.

6. For a discussion of the gradual process through which Aeneas learns that Italy is his destination, see Cairns, *Augustan Epic*, 114ff.

7. Virgil, *Aeneid* VII.120–40. In book VIII,

86f., Aeneas journeys up the Tiber to the city of the Arcadian Evander, who occupies the future site of Rome. Evander traces the common ancestry of the Trojans and Arcadians from Jove, a concord of heritages that will become important in later applications of the myth.

8. Ibid., I.257ff. For a discussion of the episodes that reveal Rome's greatness and their relationship to Roman history, see Williams, *Aeneid*, 34ff.

9. Virgil, *Aeneid* II.268ff.: "In slumbers . . . before my eyes [stood] Hector . . . uttering words of grief: 'O light of the Dardan land, O surest hope of the Trojans, what long delay hath held thee? Ah flee, goddess-born and snatch thyself from these flames. Troy falls . . . [and] commits to thee her holy things and household gods; take them to share thy fortunes: seek for them . . . the mighty city, which, when thou has wandered over the deep, thou shalt at last establish.' So he speaks and in his hands brings forth from the inner shrine the fillets, great Vesta, and the undying fire." For Vergil's special emphasis on Aeneas's mission to rescue the Penates and bring them to Italy, see Galinsky, *Aeneas*, 3.

10. Virgil, *Aeneid* III.1f. Aeneas sails "carrying into Italy Illium's vanquished gods" (I.68). According to II.296–97, Hector entrusts to him the undying fire, the fillets, and the statue of Vesta. In III.147, Aeneas refers to "the sacred images of the gods. The Phrygian Penates whom I had borne with me from Troy." For ancient representations of this subject, see Peter Aichholzer, "Darstellungen römischer Sagen" (Ph.D. diss., University of Vienna, 1983).

The Penates were worshiped in conjunction with Vesta as the guardian numina of the royal family, see *Oxford Classical Dictionary*, ed. N. G. L. Hammond and H. H. Scullard, 2d. ed. (Oxford, 1979), 797. A confusion exists between the Penates and the Palladium, which is typically represented in scenes of Aeneas's exodus. Vergil refers to the Palladium (*Aeneid* II.166) as the image of Athena. His contemporary, Ovid contributes to the confusion, when he notes that the image of the Palladium is believed to have leapt down on Troy, and Dardanus's descendant Ilus was charged to "'Preserve the heavenly goddess, so shall ye preserve the city. She will transfer with herself the seat of empire.' Ilus preserved the image . . . whether it was . . . Ulysses, or pious

Aeneas who carried her off . . . [it] is now at Rome: Vesta guards it" (Ovid *Fasti* VI.417). For the various legends regarding the origin, the identity and the transporter of the Palladium, see Vellay, *Légendes*, 389ff.

11. Virgil, *Aeneid* III.94ff.

12. Ibid., VI.648ff. Ovid confirms Aeneas's divine ancestry that proceeds from Electra's union with Jupiter, through Dardanus, Erichthonius, Tros, Assaracus, and Capys to Anchises, out of whose union with Venus was born Aeneas (Ovid *Fasti* IV.30f).

13. Virgil, *Aeneid* VI.756ff.

14. Ibid., VI.851–53.

15. Ibid., VIII.625ff.

16. Homer *Iliad* 20.298.

17. Vergil introduces Aeneas (I.10) as *Insignem Pietate Virum*, and throughout the *Aeneid*, he is referred to as "Pius Aeneas." For the various citations of Aeneas's piety in the *Aeneid*, see Cairns, *Augustan Epic*, 59f. See also the chapter "Pius Aeneas" in Galinsky, *Aeneas*, 3–61.

18. Virgil, *Aeneid* III.278ff.

19. Ibid., V.47ff. See Cairns, *Augustan Epic*, 54ff., also regarding the relationship these bore to Augustus's recent establishment of the Actian games, already indirectly referred to in *Aeneid* III.280. A historic parallel was provided by Augustus's dedication of a temple to Julius Caesar in 29 B.C., the final element in Julius's deification.

20. In III.390 he learns of the sow with thirty piglets that are the sign of the promised land.

21. On this relief in a wider context, see Zanker, *Power*, 203f.

22. Virgil, *Aeneid* VI.56ff.

23. Ibid., I.379f.

24. For the Golden Age, see Graf, "Ad Aureae Aetatis"; and Lovejoy and Boas, *Documentary History*.

25. Virgil, *Aeneid* VIII.320f. Here Aeneas learns from Evander that this is the place to which Saturn came from Olympus to rule in the Golden Age.

26. Virgil, *Aeneid* VIII.324f.

27. Turnus, who descends from Daunus through Danae, is the betrothed of Aeneas's future spouse, Lavinia. Throughout the *Aeneid* the Danaans are a generic name for the Greeks.

28. For Vergil's introduction of the powers of hell into the Trojan myth, see Viktor Pöschl,

The Art of Virgil, trans. Gerda Seligson (Ann Arbor, 1962), 28f.

29. Virgil, *Aeneid* XII.725f.

30. For the founding of Rome under Libra, the celestial guarantor of her universal sovereignty, see Manilius *Astronomica* IV.769f. See text at n. 62.

31. Virgil, *Aeneid* VI.641f.

32. For the importance of concord in the *Aeneid* see Cairns, *Augustan Epic*, 89ff. For the association of Concordia with the emperor in public cult, see Taylor, *Divinity*, 199. Concordia was deified in Rome at least by the late third century B.C.

33. For Aeneas as priest, see Virgil, *Aeneid* V.92f and Cairns, *Augustan Epic*, 223f. For a discussion of ancient treatises on kingship, see ibid., 21ff.; for Aeneas as king and as successor of the Trojan royal house, a role Hector bestowed upon him as the next of kin, see ibid, 2ff. and 38.

34. Virgil, *Aeneid* XII.791–842.

35. For references to the Argonautic legend in Homeric literature see Beye, *Epic*, 46. The earliest complete version of the myth is Pindar's IV *Pythian Ode* on the Argonauts; see *The Odes of Pindar*, Pythian IV, 1f. See also Segal, *Pindar's Mythmaking*, 9f. At the beginning of the third century B.C. this legend was developed into a full-scale saga by Apollonius Rhodius to relate to Alexander the Great's eastern victories: Apollonius Rhodius *Argonautica*. For an annotated bibliography on this version, with an emphasis on literary criticism, see Beye, *Epic*, 169ff. For the influence of Apollonius's epic on Vergil, see Cairns, *Augustan Epic*, 195ff. The *Argonautica* of Apollonius Rhodius was translated into Latin by Varro Atacinus and copied by Vergil and Ovid, see introduction to Valerius Flaccus, *Argonautica*, xiv. Valerius Flaccus's later version of the legend affirms the hereditary link between the Julians and the Flavians and glorifies the Eastern victories of Vespasian and Titus. On the meaning of the Eastern conquest in Valerius Flaccus's *Argonautica*, see I.129f and the further references below.

36. Phrixus is the grandson of the wind-god Aeolos and the son of King Athamas; he was born with his sister Helle to Nephele. Ino is the jealous stepmother who plots Phrixus's demise.

37. According to the Scholiasts on Pindar, the cosmic ram was Phrixus's soul carried to heaven, see Roux, *Le Problème*, 292. On the constellation Aries, and for a fuller discussion of the Ar-

gonautic myth, see chapter 8.

38. On the sacred impetus in Pindar's version of the myth, see Delage, "Le Mythe des argonauts," 128, and Burton, *Pindar's Pythian Odes*, 159–60.

39. On the *Argo's* painted images of the battles and loves of the gods, see Manilius *Astronomica* 1.40f; see also 5.32.

40. The theme is developed in Valerius Flaccus *Argonautica* II.580f. See the discussion in Knight, *Vergil's Troy*, 116.

41. See Roux, *Le Problème*, 294. Catullus equates the quest for the Fleece with Aeneas's founding of a new Troy. For this and other parallels in the two legends, see Adamietz, "Komposition der Argonautica," 22–23, 108–13; Fowler, *Aeneas*, 100; and Lefèvre, "Das Pröoemium der Argonautica," 55ff.

42. Valerius Flaccus *Argonautica* I.530–56.

43. Ibid., II.570ff.

44. Octavius had become sole ruler in Italy before 37 B.C., the publication date of the *Eclogues* in their present order. On this dating see *Virgil*, trans. Fairclough, vol. 1, p. x.

45. Critics have endlessly debated the identity of the child. Some have associated the child with the marriage of Octavian and Scribonia or have identified the child with Octavian himself. For those and other opinions, see the summary in *Virgil*, Appendix, p. 577.

46. *Virgil*, vol. 1, Eclogue IV.49.

47. For a brief discussion of the sibylline books and a glance at the imagery, see Mayor, Fowler, and Conway, *Virgil's Messianic Eclogue*, 90ff.

48. *Virgil*, Eclogue IV.34–36. The repetition of the Argonautic journey and the renewal of the Trojan war are signal events that bring perpetual peace in their wake. Vergil's intention is expressed in the lines that introduce the cited passage: "Yet shall some few traces of olden sin lurk behind, to call men to essay the sea in ships." See chapters 4 and 8 for the recurrence of this topos in the later Middle Ages and beyond, uses that indicate that as late as the Renaissance this significance was understood to inhere in Vergil's text.

49. *Virgil*, Eclogue IV.10 and 39–45. For a discussion of the reign of Apollo, see chapter 12.

50. The typology is established in Aeneas's landing at Actium (*Aeneid* III.278ff.).

51. Ovid *Fasti* 1.527, refers to the transferral of this role to Augustus: "Anon pious Aeneas shall hither bring his sacred burden, and, burden no whit less sacred, his own sire; Vesta, admit the gods of Ilium! The time will come when the same hand shall guard you and the world, and when a god shall in his own person hold the sacred rites. In the line of Augustus the guardianship of the fatherland shall abide."

52. Augustus took the title *Divi Filius* and issued coins with representations of Aeneas carrying Anchises and the Palladium from Troy. See Taylor, *Divinity*, 106.

53. See *Virgil, Aeneid* I.257ff., in text of this chapter at n. 8.

54. Augustus fulfilled this vow while the *Aeneid* was being written, see Suetonius, vol. 1, *Lives of the Caesars*, bk. 2, chap. 29. In his commentary on the *Aeneid* VI.69f., Servius acknowledged that Augustus's temple to Apollo on the Palatine satisfied Aeneas's vow, a fact celebrated as well in Horace and Propertius. See citations in Ussani, *Studi su Valerio Flacco*, 110f. For a discussion of Augustus's temple to Apollo, to which the emperor transferred the Sibylline books, see Gagé, *Apollon Romain*, 523ff. On Apollo, see chapter 12.

55. In *Virgil, Aeneid* I.285ff., Jove decrees the Julian descent from Ascanius Iulus, the son of Aeneas. In *Aeneid* IX.638, Apollo identifies Iulus as the son and sire of gods. See also chapter 5.

56. Augustus dedicated a temple to the divine Julius Caesar. On Augustus's institution of a cult to the *divus Iulius* and the *Genius Augusti*, his most important acts for establishing a new imperial cult, see Ussani, *Studi*, 85. For Augustus's own reception of worship in conjunction with the household gods, see Taylor, *Divinity*, 182. In the *Georgics*, III.12f., Vergil envisioned his own allegorical temple to Augustus, in which a cult statue of the emperor will occupy the center and receive sacrifice. The doors would be decorated with images of Augustus's divine ancestors.

57. While Vergil intended Aeneas's battle against Turnus to stand for the earthly conquest of virtue over vice, Horace remade the metaphor by equating the emperor's triumphs with the gods' conquest of the Giants. For both poets, the goal of universal sovereignty was everlasting peace and Horace added his eloquence to Vergil's in declaring that here in Rome, the original home of the gods and cradle of the Trojan race, Augustus had revived Saturn's Golden Age (Horace *Odes* III.4). For a discussion of this appli-

cation and of its religious implications see J. Aymard, "La Politique d'Auguste et l'Ode III 4 d'Horace," *Latomus* 15 (1956): 26–36.

58. For the identification of the Parthian victory with the Sibyl's prophecy of an oriental triumph, a connection that gave positive form to the *Renovatio* announced in the *Fourth Eclogue*, see Gagé, *Apollon Romain*, 583. Secular games initiated in 17 B.C. marked the formal designation of the *Renovatio*.

59. On the powers of the Pontifex Maximus, including the interpretation of sacred law, and his ministering to the cult of Vesta and the Penates, see Taylor, *Divinity*, 60. See the discussion of the date of this appointment in ibid., 183.

60. For a broader perspective on this frieze, see Zanker, *Power*, 120f.

61. On Augustus's personal cult of Apollo and the Penates, see Gagé, *Apollon Romain*, 570ff.

62. Virgil, vol. 1, *Georgics* 1.32f.: ". . . whether thou add thyself as a new star to the lingering months, where, between the Virgin and the grasping Claws, a space is opening (lo! for thee even now the blazing Scorpion draws in his arms, and has left more than a due share of the heaven!)." After the battle of Actium, Octavian's birthday on 23 September—the date which since the first century B.C. has marked the sun's entry into the zodiacal sign of Libra—was celebrated as a public feast; the honor was later accorded divine status when the date was commemorated by circus games.

63. Virgil, *Aeneid* XII.725f.

64. Deification is promised by Jove to all the Julian house in *Aeneid* VI.789f.

CHAPTER 2

1. For pagan precedents asserting Rome's divine mission, see chapter 1.

2. Origen *Contra Celsum* ii.30, from the text in *From Alexander to Constantine*, ed. and trans. Ernest Barker, pp. 10–11, 439f. See ibid, pp. 439–40 for Melitó of Sardo's earlier statement that Augustus and Christ were both bringers of peace. See also Mommsen, "Aponius and Orosius," 309f.

3. The prophecy appears in the book of Daniel 2:31–45. For the development of the theme that the Roman Empire postponed the coming of the Antichrist, see chapter 6.

4. See the discussion in McGinn, *Visions of the End*, 11ff.

5. Prudentius (vol. 1, *The Divinity of Christ* ll. 446–48) placed the Christian Roman emperor in the traditional line of descent from Aeneas, see "Theodosius and the Christian Empire" this chapter.

6. The association occurs in the prologue of the *Argonautica*, where Valerius Flaccus invokes Vespasian's extension of the Roman Empire and Titus's conquest of Jerusalem (1.11–13). The relationship to the Flavians and to the destruction of Jerusalem is discussed in Ussani, *Studi*, 87ff., and Lefèvre, "Pröoemium," 55–63. Valerius's text appears to be the locus classicus for the association between the conquest of Jerusalem and the capture of the Fleece, an idea that is fundamental to the medieval adaptations of the Trojan legend, discussed in chapter 4.

For parallels that Valerius established between the Argonautic journey and the *Aeneid* to connote the legitimate transfer of the empire to the Flavians, see Adamietz, "Zur Komposition," 22–23, 85; other parallels with the *Aeneid* are discussed on pp. 108–13.

7. See chapters 4 and 8.

8. For a comprehensive treatment of Prudentius's importance and influence, see Vest, "Psychomachia of Prudentius," and "Prudentius in the Middle Ages." For his relationship with Theodosius, see Harries, "Prudentius and Theodosius."

9. Prudentius, vol. 1, *Psychomachia*. While critics have analyzed the Roman political content of Prudentius's other works, only scant attention has been paid to these ideas in the *Psychomachia*. A number of other writings where Prudentius connects the Trojan myth to Roman imperial history are cited below and in chapter 9.

On Vergil's *Aeneid* as a literary source for the *Psychomachia*, see the suggestions of Smith, *Prudentius' Psychomachia*, 150, 240, 271ff. However he considers the borrowings ironic and does not develop their political ramifications. Unless otherwise noted, Prudentius's transformation of the *Aeneid* in the *Psychomachia* and the citations that substantiate this line of thought are my investigations. For a discussion of Prudentius's use of Vergil's *Fourth Eclogue*, see Salvatore, *Studi Prudenziani*, 80–83. On pages 38ff. he discusses other echoes of the *Fourth Eclogue* and of the imperial myth in the *Liber Cathemerinon* and *Hamartigenia*. See also Dexel, "Des Prudentius Verhältnis zu Vergil." Albertus Mahoney, *Vergil in the Works of Prudentius*, The Catholic University of America Patristic Studies, no. 39 (Washington, D.C., 1934), is mainly concerned with etymology and poetic structure. For further bibliography concerning Vergil's influence on Prudentius, see Salvatore, *Studi Prudenziani*, 82 n. 73, and chapter 9.

10. For this suggestion, see Emile Male, *Gothic Image* (New York, 1958), 102. On sources for Prudentius's personification of the virtues and vices in earlier Christian writers, see Gnilka, *Studien*, 9.

11. Prudentius, *Psychomachia* l. 113f; Virgil, *Aeneid* XII.6ff.; see also XII.45. Again in *Aeneid* I.294, we are informed that when Peace is achieved, "The gates of war, grim with iron and close-fitting bars, shall be closed; within, impious Rage . . . shall roar in the ghastliness of blood-stained lips." For Prudentius's reference to the chaining of Fury under the Christian Augustus, Theodosius, see chapter 9. In Vergil, Allecto and the Furies emerge from Tartarus to infect Turnus. Prudentius follows suit in establishing the vices as chthonic deities.

12. Virgil, *Aeneid* XII.723–35.

13. Prudentius, *Psychomachia* ll. 128–47. For a general discussion of the Bern manuscript, see Homberger, *Handschriften*, 136ff.

14. Katznellenbogen, *Allegories*, the fundamental study of the imagery of the *Psychomachia* in the Middle Ages, notes the continuation of martial imagery into the late Middle Ages. Stettiner, *Die illustrierten Prudentiushandschriften*, gathers illustrations from the vast number of manuscripts of the *Psychomachia*. See also Woodruff, "Illustrated Manuscripts."

15. Vergil frequently refers to him as "Proud Turnus."

16. Prudentius, *Psychomachia* ll. 210f.

17. Ibid., ll. 275–305.

18. Virgil, *Aeneid* XI.887.

19. In the *Psychomachia* the battle ends when Avarice, the symbol of the Iron Age, is overcome, and Charity, which characterizes the Christian Golden Age, triumphs. Vergil is the source of the concept that greed causes the end of the Saturnian Golden Age (*Aeneid* VIII.324f).

20. For Prudentius as a fundamental exegetist in the development of Old Testament–New Testament typologies, see the Preface to *The Origins of Sin*, vol. 1, in the cited edition.

21. Prudentius, *Psychomachia* ll. 360ff.

22. Ibid., ll. 407f.

23. For Augustus as Concordia, and for Concord's importance in the *Aeneid*, see chapter 1. For the pagan iconography of Concord, and for its assimilation to Constantine and Christ in the fourth century, see the discussion in Tanner "Concordia," 6–7.

24. Prudentius, *Pyschomachia* ll. 670f.

25. Ibid., l. 756.

26. Ibid., ll. 475ff.; the author discourses on this: "Civil War makes plunder of his kin . . ." In ll. 708f. Discord identifies herself: "I am called Discord, and my other name is Heresy."

27. Ibid., ll. 645–46.

28. Compare ibid., ll. 549ff. with the song of Miriam (Exodus 15:19).

29. Prudentius, *Psychomachia* ll. 825ff. Wisdom is enthroned in the new Temple of Solomon "In her hands a living rod of green wood. This is the sceptre that was prefigured by the flowering rod of Aaron."

30. The scepter given to the sires of Latium to bear was "once a tree . . . now cased in seemly bronze" (Virgil, *Aeneid* XII.206ff.). See Gnilka, *Studien*, 121ff. for the implication that both Aaron's and Latinus's scepters are meant. He cites the similarity of Latin terms used to describe the living rod of wood in *Aeneid* XII.208 and *Psychomachia* l. 879. For Prudentius's borrowing from the imagery of the palace of the Kings of Latium for the image of the New Jerusalem see Gnilka, *Studien*, 114.

31. See Gnilka, *Studien*, 123, for the conferring of Aaron's rod on Christ to indicate the true priest. In *The Divinity of Christ* ll. 996f., Prudentius traces the progeny of the priest-kings from which Christ descended through David, Aaron, and Noah to Adam, the first of the Creator's progeny. For the assignment to Christ of David's royal insignia, see *Prudentius*, vol. 2, *Scenes from History*, no. 20: "The marvellous David's royal emblems shine bright—sceptre, oil, horn, diadem, purple robe and altar. They all befit Christ, the robe and crown, the rod of power, the horn of the cross, the altar, the oil." Gnilka, *Studien*, 118, notes that this passage indicates Christ's enthronement as the Basileus. The classic treatment on Christ as emperor is Peterson, "Christus als Imperator." See also Beskow, *Rex Gloriae*, 11ff., 24ff., 313ff.

32. *Prudentius, Psychomachia* ll. 825ff. In line 818, Prudentius refers to the city as "purgati corporis urbem." While Gnilka has observed the scene's relationship to Aeneas's laying the foundations of a Trojan settlement at Carthage, the scene also echoes and supersedes Romulus's tracing out of the boundaries of the Capitoline Temple to Jupiter. For the perpetuation of this topos, see chapter 5.

For Prudentius, the conversion of the city of Romulus into the heavenly citadel of the New Jerusalem is finalized when the first Roman martyr effects the cleansing of the Roman temple. *Prudentius*, vol. 2, *Crowns of Martyrdom*, bk. 2, ll. 410–516. For a discussion of the hymn to Lawrence, where the pagan divinities are transformed into icons of the New Faith, and for the poem's relationship to Roman imperial ideology, see chapter 9. See also *Prudentius*, vols. 1 and 2, *A Reply to the Address of Symmachus* (hereafter referred to as C.S.), bk. 1, ll. 80ff.

33. *Prudentius, Psychomachia* ll. 804ff. An extended discussion of the parallels between Prudentius's edifice, the Temple of Solomon, and the Heavenly Jerusalem of the New Faith ruled by Christ the King in the Throne of Wisdom, is provided in Gnilka, *Studien*, 94ff. He also relates this edifice to the text from Prudentius's *Scenes from History*, no. 20: "Wisdom built a Temple by Solomon's obedient hands . . . the time is at hand when Christ shall build his Temple." See also Smith, *Prudentius' Psychomachia*, 199–200.

34. *Prudentius, Psychomachia* ll. 834ff.

35. This approach is taken up in the *Divinity of Christ* ll. 446f.

36. In the C.S., a treatise praising Theodosius's defeat of the pagan factions, Prudentius expressed this interconnection: "Happy had they been had they known that all the successes were ordered by the governance of the God Christ, whose will it was that Kingdoms should run their appointed course and the triumphs of Rome grow from more to more and that He should enter the world in the fullness of time" (C.S. bk. 1, ll. 285ff.). Elsewhere in the treatise, he ascribes a divine impetus to Rome's irenic powers: "To curb . . . [war] God taught the nations everywhere to bow their heads under the same laws and become Romans . . . united in an ancestral home. For the time of Christ's coming, be assured, was the way prepared . . . under the rule of Rome . . ." (ibid., bk. 2, ll. 602ff.). Christ is in-

vited to enter "a world in harmony . . . which peace and Rome hold in a bond of union. These Thou dost command to be the heads and highest powers of the world. Rome without peace finds no favor with Thee; and it is the supremacy of Rome, keeping down disorders . . . that secures the peace" (ibid., ll. 635ff.). For other Christian parallels to the *Aeneid*'s promise of Rome's world dominion in Prudentius, see Buchheit, "Christliche Romideologie," 137f.

37. See Harries, "Prudentius," 73ff., who discusses these issues in the C.S., and reviews the background for Prudentius's treatment of the emperor and his son Honorius.

38. This idea was already formulated for Theodosius's predecessor, Constantine. Eusebius expressed the concept that the earthly ruler's perfect virtue is grounded in his divine nobility; from this springs his assimilation to Christ: "Let . . . [Constantine] be proclaimed our sole sovereign. . . . Really a Victor is he who has triumphed over the passions which have overcome mankind, who has modelled himself after the archetypal form of the Supreme Sovereign, whose thoughts mirror its virtuous ways. . . . He makes manifest the august title of monarchical authority . . . since he alone deserves to wear the royal purple" (Drake, *In Praise of Constantine*, chap. 5, 89). For a discussion of the importance of these orations as the first clear statement of the philosophy of the Christian empire, see Baynes, "Eusebius and the Christian Empire," 13ff.

39. See Seston, "Vision païenne," 381.

40. Lactantius, the tutor of Constantine's eldest son, Crispus, identified the Golden Age with Christ's return in his *Divine Institutions*. For a discussion of this idea in Lactantius and his followers, see Charles, "Eschatology," 362ff.

41. The metaphor is drawn from *Virgil*, vol. 1, *Eclogue* IV.6. This assimilation of Mary to Astraea becomes a stock analogy: see, for example, the commentary on the *Fourth Eclogue* in Iunii Philargyrii, *Appendix Serviana*, ed. Hermannus Hagen (Lipsiae, 1902), 77: "Iam redit Virgo idest Iustitia . . . vel Maria." In the same commentary the newborn child is the prophecy of Christ (78) and the serpent is the devil (80).

42. See Drake, *In Praise of Constantine*, 94.

43. *Virgil, Eclogue* IV.34f.

44. *Oratio ad Sanctos*, c. 20, 3–4, in Barker, ed. and trans., *From Alexander to Constantine*, 219. See ibid., 218, and n. 2, for the attribution both to

Eusebius and to Lactantius and for the possibility
that the Oration is a forgery, possibly belonging
to the fifth century. For discussion of Constantine's political ideology in Eusebius see Farina,
L'impero, 15–23, and Ladner, Idea of Reform, 119–25.

45. Oratio ad Sanctos, c. 19, 5–9.

46. The Vision of Octavian first occurs in
the Chronographia of Malalas, a sixth-century author. The oldest extant version of the legend in
the West appears in the twelfth century in the
Mirabilia Urbis Romae, where it accounts for the
founding of the Aracoeli Church on the Capitoline. See Mirabilia Urbis Romae: The Marvels of
Rome, trans. F. M. Nichols (London, 1889), ixf.
and 35f., and Graf, Roma nella Memoria, 8of. and
311f.

47. Eusebius Ecclesiastical History I.2, 23; III.7,
30–36.

48. Drake, In Praise of Constantine, chap. 16,
120. Eusebius provides a rationale for the existence of the Roman Empire, which "subdued
the visible governments in order to merge the
entire race into one unity and concord." In chapter 16, Eusebius continues the connection between the Roman Empire and Christianity. See,
for passages, Barker, ed. and trans., From Alexander
to Constantine, 474ff.

49. Barker, ed. and trans., From Alexander to
Constantine, 476. On the chronicle, see chapter 4.

50. Eusebius Ecclesiastical History IX.3, 11, cited
in Grabar, L'Empereur, 95f. For the continuation of
such biblical parallels, see chapter 5.

51. In the Hellenistic kingdoms of the East,
the deification and adoration of the ruler became an institution of state. On Alexander's deification in 305 B.C., his divinely descended birth
from Ammon, and his attempts to introduce
worship of his person, see the citations from ancient texts in Barker, ed. and trans., From Alexander
to Constantine, 10–11.

52. See Ladner, Idea of Reform, 121ff., and
Farina, L'impero, 201, for references in Eusebius
where the emperor is compared to Christ.

53. On the eternal rule of Constantine, see
Drake, In Praise of Constantine, chap. 6 and n. 6.

54. Ibid., 92f.

55. Eusebius assigned to Constantine the
Christ-like and priestly function of offering up
his own kingly soul and the soul of his subjects,
whose good shepherd he is (Drake, In Praise of
Constantine, chap. 2, 5, 86). For the emperor's

priestly functions see also Farina, L'impero, 163 n.
6. On church reforms effected by the emperor's
command, especially with Constantine, Justinian
I, and the iconoclastic emperors, see Ladner, Idea
of Reform, 123 and nn. 44, 48.

56. The analogies are extended in specific
parallels: Christ fights the demon, Constantine
the enemies of Truth; Christ teaches his disciples, Constantine all his subjects; Christ opens
the portals of heaven, Constantine the doors of
the Holy Places.

57. Drake, In Praise of Constantine, chap. 3, 86f.

58. "The Only-Begotten Logos of God Endures with His Father as Co-ruler" (Drake, In
Praise of Constantine, chap. 2, 85). For the position
that the imperium belongs to the emperor and
he can give it and the title to his children, see discussion in Farina, L'impero, 169. Although it was
condemned at the Nicene Councils, Arianism figured in the ideology of Eusebius. According to
Arian theology, the Son is subordinate to the Father. This doctrine facilitated the equation Christ-
Constantine, which required reducing the Son to
a vice-regent of God. A further imperial advan-
tage could be derived from the Arian doctrine.
According to this line of thinking, the church is
not a transcendental but a terrestrial institution
that aids the empire in establishing a social and
moral order. For Eusebius's Arian viewpoint, see
Beskow, Rex Gloriae, 313ff., and Seston, "Vision
païenne," 380ff. For the continuation into the Renaissance of the Byzantine support of a subordinate role for Christ that was countered by the
Latin church's doctrine of the Filioque, see discussion in Tanner, "Concordia," 8ff.

59. "Heavenly armies encircle Him, . . . as
Supreme Commander and Chief High Priest"
(Drake, In Praise of Constantine, chap. 3, 87).

60. Ibid., chap. 6, 94.

61. See Grabar, L'Empereur, 32f., and Dinkler,
"Kreuz," 1ff.

62. See Beskow, Rex Gloriae, 11ff. In the Seven
Books of Histories against the Pagans (ca. 417), Prudentius's contemporary Orosius established new parallels between Christ and Augustus that bolstered
Jesus' imperial status. He noted that Octavian,
who would soon take the name "Augustus," a
title that signified his supreme sovereignty over
the Roman Empire, returned from the East to enter Rome in triumph on 6 January 29 B.C. That
was the same day as the Epiphany, when the

Magi arrived in Bethlehem to recognize in Christ the supreme sovereign of the universe. Orosius accommodated the date of Augustus's entry, which actually occurred on 13 August, to the date established in the fourth century for Christ's Epiphany. See Mommsen, "Aponius and Orosius," 312.

63. Prudentius, *The Divinity of Christ*, ll. 446ff. Similar ideas are expressed in C.S., bk. 1, ll. 287–90, 587–90; bk. 2, ll. 583ff. (see also discussion in introduction to Loeb edition, ix, and Smith, *Prudentius' Psychomachia*, 5, 9, 17). This theme is developed in chapter 6.

CHAPTER 3

1. For a corrective to this idea of the imperium's quiescent state, see the discussion of Clovis's quasi-imperial status in chapter 5.

2. See the discussion in Borchardt, *German Antiquity*, 190. Charlemagne brought the equestrian statue of Theoderic the Goth from Ravenna to Aachen in 801.

3. Gregory of Tours *Historia Francorum*, bk. 2, chap. 31. This passage is cited in Kurth, *Clovis*, 326f. See Kurth's appendix, 589ff., for the sources of Gregory's knowledge of Clovis. For the ramifications of this assimilation, see chapter 10. On Gregory's presentation of Clovis see Reydellet, *Royauté*, 399ff.

4. See Kurth, *Clovis*, 351. For a discussion of the Arian-Orthodox distinction, see Beskow, *Rex Gloriae*, 1ff.

5. For Avit's comparison between Clovis and the emperor, and for the distinction he makes between the rulers of the East and the West, see Tessier, *Baptême*, 110. See also Bloch, *Les Rois*, 496, for discussion of the letter that uses imperial terminology for Clovis.

6. Gregory of Tours, *Historia Francorum*, bk. 2, chap. 38. See text in chapter 5 at n. 37.

7. This attitude towards the Byzantine Empire would change with the growing pretensions to Byzantine ancestry among the northern emperors, see chapter 5.

8. The oldest account of this apparition occurs in Hincmar de Reims's *Life of St. Remi* composed in 877. The baptism of Clovis is the central focus of the *Life*, and Hincmar glosses the legend of the Holy Vial and the victories following the baptism. See the citations from Hincmar's text in

Devisse, *Hincmar*, 1043ff. On the legend and the source, see Bloch, *Les Rois*, 196, 224ff.

The disrobing of the old man, traditionally associated with the baptismal liturgy, became a symbol of the abandonment of the old Germanic royalty. On this see Tessier, *Baptême*, 109.

9. The unction is an indication of Christ's royalty. Referring to Eusebius's authority, John of Paris (1306) explains the divinity, the royalty, and the eternity implied by Christ's baptism: "Si vero . . . quod Christus rex fuerit . . . rex dico temporalis regni. . . . Eusebius dicit . . . Christo, quia unctus, quod errant Herodiani, esse regem temporaliū bonorō, quia non est unctus materiali e unguento . . . sed spirituali . . . & a ideo non est rex huius seculi, sed illius seculi de quo dicit propheta Daniel: potestas aeterna est regnum eius quod non corrompetur" (*Tractatus de Postestate Regia et Papali*, in Schardius, *De Iurisdictione*, chap. 3).

10. For the events commemorated by the Liturgy on Baptism that include the Epiphany and the Miracle of Cana, see Tanner, "Concordia," 13f.

11. For a discussion of this tradition in the Carolingian era, and for the dependence of the coronation rites on the Byzantine tradition, see Poupardin, "L'Onction," 114f.

12. On Hincmar, see n. 8. See also Bloch, *Les Rois*, 226, for a discussion of the parallels between Clovis's and Christ's baptisms. At Christ's baptism, a dove appeared and a voice announced "Thou art my beloved son" (Luke 3:21). The parallel appearance of the dove for Clovis may allude to a similar filial acknowledgment; for the genealogical connections that were developed between Christ and Clovis, see chapter 5.

13. I Chronicles 11; I Kings 10:6. Samuel anoints David in accordance with the mandate of Yahweh. For biblical citations and a discussion of the anointing of all the Jewish kings as an act which established their special relationship with God, see De Vaux, "Le Roi d'Israël," 133.

The principle of primogeniture is established in Genesis 17:5 when God makes a covenant with Abraham, promising him the land of Cana as the everlasting possession of his descendants. In Psalms 89, God makes a permanent covenant with David: "I will establish your descendants forever. . . . I have anointed [David]. . . . I will crush his foes . . . and he shall say to me 'Thou art my Father.' . . . I will make him the . . . highest of the Kings of the earth." For the Jewish king as the *Imago Dei*, see Beskow, *Rex Gloriae*, 117, 253.

14. On the desire of Clovis's minister Avit to compare the king's baptism to the ritual of the kings of Israel, see Tessier, *Baptême*, n. 84; this association is evoked by Avit's words: "membra regia . . . cum se servis Dei inflecteret timendum gentibus caput, cum sub casside crinis nutritus salutarem galeam sacrae unctionis indueret, cum intermisso loricarum immaculati artus simili vestium candore fulgerent," (108). On the meaning of the unction, see Goelzer, *Latin*, 450–51, and Bloch, *Les Rois*, 196.

15. Luke 3:21 traces Jesus' heritage through Adam, Noah, Abraham, Saul, David, and Solomon to Joseph, the husband of Mary. Also in Revelations 21:16, Christ declares "I am the root and the offspring of David." See also Matthew 1:1, Acts 2:30, II Corinthians 6:18, and Hebrews 1:5. For the sources which variously claim this descent through Joseph or Mary and for a discussion of the messianic significance of this heritage, see Beskow, *Rex Gloriae*, 90ff. For the dual descent as the basis of His legitimacy as both priest and king, see ibid., 110f.

16. For differences between Arianism and Orthodox Catholicism as they affect the imperial position, see Beskow, *Rex Gloriae*, 314.

17. According to a legend developed in the fourteenth century, the fleur-de-lis which decorated Clovis's shield and which guaranteed his victory, was either brought to him by an angel or revealed to his wife by a prophet. For a discussion of these legends see Bloch, *Les Rois*, 229ff.; these and other legends about Clovis are discussed and dated in Beaune, "Saint Clovis," 139–56.

18. See chapter 5 for the genealogical link that Einhard established between Charlemagne and Clovis.

19. The imperial position is discussed throughout the chapters of this book. For the tradition as it applies to the French kings, see the discussion in Bloch, *Les Rois*, 229ff. French pretensions are also discussed in Zeller, "Rois de France," 237–342, 497–535; and more recently by Robert Scheller in a series of articles in *Simiolus* (1981–82 and 1983). These authors do not seize

on the significance of the blood-link for these pretensions; this important link will be discussed in chapter 5.

20. Scholz, trans., *Carolingian Chronicles*, 81.

21. For Charlemagne as the successor of Constantine and Theodosius and for his empire as a prefiguration on earth of the City of God, see Ganshof, *Carolingians*, chapter 4, citing early bibliography. In the Renaissance, the German humanist Wimpfeling asserted that the empire was not actually transferred to the Germans since Diocletian, Decus, Probus, Justinian, and Valentinian were all German. It was not their warlike valor which won back the empire, he said, but German piety. Constantinople lacked similar piety; therefore the empire was removed from the Byzantines and given to the Germans. Wimpfeling's statement is cited in Borchardt, *German Antiquity*, 102.

22. Replaced in an eighteenth-century redecoration, the original image is known only from drawings, the earliest of which is the sixteenth-century drawing illustrated here. See Schramm, *Die deutschen Kaiser*, 150f.; Belting, "Die beiden Palastaulen," 55–83; and Hauck, "Missionsauftrag," 294f.

23. See Mütherich, "Book Illumination," 601ff.

24. For Aachen as the "New Rome," see Hammer, "Concept," 62. Given the tribal arguments regarding the indigenous home of the Trojans, it is likely that each transfer was conceived as a return to origins. Support for this idea appears in chapter 5.

25. See the introduction to Einhard, *Life of Charlemagne*, 11.

26. Einhard, "Karolus Magnus," ll. 92ff. Portions of the text and translation appear in Godman, *Poetry*, 196ff.

27. Otto Zwierlein interprets the lines as a reference to Aeneas's founding of sites in Carthage, Sicily, and Rome, see "Karolus Magnus–Alter Aeneas," 45ff. He makes additional references to the *Aeneid* in the poem and to Einhard's role in refashioning the image of Charlemagne after this epic. See also Godman, *Poets and Emperors*, 85ff. The lines also evoke Romulus's outlining of the walls in the culminating Trojan settlement in Rome, where he marked the boundaries of a temple to Jupiter on the Cap-

itoline (Ovid *Fasti* IV.820f., and Livy *Roman History* I.10.5). Charlemagne is compared to Romulus and proclaimed the restorer of Rome's Golden Age by Charlemagne's court poet Hibernicus: "Charlemagne revives the pristine era . . . in which Romulus governed" (Hibernici Exulis, in "Versus Karoli Imperatoris," *Monumenta Germaniae Historia* [hereafter referred to as MGH], *Poetarum Latinorum Medii Aevi*, vol. 1, no. 2, pp. 400–401).

28. Important Carolingian corrections to the manuscript are attributed to scholars at Tours in the second quarter of the ninth century. See Wright, *Vergilius Vaticanus*, 35f.

29. Einhard, "Karolus Magnus," ll. 93–114, in Godman, *Poetry*, 203; see n. 93 on p. 202 for the reference to Augustus in *Virgil, Aeneid* V.358; see also Zwierlein, "Karolus Magnus," 44ff.

30. On Alcuin's letter, see Godman, *Poets and Emperors*, 75. The same phrase is recalled by the court poet Ermoldus Nigellus, who applies its meaning to Charlemagne's son: "Illic ergo pius Caesar dat iura subactis more suo regni rite revoluit opus" (*In honorem Hludlowici* IV.285–86).

31. *Virgil, Aeneid* VI.853; see chapter 1.

32. See Wright, *Vergilius Vaticanus*, 17, 36f.

33. See Zwierlein, "Karolus Magnus," 48; he also draws attention to Charlemagne's sense of the antique in the naming of his court humanists: Alcuin was called Flaccus; Moduin, Naso.

34. For the tradition that Charlemagne received the unction with the crowning and for its sacramental aspect, see Bloch, *Les Rois*, 464. For the tradition that the Carolingians were anointed as kings in imitation of Saul and David, see Poupardin, "L'Onction," 113f. This parallel is drawn, for example, in a ninth-century account of the emperor's coronation: "Modicum post en diodema / Caesar habet capiti gemmis auroque levatum / Unguine nectarei simul est respersus olivi. Caelicolis qui mos olim succrevit Hebraeis, Lege sacra solitis reges atque ungere vaturus quod Christus erat dux atque sacerdos" (*In Gesta Berengarii*, ed. Ernestus Dümmler, MGH, vol. 1, bk. 4, vv. 176–78). On the miracle of the sword, see Borchardt, *German Antiquity*, 51; for the Holy Blood, 86. For the miraculous Oriflamme, see Gervais Chronicle, in Richeri, *Gesta Senoniensis Ecclesia*, MGH. *Scriptorum rerum Germanicarum*, vol. 25, p. 295. A Langobardian-Carolingian, eighth-

century lance containing a nail from the Cross is thought to have been in the possession of Charlemagne; it was later revered as the lance with which Longinus opened the side of Christ. Regarding the translation of the lance to Charlemagne see Bloch, *Les Rois*, p. 234f. This lance, named *Monjoie* in honor of the wood of the Cross contained in its hilt, was considered the *signum regis Karolis*.

35. See Dempf, *Sacrum Imperium*, 87. Isidore of Seville (570–636) had defined the Christian emperor's status when he reminded his readers that the kings and emperors of old were also priests or pontiffs and emperors. See the discussion in Borchardt, *German Antiquity*, 194.

36. On Charlemagne's kingly and priestly roles and for his acclamation as *Rex et Sacerdos*, see Kantorowicz, *Laudes Regiae*, 47, 70, 142. The title Holy Roman emperor was developed by the Hohenstaufen emperors and applied retroactively to Charlemagne.

37. For the background to Eastern emperor worship see Delatte, *Traités*, 47ff.

38. On the development of these legends, see the editorial notes in Einhard, *Vita*, 26f., 126ff. On the Medieval ruler cult, see Kantorowicz, *Laudes Regiae*, 62f.

39. See notes to Einhard, *Vita*, 130.

40. See Owen, trans., *Legend of Roland*, 167. For the use of the Moses metaphor to apply to Constantine's victory, see chapter 2 at n. 50.

41. See Sears, "Louis the Pious," 616f. She notes that the drawing follows ten pairs of combatants modeled on Prudentian types that are contained in a separate but contemporary quire of the Prudentius manuscript.

42. See Hauck, "Missionsauftrag," 276f. For a general discussion of the Byzantine inspiration of Carolingian art and ceremony, see Beckwith, "Byzantine Influence," 288–300.

43. See Scholz, trans., *Carolingian Chronicles*, 80, and notes to Einhard, *Vita*, 129.

44. The list of relics Charlemagne received from the Byzantine emperor includes others which similarly attest to the divinity, the priesthood, and the humanity of Christ: drops of Mary's milk, Christ's swaddling cloth, the knife and dish with which Christ ate on Maundy Thursday, wood and nails from the Cross, the spear of Longinus, the shroud which covered

His head. In the most important of these legends, the twelfth-century account attributed to
the Pseudo-Turpin, the archbishop of Reims—
which also includes the apparition of Saint
James—these are awarded at Constantinople,
where the ruler, named Constantine, recognizes
Charlemagne as the Roman emperor. On the legend of Pseudo-Turpin, see Owen, trans., *Legend of
Roland*, 45, 167f. For a fifteenth-century recapitulation of the legends, see Dynter, *Chronique*, bk. 2,
chap. 23, p. 373ff. On the acclamation of the day
of Resurrection, see ibid., 376.

45. In the *Psychomachia*, Prudentius recounts
the parallel legend of the flowering rod of Aaron
which is given to the ruler of the New Rome, see
chapter 2.

46. In the introduction to his translation of
the *Anticlaudian*, William Hafner Cornog (Alain de
Lille, "Anticlaudian," 9ff.) discusses the scant bio-
graphical details on Alain that include problems
of nationality, date and place of birth, education,
and career. It is postulated that he had connections with Theoderic, who took possession of
Flanders, superseding William the Norman, in
the year 1128. Other critics connect him with
Aquitaine. Quotations from the *Anticlaudian* are
taken from Cornog's translation.

47. John of Garland refers to Alain as
"Vergilio melior and Homero certior." The
phrase is quoted in Cornog's introduction to the
Anticlaudian, 20. Cornog notes that many scholars
of the thirteenth century considered Alain one
of the great poets of their age. See Bossuat (Alain
de Lille, *Anticlaudianus*, ed. Bossuat, 43) on Alain's
immediate and lasting success; he notes that few
authors were so often copied from the thirteenth
to the fifteenth centuries. There were two contemporary glosses on Alain's work: the earlier
by Ralph de Longo Campo in ca. 1216 and the
second, a chiefly marginal commentary, by
William of Auxerre in 1231.

48. The Virtues take on the identification
given them in Prudentius's text where they are
called supernal soldiers (book 1). Bossuat, who
notes that Vergil is Alain's most frequently cited
author, also notes that Alain takes the battle of
the Virtues and Vices directly from Prudentius;
Bossuat cites specific borrowings from the *Aeneid*
and from the *Psychomachia* for the characteristics
of the Vices (Alain de Lille, *Anticlaudianus*, ed.
Bossuat, notes to bk. VIII, ll. 232, 289). Cornog

(Alain de Lille, "Anticlaudian," trans. Cornog, intro., 39) notes that "Alain's allegory of the perfect
youth's battle with the vices recalls Prudentius'
Psychomachia in general outline but has the individual variation of the youth, the embodiment
of all the virtues, combating the hosts of evil."
He does not develop the analogy beyond this
comment. Neither of these critics considers
Alain's poem in the context of the developing
topos of the Roman imperial myth that is the
concern of this chapter. Unless otherwise noted,
the interpretation of the text and the citations
that substantiate this line of thought are my own
contributions.

49. For an interpretation of the *Anticlaudian*
as an epic of knightly adventure, in which the
Virtues send Prudence as an emissary on behalf
of Nature, the feudal suzerain, to God, for assistance in putting the vassalage back in order, see
the critical comments in Alanus de Insulis, *Anticlaudianus*, ed. Sheridan, 70. This interpretation is
sustained by the courtly imagery of the courts of
nature and of God.

50. See Alain de Lille, "Anticlaudian," trans.
Cornog, intro., 27.

51. The concept of man as microcosm,
which has its roots in Chalcidius's commentary
on Plato's *Timaeus*, finds its application to the
ruler in Macrobius's *Commentary on the Dream of
Scipio*, the classical literary description of the apotheosis of the prince. In *The Cosmographia* of
Bernard Silvestris (trans. Wetherbee, 3), which is
divided into books on the Megacosmos and the
Microcosmos, Silvestris (fl. 1145–53), an important influence on Alain, provides a formal ordering of Nature as a reflection of the mind of God.
Silvestris's microcosmic man is created before
the beginning of time (*Cosmographia*, 107). Alain's
new microcosmic man is a corrective to the errors of human nature.

52. For the positive attitudes towards the
Goths of both Honorius and his regent Stilicho,
see Reydellet, *Royauté*, 138f. This attitude seems to
have endeared Honorius to a medieval author
writing in support of northern imperial sovereignty.

53. Cited in Borchardt, *German Antiquity*, 241.

54. Alain defines his source and his intention in the introduction to his poem. In *In
Rufinum* (396) Claudian used the topos of the warring moral states to refer to Stilicho's battle

against Rufinus, who is represented as the epitome of vice. In this poem, revising Horace (*Ode* III, 4), the author adapted the Gigantomachia to the Christian cause to refer to the battle between the ministers of emperors Honorius and Arcadius for the universal sovereignty of Rome. In the *Anticlaudian*, which sustained the northern empire's claim to imperial legitimacy, the Vices are chthonic deities, following Prudentius.

55. See Pierre Duhem, *Le Système du monde*, vol. 3 (Paris, 1915), 223. This inspiration is discussed in Lottin, "Traité," 37–38. The position is supported by Alain's dependence on Bernard Silvestris's microcosmic man, who is the first human creation. Christel Meier discusses a new interpretation in the later commentary of William of Auxerre, where the New Man is identified with the incarnated Christ, and the war against the Vices with Christ's battle against the devil ("Rezeption," 474).

56. Alain de Lille, *Anticlaudianus*, ed. Bossuat, 38, refers the description to Vergil's *Fourth Eclogue*.

57. Alain de Lille, "Anticlaudian," trans. Cornog, bk. I, chap. 5, p. 56: "Here [in Nature's cosmic throne room] our Ennius intones the fortunes of Priam. Here a Maevius . . . portray[s] the gests of the duke of Macedon. . . . Here Nero blasts the world. . . . Broken by love, Paris . . . makes war in the service of Venus . . . Nature . . . holds her rights in these seats and . . . designs laws." Together with philosophers and authors of ancient history and myth are mythical figures drawn from the Trojan myth: "Alcides, cunning Ulysses . . . Turnus . . . and Cytherea" (ibid., bk. I, chap. 4, p. 55).

58. Ibid., bk. II, chap. 5, p. 70.

59. Ibid. The Emperor Nero is condemned by the Counsel for spreading crime through the world; he has been identified by some critics with the English King Henry II (d. 1183), who was planning a Syrian expedition in alliance with Frederick Barbarossa; on this see the discussion of the poem's allusion to historical personages in Alain de Lille, "Anticlaudian," trans. Cornog, intro., 28.

60. Alain de Lille, "Anticlaudian", trans. Cornog, bk. II, chap. 5, p. 70.

61. Ibid., bk. I, chap. 6, p. 57.

62. Ibid., bk. II, chap. 7, p. 74. For Alain's dependence on the fifth-century author Martianus Capella's *De nuptiis Philologiae et Mercurii* for the con-

cept that the Liberal Arts are the indispensable instruments of philosophy and necessary to the journey towards the throne of God, see Alain de Lille, "Anticlaudian," trans. Cornog, intro., 32–34. For a discussion of illustrations to Alain's text, see Meier, ed., "Rezeption," 474–75.

63. Alain de Lille, "Anticlaudian," trans. Cornog, bk. V, chap. 1, p. 103.

64. Noted in Alain de Lille, *Anticlaudianus*, ed. Bossuat, 223.

65. Alain de Lille, "Anticlaudian," trans. Cornog, bk. V, chap. 9, p. 115.

66. Ibid., bk. VI, chap. 2, p. 119.

67. Ibid., bk. VI, chap. 4, p. 122. For a precedent for placing these heroes in the empyrean, see Silvestris, *Cosmographia*, 76.

68. Alain de Lille, "Anticlaudian," trans. Cornog, bk. VI, chap. 6, p. 125.

69. Ibid., bk. VI, chap. 7, p. 126.

70. Ibid., bk. VI, chap. 8, p. 127.

71. Ibid, bk. VII, chap. 1, p. 129.

72. Ibid, bk. VII, chaps. 1–2, pp. 129–31. Here Alain adapts the topos of the *puer-senex* to the New Man.

73. Ibid., bk. VII, chaps. 5–6, pp. 135–36.

74. Ibid., bk. VII, chap. 6, p. 137.

75. For a discussion of Alain's source in Boethius, for a brief discussion of visual and literary traditions, and for a Renaissance representation of the goddess that conforms with Alain's description, see Tanner, "Chance and Coincidence," 542.

76. Alain de Lille, "Anticlaudian," trans. Cornog, bk. VIII, chap. 1, p. 141f. See Meier, ed., "Rezeption," 510, n. 307, for a reference to a manuscript illumination in which the wheel of fortune is ridden by Roman emperors. For the prominence of wheel of fortune imagery in a poem for Lothar II, Charlemagne's grandson, see Godman, *Poets and Emperors*, 162. For the application of the topos to Emperor Charles V, see chapter 4.

77. Alain de Lille, "Anticlaudian," trans. Cornog, bk. VIII, chap. 2, p. 143.

78. Ibid., bk. VIII, chap. 3, p. 145.

79. Ibid., bk. VIII, chap. 4, p. 146.

80. Ibid., bk. VIII, chap. 7, pp. 149–50.

81. Ibid., bk. VIII, chap. 6, p. 149. See Alain de Lille, *Anticlaudianus*, ed. Bossuat, notes to l. 320 for the correspondences to Vergil's description of Aeneas's divinely factored shield.

82. Alain de Lille, "Anticlaudian," trans. Cornog, bk. VIII, chap. 7. The New Man emerges in bk. 8, chap. 7, p. 150, to become the epic hero.

83. Ibid., bk. IX, chaps. 1–7, pp. 150–59.

84. Ibid., bk. IX, chap. 8, pp. 160–61.

85. Ibid., bk. IX, chap. 8, pp. 159–60: "The clamor of Avarice remains. . . . But Virtue who rains gifts, who lavishes endowments, does not bury her moneys nor imprison her resources in a coffer, but pours forth her riches freely without hope of return. . . . She attacks Avarice. Now the routed cohort of crimes bears back its arms into the realm of the dead, and is amazed at itself conquered. Victory accrues to the youth."

86. Ibid., bk. IX, chap. 8, p. 160.

87. For the anticipation of this in Bernard Silvestris, see introduction to the *Cosmographia*, 58.

88. Alain is one of the first medieval Latin writers influenced by Arab astrology; that influence is felt in the theory of zodiacal influences. For the glosses on Alain that expand the identification of the constellations with the pagan myths, see Alain de Lille, "Anticlaudian," trans. Cornog, notes to bk. V, chap. 1, p. 179.

89. "to him God reveals the universe's development from its beginnings . . ." Einhard, "Karolus Magnus," l. 81, in Godman, *Poetry*, 203.

90. "He has discovered every path of learning and all the recondite aspects of the disciplines and the secret hidden words. He alone was capable in his piety of taking up all talents and leaving all masters behind him in his accomplishments; for just as he surpasses other kings in the loftiness of his power, so he outstrips everyone else in his culture" (ibid, ll. 82–87). See also Einhard, *Life*, trans. Turner, 54ff.: "He took lessons in grammar [from] Alcuin, the greatest scholar of his day. . . . The King spent much time and labor with him studying rhetoric, dialectics, and especially astronomy. . . . The plan that he adopted for his children's education was . . . to have both boys and girls instructed in the Liberal Arts, to which he also turned his own attention." The earliest representation of the Liberal Arts appears in a manuscript of Theodulf's poems. For the Virtues in the planets, see Theodulf's poem *De Septem Liberalibus Artibus in Quadam Pictura Depictis*, p. 544, n. 2, and p. 546, n. 2, in MGH. *Poetarum Latinorum Medii Aevi*, vol. 1, ed. Dümmler. For one example of the revival of astrology under Charlemagne, where the stars are given a Christian significance, see chapter 8.

91. "What wonder is it if the eternal shepherd made so great a man His pastor to tend His flocks . . . your noble understanding [reminds us of] Solomon's, your strength reminds us of David and your beauty is Joseph's own. Guardian of treasure, avenger of crimes" (Theodulf *On the Court* ll. 29ff., text in Godman, *Poetry*, 151). See editor's note, 29–30, regarding the common application of these biblical pseudonyms to Charlemagne after 794. See also the discussion of the biblical parallels in Prudentius in chapter 2.

92. For Carolingian uses of the topos of the Virtues who victoriously defeat the Vices, see Wallach, *Alcuin and Charlemagne*, 231ff. For examples of the visual tradition in which the Virtues surround the Carolingian kings, see Katznellenbogen, *Allegories*, 31f.

93. See Schramm, *Die deutschen Kaiser*, 60f. Hrabanus Maurus, archbishop of Mainz and one of the most illustrious thinkers of the Middle Ages, was active at the court of Charlemagne's son Louis the Pious. In the *De rerum naturis* he took up the theme of the psychomachia, identifying the soldiers of Christ as those who fight against the devil and the Vices. See Sears, "Louis the Pious," 622f. On Hrabanus and Louis, see chapter 10.

94. For Alcuin's acquaintance and dependence on Prudentius's *Psychomachia*, which he used in his own treatise on the Virtues and Vices, see Wallach, *Alcuin and Charlemagne*, 235. For the frequent citations of Prudentius's *Psychomachia* and other of his works by Theodulf, see the notes to his poems in MGH. *Poetarum Latinorum Medii Aevi*, vol. 1, ed. Dümmler, pp. 446ff. In Theodulf's "Books I Used to Read," Vergil, Donatus, and Prudentius are held in the highest esteem; the poem also expresses his familiarity with the Roman imperial myth. For Theodulf's and Dungal's use of Prudentius, see Vest, "Prudentius in the Middle Ages," 86f. and 90ff. Vest notes the critics who identify Dungal with the author called Hibernicus Exul.

95. For Alain as the first author to introduce a central figure to replace Prudentius's personified Virtues, see Vest, "Prudentius in the Middle Ages," 140. For Alain's dependence on Prudentius, see ibid., 169f.

96. See Nigel Morgan, *Early Gothic Manuscripts* (I) 1190–1250 (Oxford, 1982), 127f.

97. See chapter 5.

CHAPTER 4

1. For a brief summary of these divisions
see Bloch, *Feudal Society*, 376–77.

2. There is a vast literature on the related
legends that deal with Trojan material. The *Brut*,
Eneas, and *Roman de Thebes* all belong to the mid–
twelfth century and are connected to various European courts. See Angeli, *L'Eneas*, 22, 62, 104, for
a history of this epic literature. For the *Eneas* as
the earliest of the vernacular reworkings of
Vergil's text, see Jerome E. Singerman, *Under
Clouds of Poetry: French and English Reworkings of the
Aeneid 1160–1513* (New York, 1985), 33. For the
discussion of two distinct genres—the *History of
the Caesars*, supposedly composed in antiquity,
and the *Faits de Romains*, a chivalric romance—that
were joined in the fourteenth century, see Meyer,
"Les Premières Compilations." See also Louis-
Fernand Flutre, "Le Fait des romains dans littérature française et italienne du XIII au XVI siècle"
(Ph.D diss., Paris, 1932); Buchthal, *Historia Troiana*,
briefly discusses the medieval accounts and some
of their ancient sources.

3. Though a precise dating is disputed,
both texts have been dated to the later Roman
empire. See for texts as well as questions of dating Griffin, *Dares and Dictys*. Angeli, (*L'Eneas*, 62)
notes that Dares and Dictys were in circulation
by the first half of the twelfth century. For earlier
references to Dares' history in the Merovingian
chronicle of Fredegarius, see chapter 5. An earlier version of the Troy myth, the *Excidium
Troiae*—a text whose earliest extant manuscript
may date to the end of the ninth century—does
not follow Dares and Dictys but rather a more
classical sequence of events, see E. Bagby At-
wood and Virgil K. Whitaker, eds., *Excidium Troiae*,
The Mediaeval Academy of America (Cambridge,
Mass., 1944), xi.

4. Dictys also traced the ancestry of the
rulers of Troy and Greece to a common seed.
Helena reveals that Danaos and Agenor were
both Priam's and her progenitors, because
Danaos's daughter Electra was impregnated by
Jove and gave birth to Dardanus, from whom all
the kings of Troy were descended. In a Renais-
sance Venetian edition of Dictys, Berosus the
Chaldean is cited as the source of this genealogy,
Ditte Candiotto et Darete Frigio della Guerra Troiana
(Venice, 1543), 121.

5. Meyer, "Les Premières Compilations,"

38ff. discusses this amalgam in which profane
history, which begins with the kings of Assyria
and the reign of Egypt and the history of Danaus,
is coordinated with sacred history. See ibid., 55,
for other typical interpolations of Christian
meaning into the texts.

6. See ibid., esp. 37ff., for the compilations
that amalgamate the Trojan legend with Roman
history.

7. The use of Berosus as a common source
has not been observed in the literature on this
topos. Berosus is cited as the authoritative voice
of history by Guido della Colonna, Raoul
Lefèvre, and Jean Lemaire de Belges, inter alia.
See chapter 5 for a further discussion of this
issue.

8. See the citations from Berosus in Müllerus, *Fragmenta Historicorum Graecorum*, 495–505.
For a discussion of Eusebius's *Chronographia*—
which was preserved and updated to 378 in Jerome's Latin translation, the *Interpretatio Chronicae
Eusebii Pamphili*, PL 27 (1846) col. 67, and to later
dates by other writers—as the dominant model
of world history, see Bloch, "Genealogy," 135ff.

9. See chapter 5.

10. See Joly, *Benoit*. Benoit himself indicates
Dares as his source in the Prologue, see this edition, p. 192. For problems of attribution and
chronology, see Angeli, *L'Eneas*, ix. Buchthal, *Historia Troiana*, 5, suggests that it was probably because of Benoit's literary success that interest in
the Trojan ancestry, which had flourished mainly
in the north, now spread to Italy. For the dating
and attribution of other Troy-related accounts to
the Anglo-Angevin court, see ibid., 22ff., and
101ff. The Carolingian Pippin the Short, king of
the Franks, united the Frankish realms with Aquitaine in 768. Eleanor of Aquitaine married
Henry Plantagenet, and Aquitania remained
united with England until 1453.

11. For the Latin text see Guido de Colum-
nis, *Historia Destructionis Troiae*, ed. Nathaniel Ed-
ward Griffin (Cambridge, Mass., 1936). For
English translations, see Guido delle Colonne,
Destruction of Troy, and *Historia Destructionis Troiae*.
The authors who follow Guido include Raoul
Lefèvre and Jean Lemaire de Belges, who are dis-
cussed below.

12. See Bayot, *La Légende de Troie*, 36, and
Guido de Columnis, *Historia Destructionis Troiae*, ed.
Griffin, xvii, regarding this supersession of influ-

ence. In England, Guido's version was used by Chaucer, Caxton, and Shakespeare. A German prose version of Guido's Latin work by Hans Mair was produced in 1391. For this, and the vernacular Trojan tradition in Germany, see Karin Schneider "Der 'Trojanische Krieg,'" 66, 73. For early Spanish versions of Guido's text, see *La Coronica Troyana: A Medieval Spanish Translation of Guido de Colonna's Historia Destructionis Troiae*, ed. Frank Pelletier Norris II, University of North Carolina Studies in the Romance Languages and Literatures, no. 90 (Chapel Hill, 1970), 14ff. The most complete Spanish version was prepared for Alonso X the Wise, king of the Germans and of Castile, see ibid, 13.

13. Guido himself refers his readers to the *Aeneid* in bk. XXXIII; he also records the Sibyl's admonition to Aeneas to seek the land of his ancient mother, which he learned was Italy, and he notes that Saturn was an ancestor (bk. LIX) (*Historia Destructionis Troiae*, ed. Griffin).

14. Guido begins his Trojan tale at the equinox, when the sun enters Aries, the constellation that commemorates the Golden Fleece. See chapter 8 for the crusading motives attached to the legend and to this cosmic emblem.

15. Buchthal, *Historia Troiana*, 6, notes that Guido belonged to the group of high officials at the court of Emperor Frederick II and later of his son Manfred. See also Bayot, *La Légende de Troie*, 18.

16. In book IV Guido recounts the first destruction of Troy by Jason and Hercules. For the Argonautic story outline, see chapter 1. Buchthal, *Historia Troiana*, 40, suggests that the classicizing illustrations to the earliest Guido manuscripts may depend on Vergil's *Aeneid*, and mentions the famous illustrations in the *Vaticanus* and *Romanus* manuscripts (cf. figs. 2 and 3 for examples from the *Vergil Vaticanus*).

17. For Berosus as the source of this syncretism in the historical chronicles of Emperor Frederick I, see chapter 5.

18. See chapter 8. I have discussed the Order's Christian and imperial meanings in a talk entitled "Titian's *Danae* for Philip II and the Order of the Golden Fleece," College Art Association Annual Meeting, New York, 1985.

19. Guillaume Fillastre, *Le Premier Volume*, 9 verso. The *Argo* is called "an ark like Noah's." For fuller discussion of Fillastre's treatise, see chapter 8.

20. Lefèvre, *L'Histoire de Jason*. See ibid, 99, for a discussion of Philip's manuscripts of Trojan romances. For a visual example see chapter 8. The Burgundian Throne Room was decorated with a series of tapestries drawn from the extended medieval accounts of Troy (Tournai 1465–70), in which Caesar appears as a Burgundian duke. On the Argonautic tapestries, see Lefèvre, *L'Histoire de Jason*, 98ff.

21. Lefèvre, *Recueyell*, 9f. For the Burgundian imperial heritage, see chapter 5 and Bayot "Sur l'exemplaire," 183–90.

22. Lemaire de Belges, *Illustrations*. For a summary of content, see Doutrepont, *Jean Lemaire de Belges*, 41ff.

23. The commission was provided by Charles's aunt Margaret, who would later be his staunchest supporter in the battle to transfer the empire to Philip II. For Lemaire's subsequent attachment to the court of France see Abelard, *Illustrations*, 26. In a letter to Margaret of 1508 Lemaire announced that he was removing any anti-French statements previously contained in the legend and including passages that referred to the Peace of Cambrai, see Lemaire de Belges, *Illustrations*, 219. The Trojan legend was celebrated at the French courts of the sixteenth century by Ronsard and others who perpetuated a French version of the myth.

24. Lemaire showed how the blood of Burgundy was joined with that of France in the person of Blichilde, a descendent of Clovis and Clothilde who belonged to both lines, and how these lines were joined with those of Rome and of the house of Austria; see Doutrepont, *Jean Lemaire de Belges*, 73. Lemaire also traced the Trojans back to the original Italic races, who are descendants of Saturn, the grandson of Noah (*Illustrations*, bk. I, p. 32ff.). A parallel resolution between indigenous and classical tales of origin is provided in the Hapsburgs' mythical genealogies, see chapter 5. See also the link between this and the prophetic traditions, in chapter 6.

25. Lemaire de Belges, *Illustrations*, 272ff., 312ff.

26. Steppe ("Vlaams Tapijtwerk," 719–65) discusses the tapestries' dating, their relationship to Charles V, and the possible humanists who contributed to the program. Guy Delmarcel published a brief study of the tapestries as a didactic allegory for the emperor ("Los Honores"), drawn from his dissertation, "De Brusselse wandtapi-

jreeks *Los Honores* (1520–25): Een vortenspiegel voor de jonge keizer Karel V" (Ph.D. diss., Catholic University of Louvain, 1981). The dissertation has not been made available to the public, but he kindly informed me that his findings will be published in a forthcoming book. I have previously discussed the tapestries' dynastic context in "Titian," 160f. See also Junquera de Vega and Carretero, eds., *Catálogo*, 35–44.

27. Male, *L'Art religieux*, 367ff., first observed the relationship between the tapestries and Alain's *Anticlaudianus*, noting the correspondences in Prudence's journey to the realm of Divine Wisdom, in Fortune's realm, and in the battle of Virtues and Vices. See the discussion of various literary sources in Tormo y Monzó and Canton, *Los tapices*.

28. See chapter 5.

29. The inscription is transcribed in Juan Battista Crooke and Navarrot Valencia de Don Juan, *Tapices de la corona de Espana*, 2 vols. (Madrid, 1903), 1:24.

CHAPTER 5

1. There are many fascinating studies devoted to the mythic history of individual cultures—Roman, Byzantine, Frankish, and so forth. Bibliography on these subjects is provided in the individual notes. Among these, Frank L. Borchardt's *German Antiquity* is an outstanding introduction to the Franks' legendary past. Although Borchardt is interested in a broader range of subjects, references to important ancient, medieval, and Renaissance sources for the Trojan legend are scattered throughout his book. By exploring the mythical elements that contributed to the shaping of a national image, Borchardt alerts the reader to a body of imaginative literature that is generally ignored by the factual historian.

On the specific subject of Hapsburg genealogy, Simon Laschitzer wrote a number of excellent critical studies that appeared at the end of the nineteenth century: "Heiligen," and "Genealogie." In a pivotal article, Lhotsky ("Apis Colonna") continued these investigations. Although Lhotsky does not synthesize the significance of his findings, he restructures the contributing sources that describe the development of a Hapsburg legendary past. He also cites

earlier sources for the Franks' Trojan origins. Lhotsky's work served as the basis for a series of synthetic studies by Anna Coreth. For this chapter I have used chiefly "Dynastisch-politische Ideen," and "Wappenbuch." Through her insights into the significance of Lhotsky's findings—which she expands with additional sources—Coreth isolated a number of important ideological positions that the Hapsburgs developed on the basis of a legendary past.

2. The Holy Roman Empire ended when Napoleon forced the Hapsburg Emperor Franz I to abdicate in 1806 (Napoléon then appropriated the Roman imperial myth for himself), but the Hapsburgs continued to effectively perpetuate the imperial myth in their rule of the Austro-Hungarian Empire, which lasted until the monarchy's dissolution under Carl Franz Joseph at the end of World War I. Borchardt, *German Antiquity*, 314, notes that efforts to prove Trojan ancestry continued until the later nineteenth century.

3. See Ussani, *Studi*, 85ff., regarding the institution of the cult of the *divus Iulius* and the *genius Augusti*, and for the perpetuation of this cult by Tiberius who established a college of priests to tend the rites. See ibid., 88–89, regarding the basing of this religious stature on their mythic and epic genealogy, a status confirmed by the apotheosis of Julius Caesar and Augustus. The tradition is continued by the Flavians with the elevation of a temple to the *gens Flavia*; see ibid., 89 and 106. For the reference to this temple in Valerius Flaccus's *Argonautica*, see introduction to cited edition.

4. Virgil, *Aeneid* V.62, see chapter 1. Vergil created an imaginary temple to Augustus, who "shall possess the shrine," and he adorned it with Jove's Trojan progeny, "statues that breathe" of "the seed of Assaracus and the great names of the race sprung from Jove . . ." *Georgics* III.12ff.

5. For the Penates as gods of the Julian family, and again as the gods of the Roman state, see Fowler, *Aeneas*, 110. The Penates were, with the fillets of Vesta, among the seven signs of the perdurability of the Roman Empire. On Aeneas's shield, Augustus wins the battle of Actium with the great gods and the Penates by his side (*Aeneid* VIII.626ff.). On the occasion of Augustus's elevation to the office of Pontifex Maximus, Ovid proclaims these gods the emperor's kin: "Ye gods of ancient Troy, ye worthiest prize to him who bore ye . . . whose weight did save Aeneas from the

foe, a priest of the line of Aeneas handles your kindred divinities; Vesta, do thou guard his kindred head" (Ovid *Fasti* III.425f.). For Vesta's chapel in Augustus's own house on the Palatine, see *Fasti* IV.949f. For a learned exegesis on Vesta and the Penates, see Lipsius *De Vesta*.

6. See chapter 12.

7. On Aeneas's and Augustus's apotheoses, see chapter 1. Clovis's minister Avit asserted that the king's conversion assured for himself and for his posterity a place among the elect in heaven, see n. 35 this chapter. See the examples of the promise of a reign in heaven for Constantine, Theodosius, Charlemagne, and for the Saxons in Schramm, "Mitherrschaft im Himmel."

8. On Clovis, see Beaune, "Saint Clovis," 117f.; on Charlemagne, see *Die Ausstellung Karl der Grosse—Werk und Werkung*, Exhibition Catalogue (Aachen, 1965), entry 740. On ancient ruler worship in Byzantium and among the Carolingians, see Kantorowicz, *Laudes Regiae*, 62.

9. *Virgil, Aeneid* I.257–97. According to the interpretation of Donatus, the opening lines of Vergil's epic "Arms and the man" (*Aeneid* I.4) refer to Aeneas's divinely factored shield. The shield centered on the image of Aeneas's progeny Augustus in triumph: "Arma: scilicet, hoc est scutum et alia quae aenea Vulcanum fabricasse perscripsit. Virum; non ut sexum significaret sed virum qui talia arma tam magna pulchra habere vel gestare potuit" (Donati *Interpretationes Vergilianae*, I.1). For the shield, and for other genealogical references in the *Aeneid*, see chapter 1. For bibliographical references to sources and critical studies of Trojan ancestry among the ancients, see Taeger, *Charisma*, 49. The Julians claimed a dual divine descent, inheriting the divinity of Venus through Aeneas and that of Mars through Romulus. For claims to Trojan ancestry during the Roman Republic, see T. P. Wiseman, "Legendary Genealogies in Late-Republican Rome," *Greece and Rome* 21 (1974): 153–64.

10. See *Ausonius*, trans. Hugh G. Evelyn White, 2 vols., Loeb Classical Library (London, 1951), vol. 1: *On the Twelve Caesars*, bk. 14, chap. 6, Nero, II.5–6, who calls "nero saevus ultimus Aeneadum."

11. Prudentius, vols. 1 and 2, *A Reply to the Address of Symmachus*, bk. 2, ll. 586ff.: to "bring into partnership peoples of different speech and realms of discordant manners, determined that

all the civilized world should be harnessed to one ruling power . . . for no bond is made that is worthy of Christ unless unity of spirit leagues together the nations it associates."

12. Ibid., bk. 1, ll. 286ff. The phrase continues: "whose will it was that kingdoms should run their appointed courses and the triumphs of Rome grow from more to more, and that He should enter the world in the fullness of time."

13. *Prudentius*, vol. 1, *Apotheosis*, 446–48; see chapter 1. See also the introduction to the Loeb edition, p. ix. For another example of this idea, see *Prudentius*, vol. 2, *Crowns of Martyrdom*, bk. 2, ll. 425f., in my chapter 9.

14. See Coleman, *Constantine*, 149. See chapter 1, n. 4, for the topos of Dardanus's receipt of Troy in exchange for Italic lands in the medieval legends of Troy.

15. The rhetorician Eumenius asserted Constantine's Claudian descent in a panegyric delivered before the emperor in 310, see Coleman, *Constantine*, 113. Constantine's descent from Aeneas as the kin of the noble Eutropius, is recorded by the fifteenth-century antiquarian Pomponio Leto in connection with Constantius Clorus: "Ille Constantius Cloros natus est patre Eutropio Romana gentis nobilissimo, qui genus ab Aenea deducebat . . .et matie Claudia Claudii aug. f. [augusti filia]" (Leto, *Romanae Historiae Compendium*, fol. 45r). For this gens, for Justinian as one of the Aeneadae, and for a retroactive construction of the Hapsburgs' Constantinian and other Byzantine ancestry, see chapter 10.

16. "Ilus, descendant of Dardanus, had lately founded [Troy]. . . . a celestial image of armed Minerva is believed to have leaped down on [its] hills. Apollo . . . gave this answer: 'Preserve the heavenly goddess, so shall ye preserve the city. She will transfer with herself the seat of empire'" (Ovid *Fasti* VI.419f.). See the Prologue for an instance of the continuing identification of Constantinople with Troy.

17. Constantine's transfer of the Palladium is elaborately described by Leto, *Romanae Historiae Compendium*, 55r–56r. He notes the various traditions of its heavenly origin, its form and its transfer by Constantine: "Quid & etiam Constantinopolim Palladium Roma translatum . . . 'Ex urbe Roma genitrice coclidem columnam porphyriam transferri insit, & locari in foro lapidibus strato, & variis signis circundato: & ex Troade de Aeneam

statuam Apollinis mirandae magnitudinis sup-
posito . . . sublato capite suum acommodavit co-
lumnaeque superposuit . . . necnon e clavum
tormenti Salvatoris . . . Palladium, ut credidit
varia coelo lapsum in . . . urbe Phrygia . . . Ubique inde Constantinus ferri iussit Constantinopolim, & locari in foro' . . ." He appears to
expand the account found in George Codrenos,
Historia Compendiae, in *Corpus Scriptorum Historia By-
zantinae,* ed. Immanuel Bekkero (Bonn, 1839).
Codrenos's account is noted in Vellay, *Légendes,*
481. For a parallel to the Palladium's powers, see
Eusebius's apotropeic definition of the Cross in
Drake, *In Praise of Constantine,* 94. For the continuing interchangeability of the Palladium with
Christ's insignia, see chapters 10 and 11.

18. For the designation of Constantinople as
"Rome" or the "New Rome" see Hammer, "Concept," 53f.

19. "Ast ab avus Anchise potens, qui ducit ab
illo / Troiano Anchisa longa post tempore nomen." Cited in Roth, "Trojansage," 36. The relationship is elaborated in later chronicles, such as
that by Ekkehard of Aura (d. 1125).

20. See Borchardt, *German Antiquity,* 204. On
Dungal (variously referred to as Hibernicus Exul),
see also Roth, "Trojansage," 36. See also Godman,
Poets and Emperors, 62, for the panegyric of Dungal
in which Charlemagne rouses the Franks to battle by recalling the Trojan origins of the race.

21. See chapter 3.

22. "Mensibus etiam iuxta propriam linguam
vocabula imposuit. Ianuarium wintarmanoth . . ."
(Einhard, *Vita,* 100). On Romulus, see Ovid *Fasti*
IV.23ff.

23. Ermoldus Nigellus, *Ad Pippinum Regum* II,
86: "Si Veneris soboles Priami si filius adsit Hector
et Aeneas cedet uterque tibi."

24. "Hoc patre Flodufus. . . . Huic erat Anchi-
sus frater [Flodulfo Harnulfi filio] / memorabilis
aevo, viribus infractis surgit quo patre Pippinus"
("Carmen de Exordio Gentis Francorum," p. 141,
l. 78f). The editor, Dümmler, notes the date of
ca. 844 and identifies the sources in Vergil and
Ovid.

25. See Devisse, *Hincmar,* 455ff.

26. For the Macedonian connection, see
Fredegarius *Chronicarum,* 45. Expanding on the
earlier account of Priam's Macedonian detour to
conclude that the Trojans, the Macedonians, and
the Franks are all of one seed, Ottfried von

Weissenburg (fl. 865) provided the first known
record of Charlemagne's descent from Alexander the Great, see Borchardt, *German Antiquity,*
201.

27. "Berta Caroli Mater Heraclitis Constantine politani Imperatoris filia. In duo divisa
Troiana propago parente / Iungitur in Berte
Pepini semine ventre, semine Pepini Troia sit una
sibi" (Godefridi Viterbiensis, *Speculum Regum,* 92–
93). This is recorded, for example, for the Saxon
Emperor Otto III, see Coreth, "Dynastisch-
politische Ideen," 87. For Charlemagne's adaptation of Constantine's cognomen, for other Constantinian appropriations by the Carolingian
court, and for the perpetuation of this tradition,
see chapter 10. For the identification of the imperial palace at Aachen with Constantinople, see
H. Fichtenau, "Byzanz und die Pfalz zu Aachen,"
*Mitteilungen des Instituts für österreichische Geschichts-
schreibung* 59 (1951): 195, and Beumann, "Nomen
imperatoris," 52f.

28. See Borchardt, *German Antiquity,* 32.

29. *The Germania of Tacitus,* ed. Rodney Potter
Robinson, Philological Monographs published by
the American Philological Association, no. 5
(Middletown, Conn., 1935), 272. A great deal
of literature has been devoted to the rediscovery
of Tacitus in the Renaissance, but the legend of
Tuisco already informs the medieval legends of
Troy.

30. See Karl Domanig, "Peter Flötner als
Plastiker und Medailleur," *Jahrbuch der
kunsthistorischen Sammlungen des allerhöchsten Kaiserhauses* 16 (1895): 11–19.

31. The *Alsatian Anonymous,* cited in Borchardt, *German Antiquity,* 116–17. We may see a
corollary to this tradition in the development of
an architectural style that appropriated the rustic
elements of Adam's house in Paradise as an indigenous "Gothic" style in Francia. The rustic
style accords with Vitruvius's definition of the origins of architecture. See Joseph Rykwert, *On
Adam's House in Paradise,* 2d ed. (Cambridge, Mass.,
1989), for a general discussion of Adam's primi-
tive dwelling. See p. 105 for Vitruvius's conception of architecture's origins, and p. 212 for the
popularity of Vitruvius in the ninth century.

32. Fredegarius *Chronicarum,* 47. For the legend that the Palladium was brought to Rome by
Fimbria, see Vellay, *Légendes,* 45.

33. On the *Liber Chronicarum,* popularly

known as the *Nuremberg Chronicle*, as the best
known of all items printed in the fifteenth century, with the exception of the Gutenberg Bible,
see Janet Ing, *Johann Gutenberg and His Bible* (New
York, 1988), 26. Ellen Shaffer, *The Nuremberg Chronicle* (Los Angeles, 1950), 22, notes that the chronicle's patron, Sebald Schreyer, had grown up at
the court of Frederick III and had witnessed the
emperor's coronation in Italy.

34. See Godefridi Viterbiensis *Speculum Regum*, 61–62.

35. Avit, Epistle 36, cited in Tessier, *Baptême*,
106 n. 72. Avit declared that by his conversion
Clovis became the founder of a new dynasty and
assured for himself and for his posterity a celestial royalty among the elect.

36. Fredegarius *Chronicarum*, 26ff. For Fredegarius's account that Meroveus was born from his
mother's union with a marine divinity, see Kurth,
Histoire poétique, 151.

37. "Igitur ab Anastasio codecillos de consola-
lata accepit, et . . . blattera indutus et clamide im-
ponens vertice diadema ab . . . ea die Tamquam
consul aut Augustus vocitatus est." (Gregory of
Tours, *Historia Francorum*, bk. 2, chap. 38, pp. 102f.).

38. See Brennan, "Image of the Frankish
Kings," and Godman, *Poets and Emperors*, 24ff. For a
more extensive discussion of Fortunatus's poetry
with an eye to its political content, see Hoeflich,
"Between Gothia and Romania,"123ff. Hoeflich,
p. 125f., discusses Fortunatus's constant stress on
the royal stirps of the Merovingian gens. On
Venantius, see also chapter 10.

39. On Hunibald, see Roth, "Trojansage," 38,
and for earlier sources that sustain a Trojan origin
for the Franks, see ibid., 50. Later texts proclaimed Clovis's direct descent from Aeneas.

40. The Sicilian Diodorus composed a universal history in Greek; another contemporary,
Pompeius Trogus, a native of Gaul and contemporary of Augustus, composed the first universal
history in Latin. He includes the Assyrians,
Medes, Persians, and Greeks and ends with Augustus's conquest of the Cantabri. This lost work
was abridged by Justin in the second or third
century A.D. See Moses Hadas, *A History of Latin Literature* (New York, 1952). For Berosus's contribution to the genre, see chapter 4.

On Eusebius's chronicle, which was embellished by Orosius and others, see my chapter 4.

41. Fredegarius calls Adam the first pontifex
of the Jews (*Chronicarum*, 20f.). On the anonymous compilers who go under the name Fredegarius and on the dating of this chronicle, see
Roth, "Trojansage," 34; Kurth, *Histoire poétique*,
507ff.; and Borchardt, *German Antiquity*, 195f., who
discusses the various ways in which Troy was
used as a German foundation myth. For similar
claims to Trojan heritage among other European
countries, see Borchardt, *German Antiquity*, 312.

42. Fredegarius *Chronicarum*, 26ff.

43. Ibid., 45ff. For preexistent implications
in the writing of Gregory, bishop of Tours (538–
94), who grafted Frankish history onto that of
the universal chronicle, see Coreth "Dynastisch-
politische Ideen," 84. A popular medieval source
for disseminating the Trojan origins of the
Franks was the *Speculum Historialium* of Vincent of
Beauvais (1244) which had been published eight
times by the end of the fifteenth century.

44. Fredegarius *Chronicarum*, 45ff. The text of
Dares history is appended to Fredegarius's
chronicle in the cited edition (*Chronicarum*, 194ff.).
On Dares, see chapter 4.

45. See the continuation of Fredegarius's account (*Chronicarum*, 168ff.) and the ninth-century
genealogy of the Frankish kings, beginning with
Priam and proceeding through Clovis to present
times in G. H. Pertz, ed., *Regum Francorum Genealogiae*, MGH. *Scriptorum rerum Germanicarum*, vol. 2,
310–11 (Hannover, 1829), cited in Borchardt, *German Antiquity*, 201.

46. For further bibliography on the Byzantine, Merovingian, Carolingian, and Ottonian emperors' identification with David, and for images
that express the concept, see Steger, *David Rex*,
121ff.

47. See Weitzmann, *Joshua Roll*, 102ff. and
114, and Shapiro, "Joshua Roll," 57ff.

48. Shapiro, "Joshua Roll," 58.

49. For the application to Clovis of imagery
derived from the panegyric of Corippus on Justin II, see Brennan, "Image," 3f.

50. Cited in Brennan, "Image," 8, who notes
that the church was founded by the king.

51. For the association of Clovis's baptism—
which is prefigured in the Old Testament
anointing—with royal coronation, see W. M.
Hinckle, *The Portal of the Saints of Reims Cathedral*
(n.p., 1965), 37f., and Beskow, *Rex Gloriae*, 247f.
and 133 n. 1.

52. See Watson, *Early Iconography*, 134ff. and plate 32, and Beskow, *Rex Gloriae*, 110.

53. The Tree of Jesse was first figured at Saint Denis ca. 1140, see Watson, *Early Iconography* 77, 166–67.

54. This is recorded by Hincmar de Reims, archbishop of Metz, on the occasion of the coronation of Charles the Bald in 869, see Devisse, *Hincmar*, 455. For the Carolingian-Merovingian "kinship by adoption," see Steger, *David Rex*, 131.

55. For a discussion of Charlemagne's regnum Davidicum, see Kantorowicz, *Laudes Regiae*, 55ff., and *King's Two Bodies*, 77ff., where he characterizes the emperor's reign as "haloed by the perennitas of the pious Kings of Israel, in whom the Carolingian imperial idea of the regnum Davidicum became manifest." For images of Carolingian rulers that carry this significance, see Steger, *David Rex*, 113, 127f. Alcuin expressed this inheritance when he praised "Charlemagne who both uses the sword of triumphal power . . . like his biblical prototype David and who appears before the people as the predicator of God's law" (Alcuin, Epistle 41, in *MGH. Epistolae Karolini Aevi*, vol. 4, bk. 2, ed. Ernestus Dümmler [Berlin, 1895]). For other literary examples, see Godman, *Poets and Emperors*, 65ff. Steger, *David Rex*, 127f., notes Pippin's identification with David in a contemporary papal document, while Kantorowicz, *Laudes Regiae*, 64, observes that the donation of Constantine was invented at the time of Pippin's anointment, when the homage to the Davidian kings becomes associated with the popes.

56. Schramm, *Herrschaftszeichen*, vol. 1, n. 44, and Folz, *Couronnement*, 324 and fig. 7.

57. See chapter 3. These miracles continue to be cited in support of dynastic claims; see, for example, Dynter's chronicle, n. 134.

58. For the tradition that the sword from heaven remained in the imperial regalia, see Borchardt, *German Antiquity*, 51. For the connection between Clovis's arms and Charlemagne's lance, see Bloch, *Les Rois*, 234, n. 5.

59. On this Bible, see Schramm, *Die deutschen Kaiser*, 170ff. For the Carolingian's lily crown as one of David's attributes, see Steger, *David Rex*, 12.

60. For recall of both traditions in the literature of the court, see Zwierlein, "Karolus Magnus–Alter Aeneas," 48ff.

61. See text at n. 97.

62. See chapter 2 for Prudentius's poetic formulation of this concept.

63. Sedulius Scotus, "Carmina," 151. For the phrases comparing Charlemagne and Augustus, the editor notes the poet's reliance on Vergil and Ovid.

64. Ermoldus Nigellus, *In honorem Hludlowici*. See the notes by Dümmler, for Ermoldus's frequent borrowings from Vergil. A portion of the poem is translated by Godman, *Poetry*, 251–55, who notes that a comparable cycle of narrative paintings survives in the Church of Saint John in Müstair, Graubünden (see W. Braufels, *Die Welt der Karolinger und ihr Kunst* [Munich, 1958], 94, 220ff., and plates XV–XVI). The Ingelheim cycle is discussed in Lammers, "Bildprogramm," 226–89.

65. Ermoldus Nigellus, *In honorem Hludlowici*, ll. 179ff., in Godman, *Poetry*, 251.

66. Lammers, "Bildprogramm," 257ff. Lammers cites Orosius for the schema of the Four World Monarchies, but it is important to be aware of Fredegarius's intermediary adaptation of the topos to the Frankish kings.

67. Ermoldus Nigellus, *In honorem Hludlowici*, in Godman, *Poetry*, 255.

68. Ermoldus Nigellus, *In honorem Hludlowici*, 66f.

69. Virgil, *Aeneid* VI.851–53, see chapter 1.

70. Ermoldus Nigellus, *In honorem Hludlowici*, in Godman, *Poetry*, 255.

71. Lammers, "Bildprogramm," 251ff., and charts on 286ff. Although Lammers hints at an ancestral link between Charlemagne and the Byzantine emperors, whom he places on a common wall, he does not suggest a link between the pagan and the biblical antetypes.

72. Ibid., 278. For a further discussion of Charlemagne as the "New Constantine," see chapter 10.

73. For the consolidation of these possessions, through Otto II's marriage to the Byzantine princess Teofane, see Leo Santifaller, "Ottone I, l'impero e l'Europa," *Römische historische Mitteilungen* 5 (1961–62): 13.

74. For both designations, see Hammer, "Concept," 57f. For the legend that the city was founded by Constantine's mother, Saint Helena, see ibid., 57.

75. Citing relevant sources, Anna Coreth discusses these tenth-century claims to both Greek and Roman heritage in "Dynastisch-politische Ideen," 87.

76. For some examples of this use, see Schramm, *Die deutschen Kaiser*, 74ff. For a discus-

sion of the heights to which the Ottonians brought the imperial powers in both the secular and sacred spheres, see Santifaller, "Ottone I," 10ff.

77. Gerhard B. Ladner, *L'Immagine dell'Imperatore Ottone III* (Rome, 1988), 45, notes the adaptation here of the *Majestas Domini* scheme that was used in late antiquity for the emperor and for Christ; here the formula is emphasized: his body is enclosed in a mandorla, and he is suspended between heaven and earth. Kantorowicz, *King's Two Bodies*, 61, notes that the image reflects the imperial *christomimetes'* two natures. See also L'Orange, *Apotheosis*, 122–24.

78. See Lhotsky, "Apis Colonna," 203, for the extension of the Trojan roots to the German stem in the tenth century. Alexander the Great continues to be counted among these ancestors.

79. See the citations and commentary on Widukind's history of the Ottonians in Poupardin, "L'Onction," 125.

80. See Kantorowicz, *King's Two Bodies*, 117, who notes that in the *Norman Anonymous*, the phrase "eminence of deification" that is applied to the ruler is described as coterminous with the Greek apotheosis. This eminence provided the king with a body of grace by which he became "another" man who eclipsed all others, see ibid., 47.

81. See Kantorowicz, *King's Two Bodies*, 46ff.

82. The inscription was added under Conrad II (1024–39). On their scrolls appear phrases from the coronation liturgy; these phrases include the words *rex regem*, drawn from Proverbs 8:15, to proclaim that kings and princes are from God. Apocryphal iconography is represented by the crown's circlet, which consists of eight stone-studded plaques, to recall the Heavenly Jerusalem. For the dating and for a description of the crown, see Leithe-Jasper and Distelberger, *Kunsthistorische Museum*, 8f.; for traditions concerning the crown, see Rosenthal, "Die 'Reichskrone.'" See also Schramm, *Herrschaftszeichen*, 2:560ff., esp. 611ff.

83. See L'Orange, *Apotheosis*, 119f., and Katznellenbogen, *Allegories*, 36 and 31ff., for the tradition of the Virtues surrounding the emperor.

84. *Ekkehardi. Uraugiensis chronica*, 33ff. Ekkehard includes the account that the Franks and Trojans were brothers, "Germani dicta sunt." Noting that Charlemagne was crowned by God

(178), Ekkehard diagrammed a family tree (188) that extended from the Carolingians to Conrad. See Borchardt, *German Antiquity*, 222 n. 102, who uses the term *bestseller* to characterize the chronicle's enormous popularity; Borchardt notes (223) that it is Ekkehard who identifies Charlemagne's ancestor Ansgisus as the namesake of the family's Trojan ancestor Anchises.

85. See discussion in Fuhrmann, *Germany*, 132.

86. On the papal support of the Capetians, see Zeller, "Rois de France," 285, 290.

87. On these restorations, see notes to Einhard, *Vita*, 130. These actions were precipitated by the birth of a son to Louis VII of France and an heiress of the Carolingian line; see Zeller, "Rois de France," 279.

88. The *leges imperiales* were held suspect by the Capetians, and a papal bull forbade the teaching of Roman law at the University of Paris, an interdiction removed only in 1679 by Louis XIV. See Zeller, "Rois de France," 280, 290. For other examples of historical continuity between Rome and the Hohenstaufen in secular and sacred matters, see Benson, "Political Renovatio,"370f., 382f.

89. See chapter 4.

90. For this point of view, see Borchardt, *German Antiquity*, 90–91. Annius was in service to the Borgia Pope Alexander VI. For a bibliography on the historical literature that accuses Annius of this forgery, see Don Cameron Allen, *The Legend of Noah* (Urbana, 1949), 114.

91. The attribution of Berosus's writings to Annius of Viterbo is related to the Renaissance discovery of Tacitus. Tacitus was also known in the Middle Ages, however. For a discussion of this knowledge of Tacitus and the detection of his influence in the work of Einhard and others, see Schellhase, *Tacitus*, 5ff.

92. *Ottonis Episcopi Frisingensis Chronica*. Borchardt, *German Antiquity*, 230, considers this work the greatest synthesis in medieval historical writing. Otto's importance is also discussed by Fuhrmann, *Germany*, 136. For a brief consideration of the place of Otto's work in the history of the universal chronicle, see Classen, "Res Gestae," 400ff.

93. *Ottonis Episcopi Frisingensis Chronica*, bk. 1, chap. 25: "De raptu Helenae et subversione Troiae et inicio Gentis Romanorum et Francorum et fundatione Patavi . . . Troianis Antenor

. . . fundator Patavi." Otto mentions Berosus's history (bk. 1, chap. 3) and cites Josephus (bk. 1, chap. 4) for the knowledge that Janus was Japhet's son.

94. Ibid., bk. 1, chap. 4.

95. Godefridi Viterbiensis *Speculum Regum*, bk. 1 64: "Germani et Romani facti sunt socii . . . Nam quos Troia suos olim retinebat alumpnos . . ." And on p. 82: "Romanam fore Troianum natura fatetur; Germanus patriota suus frateque videtur. Troia suis populis mater utrisque fuit . . . Germanus populus civis Romanis habetur. Communis patrie regnum commune tenetur . . . Romani quam Germani de uno patre ex semini . . . de priamo magno rege Troianorum. . . . procisserunt Germani . . . et Antenor ac Romani ea Enea est Ascanio geniti, quasi fratres. . . . ut populus Romani et Germanius quasi unos populus . . ."

96. Ibid., 61–62, 64. Coreth, "Dynastisch-politische Ideen," 80f., points to this statement as the basis for the Frankish claims to the Eastern Empire.

97. Godefridi Viterbiensis *Speculum Regum*, bk. 1 30ff.: "De generatione processa a filiis Noe . . . quod prognies imperialis a primo rege, qui primus tempore fuit, descendit. . . . prima tui generis, fuit hec, Henrice, corona. Cui celebris post Roma dedit sua climata prona. . . . Principium regum, quo descendisse videris, et genus imperii Troianaque . . . imperiale genus. . . . Romulus atque Remus Gentis Hebreorum loca, tempora regna tacemus. Vertimur ad Grecos, gentilia gesta canemus . . . unde sit imperii linea, norma, genus.

In his *Pantheon* (300ff.), Godfried showed the genealogical connections that underlay the parallel history of the universal chronicle that he had reconstructed in the *Speculum Regum* by tracing Henry's genealogy from Adam through Noah, Sem, Saturn, Jupiter, Priam, and Charlemagne: "Origo regum Francorum ab Adam usque ad Karolum Magnum et usque ad imperatorem Fredericum et filium eius Henricum: Adam, Seth . . . Noe . . . Nembrot . . . Saturnum . . . Iovem . . . Eneam . . . Meroveus . . . Clodoveus . . . Arnuldus . . . Pipinus . . . Karolus Magnus . . . Otto . . . Henricus II . . . Fredericus I. Ecce habes lector, ab Adam usque ad Fredericum I et filium eius Henricum plenam genealogiam et plenum cathalogum regum sive imperatorum Francorum."

98. See chapter 6.

99. For Frederick's claims to the title, for the attempts to make Jerusalem a hereditary fief, and for the Norman kings' contested claims, see sources and discussion in LaMonte, *Feudal Monarchy*, 4ff., 56ff.

100. Cited in Kantorowicz, *Frederick II*, 201ff.

101. For these two descriptions, see ibid., 259 and 442f.

102. Ibid., 448–49 and 259.

103. Ibid., 441, characterizes Gregory VII (1073–81) as the founder of the imperial Papacy and charts a straight line in this development through Innocent III and Boniface VIII, who called himself Caesar and Imperator, to Julius II. A continuing clash between temporal and ecclesiastical powers had characterized relations between emperor and pope since the eighth century when the famous forgery of the Donation of Constantine purported to transfer secular rights, titles, and dignities from Constantine to the church.

104. Charles's ancestry is traced through the following direct line from Charlemagne: Louis the Pious, Charles the Bald, Louis the Stammerer, Charles the Simple, Louis, Charles the duke of Lotharingia, possessor of Brabant, and heir to the throne of France.

105. *Genealogie Ducum Brabantiae*, 385: "Arnulfum genuit Ansigisum qui duxit sanctam Beggam, filiam Pipini primi ducies Brabantiae qui erat etiam maior domus . . . in regno iure hereditario. Consanguineam etiam suam Sanctam Gudulam. . . . In ipsa etiam terra, scilicet Aquisgrani, tronum imperialem instituit." The text recalls that Charlemagne's son Pippin made Lotharingia a hereditary realm and mentions the transfer of the imperium to Aachen and Pippin's blood link to Saint Gudule, patron saint of Brussels. (On the Church of Saint Gudule in Brussels, see chapter 11.)

106. "Priamus genuit Pharamundum . . . genuit Clodionem . . . successit ei nepos eius Meroveus . . . [and following several begats the heritage reaches Clovis] quem sanctus Remigiis baptizavit et oleo celitus misso consecravit" (*Genealogie Ducum Brabantiae*, 387).

107. *Genealogie Ducum Brabantiae*: "usque ad Karolingos ascendit clarius pateat, ducis non solum totium Lotharingiae, sed etiam regni Francici legitimos esse heredis . . ." (385). "Hec est prosapia regnum Francorum a tempore Priami

primi regis Francie usque ad tempus Iohannis ducis Lotharingie . . . qui est heres regni Francorum hereditario iure, sicut primagenito Karoli Magni stirpes. Cuius stirpis generatio non derelinquetur in saecula" (391). ". . . cuius progenies duces erant Austrie . . . que nunc Brabantia vocantur. . . . Reges vero solo . . . sed duces Brabantie" (387). For John as the hero of Minnesang and related literature, see Seibt, *Karl IV*, 52f. For the designation of Tournai as the New Rome, see Hammer, "Concept," 61.

108. On the duke's Trojan patronage, see Bayot, *La Légende de Troie*, 36ff. On Philip's chronicle, see Camille Gaspar and Frédéric Lyna, *Les Principaux Manuscrits a peintures de la Bibliothàque Royale de Belgique*, vol. 1 (Brussels, 1984), 358f.

109. Jan de Klerk (d. 1351) (*Gestes*) chronicled this pedigree for John III of Brabant, Henry VII's son. He traces John's ancestry from Noah through his offspring Saturn to the Trojan Franks and then to Charlemagne. On this chronicle see also Lhotsky, "Apis Colonna," 210.

110. For a general discussion and for citations of Dante's support of Henry VII as Aeneas's heir, see the classic study by Lenkeith, *Dante*, from which I have drawn many of these citations. Other citations directly applicable to the themes of this study are drawn from the text of *De Monarchia*, in Moore, ed., *Tutte le opere di Dante*. Borchardt (*German Antiquity*, 269, n. 65) notes that *De Monarchia* was largely suppressed in Catholic Europe and was not printed until 1559 when Oporinus printed it with a German translation in Basel.

111. Dante *De Monarchia* III, chap. 4.

112. Ibid., II, chap. 9. Vergil is Dante's infallible authority on the divine origins of Rome (*De Monarchia* II, chap. 6); the Mantuan reveals to him that the Roman Empire is intended to endure forever (Dante *Convivium* IV.iv.11, cited in Lenkeith, *Dante*, 84).

113. Cited in Lenkeith, *Dante*, 107.

114. Dante *De Monarchia* II, chap. 7, quoting from the *Aeneid* VI.851f.

115. Dante *De Monarchia* II, chap. 9. He quotes from Luke that Christ submitted himself to Roman law. On the importance Dante places on Roman law for the return of the Augustan Golden Age, see Kantorowicz, *King's Two Bodies*, 444.

116. Dante *De Monarchia* II, chap. 12. See also a similar statement cited in Lenkeith, *Dante*, 89.

117. Dante *De Monarchia* I, chap. 16.

118. Ibid., II, chap. 3.

119. Epistle VII.1, cited in Lenkeith, *Dante*, 84–85. She also cites Epistle VII.3, where Dante calls Henry the heir to the prophecy that "from the fair line of Troy a Caesar shall be born." For Dante's treatment of Astraea, see Yates, *Astraea*, 36f. For the terrestrial paradise as a vision of the Golden Age, see Dante *Purgatory* XXVIII.139, cited in Lenkeith, *Dante*, 58. In support of the Frankish emperor, Dante refers to Charlemagne's liberation of the church from the Lombards.

120. "In quel gran seggio, a che tu gli occhi tieni, Per la corona che già v' è su posta, Prima che a tu a queste nozze ceni. Sederà l'alma, che sia giù agosta, Del'alto Arrigo, ch'a drizzare Italia / Verra' in prima ch'ella sia disposta" (Dante *Paradiso* XXX.136f.). Vergil is Dante's guide throughout the *Divine Comedy*; he is replaced by Beatrice for the last leg of the journey which reveals the Christian Empyrium. Beatrice addresses Henry as the successor of Caesar and Augustus, the king of the Romans by Divine Providence (Epistle VII, salutation). See the discussion of Henry's place in the Empyrium in Seibt, *Karl IV*, 55.

121. Prague, State Archives, see *Die Parler und der Schöne Stil 1350–1400*, Cologne Exhibition Catalogue (Cologne, 1980), vol. 1, pt. 2, pp. 154–55. On the translation of the empire to Bohemia, see also Seibt, *Karl IV*, 65.

122. "Legitur itaque in Chronica Eusebii, . . . ubi plena prosequitur Eusebius de origine gentis & regum Francorum, quod post excidiũ Troiae, illo tempore quo Aeneas in Italiam venit . . . fuerunt autem inter eos tunc duo principes . . . Priamus & Antenor . . . venerunt in terram Germaniae . . . ut refert Eusebius . . . quod Aeneas & Phryges, qui regnavit in Phrygia, fratres erant . . . et successit Pharamundus . . . cui successit Meroveus . . . & Pipinus . . . & Carolus . . . a domino coronato et pacifico imperatori Romanorum . . ." (Lupoldus de Babenberg, "De origini regni Francorum," in Schardius, *De Iurisdictione*, 333ff.).

123. "Carolus duodecim mensibus, & duodecim ventis, iuxta propria linguam vocabula imposuit" (ibid., 341). The German possession of the Roman Empire is verified with the reign of the Ottonions, ibid., 339.

124. Here Lupold reverts to the authority of the Hohenstaufen historian Godfried of Viterbo, ibid., 340.

125. Marignola, *Kronika Marignolova*, 577ff. He credits Josephus for the information that Janus is called Janan in Genesis: "Janus, filius Noe, pater Ytalie, iste in Genesi dicitur Janan" (ibid., 507). See the parallels between Lupold and Marignola in Neuwirth, *Bildercyklus*, 25f. On the dating of Marignola's chronicle to 1355–62, see Neuwirth, *Bildercyklus*, 24. On Marignola, see also the discussion in Lhotsky, "Apis Colonna," 210, 243, and Seibt, *Karl IV*, 393. Marignola (*Kronika Marignolova*, 588f.) also recorded the legend of the vision of the Virgin and Christ that appeared to Augustus as a revelation of the Christian meaning of the enigmatic *Fourth Eclogue*; he testified to Augustus's prescient acknowledgment of Christ through his dedication of the Aracoeli altar on the Capitoline.

126. Marignola (*Kronika Marignolova*, 588) notes that Joseph is of the house of David, whose members were kings, but Mary was born of the house of Levi, whose members were priests. Dante had referred the Old Testament roles to the words of Moses, who traced the root of the priest-kings to Jacob. Of Jacob's sons Levi and Judah, one was the father of secular kings; the other of priests (*De Monarchia* III, chap. 5).

127. "Karolus autem ex deorum gentilium Saturni et jovis recta linea per Troyanos noscitur descendisse et de qua per Enee filium . . . per Laviniam, filiam regis Jani . . . atraxit originem" (Marignola, *Kronika Marignolova*, 520).

128. For Charles IV's influence on the Hapsburgs' construction of a mythic genealogy, see Neuwirth, *Bildercyklus*, 11ff.

129. A reconstructed model at Karlstein castle that is based on the later manuscript (see n. 130) shows the sacred and secular figures beside each other on the walls of the throne room. On this reconstruction see *Charles IV, 1316–1378*, Centre for State Care of Historic Monuments and Nature Conservation of the Central Bohemia District (Karlstein, 1978), without pagination. On the palace decorations, see also Seibt, *Karl IV*, 54ff. On precedents in the imagery of Byzantine rulers, Charlemagne, and Frederick II, see ibid., 390ff. On the precedents that include the palace of Henry IV at Trier, see Neuwirth, *Bildercyklus*, 12f.

130. The whole cycle vanished in the Renaissance, but was preserved in two Renaissance copies. These images are drawn from a manuscript (Cod. Vind. Palat. n. 8330.) made for Em-

peror Maximilian II, circa 1575. On the manuscript, and for a lengthy discussion of Charles's genealogy and of these images, see Neuwirth, *Bildercyklus*, 5ff. The manuscript includes intermediary descendants between Noah and Janus; among these are Nembroth and Ninus.

131. Blichilde was the descendant of Clovis, and Ansibert had imperial roots and was himself the root of the Carolingian dynasty. See the prior discussion of these marital links in text following n. 20.

132. Begga was duchess of Lotharingia and Brabant; she gave birth to the younger Pippin.

133. Gerberga, who was descended from Charles the Bald, preserved the Clovian and Carolingian pedigrees.

134. His claims were sustained in the *Chronica ducem Lotharingia et Brabant* that he ordered from Edward de Dynter; the work was presented to the duke in 1447. De Dynter's work was published in the contemporary French translation of Jehan Wauquelin, clerk and secretary to Philip the Good. See the introduction to this edition for a biography of de Dynter, notes on his sources, and details of the commission. In addition to recapitulating the Trojan genealogy that descended to the Burgundian dukes from Clovis and the Carolingians, de Dynter repeated the reasons for preserving the Roman Empire. These lay in Christ's sanctification of its rule—by submitting Himself to the imperial census, by rendering tribute, and by bringing universal peace in Augustus's reign. See Dynter, *Chronique*, bk. 2, pp. 348ff. Following the admonition of Scripture, de Dynter restates that the continuation of the Roman Empire is necessary to keep the Antichrist at bay. De Dynter asserts once again that the empire was transferred to the Germans ". . . descendants of Aeneas and Priam the Younger . . . in the time of Charlemagne" (ibid., bk. 2, pp. 346ff). Charlemagne's sanctity is proven by the repetition of the legend of Turpin (ibid., bk. 2, pp. 331ff., 372ff.). In delivering Jerusalem from the Saracens, Charlemagne obtained Christ's Crown of Thorns, it flowered and healed the sick in his presence (ibid., 372ff.). On de Dynter, see also Neuwirth, *Bildercyklus*, 21f.

135. See Lhotsky, "Apis Colonna," 182ff., regarding the establishment of Rudolf's Roman origins as early as the thirteenth century, a link

strengthened when his granddaughter was engaged to a descendant of the Colonna family, professed descendants of the Julio-Claudians. Rudolf, who had married Elizabeth, the daughter of the duke of Burgundy, was also related to Emperor Charles IV, see Seibt, *Karl IV,* 52. On Rudolf's contributions to the imperial myth, see chapters 10 and 11. Heinrich von Klingenberg's fifteenth-century chronicle directly asserted the Trojan origins of the Hapsburgs, see Peter P. Albert, "Die habsburgische Chronik des Konstanzer Bischofs Heinrich von Klingenberg," *Zeitschrift für Geschichte des Oberrheines,* n.s. 20 (1905). Klingenberg traces the Trojan heritage through Priam to Clovis, Charlemagne, and the Hapsburgs. On this chronicle's importance for Maximilian, see Lhotsky, "Apis Colonna," 205f.

136. Roo, *Annales,* B2: "Arborum . . . et licet à Phrygiis genus hoc detraxerit ortum."

137. Ibid., A2.

138. See Ovid *Fasti* IV.51–52.

139. See Lhotsky, "Apis Colonna," 208f., for the marriage's importance for Maximilian's genealogical presumptions. On the celebrations of the marriage, see Molinet, *Chroniques,* 1:224f. On the Trojan imagery that decorated the most important of the emperor's public ceremonies, see ibid., 2:479, 560. This union strengthened existing ties to the dukes of Brabant, for Rudolf I was already related to the Burgundians through marriage. For the importance of the Burgundian heritage and territories for Maximilian, see Emil Dürr, "Karl der Kuhn und der Ursprung des habsburg-spanischen Imperiums," *Historische Zeitschrift* 113 (1914): 22–23.

140. On Maximilian's denunciation of the Capetian usurpation, see Coreth, "Dynastisch-politische Ideen," 85.

141. See Coreth, "Wappenbuch," 294. This was supported by gathering and adding to the ties to Greek ancestry already claimed for earlier Frankish emperors.

142. See Creighton, *History of the Papacy,* 108, who quotes from both letters.

143. Quoted in Schulte, *Kaiser Maximilian I,* 77ff.: "Il signor Prospero Colona partira per Roma, intexo maxime il Papa stava malissimo, et il viceré non voria esser in Milan. Si dice, etiam lui anderá a Roma a far Papa Maximian imperator." On Nagonius's poem, see *Hispania-Austria,* 271f. For an analysis of its content and a dating to

1498, see Paul Gwynne's forthcoming study, "Tu alter Caeser erit: Nagonius and the Renovatio Imperii."

144. Laschitzer, "Genealogie," 10f., traces Maximilian's earliest interest in constructing his genealogy to 1498; he reconstructs the steps in this development through the second decade of the sixteenth century. For the additions of Philip II which expanded this configuration into its final format, see chapter 10.

145. In his *Oratio ad Maximilian* (1504) Bebel resorts to Maximilian's Trojan heritage, which was variously claimed to come from Priam, from Hector, and from Aeneas. See Borchardt, *German Antiquity,* 154ff.

146. Celtis's contributions included giving German origins to the Demogorgon and the Greek-speaking Druids. See Borchardt, *German Antiquity,* 106–8.

147. In the *Libertas Germaniae* of 1519, Hieronymus Gebwiler accepts both the Trojan myths and the Berosus myths; Tuisco is claimed the ancestor of the Hapsburgs, who stem from Troy by way of the younger Priam as well. On Gebwiler, see Lhotsky, "Apis Colonna," 221.

148. Wolfgang Lazius, *Commentarium in Genalogiam Austriam* (Basel, 1564). Lazius (1514–65) was a professor at Vienna and counselor and historian of the Roman Empire. On p. 19ff., he traces the Noah-Saturn genealogy and recapitulates the contributions of other humanists to this construct.

149. See Lhotsky, "Apis Colonna," 205 and chart on 238; also 213 and chart on 239 for Mennel's chronicles.

150. In Johannes Naucler's *Chronicarum* (Tübingen, 1516), a major monument of Renaissance historiography that was published in 1516 under the supervision of Erasmus, Noah is identified with Janus and called the father of Saturn, the ruler of Latium during the Golden Age.

151. Conrad Peutinger follows Tacitus in claiming Tuisco the eponymous father of the race, but Berosus is his authority for Tuisco's identification as Noah's son; he draws on the medieval legends for the Franks' Trojan ancestry. See Borchardt, *German Antiquity,* 114ff. For the dissemination of Tacitus in Renaissance Germany, see Schellhase, *Tacitus,* 5f.

152. As early as 1503, when he locates Maximilian's seed in Noah, Stabius follows the direction set by Charles IV. Stabius continues this

heritage from Noah to Tuisco and his Trojan heirs. Stabius extends Maximilian's genealogy to include the Egyptian god Osiris whose reign is placed between that of Noah and Dardanus; and again to encompass a Greek line that passes to Turnus from Hector. See Lhotsky, "Apis Colonna," 214, 219f. The emperor appears as an ancient Egyptian monarch with hieroglyphic attributes in Dürer's *Triumphal Arch*; see ibid., 221.

153. Francisco Irenico, *Germaniae*, bk. 1, p. A4. On Irenico, see Borchardt, *German Antiquity*, 144f.

154. Gebwiler, *Epitome Regii*, opposite p. B.: "Hunc Noam vetustas ipsa sub Iani nomine bifrontem figurans."

155. Gebwiler finds testimony in Berosus to include Osiris, known as Moses Mesraim: "Cham . . . cui pareter Osirim innumeram prolem fuisse Berosus testatur . . . Osiris praefati Chami seu Aegyptii Saturni ex Rhea filius quem Moses Mesraim vocat, Aegypti rex constitutus . . ." See Gebwiler, *Libertas Germaniae*, n.p. See also Lhotsky, "Apis Colonna," 221, n. 219.

156. Laschitzer, "Genealogie," 12ff.

157. Jacob Mennel, a student of Johannes Naucler, begins Maximilian's Greek heritage with Hector, the lineage continues through Troilus, Turnus, and Diomedes to the Merovingian and Ottonian emperors. His Trojan ancestry originates with Dardanus, proceeding through the Frankish and Roman heirs of Troy to Maximilian's grandson, Emperor Charles V (see Laschitzer, "Genealogie," 11). On Mennel, see also Lhotsky, "Apis Colonna," 79ff., and Albert, "Chronik," 182ff., for Mennel's debt to Klingenburg. Mennel wrote a number of chronicles for Maximilian, each exceeding its predecessor in the number of illustrious ancestors. See Laschitzer, "Genealogie," 32f.

158. Under Maximilian, the legends of Charlemagne's and Otto II's Greek parentage swelled to include indigenous elements. On the development of these indigenous legends, and for Maximilian's recall of the Franks' Greek past established in Godfried of Viterbo and others, see Coreth, "Dynastisch-politische Ideen," 86f. For the projection of the Greek strain in German history through Maximilian's assimilation to Constantine and Justinian, see chapter 10.

159. The theological faculty deliberated on and accepted these origins: "1518 . . . 16 Dec . . .

doctor Petrus Thonnhauser litteras sacre caesaree maiestatis presentavit facultati, . . . Deliberatione . . . satisfaceruntur. Erat intentio cesaree maiestatis voluitque . . . examinavit singulas generationis procerum et familiarum et successione eorundem a Noe inclusive usque ad Sicambrum . . . serie procerum a Noe usque ad Sicambrum . . ." (Archiv der Wiener Universität, Mspt. sig. III, fol. 49: [16 Dec. 1518], text in Laschitzer, "Genealogie," 30, n. 1).

160. Completed in 1515, the enormous project apparently involved Dürer, Pirckheimer, Stabius, and others for several years. See Panofsky, *Life and Art*, 175ff. and *Hispania-Austria*, 320. See also Silver, "Paper Pageants," 299f., for a detailed description of the program and for the arch as a visual claim to the Eastern and Western imperial office.

161. See Vinzenz Oberhammer, *Die Bronzstandbilder des Maximilian-Grabmales in der Hofkirche zu Innsbruck* (Innsbruck, 1935), and *Hispania-Austria*, 342ff. As originally planned, the project contained more than forty statues, including Julius Caesar, Theoderic the Great, and Clovis.

162. Vienna, Cod. Vind. Palat 3072, fol. 44–48. For a discussion of the image see Laschitzer, "Genealogie," 12f., 34; and Coreth, "Dynastisch-politische Ideen," 88f.

163. See Coreth, "Dynastisch-politische Ideen," 92f.

164. Cited in ibid., 88f.

165. See Schulte, *Kaiser Maximilian I*, 77.

166. These appear in the latest versions of Mennel's chronicle (1518). On this work, see Laschitzer, "Heiligen," 4:70ff., 5:117ff. and *Hispania-Austria*, 311.

167. See *Decensus Averno* (Sebastian Brant's Vergil), ed. Anna Cox Brenton (Stanford, 1930), woodcut 13, illustrating the glory destined to follow the Dardanian line (from *Aeneid* VI.752–853). See also Theodore K. Rabb, "Sebastian Brant and the First Illustrated Edition of Vergil," *The Princeton University Library Chronicle* 21, no. 4 (1960): 187–94. In connection with Brant's Vergil, it is interesting that the *Vatican Vergil* (see figs. 2, 3, and 129) was reputedly in the possession of Giovanni Pontano in the fifteenth century (see Stevenson, *Miniature Decoration*, 12). The Neapolitan Pontano had close associations with Maximilian and dedicated his famous poem *Urania* to him. On Maximilian as the heir to prophecies connected with Aeneas's

settlement of Rome, see Warburg's discussion of Dürer's *Scofa Virgiliana,* "Divinazione," 353.

168. His maternal grandfather, Ferdinand, who led a drive to recover Jerusalem, acquired the title king of Jerusalem for the Spanish crown. The Paleologan donation is recorded in Valdesius *Praerogativa Hispaniae,* 245.

169. Charles's efforts to revive the dream of universal empire have been brilliantly studied by Yates, *Astraea,* 1–28.

170. See chapter 8.

171. A. F. Doni's edition of this treatise appeared in 1547.

172. See Borchardt, *German Antiquity,* 186.

173. This is recorded in a treatise dedicated to Philip II by Contile, *Ragionamento,* 44r.

174. Ariosto *Orlando Furioso,* canto 15, stanza 21ff. For the application of the Astraea theme to Charles V, see Yates, *Astraea,* 53f. For Charles's use of Augustan imagery, see also Strong, *Splendour at Court,* 79ff.

175. Leoni identified the *Aeneid* as the literary source for the statue; these implications for Charles are developed by Mezzatesta, "Imperial Themes," 41ff.

176. On Charles's assimilation to Marcus Aurelius, while he yet bears the arms of the Christian knight, see Panofsky, *Problems in Titian,* 48.

177. Fernández de Oviedo y de Valdés, *Catálogo real de Castilla,* 5v., "segundo Beroso . . ." On p. 6v., the descent of the Spanish kings from Aeneas and Cham is traced: "Españoles sucedieró los Troyanos, de quien procediero los reyes de Roma . . . pero pues ellos dizen per Eneas hijo di Venus [que] conforme atal madre per descendido da stirpe de Cam." The author delineates the emperor's descent from Tuisco, the eponymous father of the German race and the grandson of Noah-Janus, through Dardanus who settled Troy in Phrygia to Priam, Clovis, and Charlemagne. A precedent for such a heritage for the Spanish branch of his family was established in the universal chronicle commissioned by Alfonso the Wise following his contested election as king of the Germans in 1254 (*Primera crónica general de España,* reprinted Madrid, 1955). See also for Charles V's mythic genealogy, Campo, *Crónica general de España,* and its continuation by Ambrosio de Morales, Cordova, 1586.

178. Mareno, *Compendio,* A ii verso. Researching the history of Tuscany, the author shows that

two princes possessed it: Charlemagne and Charles V. "Ma essaminando poi la loro origine ho conosciuto l'uno e l'altro nascere da una medesima stirpe; discesa da Tusco, Re di Toscana . . . Etruria & Tirrenia . . ." The heritage continues on p. B ii to recount that Tuisco came to Tuscany in the year of the Flood; his progeny Janus bore Dardanus.

179. Ibid., ii verso: "Conoscendo quelle essere ben inclinato . . . al servigio di sua Cesarea e Cattolica Maesta . . . & . . . simigliando gli loro antenati della casate de Medici & Toledo; quella tutta inclinosi farvi padroni del stato di Firenze qual possedete." The Medici were restored to power in 1512, and the city was placed under the protection of the imperial league in 1519; they commissioned important artistic monuments following this date. The Medici were overthrown in 1527; they were reinstated to power and given ducal status by Charles in 1532. The emperor gave his natural daughter, Margaret, in marriage to Alessandro de' Medici, first duke of Florence, in 1536; Alessandro died in 1537. In 1539 Cosimo I, second duke of Florence, married Eleanor of Toledo, whose family were the emperor's powerful allies. Charles became the godfather to Francesco de Medici (b. 1541), and he elected Cosimo to the Order of the Golden Fleece in 1544. On this history, see J. N. Stephens *The Fall of the Florentine Republic, 1512–1530* (Oxford, 1983), 74f.

180. For the vassal obligations of this status, see chapter 8.

181. See Davidson, "Navigation," 35ff. She mentions that the palace at Genoa served as an imperial residence (35).

182. For Horace's appropriation of the theme of Jupiter's destruction of the giants to Augustus, see chapter 1.

183. Federigo decorated his villa for Charles's impending imperial visit, see Frederick Hartt, *Giulio Romano* (New Haven, 1958), 152ff., E. H. Gombrich, "The Sala dei Venti in the Palazzo del Té," *Journal of the Warburg and Courtauld Institute* 13, nos. 3–4 (1950): 199, and the discussion in Tanner, "Titian," 151. Eisler ("The Impact of Charles V," 93–110) has also discussed imperial patronage at Genoa, Mantua, and Trent.

184. The text was amended in 1529 for this inclusion as soon as the enmity between the duke and the emperor—caused when the duke

entered the Holy League against Charles—
ended. See Michele Catalano, *Vita di Ludovico
Ariosto* (Genoa, 1930), 1:600.

185. See chapter 12.

186. Aspects of the *Los Honores* tapestries are
discussed in relationship to Alain de Lille's *Anticlaudian*, in chapter 4.

187. The first nine cantos were completed
in 1547 and dedicated to Charles; the remaining
eighteen cantos were published in Venice in 1548
and presented to Charles in Brussels in March of
1549. See Faggin, "Giangiorgio Trissino," 33–34.

CHAPTER 6

1. Only a single page known as the *Sibyllenbuch Fragment* survives. On the scholarly opinion
regarding the book's precedence over the Bible,
see the *New York Times*, 12 May 1987, p. c1.

2. For a general view of the subject, see the
fundamental studies by Reeves, *Influence of Prophecy*, and *Joachim of Fiore*. The work of McGinn, *Visions of the End*, is invaluable both for the gathering
and the English translation of diverse prophetic
texts in a single work. For the German imperial
position, see pertinent documents and discussion in Kampers, *Die deutsche Kaiseridee*. While
Reeves and McGinn have considered the entire
messianic tradition—both papal and imperial—
my discussion is geared to the development of
the imperial strand and, in a later chapter, to developing a culminating stage in the tradition that
was reached with Philip II.

3. Daniel 2:31–45. See chapter 2.

4. For the apocalyptic texts ascribed to
Jesus, for apocalyptic reflections in the Gospels,
and for earlier Judaic, Hellenistic, and Christian
apocalyptic sources, see McGinn, *Visions of the
End*, 11ff., 21ff.

5. 2 Thessalonians 2.

6. Tertullian *Apologeticus* c.32 I, text in
Barker, ed. and trans., *From Alexander to Constantine*,
455. For instances of an anti-imperial position,
see McGinn, *Visions of the End*, 66.

7. See McGinn, *Visions of the End*, 23ff.

8. Virgil, vol. 1, *Eclogue* IV.4–5. For Varro's
discussion of the history of the Sibyls, the most
important of which was the Erythrean, who was
supposed to have lived during the Trojan War
and to have migrated to Cumae, near Naples, to
become Aeneas's guide and the prophetess of

the Golden Age, see McGinn, *Visions of the End*, 19.
Augustus placed the Sibylline texts in the Temple
of Apollo on the Palatine.

9. "Then will arise a King . . . whose name
is Constans. He will be the king of the Romans
and the Greeks. . . . [He] will claim the whole
Christian Empire for himself . . . destroy all idol-
atrous temples; he will call all pagans to baptism,
and in every temple the Cross of Christ will be
erected. . . . At that time . . . Gog and Magog [will
come forth]. When the king of the Romans hears
of this he will . . . vanquish and utterly destroy
them. After this he will come to Jerusalem, and
having put off the diadem from his head and laid
aside the whole imperial garb, he will hand over
the empire of the Christians to God . . . and
Christ. . . . When the Roman Empire shall have
ceased, then the Antichrist will be openly revealed and will sit in the House of the Lord
in Jerusalem. . . . Then there will be a great persecution . . . and the Antichrist will be slain by
the power of God through Michael the Archan-
gel on the Mount of Olives" (*The Tiburtine Sibyl*,
text translated in McGinn, *Visions of the End*, 49–
50).

10. I have drawn this summary from both
Greek and Latin versions of the *Tiburtine Sibyl*
(texts in McGinn, *Visions of the End*, 43ff., 49ff.).

11. For the dating of the *Tiburtine Sibyl* to the
reign of Theodosius, see McGinn, *Visions of the
End*, 43. See also citations in Reeves, *Influence of
Prophecy*, 299f. The text of the *Tiburtine Sibyl*, the
most cogent proof of the revival of apocalyptic
doctrine in the Christian Roman Empire of the
fourth century, was written in Greek and translated into Latin, which only survives in later
manuscripts. For arguments concerning the dating and the contents of the Latin version, and for
their relationship to the seventh-century text of
the Pseudo-Methodius, see McGinn, *Visions of the
End*, 43ff.

12. Prudentius, vol. 1, *Apotheosis*, ll. 446ff. Similar ideas are expressed in *Prudentius*, vols. 1 and 2,
A Reply to the Address of Symmachus, bk. I, ll. 287–90,
587–90; bk. II, ll. 583ff. Referring to the emperor's defeat of the pagan faction, Prudentius
took up the theme of a Christian Rome in which
the pagan divinities are transformed into icons
of the new faith, and Christ is invited to enter "a
world in harmony . . . which peace and Rome
hold in a bond of union." The passage con-

tinues: "These Thou dost command to be the heads and highest powers of the world. Rome without peace finds no favor with Thee; and it is the supremacy of Rome, keeping down disorders . . . that secures the peace . . ." (ibid., bk. II, ll. 636ff.). Allegory and symbol, abstractions in which he excels, are fundamental elements of this tradition. On Prudentius's Roman political ideology see also chapters 2 and 9.

13. For the inclusion of Macedonian, Greek, and Roman history, see texts and discussion in McGinn, *Visions of the End*, 66–76.

14. See text in ibid., 74f. and discussion on 34 and 70f. Ten editions of the Pseudo-Methodius were printed between 1470–75 and 1677; the most important was the 1498 Basel edition with woodcuts by Sebastian Brant, see ibid., 302, n. 21. On Brant, see also chapter 5.

15. See Reeves, *Influence of Prophecy*, 300. For the reflection of Adso's version of the legend in earlier Carolingian apocalyptic ideas, see McGinn, *Visions of the End*, 83–84. For Charlemagne as the new golden head of Daniel's monolith of the four empires, see the passage in Notker the Stammerer's *Life of Charlemagne*, cited in McGinn, *Visions of the End*, 304, n. 17.

16. See McGinn, *Visions of the End*, 82ff. He notes that Adso's *Letter* was dedicated to Gerberga, the sister of Otto the Saxon and the wife of Louis IV, one of the last descendents of the Carolingians. For the application of Adso's prophecy to Emperor Otto I, see Grauert, "Der deutschen Kaisersage," 106.

17. Text in McGinn, *Visions of the End*, 85–86. For apocalyptic themes in the writing of the same Ekkehard of Aura who had applied the Trojan myth to the Saxons, see ibid., 92, and Reeves, *Influence of Prophecy*, 301.

18. See discussion in McGinn, *Visions of the End*, 88.

19. See text and discussion in ibid., 122ff. For other instances of apocalyptic ideology in the literature of the court, including Otto of Freising and Godfried of Viterbo (on whom, see chapter 5), see McGinn, *Visions of the End*, 117ff., and Reeves, *Influence of Prophecy*, 302. Godfried of Viterbo's apocalyptic ideas are also discussed in Lhotsky, "Apis Colonna," 177.

20. The late medieval papacy, when it was not endorsing its own rights to imperial identity, generally supported the French position. For French support in the writings of the Franciscan John of Rupescissa, one of the best-known apocalyptic publicists of the Avignon papacy (1308–77), see text and discussion in McGinn, *Visions of the End*, 230f.

21. Text translated in ibid., 250. It contains the details cited here and continues the concept of the emperor's journey to Jerusalem, the ascent of the Mount of Olives, and the rendering of his crown back to Christ. On the prophecy concerning a second Charlemagne, which dates to the eleventh century and alternately reflects the claims of the German and French kings, see also Reeves, *Influence of Prophecy*, 301, 320ff. She quotes from the final form of the prophecy as it appears in 1644 to note the consistency of the circumstantial details, especially the physical features: "a long forehead, high brows, great eyes, an Eagle's Nose: He shall . . . destroy all Tyrants. . . . the greatest Clergymen who have invaded Peter's Seat he shall put to death: and in that year obtaine a double Crowne. At last . . . he shall enter Greece, and be named King of the Greeks. The Turks and Barbarians he shall subdue. . . . And he shall possesse the Dominion of the Earth" (392). The aquiline nose, the most distinctive of the features, would have a likely source in Suetonius's description of Augustus (*Suetonius*, vol. 1, *Lives of the Caesars*, bk. 2, chap. 79, p. 245).

22. For the legends surrounding the resurrection of Frederick II (d. 1250), which served the German cause, see Reeves, *Influence of Prophecy*, 332ff. Reeves also discusses the anti-German position that described the third Frederick as the Antichrist.

23. His contributions to the legend are analyzed by Reeves, *Influence of Prophecy*, 303ff., and succinctly summarized in McGinn, *Visions of the End*, 126ff. An interesting literary parallel occurs in Alain de Lille's contemporary *Anticlaudian*, where the Perfect Man, a metaphor for the temporal ruler, alone fights and overcomes the chthonic deities and restores Edenic peace to the earth.

24. See Joachim's text in McGinn, *Visions of the End*, 134f. On the Angelic Pope, see ibid., 186ff., and Reeves, *Influence of Prophecy*, 395ff. On the visions, see the discussions and the citations from Joachim's text in McGinn, *Visions of the End*, 126ff., and Reeves, *Influence of Prophecy*, 302ff.

25. See the discussion in McGinn, *Visions of the End*, 168, who also reviews the political issues in the conflict between Frederick II and the papacy.

26. For Frederick II's letter that calls the reigning pope, Innocent IV, the Antichrist and makes other similar charges, see ibid., 172ff.

27. Reeves, *Joachim of Fiore*, 60, points to Frederick II as the first emperor to be placed in a Joachimite context.

28. On Frederick II's encouragement of messianic adulation towards his person, see Reeves, *Joachim of Fiore*, 61. See Kantorowicz, *Frederick II*, 258ff., for the likening of Frederick's stainless nature to that of Adam and Christ.

29. On the thirteenth-century use of astrological predictions to determine the time of the End, see McGinn, *Visions of the End*, 150ff.

30. On Brigid, see Reeves, *Influence of Prophecy*, 338ff.

31. For Gamaléon as a fictitious character, and for his prophecy, see McGinn, *Visions of the End*, 248ff.

32. See Borchardt, *German Antiquity*, 256f., for the various applications of the legend in the period between the Interregnum and the Council of Florence. For the application of the legend to the Luxembourger emperor Sigismund, see Reeves, *Influence of Prophecy*, 340f.

33. See Reeves, *Influence of Prophecy*, 350f. For the revival of the "Frederick" prophecies in the fifteenth century, see Borchardt, *German Antiquity*, 150.

34. For the concept that Maximilian's identification with Constantine implied that he was the Last World Emperor, see Reeves, *Influence of Prophecy*, 352, n. 1, with bibliography.

35. See ibid., 352, n.1.

36. The text of Lichtenberger's *Prognosticatio*, which refers to Maximilian, is quoted in McGinn, *Visions of the End*, 272. On Lichtenberger, see Kurze, *Johannes Lichtenberger*. See also Reeves, *Influence of Prophecy*, 347ff., also for his predilection for a Burgundian savior. Lichtenberger's *Prognosticatio* is astrological in conception and deals with the effects of planetary conjunction on the fate of the empire. Lichtenberger defines the breakup of the empire as the schism that announces the Antichrist's arrival. The basis for its continuity to that time is succintly phrased by Paracelsus (cited in Kurze, "Prophecy," 76): "The Roman Empire has survived and is to survive until the end of time because Christ has sanctified it and endowed it with permanence."

37. See n. 21 above.

38. The portait is based on Dürer's own drawing of Maximilian, which is inscribed "Divus." See *Gothic and Renaissance Art in Nuremberg 1300–1550* (Catalogue of an exhibition held at the Metropolitan Museum of Art, New York, and at the Germanisches Museum, Nuremberg, 1986), 322 and fig. 131.

39. See chapter 5.

40. See Britnell, "Jean Lemaire de Belges," 151. On Aytinger, who also revived the mystical name "P" and "C" prophecies to apply to the Hapsburg rulers, see Kampers, "Kaiserprophetien," 49ff., and McGinn, *Visions of the End*, 271–76.

41. This interpretation was advanced by Rudolf Chadraba, *Dürer's Apocalypse* (Prague, 1964).

42. John Lichtenberger, *Prognosticatio*, bk. 2, chap. 16, trans. in McGinn, *Visions of the End*, 273, and cited in Reeves, *Joachim of Fiore*, 111. In his commentary on Methodius (the 1498 edition is cited in Kampers, *Die deutsche Kaiseridee*, 12, n. 18), Aytinger, Maximilian's historian, drew up a genealogical table, showing the prince's descent from the kings of France on his mother's side and noted that he fitted the prophecy of the ruler with the name P, "Paria laudabilis virtutis dicuntur de filio, cuius nomen incipit a P littera et ex matre sit de stirpe regum Francie." Following Lichtenberger, Aytinger identifies Philip of Burgundy as the ruler of the last days. See also McGinn, *Visions of the End*, 271ff., for other examples of this status.

43. Reeves advocates this idea in *Influence of Prophecy*, 359ff., which is devoted to the discussion of the constellation of prophecies that devolved on Charles V in the works of Peutinger, Gebwiler, Egidio da Viterbo, Wolfgang Lazius, and others.

44. A contemporary redaction of Telephorus's prophecy applies this destiny to Maximilian (quoted in Kampers, *Die deutsche Kaiseridee*, 216): "intrabit Greciam et rex Grecorum nominabitur. Caldeos, . . . Palestinios . . . subiugabit. Hiis factis sanctus sanctorum vocabitur veniens ad sanctam Jheruslaem et accedens ad montem Oliveti orans ad patrem deponesque coronam de capite, Deo gratias agens cum magno terre motu, signis et mirabilibus emittet. . . . Hic coronatus erit ab angelico pastore et primus imperator post Friedericum III, post presens scisma et tribula-

ciones pseudoprophetarum et dicti Friderici."

45. See LaMonte, *Feudal Monarchy*, 4ff., for the crown of thorns and for the discussion of the attempts to make Jerusalem a hereditary fief. Godfrey was a direct descendent of Charlemagne. He appears wearing the crown of thorns among the figures at Maximilian's tomb in Innsbruck. See also Kampers, *Die deutsche Kaiseridee*, 216, n. 17: "Hic Imperator renuet coronari corona aurea ad honorem spinarum Coronae Jesu Christi."

46. "Ya dise que para la hesecucion de la ynpresa de las Yndias no me aprovechó rasón, ni matemática, ny mapamundos: llenamente se cunplió lo quediso Ysayas . . ." (Cristoforo Columbo, *Libro de las profecías*, 82).

47. ibid., 80: "Yo dise que diría la rasón que tengo, de la restituçión de la Casa santa á la santa Yglesia: digo que yo deso todo mi navegar desde hedad nueva . . ."

48. On this, see the text of the *Schechina* of Egidio of Viterbo quoted in Reeves, *Influence of Prophecy*, 365.

49. See chapter 3.

50. Columbo, *Libro de las profecías*, 83: "El abad Johachín, calabrés, diso, que había de salir de España quien havía de redificar la Casa del monte Sion." See the discussion in McGinn, *Visions of the End*, 284–85. Reeves (*Influence of Prophecy*, 360) also quotes from this document.

51. Columbo, *Libro de las profecías*, 201.

52. ibid., 202. See also McGinn, *Visions of the End*, 285f.

53. The *Zimmer Chronicke* identifies Charles V as the Great Eagle prophesied by Saint Brigid. Similarly Wolfgang Lazius refers all current prophecies to the emperor or his brother Ferdinand. (See Kurze, "Prophecy," 79). Charles is acknowledged as the second Charlemagne in a version of this prophecy that was sent by Sanuto to Venice in 1519. On both French and German prophecies that were applied to him, see Reeves, *Influence of Prophecy*, 359ff.

54. See the discussion of Ariosto's *Orlando Furioso* in chapter 8.

55. Text cited in Britnell, "Jean Lemaire de Belges," 151. Lemaire's patroness was Margaret of Austria, daughter of Maximilian I, sister of Philip I, and aunt and guardian of the future Charles V. Britnell points out (141ff.) that only in Lemaire's second edition, when his personal ties with Margaret were loosening, does he include a pro-French verse which heralds a French Angelic Pope and a French world emperor, but these predictions were absent in the edition of 1511 which balances French and German claims. Britnell further notes that these prophecies are characteristically written in Latin and carefully constructed to be comprehensible only to the educated.

56. See Britnell, "Jean Lemaire de Belges," 144f.

57. On this interpretation, see the texts cited in Reeves, *Influence of Prophecy*, 448f.

58. Wolfgang Lazius, *Fragmentum . . . Methodi*, cited in Reeves, *Joachim of Fiore*, 114. Ariosto, among others, translates into poetic terms the satisfaction of this prophecy, see chapter 8.

59. For these observations in Titian's picture, see Panofsky, *Problems in Titian*, 84–87.

60. See ibid., 64ff., for the identification of these figures and for a discussion of the picture's disputed title, which Charles V referred to as a Last Judgment. On Luca Giordano's recapitulation of the image on the main staircase of the Escorial for Charles II, see Carr, "Luca Giordano," 16ff., 64ff. He relates Giordano's imagery to Saint Augustine's City of God.

CHAPTER 7

1. An early statement of these ambitions is provided by the chronicle of Charles's sojourn in Italy of 1529–30: "Immediately upon receiving the imperial crown from the Pope, Charles wished to return quickly to Germany . . . [following Charles's coronation the electors of the sacred imperium would immediately elect another designated king of the Romans] and Charles returned home to secure that this election would settle the title on his son, or at a minimum on his brother, so that the imperial title would rest with the House of Austria" (*Cronaca del Soggiorno di Carlo V in Italia . . . 1529–1530*, Documenti di Storia Italiana Estrato da un codice della Regia Biblioteca di Pavia [Milan, 1892], 199). For the contemporary view of the imperium as a hereditary office, see Braudel, *Mediterranean*, 912.

2. Historical criticism which reverses this tradition is discussed in Tanner, "Titian," 11f.

3. For Philip's blending of Burgundian and Spanish with papal ceremony to achieve the intention of making his kingship impressive and remote, see Elliott, *Spain*, 152ff.

4. For sources and a summary of the issues, see Braudel, *Mediterranean*, 914–16.

5. A. de Leva, *Storia documentata di Carlo V*, vol. 5 (Bologna, 1894), 163f.

6. Calvete de Estrella, *El felicíssimo viaje*. See Leo Van Puyvelde, "Les Joyeuses Entrées et la peinture flamande," 287–96, Jean Jacquot, "Panorama des fêtes et cérémonies du Règne," 450ff., and Marcel Lageirse, "La Joyeuse Entrée du Prince Philippe à Gand en 1549," 297ff., all three in Jacquot, ed. *Les Fêtes*, and Strong, *Splendour at Court*, 103ff.

7. Grapheus, *La . . . triumphante entrée du . . . Prince Philipe*, L iii verso. Philip's descent from Noah and from the Trojans was celebrated through figure and inscription, see, for examples, Calvete de Estrella, *El felicíssimo viaje*, 252ff.

8. Calvete de Estrella, *El felicíssimo viaje*, 17.

9. Ibid., 283, Leyden entry: "Como Salomon fue ungido por Rey . . ." The Solomonic imagery appeared throughout the realms, see ibid., 65f., 288. The words "Hic est filius meus dilectus" which bear a relationship to the phrase by which God acknowledges Christ's filiation at the Baptism, underscore the idea that the co-rule of father and son resides in the divine pattern. For the inscription, see ibid., 43.

10. Drake, *In Praise of Constantine*, chap. 2, para. 1. The doctrine was defined and related to imperial rule by Eusebius who declared that "similarly [God's] friend [the Emperor], supplied from above by royal streams and confirmed in the name of a divine calling, rules on earth" (ibid.). See Kantorowicz, *King's Two Bodies*, 338, regarding the monarchical principle of the oneness of Father and Son.

11. The *Gloria* adapts the formula for representing the consubstantiality and the joint rule of God Father and Christ by two nearly identical figures. For a brief discussion of the development of this tradition in the Franco-English and Flemish milieu of the twelfth century, see Panofsky, *Problems in Titian*, 67. For a previous discussion of the pictures' dynastic context, see Tanner, "Titian," 154.

12. Calvete de Estrella, *El felicíssimo viaje*, 82f.: "Ainsi que par Priam à Hector fut donnée la charge de garder Troye, e la Grecz defendre, Nostre naturel Prince est venu este année pour sur nous de son pere semblable charge prendre."

13. The lines from Vergil's *Fourth Eclogue* are applied to the prince: "Iam Redit duce; hoc et aurea aequitas et aura omnibus" (ibid., 230).

14. Ibid., 241–42.

15. *Il Philippino*, Escorial ms & iii. 12, p. ccxxxiiii.

16. For provenance, see Junquera de Vega and Carretero, eds. *Catálogo*, 328.

17. Grapheus, *Triumphe*, Hij.

18. Calvete de Estrella, *El felicíssimo viaje*, 145v. For the coincidence, see Orosius, *Contra paganos*, bk. 7.20.

19. Calvete de Estrella, *El felicíssimo viaje*, 145. For further uses of this topos, see chapter 10.

20. See Braudel, *Mediterranean*, 915–16.

21. Contile, *Ragionamento*, 43f.

22. Saxl, "Veritas," traces the religious character of the northern development of this theme of truth's rescue, its alternating use as a rallying cry, now for Protestant and now for Catholic causes, and its adaptation to refer to the triumph of the Catholic faith by the Hapsburgs. The motto carries eschatalogical implications, for it is extrapolated from the passage in Psalms which refers to the final age of peace when "Truth springs from the earth." I have discussed the application of this motif to Philip in "Titian's Calumny: The Diana and Callisto for Philip II," College Art Association Annual Meeting (New York, 1982).

23. This image is described in Fabre, *Descripción*, 19–20.

24. See chapter 8.

25. See Rosenthal, *Cathedral of Granada*, 162.

26. Ibid., 164, also 117f.

27. This appears in the dedication to the first history of the Indies that was written in the 1550s by the Spaniard Gomarra. He also recalls that this prodigious development was reserved for the reign of Charles V and that Charles's motto "Plus Ultra" implies the sovereignty of the New World. Cited in Bataillon, "Plus oultre," 13.

28. See, for example, Johan Eckius, *Sperandem. Adversus Turcam* (Augsburg, 1532), 279v.: "dictis sacrae scriptyurae, qua plaeriq; qui revelationinibus & Astronomicis praedictionibus fuit. Ecclesiam restituendam afferunt Christianis Catholis, & similiter templum S. Sophie . . . hoc est, Hispanicam, necaturam Turcum, ci multis similibus: qui . . . sub D.D. Carolo & Ferndinando turce Imperium dissolvendum. . . . Cum em Romanorum regnum peribit ante adventum Antichristi, ut Augustinus ex Paulo affirmat . . . libro

de civitate Dei, quanto magis Turcarum." See also Rosenthal, *Cathedral of Granada*, 165.

29. See Bergweiler, *Allegorie*, 186ff.

30. Garibay, *Illustraciones*, 48f., 5ff., and 60f., inter alia. See the reiteration of this claim in Chiflet, *Vindiciae Hispanicae*, 50.

31. See Chiflet, *Vindiciae Hispanicae*, 106.

32. See Braudel, *Mediterranean*, 675, for Micheli's letter to the Doge of 30 January 1563, and for the span of these intentions, which are documented as early as 1562 and as late as 1583.

33. See chapters 10 and 11.

34. See chapter 9.

35. See Tanner, "Titian," 158ff. and 174ff.

36. See chapter 12.

37. See chapter 12.

38. See chapter 9.

39. See Scheicher, "Heraldica," 49f., 56.

CHAPTER 8

1. In the catalogue of the constellations, which he dedicated to the emperor, Manilius characterizes Aries: "Painters represent him gold . . . for according to fabulous history, this was the ram of the Golden Fleece" (Manilius *Astronomica* V.32f.). In the *Fasti*, a circular calendar poem linked with a capsule history of Augustus's divine descent, Ovid begins with Aries: "On reaching the shore the ram was made a constellation but his Golden Fleece was carried to Colchian homes" (Ovid *Fasti* III.876). According to the Scholiasts, the cosmic Ram was Phrixus's soul carried to heaven.

2. Pindar (*Odes* IV.230) calls the Fleece "imperishable," as does Apollonius Rhodius *Argonautica* IV.1141. For a discussion of the Golden Fleece as the genie of Phrixus in Pindar, "who makes the motive for the voyage . . . the urgent desire of Phrixus' ghost that the fleece come back to Iolcus so that his soul can be at rest," see Beye, *Epic*, 47. In the description of Philip II's *Argo*, Mal Lara, *Descripción*, 87, quotes Pindar's phrase that the fleece was Phrixus's incorruptible spirit. For the perpetuity of the concept, see Epilogue.

3. Pindar *Odes* IV.159F. In Valerius Flaccus's *Argonautica* V.503, Jason asks Aeetes to "grudge not [the return of the Fleece], it is to Phrixus thou dost give it, that Phrixus is bearing it to his father's house." See ibid., V.475, for Jason's procla-

mation of his kinship with Phrixus; also see II.1030ff. Pindar identifies all the Argonauts as sons of the immortal gods (*Pythian* IV.I.1). In Valerius Flaccus *Argonautica* V.30, the Argonauts relate: "We are the sons of gods and this vessel is Minerva's." For a discussion of this identity and of the journey as a divine enterprise, characterized by prayer, sacrifice, and libations see Delage, "Mythe," 127f. See also Roux, *Problème*, 292.

4. See Valerius Flaccus *Argonautica* I.530, (cited in chapter 1) in which Jove reveals his providential plan for the defeat of Asia and the rise of the Roman Empire. The passage picks up and extends for the Flavians the theme announced for Augustus in Virgil, *Aeneid*, bk. I.

5. See, for example, Manilius *Astronomica* II.945f. For the adaptation of this chronology to Old and New Testament personifications of a New Time, see Chauncey Wood, *Chaucer and the Country of the Stars* (Princeton, 1970), 163. Chaucer, for example, refers to March as the month in which God made Adam and the world began (*Nun's Priest's Tale*, 3187–88).

6. For these concepts, see 37C–38C in *Plato's Cosmology*, ed. Francis M. Cornford (London, 1937).

7. *Virgil*, vol. 1, *Eclogue* IV.11–17. In his Commentary on Vergil's *Fourth Eclogue*, Servius explains that at the beginning of a new Great Year, when the prophesied reign of Apollo would be initiated, all the stars must return to the position they occupied at the Creation: "Cumana . . . saecula per metalla divisit, dixit etiam quis quo saeculo imperaret, et Solem ultimum, id est decimum voluit: novimus autem eundem esse Apollinem, unde dicit (10) 'tuus iam regnat Apollo.' Dicit etiam, finitis omnibus saeculis rursus eadam innovari: quam rem etiam philosophi hac disputatione colligunt, dicentes, completo magno anno omnia sidera in ortus suos redire et ferri rursus eodem motu . . . hoc secutus Vergilius dicit reverti aurea secula . . ." (Servii, *Grammatici*, 44–45). This concept of renewal is discussed in Carcopino, *Virgile*, 38–39, and Snell, "L'Arcadia," 319ff. Vergil's Great Cosmic Year is related to the theory of the four ages that commence with the Golden Age and end with the Iron Age. See the reference to this topos in *Eclogue VI*, wherein the New Time is heralded and the moral degradation that has taken place from the end of the Golden Age to the present is contemplated. For a

discussion that the Great Year would begin in spring and initiate a millennium, see della Corte, "La 'Proanafonesi,'" 7–9. In some sixteenth-century seasonal cycles—the Villa at Caprarola in Italy is one example—representations of the myth of Phrixius and Helle astride the Golden Fleece are used to illustrate the first season of the year, spring.

8. Virgil, *Eclogue* IV.34–43.

9. Ibid.

10. Apollonius Rhodius *Argonautica* IV.125. Although critics have pondered the meaning of the Cosmic Year in Vergil's *Fourth Eclogue*, they have not, to my knowledge, connected this renewal to the return of Aries to the heavens. The link between the Golden Fleece and Aries is sustained by the symbolism of the cosmic insignia, as pointed out here.

11. "Lord of the flock and conquerer of the sea . . . the Ram . . . even now draws *Argo* by the Poop. . . . Whoever is born . . . at the rising of *Argo* will be the captain of a ship . . . visit the deep Phasis, and better the speed of Tiphys towards the rocks. Take away the men situate beneath this constellation and you will take away the Trojan war . . . the world within Actium's bays hangs in the balance between opposing forces, and heaven's destiny floats at the mercy of the waves" (Manilius *Astronomica* V.32).

12. See Adamietz, "Komposition," 22, and Roux, *Problème*, 294, for this interpretation, also cited in chapter 1. See also Cairns, *Augustan Epic*, 195ff., for Jason as a model for Aeneas, and 222 for the characterization of the *Aeneid* as a religious poem that narrates the fulfillment of a divinely inspired mission.

13. See chapter 2.

14. This phrase is used by Lucan, *The Civil War*, trans. J. D. Duff, Loeb Classical Library (London, 1962), IV.179 "But . . . in spring [Aries the Ram] who let Helle fall received the burning sun and looked back at the other signs; and when day and night had for the second time been made equal according to the balance of . . . Libra, day gained the victory."

15. The Carolingian Hirenicus associated the lamb of God with Aries. See "De Ratione Duodecim Signorum," *MGH. Poetarum Latinorum Medii Aevi*, ed. K. Strecker, vol. 4, pt. 2 (Berlin, 1923), 693–95: "Habet fides Christiana signorum memoriam / Primum agni (Christi, quia Aries in

zodaico agmen [ed.note]) qui in celo maiestate fulgida / Regnat unicus cum patre per immensa secula."

16. In the *Iconologia*, a standard Renaissance handbook of emblematic devices, Cesare Ripa records that the birth of the sun and the creation of the world as well as the Passion and the Redemption of Christ occur in the sign of Aries: "Equinottio della Primavera . . . nel mese di Marzo . . . principio dell'anno . . . fosse la creatione del mondo, & anco l'anno della Redentione, & della Passione di N.S. & anco da quello nel primo grado dell' Ariete essere stato creato il Sole" (Ripa, *Iconologia*, 142–43).

17. Colonne, *Destruction of Troy*, bk. IV, ll. 1048ff. The Latin original is more complete in that it connects this moment with the equinox: "Tempus erat quod sol maturans sub obliquo zodiaci circulo cursum suum sub signo iam intraverat arietis, in quo noctium spatio equato diebus celebratur equinoctium primi veris, tunc cum incipit tempus blandiri mortalibus in aeris serenitate intentis" (Columnis, *Historia Destructionis Troiae*, bk. IV, ll. 1048ff.). These lines are thought to have inspired Chaucer in fixing the date for the spiritual crusade which begins the *Canterbury Tales*: "When . . . the yonge sonne / Hath in the Ram his halve cours yronne, . . . Thanne longen folk to goon on pilgrimages" (*General Prologue*, 1–12). For a discussion of Chaucer's adaptation, see Nils Erik Enkvist, *The Seasons of the Year* (Helsingford, 1957), 124, and Wood, *Chaucer*, 161ff.

18. The establishment of the Order was considered the principal act of the celebrations in honor of Philip's marriage to Isabella of Portugal. See Baron de Reiffenberg, *Histoire*, xxi and xxiv. Shortly after his marriage, Philip had a cosmic room in his palace decorated with scenes of Jason and the Golden Fleece. The establishment of the Order coincides with the duke's investiture of the Duchy of Brabant by Emperor Sigismund in 1430.

Philip the Good's father, John the Fearless, was captured on Turkish soil, near the place identified with Jason's expedition. The Turkish question is discussed in Kervyn de Lettenhove, *Toison d'or*, 15ff. For a history of the Order, see also Baron de Reiffenberg, *Histoire*. Rudolf Payer von Thurn, *Der Orden vom Goldenen Vliess* (Vienna, n.d.), and Terlinden, "Das goldene Vliess."

19. See chapter 4.

20. Fillastre, *Le Premier Volume* I:4ff. The treatise was completed in 1468. Kervyn de Lettenhove (*Toison d'or*, 13) records that chapter meetings were held in the choir of a church and began with vespers. He quotes an address to the knights by "Dame Religion" at the famous Banquet du Faisan at Lille in which the eucharistic implication of the Fleece is recalled: "Vous Chevaliers, qui portez la Toison, N'oubliez point le très divin sacrifice." V. Terlinden ("Coup d'oeil," 25f.) discusses the Order's objectives in the Holy Land. Tourneur ("Origines," 314) discusses some of Philip's political objectives and his intended crusade to oust the Turk from the Holy Land. In this connection, he mentions (314) that a mythic counterpart already existed in the *Histoire de Troyes*, a medieval Trojan chronicle transmitted to Philip by his grandfather that began with the adventures of the Argonauts to conquer the Golden Fleece.

21. Fillastre, *Le Premier Volume* I:9. On p. 8, Fillastre associates Jason with Jesus and the *Argo* with Mary's womb.

22. Ibid., I:44ff.

23. Ibid. A pagan parallel for this correspondence was provided in Manilius, who assigned the parts of the human body to the zodiac. To the ram, as chieftain of them all, is allotted the head (*Astronomica* II.453f.). This division of the human figure according to zodiacal influences with Aries commanding the head is represented in a contemporary miniature by the Limbourg Brothers in the *Très Riches Heures* of the duke de Berry. It is interesting to note that Philip the Good was related to the duke de Berry and was himself a patron of these artists.

24. See chapter 5.

25. Both saints Andrew and Gideon were also patrons of the Order.

26. Washington, D.C., National Gallery. See Panofsky, *Early Netherlandish Painting* I:139 and n. 1, II:plate 11.

27. The statutes provide that the knights cannot distance themselves from the sovereign of the Order nor undertake wars without his permission. On this, see Hommel, *L'Histoire*, 18; see further pp. 41–45 regarding the knights' privileges and rights of immunity. These include not only the receipt of bounties, the release from contributions and immunity to taxation but the implication that in matters of law, the Order would act as a tribunal affording them exclusion from other jurisdiction.

28. *Virgil, Eclogue* IV.35–36.

29. See Bergmans, "Note," 9f. A more detailed description of the reconstructed altarpiece is provided in Jarenbergh, "Fêtes," 11ff., and more recently by Jeffrey Chipps Smith, "Venir nobis pacificus Dominus: Philip the Good's Triumphal Entry into Ghent in 1458," in *Triumphal Celebrations and the Rituals of Statecraft*, ed. Barbara Wisch and Susan Scott Munshower, Papers in Art History from the Pennsylvania State University, vol. 6, pt. 1 (University Park, Penn., 1990), 258–91. For a monographic study of this altarpiece that considers other contexts, see Lotte Brand Philip, *The Ghent Altarpiece and the Art of Jan van Eyck* (Princeton, 1980).

30. "Haec Aries, haec lanificum denuciat astrum. Hoc olim dominante novi sub origine mundi. Et felix aetas, & libera secla fuere. . . . Omnibus una quies & amor simul . . ." (Pontano, *Urania* II, v. 250ff. in *Carminum*).

31. Burgundian sovereignty of the Order was dynastic and not territorial. This issue is discussed in Terlinden, "Coup d'oeil," 28. Since a female could not inherit the title, sovereignty passed to Maximilian when he married Mary; it passed through Maximilian to his Hapsburg heirs.

32. For a discussion of the contested sovereignty of the Order between Austria and Spain, which mentions Napoléon's creation of another branch of the Order, based on the assertion that he brought together in his person Burgundian and Austrian rights, see Hommel, *L'Histoire*, 54ff.

33. Rosenthal ("Invention," 201ff.) established that the device was invented for this occasion.

34. Traveling to Spain, where he destroyed the tyrant Geryon and fathered a line of noble rulers, Hercules (one of the Argonautic adventurers, and the legendary founder of Spain) set up the columns at Gibralter, which marked the farthest reaches of Africa and Europe. For the ancient sources of this tradition, see Rosenthal, "Plus Ultra." For the dependence of the emblem's inscription, "Plus Ultra," on the Trojan legend created by Raoul Lefèvre for Philip the Good of Burgundy, see ibid., 218–19; Rosenthal posits that the earliest reference to the columns of Hercules in Flanders occurs in this history

(213). He also suggests that the phrase evokes the cry of medieval pilgrims journeying to the Holy Land (222).

35. For Augustus's use of the columns of Hercules, see Rosenthal, "Invention," 217.

36. For the use of paired columns in a medal of Alfonso I of Naples, then king of Jerusalem and the grandfather of Ferdinand the Catholic, and thus Charles V's paternal grandfather twice removed, see Rosenthal, "Invention," 218. For other Spanish references, see 212ff., and for the device's references to the New World, see 217.

37. For the tradition of paired columns as a reference to Jachim and Boaz, the columns of Solomon's temple, see Rosenthal, "Invention," 220, n. 81, and fig. 34b; Rosenthal discounts this reference, however, because the disposition differs from the columns on Charles's device. With the emphasis on Jerusalem as the focus of imperial destiny, the Solomonic identification seems to be a critical motive for the iconography. On this, see also chapter 9. For Emperor Charles VI's reuse of the columns with this significance, see Maatsche, Kunst, 289.

38. Yates, Astraea, 42, signals the columns as a key symbol for the revival of the dream of universal empire; in later portions of her book she traces the adaptation of its iconography by rival courts.

39. Rosenthal, "Invention," cites and illustrates, among other examples, Dürer's medal of 1521 for the city of Nuremberg (225 and pl. 39 c.d.); and the choir stall in the cathedral of Barcelona, decorated for a meeting of the Order of the Golden Fleece. See also the combination of the columns, the firestone, and flint with the Gordian knot and yoke of Ferdinand, and the bundle of arrows of Isabella (224).

40. See ibid., 221, for the oration delivered at Charles's assumption of the Order's sovereignty on 26 October 1516 by Luigi Marliano.

41. The Burgundian statutes fixed the number of members at thirty-one; Charles V increased the power of the knighthood by raising the number to fifty-one; ten of these new knights were Spanish, the first inclusion of Spanish nobility. See Terlinden, "Coup d'oeil," 23.

42. Baldasar de Cartolari, La Entrade, de la majestad à Milano (Rome, 1541): "Al los mios aquiste el vellocino, y al mondo acquistaste el siglo

d'oro." The image above Jason represented "el castillo de la Goleta y exercitos se combattan." Similarly in Dordrecht, a representation of Jason carries this description: "Veys aqui el resplandeciente vellocino de oro de Phryxo, Serenissima Principe, al qual llevo de Colcos aquel Illustre y magnanimi Iason, a este y a sus esclarecidas hazanas, tomad por dechado por ymitarle."

43. The opening lines of Orlando Furioso— "Of Loves and Ladies, Knights and Arms I sing, . . . Who on king Charles', the Roman emperor's head / Had vowed due vengeance for Troyano dead"—echo the opening lines of the Aeneid— "Arms I sing and the man who first from the coasts of Troy, exiled by fate, came to Italy . . . whence came the lords of Alba"—and cast Charles in the mold of Aeneas (Ariosto Orlando Furioso, canto 1, stanza 11, ll. 1ff., and Virgil, Aeneid I.1ff.). Ariosto's ending lines paraphrase Aeneas's victory over proud Turnus.

The Orlando Furioso venerates Charles V as the new Aeneas and the new Charlemagne. For other Vergilian references in Ariosto see Orlando Furioso, xxxix. The poem was written for Alfonso d'Este, who derived his own claims to imperial legitimacy through his status as Charles V's vassal. The iconography of Charles V as it emerges in the poem has never been analyzed in any significant detail; in her fundamental study of Charles's imperial iconography, however, Frances Yates suggested some possible approaches (Astraea, 23f.).

44. Ariosto Orlando Furioso, canto 15, stanzas 21f.

45. See Weber, "Der österreichische Orden," 29.

46. Sixto, Genealogia, 29v–34v: "Ex eo Clodivicus . . . à Divo Remigio sacrum baptisma suscepit. . . . & per baptismum Christo adhaereret. . . . Eodemque die & inibi Angelus è coelo cunctos stupore afficiens visus est, manu altera lilia aurea gestans, altera vero' vasa miré laborata Olei plena, et inquit, hûc me Rex misit caelestis ut semper tui sit Mundo memoria, quemadmodum Christo mentem direxisti. En lilia aurea, quae domi forisque tua Regia erunt insignia, & posterum tuorum, qui Franciae sceptrum obtinebunt. . . . Insuper affero tibi hoc vas plenum liquoris rari: quo semper, & tu simul, & successores tui Regni caput ungent. . . . Quare Ludovicus liquore sancto caput aspersit, liliorum

insignia erexit toti familiae debita quidem tro-
phaea. . . . Ex quo Carolus magnus Imperator
Austriae Rex secundus, . . . Author non dico de
Hilperico, ex quo origo Carolimagni: sed de
Sigisberto, qui Austriae regno ex patria successione potitus est, qui fuit primus Rex Austriae . . .
Ridulphus ex Austriae familia primus Imperator
. . . Philippus Rex noster tempora ista Iuppiter
Christianitatis est appellandus." See also the cod-
icil to Philip's will, in which he appropriates a
fleur-de-lis reliquary and cross as a perpetual dynastic preserve: "habia vinculado expresamente
al trono, para recibir en herencia, un relicario en
forma de flor de lis, que pertenecio al Emperador, y un lignum crucis, con identica fuerza e im-
portancia, una esa donacion, de forma inse-
parable" (Campos and Fernandez de Sevilla,
"Carta de fundación," 326, n. 77). Also included is
the unicorn's horn, a symbol of the Virgin's pu-
rity.

47. See Baron de Reiffenberg, Histoire, lxxiv.

48. Hommel, L'Histoire, 71.

49. For a discussion of this decision, see
ibid., 73ff. The role played by the Order in world
politics up to 1918 and a more extensive discussion of Spanish and Austrian claims to its sovereignty are discussed in Weber, "Der österreichische Orden," 176ff.

50. See F. W. H. Holstein, Dutch and Flemish
Etchings and Engravings, ed. K. G. Boon, vol. 26 (Am-
sterdam, 1982), 51 and fig. 4.

51. Marciano, Pompe Funebri, 117.

52. For a description and more detailed
photographs of the ceiling, see Rosa López Tor-
rijos, Lucas Jordan en el Casón del Buen Retiro: La alegoria
del Toison de Oro (Madrid, n.d.).

CHAPTER 9

1. Sigüenza, Fundación, 17. Sigüenza, who
claimed that he authored the library's iconographical program, followed Arias Montano as its
librarian. The universal import of this victory
continued to be articulated into the seventeenth
century and beyond. In Padre de los Santos's account of the Escorial, he notes: "Fue esta la
primera Vatalla de el prudentíssimo Rey Philipo
Seguno . . . la primera Vitoria; y de consequen-
cias tan grandes, que ocasionó una paz en la
Christianidad la mas universal, que se ha visto en
muchos Siglos; y fue tambien el primer motivo

para edificar esta maravilla" (Santos, Descripción,
cited in Carr, "Luca Giordano," 227).

2. See Schramm, Sphaira, 51, cited in Van
der Osten Sacken, San Lorenzo, 104, n. 168.

3. The building was begun under the architect Juan Battista de Toledo; at his death in 1567
he was succeeded by Juan de Herrera. For
Philip's close supervision of the execution of
this project, see Taylor, "Architecture and Magic,"
81. For an example of Philip's involvement in the
genesis and progress of a work of art for the
main altar, see Priscille E. Muller, "Philip II,
Federigo Zuccaro, Pellegrino Tibaldi, Bartolom-
meo Caducho," and the Adoration of the Magi in the
Escorial Retablo Major, XXII Congreso Internacional
del Arte (Granada, 1973), 125. For a monographic
study of the edifice, see Kubler, Building the Escorial; a recent annotated bibliography appears in
Barghahn, Age of Gold, 1:265ff.

4. For the former image, see Barghahn, Age
of Gold, vol. 1, following p. 109. For Luca Giordano's pictorial reconstruction of the building's
foundation, which shows "the most pious King
Philip II, who with great Solemnity lays the first
stone," see Carr, "Luca Giordano," 109ff. Noting
that the subject of kings directing construction is
rare in the history of art, Carr shows the symbolic meaning of Giordano's scene which emphasizes the temple. He relates this emphasis to
Philip's identity with Solomon, the temple
builder.

5. The crypt was to include other members
of the royal family as well. The building was also
to serve as a "seminary and hospital for the Jeronomite Monks to whom my father was particularly devoted" (Campos and Fernandez de
Sevilla, "Carta de fundación," 233ff.).

6. See Hempel, Philip II, 78ff., for contemporary sources that call the Escorial a Roman
Olympus and refer to Philip as Jupiter on earth.
Sigüenza, Fundación, also applied mixed metaphors to describe the monument: "La compara-
ción . . . de este templo y casa con otros edificios
famosos, principalmente con el templo de Salomón . . . otros también se acuerdan de las siete
maravillas del mundo, y con gente más leída,
dicen que es . . . la octava" (573). Other analogies
perpetuate the Escorial's connection to the Seven
Wonders of the World: "Pues con uno que hizo
en el sitio del Escorial puede callar el Templo de
Diana en Efeso, la casa del Sol, los muros de
Babilonia, el coloso de Rodas, las Piramides de

Egipto. . . . se da el nombra de octava maravilla" (Baltasar Porreno, *Dichos y hechos del Rey don Felipe II*, text in Alvarez Turienzo, *El Escorial*, 167–68). See also Hempel, *Philip II*, 76ff., for this and other references to the Escorial as the House of the Sun, the Eighth Wonder of the World, et alia.

7. See Hempel, *Philip II*, 89, for Philip's comparison with Moses, and the Escorial with Sinai; see ibid., 85ff., for other Old Testament parallels. For Philip's identification with the pagan gods and rulers see ibid., 74, 78f., and 99.

8. "Es la planta de esta immensa fábrica cuadrada, menos por la parte del oriente donde brilla el palacio real con el immensa fabrica con el cual dio su ilustre arquitecto al conjunto del edificio la forma de las parrillas en que fue martirizado nuestro San Lorenzo" (Padre Mariana [1536–1623], *Del Rey y de la Institución Real* [Madrid, 1854], 552–53, cited in Alvarez Turienzo, *El Escorial*, 175).

9. For the Flemish source of the roofs and for perpetuation of this mixture of imperial towers with pointed slate roofs at Philip IV's Buen Retiro Palace, see Brown and Elliott, *A Palace for a King*, 84.

10. "Fastigio, usada antiguamente solamente en las fachadas de los templos, puesta despues en obra por Julio Cesar en el frontispicio de su nuevo Palacio" (Juan Caramuel Lobkowitz, *Philippus Prudens* [Antwerp, 1639], 28).

11. For the Old Testament ancestors of the Hapsburg gens, see chapter 5.

12. The six kings who built or rebuilt the temple and who appear here with inscriptions are David and Solomon, Hiskia and Josephat, Joshua and Manassah. See Sigüenza, *Fundación*, 89f., who links the sculptural decoration to Benito Arias Montano. For George Kubler (*Building the Escorial* 42f.) the biblical kings were an afterthought, and the comparison with Solomon's temple was developed after Philip was exposed to Villapando's *In Ezechielem Explanationes et Apparatus Urbis, ac Templi Hierosolymitani* (published 1598–1604) only after the building was completed. This line of thinking disregards the consistent edifice of Hapsburg theocratic thought, and it denigrates Philip's role in ideating his key monument. Referring to Arias Montano as the ideator of the sculptures, another view was provided by L. Moya Blanco: "La obra de erudición tardó más que la obra de piedra, pero es posible que los primeros resultados de la investigación estuviesen ya en condiciones de servir de base para el proyecto, en la época de Juan Bautista de Toledo" (quoted in Hempel, *Philip II*, 90f.).

13. On the towers as the emblem of a Hapsburg family name that carried the significance of invincibility, see chapter 10.

14. "Aquí como en otro templo de Salomón, a quien nuestro patron y fundador Felipe II fue imitando en esta obra, suenan de dia y de noche las divinas alabanzas, se hacen continuos sacrificios, humean siempre los inciensos, no se apaga el fuego ni faltan pannes recientes delante de la prescencia divina, y debajo de los altares reposan las cenizas y los huesos de los que fueron sacrificados por Cristo" (Sigüenza, *Fundación*, 11). Ibid., 573f., for other examples of its likeness to Solomon's temple; there Sigüenza includes the Escorial's similarity to great Christian monuments as well. For the identification of the Escorial with Solomon's temple, see the studies of Taylor, "El Padre Villalpando," 421f., and "Architecture and Magic," 90ff.; and more recently Van der Osten Sacken, *San Lorenzo*, 207ff.

15. On this distinction, see the sources cited in Van der Osten Sacken, *San Lorenzo*, 216.

16. See *El Escorial en la Biblioteca Nacional*, 110f. For a general study on Montano, see Rekers, *Benitos Arias Montano*.

17. Sigüenza, *Fundación*, 589: "A la que estaba a la diestra del templo llamó Jachim, y a la otra, Bohaz; no es lugar de deternernos a explicar tantos misterios como aquí se encierran."

18. For the connection between Charles V's emblem and the columns of Jachim and Boaz see chapter 8. For the adaptation of these two columns to other architectural monuments, see Anthony Blunt, "The Temple of Solomon with Special Reference to South Italian Baroque Art," in *Kunsthistorische Forschungen: Otto Pächt zu seinem 70. Geburtstag*, ed. A. Rosenauer and G. Weber (Salzburg, 1972), 259ff.

19. For another view of the similarities, see Van der Osten Sacken, *San Lorenzo*, 213f.

20. Santos, *Descripción*, 4.

21. See Frances Yates, *The Valois Tapestries* (London, 1975), 25. She notes the picture's connection with a meeting of the Order of the Golden Fleece. For another example, see Carr, "Luca Giordano," 132, who cites an edition of Montano's *Humanae Salutis Monumenta* with a plate depicting Solomon with the features of Philip II.

22. See Columbo, *Libro*, 311, for a discussion of Columbus's identification of the New World with Ophir. This belief was perpetuated in Spanish court circles: "En las de la Nueva España, quiere constituir el Ophir. . . . Como aun el mesmo Don Christoval Colon lo coméço à hazer en la Islas Española, luego que la descubrio, i reconocio, alabàndose, que avia hallado la Region Ophira, como Pedro Martyr afirma" (Solorzano Pereira, *Politica Indiana*, 26.

23. One example is provided by the Emperor Charles VI. Claiming the right of succession to the Spanish throne, Charles took up the Solomonic identity, calling Philip II the Second Solomon and himself the Third. See Maatsche, *Kunst*, 289. For the Escorial as the model for future Crown construction, see Brown and Elliott, *A Palace for a King*, 43 and 84.

24. From a poem by Biagio Riti, *Poemi scritti in Lode de la sacra Real Fabrica de lo Escuriale*, cited in Hempel, *Philip II*, 88.

25. Sigüenza (*Fundación*, 577ff.) compares the building not only to Solomon's temple, but to the heavenly Jerusalem of Ezekiel's vision: "Lo primero que quiero asentar . . . que el Templo de Salomón, y el que el profeta Ezequiel pinta, cuyas medidas le mostró el ángel en visión, son tan diferentes como el cielo y la tierra . . . y tan distantes como los dos arquitectos, Salomón y Jesucristo. Aquél le hicieron manos de hombres y los ojos de infinitos le vieron y le pudieron medir. Este no entraron manos de hombres en él. . . . Templo de Ezequiel, que no es según nos lo enseña, sino un Templo y perfecta Fábrica de Cristo . . . prueba el Doctor santo que este Templo no es el de Salomon . . . porque en este de Ezequiel, todo él con todo su ámbito se llama Santa Santorum . . . y que no tiene que ver esta Casa de San Lorenzo con sólo este paredon y cimientos." Another recall to Ezekiel may have been intended in the Escorial's ground plan; see text at n. 47.

26. Saint Paul defined the translation of the Old Testament into the New Testament Temple of Jerusalem as the moment when the fiend death is defeated. This concept informed Origen's formula, which contributed to the Christianization of the image, see Gnilka, *Studien*, 113, n. 47.

27. Sigüenza, *Fundación*, 577.

28. In Biagio Riti's poem cited in the text, the Escorial is described in the terms of Revelation as the bride descending to her heavenly bridegroom. He also links the Escorial's jeweled ornamentation to Saint John's description of the heavenly Jerusalem. The references are to Revelation 21:2. See Hempel, *Philip II*, 92, also 88ff. for the notation that these comparisons put the Escorial into an eschatological context.

29. Revelation 21:18; compare also with Prudentius's Roman redaction: "No building stone is there, but a single gem, a block through which much hewing has pierced a passage . . ." (*Prudentius*, vol. 1, *Psychomachia* ll. 834–36).

30. See *El Escorial en la Biblioteca Nacional*, 111ff.

31. "En el uno y en el otro [de los testeros] las armas y blasones de sus padres y antepasados, hechos de los mismos jaspes y piedras . . . estan los de parte de padre, y en el de las espaldas los de parte de la madre" (Sigüenza, *Fundación*, 471). He also quotes the inscriptions and exalts this ancestry, thus for Charles V: "Quiere decir: Estos son los blasones y armas del linaje y descendencia de parte del padre Carolos V. Emperador Romano . . . distintas por sus grados y dignidades. . . . La providencia y cuidado de los descendientes deja esta lugar vacío a los hijos y nietos."

32. For a discussion of the bronze effigies, see Mezzatesta, "Imperial Themes." By equating the imagery to sacramental tabernacles, he has developed an interpretation that is conceptually related to the meaning suggested here.

33. "Que por mi devoción y en reverencia del Santísimo Sacramento hayan de estar continuamente dos frailes delante del rogando a Diós por mi ánima y por las de mis difuntos . . . dia y noche han de estar en oración perpetua los dichos dos frailes, uno sacerdote y otro no." The quote is taken from the codicils to Philip II's will written in the year of his death 1598, regarding matters relative to San Lorenzo (Campos and Fernandez de Sevilla, "Carta de fundación," 374, n. 332).

34. Cited in Braudel, *Mediterranean*, 675.

35. *Prudentius, Psychomachia* ll. 804ff.: "One task remains [to] . . . Solomon . . . rest for the homeless Ark. . . . In our camp too let the Temple arise [for Christ's return]." See Gnilka, *Studien*, 120f., for a discussion of the temple as a metaphor for the Corpus Christi, and as a symbol of the Pax Cristiana which incorporates the sublime

Tribunal. See ibid. for the temple's imperial parallel.

36. Prudentius, *Psychomachia* l. 818.

37. See chapter 2.

38. For the conferring of kingship and priesthood through the attributes of scepter and rod, and for a discussion of the scepter's relationship to both Aaron and Latinus, see Gnilka, *Studien*, 120ff., and chapter 2. For an extended discussion of the parallels between Prudentius's edifice, the temple of Solomon and the heavenly Jerusalem of the New Faith ruled by Christ the King in the Throne of Wisdom, see ibid., 109ff. Gnilka (120–21) refers to visualizations of this concept in early Christian art. References to Prudentius's apocalyptic imagery are also made by Smith, *Prudentius' Psychomachia*, 199–200.

39. See Hempel, *Philip II*, 80.

40. For an itemization of the library's subjects, see Sigüenza, *Fundación*, 380ff. For Montano's response to the criticisms of the use of nudity and profane subjects, see his letter, cited in Rekers, *Montano*, 115.

41. For a reading that relates this imagery to Philip's horoscope, see Taylor, "Architecture and Magic," 98ff. Copies of this medal, which was designed by Jacopo da Trezzo, who created Philip's personal emblem, were placed in the cornice and in the foundations of the tabernacle in the church. On this see ibid, 101.

For a medieval vision of a temple of justice in which the Eucharist is preserved and protected by the statutes of Roman law, see Kantorowicz, *King's Two Bodies*, 107ff. Here, the shrine reserved for the Holy of Holies was separated by a wall of glass on which the texts of Justinian's law books were inscribed.

42. The poem is quoted and discussed in Hempel, *Philip II*, 59.

43. For Chueca Goitia (*Casas reales*, 142ff.) the cloister-residence is the apex of a long tradition of politico-religious complexes combining a mausoleum with a temple, palace, and college that began with Diocletian's palace at Split; he notes the evocation of this model at Aachen.

44. Suetonius, vol. 1, *Lives of the Caesars*, bk. 2, chap. 29, p. 167.

45. "In Eucharistico succo Austriae familiae arbori. . . . Hoc verae Palladis . . . genitae. . . . Hoc . . . est gentilitum magnae tuae gentis em-

blema" (Palavicino, *Austriaci Caesares*, 44–45). For other examples, see chapter 11.

46. Prudentius, vol. 2, *Crowns of Martyrdom*, bk. 2, ll. 109–43, was the most popular version of the legend, and was known to Philip II. For other sources of the Lawrence legend, see *Analecta Bollandiana*, vol. 51, fasc. I and II, ed. Hippolyte Delehaye (Brussels, 1933), pp. 34–98.

47. Condemned to a slow torturous death on the gridiron, Lawrence, who remained steadfast in his faith to the end, called out when the heat had consumed his body for a long time: "This part of my body has been burned long enough; turn it round and try what your hot god of fire has done" (Prudentius, *Crowns of Martyrdom*, bk. 2, ll. 400ff.).

In Ezekiel 4:1, the Lord appears to Ezekiel and tells him to trace out Jerusalem and set up siegeworks and battering rams about it. "And take . . . an iron griddle, and set it as an iron wall between you and the city, and set your face toward it, and let it be in a state of siege, and press the siege against it. This is a sign for the house of Israel. Then lie upon your left side, and I will lay the punishment of the house of Israel upon you. . . . And when you have completed these [years of punishment], you shall lie down a second time, but on your right side and bear the punishment of the house of Judah." The vision of the temple begins at Ezekiel 8:1.

48. Prudentius, *Crowns of Martyrdom*, bk. 2, l. 39.

49. Ibid., ll. 397f. Lawrence's offer of his flesh, "It is done, eat it up, try whether it is nicer raw or roasted," establishes the martyr's assimilation to Christ. He is also compared with Moses, (with references to Exodus 32, 34:29–30, and 10:22–23): "Lawrence's . . . face shone with beauty and a glory was shed around him. Such was the countenance that the bearer of the law brought down from the mountain on his return, and the Jewish people having stained and tarnished itself with the golden ox, was greatly afraid. . . . It was like the Egyptian plague, which, while it condemned the barbarians to darkness, gave to the Hebrews the clear light of day."

50. Prudentius, *Crowns of Martyrdom*, bk. 2, ll. 46f. When commanded to yield the treasures of the church by the imperial prefect, Lawrence produced instead "noble jewels . . . the consecrated virgins . . . and pure old women. . . . These are the Church's necklace."

51. For Prudentius's dependence on *Aeneid* VI.756ff., which emphasizes the coming imperium, and for a general discussion of Prudentius's adaptation of Vergil's concept of Rome's destiny to Christianity, see Buchheit, "Christliche Romideologie," 125ff., and Palmer, *Prudentius*, 121ff.

52. *Prudentius, Crowns of Martyrdom*, bk. 2, ll. 413f. For Prudentius's source in Anchises' parade of hero-ancestors (*Aeneid* VI.851–53), see Buchheit, "Christliche Romideologie," 127f.

53. For Theodosius as the promised emperor, and for Prudentius's sources for the concept in the *Aeneid*, see Buchheit, "Christliche Romideologie," 138ff. Prudentius expressed a similar concept in *A Reply to the Address of Symmachus* where—referring to the emperor's defeat of the pagan faction—Prudentius took up the theme of a Christian Rome in which the pagan divinities are transformed into icons of the New Faith, and Christ is invited to enter "a world in harmony . . . which peace and Rome hold in a bond of union." The passage continues: "These Thou dost command to be the heads and highest powers of the world. Rome without peace finds no favor with Thee; and it is the supremacy of Rome, keeping down disorders . . . that secures the peace" (*Prudentius*, vols. 1 and 2, *A Reply to the Address of Symmachus*, bk. 2, ll. 636ff.).

54. *Prudentius, Crowns of Martyrdom*, bk. 2, ll. 443–87. "Julus" is a reference to Aeneas's son, who was the paterfamilias of the Julio-Claudian dynasty.

55. Ibid., ll. 497–520. For the relationship between Vesta and the Penates, see chapter 1.

56. According to the *Res Gestae*, Octavian was awarded the civic crown together with the title Augustus for ending the Civil War and establishing his universal sovereignty: ". . . after I had extinguished civil wars, and at a time when with universal consent I was in complete control of affairs. . . . For this service of mine I was named Augustus . . . and the doorposts of my house were publicly wreathed with bay leaves, and a civic crown was fixed over my door" (P. A. Brunt and J. M. More, *Res Gestae Divi Augusti: The Achievements of the Divine Augustus* [Oxford, 1967], 34–35). For the link established between Lawrence and Augustus by the corona, see Buchheit, "Christliche Romideologie," 143.

57. Prudentius, *Crowns of Martyrdom*, bk. 2, ll. 547f.

58. Panofsky, *Problems in Titian*, 53–57, observed that Prudentius's legend served as the text informing the picture. Begun by 1564, the picture was installed as early as 1567. In connection with Lawrence's importance for Roman imperial iconography, it is interesting that Titian's earlier Lawrence (Venice, Gesuiti) has recently been connected with the Querini family's pretensions to descend from the Emperor Galba and that the statue of Vesta-Claudia is a direct allusion to the patroness of the picture, Elizabeth Querini; see *Tiziano*, Exhibition catalogue Palazzo Ducale (Venice, 1990), 311. Another painting of Lawrence by Pellegrino Tibaldi forms the center of the altarpiece at the Basilica of the Escorial. It is modeled on Titian's picture.

59. This rededication of pagan to Christian had its parallel in Christ's cleansing of the temple. The topos was later identified with the capture of the Holy Sepulchre, a feat accomplished by Philip's ancestors, the Latin kings of Jerusalem. In Saint Mark's Gospel, the first reference to Jesus as the son of David is preceded by his anointing—which bestows on him the powers of king and priest—and immediately followed by his Solomonic entry into Jerusalem and the cleansing of the temple.

60. See chapter 12.

61. Campanella, *Monarchia*, vol. 1, *Proemium*. In addition to the *Monarchia di Spagna* (1598–1601) Campanella also authored other political works that glorified the Spanish rulers, including the *Discorso sui Paesi Bassi* (1594), the *Città del Sole* (1602), and the *Discorso dei diritti del Re Catollico sul Mondo Nuovo* (1605).

62. Campanella, *Monarchia*, 93.

63. Ibid., 95.

64. Ibid., 102.

65. Ibid.

66. Ibid., 93.

67. See Junquera de Vega and Carretero, eds. *Catálogo*, 279.

68. For the provenance, see ibid., 269f.

69. Philip inherited this tapestry from his aunt Mary of Hungary. For provenance, see ibid., 171.

70. Campanella, *Monarchia*, 216.

71. See Reeves, *Influence of Prophecy*, 465ff.

72. Campanella, *Monarchia*, 91f.

73. Ibid., 95.

74. Ibid.

75. "& Turcicae . . . & totius Orientalis Ecclesiae cum terra sancta recuperandae, ut non tituli nomen inane Regni Hierosolomitani, sed ipsum una cum titulo possideat & gubern. Regnum. . . . Ille autem & (ut ad te Ser. Princeps, nostre sermo reducat) Pater tuus, Carolus V., Ro. Imp. Aug., . . . hostem illum Turcum devicerit . . . Aut tu unicus ipsius filius, potentia post ipsum nec future inferior . . . Ac tum reaedificata Sione Ecclesia Christi, sub uno pastore, in uno ovile, orbi illuscescet ultimus ille dies, fine mundum clausurus, in quo Christus Maiest. sua orbi apparebit iudicature" (Campanella, *Monarchia*, appendix). These prophecies were typically applied to Philip from the time of his triumphal journey through the empire in 1549. See also Hempel, *Philip II*, 99f., regarding the dominant themes of the king's vanquishing the infidel and the crusade and wars against the infidel in Philippean literature.

76. For a history of the commission and for Philip's earlier set of Apocalypse tapestries see Ortiz, Carretero, and Godoy, *Resplendence of the Spanish Monarchy*, 41ff.

77. Scott, "Catafalques," 128. For references to the Holy Sepulchre in the crypt of the Escorial, see Barghahn, *Age of Gold*, 71. For a precedent for the adaptation of the Holy Sepulchre in the mausoleum of Ferdinand and Isabella at Granada Cathedral, see Rosenthal, *Cathedral of Granada*, 114ff. and 162ff.

CHAPTER 10

1. For this and the following chapter, I have drawn from both the sources indicated and the analysis provided by Coreth, *Geschichteschreibung*, "Pietas Austriaca," and *Pietas Austriaca*. Although Coreth focuses on the Baroque era in these exemplary works of clarity and insight, she scans earlier traditions and lays the groundwork for any future discussions of Hapsburg piety as a dynastic concept. Coreth also discusses another expression of Hapsburg dynastic piety: Marian worship.

2. For Augustus's piety, see chapter 1; for Eusebius's expressions of Constantine's hereditary piety, see Seston, "Vision païenne," 382, n. 4.

3. Christ's monogram on the Labarum is composed of the intersection of the first two let-

ters of the Greek word of His name, Χριστος. Lactantius, who provides the earliest account, describes the apparition not as a cross, but as the monogram of Christ: "Constantinus, ut caeleste signum Dei notaret in scutis . . . et transversa X literra summo capite circumflexo, Christum in scutis notat. Quo signo armatus, exercitus capit ferrum" (*De mortibus persecutorum*, 44, cited in Seston, "Vision païenne," 374). Problems arose regarding the form of the vision, and Eusebius said it was not a chi-rho but a Cross. On the Labarum, see also Grabar, *Christian Iconography*, 38f., and Dinkler, "Das Kreuz," 1ff.

For a sixteenth-century summary of various points of view regarding the form of the Constantinian vision, see Justus Lipsius, *De Cruce* (Antwerp, 1594), 89–90. The Jesuit Lipsius (1547–1606) was historiographer to Philip II. On Lipsius as the originator of a widespread literary topos that proclaims "Pietas" as the basis of Hapsburg world dominion, see Coreth, "Pietas Austriaca," 93f.

4. Seston ("Vision païenne," 373) provides sources who suggest that the details of the Cross legend may have been gathered only under Theodosius, following the deliberations of the Nicene Council. See also Beskow, *Rex Gloriae*, 16.

5. Prudentius, vols. 1 and 2, *A Reply to the Address of Symmachus* (hereafter referred to as C.S.), bk. 1, ll. 464ff.

6. Gregory of Tours, *Historia Francorum*, bk. 2, pp. 92–93. "Rex ergo prior poposcit, se a pontefeci baptizare. Procedit novos Constantinus ad lavacrum, deleturus leprae veteris morbum . . . sanctus Remegius, episcopus egregiae . . . ut Silvestri virtutebus equaretur."

7. See Brennan, "Image of the Frankish Kings," 6. Iacobo Chiflet reverts to Gregory of Tours for the knowledge that, from the day of his baptism, Clovis was called Augustus, and he endorsed the purple tunic and insignia of power. Gregory noted that Clovis was not the absolute Augustus but was called Consul and Augustus, and this was decreed by God, according to the testimony of Saint Remi (Chiflet, *Vindiciae Hispanicae*, 181–83).

8. See Bloch, *Les Rois*, 229, regarding the fourteenth-century legend of the miraculous appearance of the fleur-de-lis as the guarantor of Clovis's victory. For its equation with Constantine's vision, see text at n. 40.

9. See chapter 3.

10. See Godman, *Poets and Emperors*, 58, and n. 106, for further bibliography on the subject.

11. See Leithe-Jasper and Distelberger, *Kunsthistorische Museum*, 15.

12. In the *Chanson de Roland*, the Oriflamme was associated with the Roman Vexillium that Pope Leo III offered to Charlemagne. For the legend of Charlemagne and the Oriflamme, see Bloch, *Les Rois*, 235. See the connection between Clovis's arms and Charlemagne's lance, ibid., 236. The sources that equate Constantine's, Clovis's, and Charlemagne's visions and insignia are gathered in a treatise for Philip III by Valdesius *Praerogativa Hispaniae*; see also n. 40 this chapter.

13. The miracle is depicted in the emperor's window at the Church of Saint Lawrence, Nuremberg (ca. 1477). Portraits of Emperor Frederick III and his consort Eleanor of Portugal appear in the two bottom registers. Other scenes depict the conversion and baptism of Constantine and various scenes from the Legend of the Cross. See *Gothic and Renaissance Art in Nuremberg, 1300–1550*, Exhibition Catalogue, The Metropolitan Museum of Art, New York, and Germanisches Nationalmuseum, Nuremberg (Munich, 1986), 176f. and fig. 44.

14. On the poem, see Godman, *Poets and Emperors*, 58f. He raises the question of whether Alcuin intended to draw a direct parallel between his patron and the emperor whose encomiast he imitated and suggests that "this nomenclature gives substance to [Alcuin's] assertion that he is attributing to Charlemagne the proper ancestral names which he restores." He notes that the name of the Flavians had been adopted in the coterie language of the Carolingian courts. The Flavian name takes on additional meaning in the context of this study in view of the meaning applied to Titus's conquest of Jerusalem. The Flavians are integrated into the Byzantine ancestry by later authors, see n. 41 this chapter. See Godman, *Poets and Emperors*, 56, for Porfyrius's use of the format in a cycle of twenty-two such poems to Constantine the Great, and for the adaptation of the format by Venantius Fortunatus. On Venantius, see also chapter 5.

15. For a discussion of the poem and the image, see Sears, "Louis the Pious," 605ff. For a general discussion of Byzantine influence on Carolingian ceremony and art, see Beckwith, "Byzantine Influence," 288ff. He also mentions the possible modeling of Aachen on Constantine's palace in Constantinople. For the relationship of the images of Charlemagne and his son (fig. 22) and Honorius (fig. 99), see Schramm, *Die deutschen Kaiser*, 156.

16. The *Historia Hierosolmitana*, written in 1118 by Roberto, Monaco de Reims, and dedicated to Frederick I. See also Schramm, *Die deutschen Kaiser*, 267ff. For Constantine as a model for the Hohenstaufen, see Benson, "Political Renovatio," 372f.

17. "Cum . . . Rudolffus fuisset in virglia omnium sanctorum (in regem Tewthonye coronatus) apparuit hora nona magna nubes candida in modem crucis formata, que postea fuit in ruborem sanguinis transformata." Hermanni Athanenses, *Chronicon*, 244.

18. "Anno 1273 . . . electus est Rudolfus comes de Habspurch in Romanum regem, postea in imperatorem consecrandus. Qui Rudolfus statim exegit a principibus clericis ac laicis fidei iuramentum. Quod cum recusarent propter sceptri absenciam, ipse electus signum crucis accipiens talia dixisse fertur: 'Ecce signum, in quo nos et totus mundus est redemptus; et hoc signo utamur loco sceptri'" (ibid., 408). For a discussion of the legend, which was circulated by the middle of the fourteenth century, see Redlich, "Rudolf von Habsburg," 3f.

19. The tradition that Constantine's vision was duplicated for Rudolf is summarized by Juan Solorzano Pereira. The author first relates Constantine's vision: "Magni Constantini victoriae contra Maxentiũ, Maximinum, Licinum, & alios ostendunt. In quarũ prima, Crucis signum coelistus sibi apparuisse, Eusebius, & alii apud Baronium testantur, hoc Elogio repetitis vicibus ac vocibus addito, In hoc Signo vinces" (Solorzano Pereira, *Emblemata*, 81). The miracle is repeated for Rudolf: "Christi Cruci . . . pro Sceptro . . . noster Rodulphus dixit, & . . . revereantur. Constantinũ Imperatorem sequuti, qui in memoriã illius auxiliaris, sibi coelitus . . . demonstratae, eandem posteà super suam Coronã apposuit, & militaribus vexillis, quae *Labarà* dicta fuerunt" (ibid., 84). The text accompanies the illustration of Rudolf that appears here. Other sixteenth- and seventeenth-century authors similarly record this analogy.

20. For the picture's connection with Maximilian's planned coronation at Rome in 1507, see Gertrud Otto, *Bernard Strigel* (Munich, 1964), 31ff.

21. Vernulaei *Virtutum*, 33f.

22. The scenario is described in Strong, *Splendour at Court*, 94.

23. For the provenance of this painting, now lost, see Jochen Sander, "Reconstruction of Old Master Paintings of King Willem II," *Simiolus* 19, no. 1 (1989): 64. Justus Lipsius notes the eagle's symbolism as the sign of dominion over East and West and traces the motif to its Roman origins, see Lipsius *Analecta ad Militam Romanum in Opera Omnia*, 435. In the time of Heraclius (610–41), the Byzantine emperors adopted Jupiter's emblem of an eagle as their crest. In the fourteenth century this became a double-headed eagle to symbolize the Eastern and Western territories.

24. The discovery and the festivities that Philip established for their exaltation is discussed by Philippus Gothus Siculus in a treatise dedicated to Prince Philip (Gotho, *Breve Reguaglio*, intro.): "suo Invittissimo Padre, che Dio N. Signore per donarli particolari protettori nel Cielo, acciò guidino l'attioni sue felicemente in terra, gli ha scoperti." Noting that "in tractato vulgari Italico . . . quem de Inventione SS. Placidi Anicii . . . composuit. Et primo in epistola dedicatoria, quae est ad Philippum Principem," the passage is quoted in a contemporary text by Arnoldo Wion (1554–1603), a Belgian monk of the Order of Saint Benedict in Mantua, see Wion, *Lignum Vitae*, vol. 1, e7.ff.

25. The chapel is located in San Giovanni Evangelista. I have not yet investigated the Hapsburg connection to Placido del Bono, the presumed patron. For a brief discussion of the provenance, see *The Age of Correggio and the Carracci: Emilian Painting of the Sixteenth and Seventeenth Centuries*, Exhibition Catalogue (Washington, D.C., 1986), 104.

26. "Scoperti miracolosamente questi 37 gloriosi Santi, 1047 anni fa' martirizati; tra i quali Placido, Eutichio, Vittorino, & Flavia fratelli, & sorella, sono dell' istesso, & antichissimo Sangue Anicio, donde tiene origine la Serenissima Casa d'Austria . . . congionta di sangue con questi santi Martiri . . . come, perche quei invitti guerrieri di Christo sono dell' istesso sangue Anicio, dalquale la Serenissima Casa d'Austria degnissima prosapia dell'Altezza Vostra trahe l'origine" (Wion, *Lignum Vitae*, vol. 1, e7ff.). Wion, quoting the Italian of Philippus Gothus Siculus, notes that Silicus drew on Antonio Colonna's and Luca Contile's *Symbolum Philippi II*.

27. Ibid, fvoff., citing *Virgil, Aeneid* I: "Anicios vero originem suam á Troianis traxisse, . . . qui de Sergesto Aeneae socio loquens."

28. Ibid., opp. p. b; he quotes Prudentius C.S. bk. 1. Prudentius's text reads: "For it is said that a noble Anicius before all others shed lustre on the city's head . . . and the inheritor of the blood and name of Olybrius . . . was eager to . . . humble the Ausonian axe to Christ" (C.S. bk. 1, ll. 551f.). This treatise opens with a panegyric to Theodosius who had brought the triumph of the true religion and opposed the return to pagan idols that was initiated with Julian the Apostate. Julian removed Christ's name and the Cross from the Labarum.

29. Cassiodorus is cited for this information, see Wion, *Lignum Vitae*, vol. 1, a7vo; here he also notes that the Emperor Justinian sprang from this ancestry and quotes an inscription that testifies that Justinian used the cognomen "Aeneida": "Imperator Iustinianus, qui ex eodem sanguine Anicio linea ducens, ubique Aeneidam se appelat."

30. Wion, *Lignum Vitae*, vol. 1, bvoff.: "duo fratres Anicii, Comitis Aventini fillii (de quibus infra in Genealogia Austriaca dicemus) in Germaniam venirent. . . . Ex hac familia cum tibi nasci contigerit, Philippe Rex." Drawing on Gregory of Tours for the Trojan origins of the Franks and following Maximilian I's historians for the subsequent history, he extends that descent from Pharamund through Clovis to the Hapsburgs: "familia Austriaca nobilissima originem traxerit . . . á Pharamundo Francorum Rege" (ibid., c.ff.). He also traces the Anici heritage beyond the Trojans to the Anysi, kings of Egypt (ibid. f2f.).

31. Noting that the Hapsburg relationship to the Anicio family had been suggested, as Seifried notes, by the fifteenth-century historiographer Bonstetten, Seifried (Seifried, *Arbor Aniciana*, bk. 2, p. 37) follows Wion (*Lignum Vitae*, vol. 1, e.ff.) in documenting that relationship by the intermarriage with other noble families: "Quando è pur certo, che gli antecessori di V.A. i quali dallo acquisto dell' Austria procreorno da se il cognome d'Austria . . . discendono per legitima successione dalli Fregepani [and Perleoni, etc.], . . . & questi da gli Anicii, paterni maggiori di San Placido." The interchangeability of the cogno-

men Hapsburg and "House of Austria" followed the family's acquisition of Austria in the early fourteenth century.

32. "Hoc declaravit nepos eiusdem, Constantinus Magnus, quippè qui Aeneae, rerúmque Trojanarum studiossimus fuit. Unde novam conditurus Urbem, eam primùm in Dardania exaedificandam statuit, verùm indè omine & augurio quodam ad Bizantinam civitatem amplificandam rejectus, in eam Palladium, quod ab Aenea unà cum signis magnorum Deorum ex Ilio in Italiam transvectum & hactenus Romae in templo Vestae asservatum fuerat . . . deportati curavit . . . familiae Anicianae omnino ad Aeneam Achises . . . referendam esse" (Seifried, *Arbor Aniciana*, bk. 2, p. 40).

33. Ibid., bk. 3, p. 53. On the sarcophagus, see Beskow, *Rex Gloriae*, 23 and 293.

34. Seifried, *Arbor Aniciana*, bk. 2, p. 44.

35. Garibay, *Illustraciones*, 280ff. Garibay culls his information from dozens of ancient and contemporary authors and notes that his genealogy has been approved by Father Juan de Mariana, S.J., and by Benito Arias Montano.

36. "Imperii sedes . . . quam per Olybriam ac Perleoniam gentem in Habsburgiam Austriam derivatam in eáque fascibus & sceptris Imperi in Occidēte, quae dudùm in Oriente moderata fuerat, restitutà esse, infrà manifestis validisque argumentis convincemus. Quocircà cùm ex eàdem stirps ex qua Domus Austria orta est" (Seifried, *Arbor Aniciana*, intro., 2r).

37. An assertion of Burgundian preemption derived from the Belgians having been instructed in Christian concepts before Clovis baptized the Franks in the West because when Constantine crossed the Alps with the Labarum he traveled to Belgium. This journey as recorded in Prudentius, *C.S.* bk. 1, ll. 467–68, is cited in Chiflet, *Vindiciae Hispanicae*, 244.

38. On the medal, see Lipsius *De Cruce*, 93. It was reproduced in Octavio de Strada, *Genealogia. Austriacae Ducum* (Frankfurt, 1629). On these medals, see Stephen K. Sher, "The Medals in the Collection of the Duke de Berry" (M.A. thesis, New York University, 1961), 60, 66, 129f., for the use of Heraclian medals for church celebrations of the Cross's exaltation. For the suggestion that the medal was a Flemish forgery, see J. von Schlosser, "Die ältesten Medaillen und die Antike." *Jahrbuch der kunsthistorischen Sammlungen des Allerhöchsten Kaiserhauses* 18 (1897): 92.

39. Lipsius *De Cruce*, 9, 15. Lipsius caps a short illustrated list of Byzantine emperors who venerate the Cross Labarum with an account of Rudolph's devotion to the Cross. Lipsius was a secretary to Granvelle in the 1560s, and in the 1590s was named historiographer to the king of Spain. See Nisard, *Juste Lipse*, 100f., for Philip's appointment of Lipsius as historiographer, and for Lipsius's reputation as a humanist. The title of Nisard's book refers to the three men who were considered the literary triumvirate of the sixteenth century.

40. Valdesius *Praerogativa Hispaniae*, 317ff.: "Auriflamma . . . & auctores alii asserunt fuisse Labarum & vexillum Constantino concessum, cum vidit signum crucis in victoria . . . alii affirmant, quod Angelus é coelo Clodovaeo attulit." Similarly in Chiflet, *Vindiciae Hispaniae*, 158, the sacred Ampoule, Lily Shield, and Oriflamme conceded to Clovis are Philip's birthright. See the Epilogue for fuller quotations. Because Salic law, which prevented a woman from inheriting the realm, was honored among the Franks, Chiflet asserts that Capetian blood was first mixed with the blood of Charlemagne's legitimate heir in Philip II: "Certum . . . Capetinum sanguinem . . . Caroline legitimé non fuisse permixtum ante Philippi II . . . Hugo Capetium Regnum usurpavit" (ibid., 50f.). This had earlier been advocated at the Tridentine Council by Jacob Mendoza. Rejecting the French claims presented by Peter Damian, Mendoza replied that Francis I was not descended from Clovis by the male line but by the female line and that the Austrian-Spanish kings preserved the first and second pedigree to the French realms and prerogatives (ibid., 147).

41. Sixto, *Genealogia*, 17v.f. The author characteristically identifies Berosus as a source of this syncretism: "Duae sunt opiniones circa Genealogiam Familiae Austriae. Altera ex Cam per Troianos; altera ex Sem per Graecos. . . . Cam genuit Osiridem, seu aliter dictum Apim: qui genuit Herculem Lybicum. . . . et ipse Dardanum . . . Priamum . . . Hectorem. . . . Et hic Clodoniem . . . post quos Pharamundus regnavit in Francia ipse." Sixto (27–31) also notes the derivation of the Hapsburg name from Mount Aventine. "Comes Avenburch dictus, & castrum istud ab Aventino . . . est ab Aventino & ei nomen indidit Aventburch: cùm postea ab oïbus dicitur Asburch, . . . cúm de Aventino diceremus."

See also Seifried, *Arbor Aniciana*, bk. 2, pp. 37ff., who cites earlier authors among his sources: "Habsburgios Perleonum & Aniciorum posteros ab Aenea & Trojana stirpe oriundos esse . . . ex Aenea atque Trojana linea illorumque Leonem . . . Porrò Perleones ex eadem Aeneae stirpe generatos fuisse . . . ex gente Iulii Caesaris. . . . Certum est Eutropium Constantii Imp. patrem, ac Constantini Magni avum genus suum, ad Aeneam retulisse . . . testimonia . . . Pomponii Laeti, qui in Romanae Historiae compendio Constantii Chlori parentes sic describit." He also links Constantine to the Flavian gens and Vespasian. Seifried is referring to Pomponio Leto's *Romanae Historiae Compendium*, in which Constantine's ancestry was traced to Aeneas and beyond him to Eutropius, the paterfamilias of the Anicio family, and to Dardanus, the founder of Troy. To form these genealogical conclusions, the king's historians brought the heritage forward through two strands of inquiry that met in the Trojan ancestry: the Burgundian and the Constantinian links to Troy.

He also takes the Anicio roots through Dardanus, the founder of Troy, to Noah. "Perducta igitur clarissimae stirpis Aniciae antiquitate ad Trojana tempora, plus ultra provehi non sedet animo, cùm quia ipsi Caesares Iulius & Augustus non altiùs genus suum, quàm ad Aenĕam retulere . . . velle ab Adamo vel Noacho, a quibus universum hominum genus tanquam á fonte & capite descendit, generis sui claritatem derivare; ipsiq' belli Trojani Scriptores, ut Dictes Cretensis & Dares Phrygiius non altiùs Aenea genus repetunt, quam a Dardano Iovis & Electrae filio. . . . Origo Trojanorum Dardanus fuit . . . ab Italia . . . commutans . . . ad Phrygiam devenit . . . ex hoc . . . Aeneas" (Seifried, *Arbor Aniciana*, 44). As he suggestively unravels the strands of the family's heritage "plus ultra" to its source in Adam, we may discover a recondite meaning for these words that constitute the motto on Charles V's twin-columned personal emblem.

42. For a summary of the premise that the right to universal sovereignty resides solely in the blood of the Hapsburg clan, and a declaration that Philip II effected the concord of the whole world when he brought together in his person the strands of this inheritance, see Chiflet, *Vindiciae Hispanicae*, 242ff. As precedents, the author cites the standard topoi of Charlemagne's Greek

mother, and Baldwin's sovereignty of Jerusalem and Constantinople; to these he adds the donation of the Eastern Empire made by Emperor Andrea Paleologus to the kings of Aragon and the union of bloodlines in Philip II. For the significance of Christ's title *Concordia Mundi*, and for its appropriation by Constantine to symbolize the unification of the East and the West, see Tanner "Concordia," 7f.

43. Didaco di Lequile, *Colossus Angelicus*, centerfold, with explanatory appendix, pp. 1–13.

44. The coin is represented in Seifried, *Arbor Aniciana*, bk. 2, p. 32; he cites Wion for its significance: "argenteis . . . numismatibus . . . ex una quidem parte effigiem Constantini, in altera autem facie praefert Anicianae Domùs insignia . . . Turrim enim argenteam in rubro campo Aniciis prostemmate fuisse tradit Arnoldus Wion, quâ fortè eò libentiùs usi sunt, quòd congruentem nomini Anicio significationem, quo designari invictum quoddam robur ac insuperabilem animi vel corporis fortitudinem." The tower emblem illustrated here is taken from Didaco di Lequile, *Colossus Angelicus*, 192; he also cites the meaning derived from Wion.

45. Valdesius, *Praerogativa Hispaniae*, 309: "insignia fuisse leonem rubrum in campo albo . . . & etiam leo fuit stemma Regum Iuda, & signum Jacob, Genesis 49 quo significatus fuit Christus Apocalypse 5 vicit leo de tribu Iuda."

46. Didaco di Lequile, *Colossus Angelicus*, 185ff. He cites the ancient sources for the knowledge of the Phrygians' association with the lion, and therefore for its adaptation in the arms of the Julio-Claudians. The lion is recorded as a heraldic Trojan symbol from the earliest treatises on heraldry in the fourteenth century. See Van den Bergen-Pantens, "Guerre de Troie," 13.

47. Valdesius, *Praerogativa Hispaniae*, 309: "Cantabros Hispanos ante Christum natum usos fuisse signo crucis, & vexillo, dum praesagium esset, quod illud Hispaniam salvam faceret omni seculo, & imperium eius in cruce stabilitetur. Post Hispaniam vero à Sarracenis capta & recuperari incepta crux fuit Hispanoru signum & vexillum."

48. Christique Crucem pro Sceptro principes habentes in hoc et in alio saeculo maneant" (Solorzano Pereira, *Emblemata*, 82).

49. "Quasi dictum Austriacis Principibus esset, quod olim Constantino Magno, IN HOC SIGNO VINCES, ita singulari in Christi Servatoris

Crucem fiduciá semper fuĕre. Neque sané frustra. Cum enim Crucem hanc praeferri sibi ad
pugnam ituris voluerint, in ejus signo saepe vice-
runt & de suis hostibus triumpharunt" (Vernulaei,
Virtutum, 32). The author, who was a student of
Philip II's historiographer Justus Lipsius, himself
became the imperial historiographer to Emperor
Ferdinand III. Vernulaei dedicated this work to
Ferdinand, to Philip IV of Spain, and to other
members of the Hapsburg family. Vernulaei sustains their right to this motto by recounting inci-
dents of the family's devotion to the Cross
beginning with Rudolf.

50. With Calderon and the Jesuit theater,
these concepts were disseminated in Spain,
thereby affecting the development of lay piety.
For this development, and for the role of the
new clerical orders in its dissemination, see
Coreth, "Pietas Austriaca," 96. For the similar
spread of Eucharistic veneration in connection
with the House of Austria, see chapter 11.

51. See Coreth, "Pietas Austriaca," 94.

52. The play was written for the crowning
of Emperor Ferdinand III in 1627; the second act
was set in Constantine's camp. For the sixteenth-
century roots of Constantinian drama in the circle of the Jesuits, and for a description of the
play, see J. W. Nagl and Jakob Zeidler, *Deutsch-
Osterrreichische Literaturgeschichte* (Vienna, 1898),
665ff.

53. Grapheus, *La . . . triumphante entrée du . . .
Prince Philipe*, K2 verso.

54. The image was invented by San Bernardino of Siena. See Pacelli, "Il 'Monogramma,'"
259f. See also Blunt, "El Greco's 'Dream of
Philip,'" 58f., regarding the Jesuit adoption and
addition of the nails; for a brief history of the
Jesuit veneration of the name of Jesus; for their
association of His name with the inscription "In
hoc signo vinces," and for the esteem held for
this worship in Spain. He does not develop
Philip's relationship to Constantine, nor relate
the picture to contemporary Jesuit theater.

55. See Blunt, "El Greco's 'Dream of Philip,'"
66, for the repeated references to the power of
the name of Jesus to conquer the devil, death,
and hell in the rhetoric of the sixteenth-century
Spaniard Luis de Granada. Interesting in the Constantinian connection is the anachronistic borrowing from Byzantine art for the formula of the
Demon of Hell. On the pros and cons for a

Byzantine source, see ibid., 59 and n. 2. For an
interesting parallel to El Greco's picture, where
there is another direct connection between the
emperor, the apparition of the name of Jesus,
and the victory over the Turks, see the engraving
by Pieter Balten from the end of the sixteenth
century discussed in ibid., 66f. Blunt also suggests
(67, n. 2) that the emperor, who treads a Turkish
crescent under foot, may represent Frederick
Barbarossa.

56. Ibid., 68, n. 1. Blunt discredits this suggestion on stylistic grounds.

57. Corrado, *Descripción*, 182f.

58. These objectives are specifically expressed in a treatise dedicated to the Emperor
Ferdinand III's daughter, Maria Anna of Austria,
who was the wife of the deceased Philip IV, regent of Spain: "& vincet cum Magno Constantino
Rudolphus Magnus atque in ipso coronata poste-
ritas crucis auspiciis initiata ad triumphos: en quo
titulo & sceptro regnatis Austriaci Caesares . . .
cui crux pro sceptro imperatricem manum re-
gebat. . . . Adoro dominatorem horoscopum na-
scentis Austriaci imperii, stellantem crucem
propagandi non solum ad . . . solis orientis & oc-
cidentis thalamum sed ab arctico & antarcticum
cardinem cruce sidereá insignem, ab Austriacá
potentia crucis regni luculentum auspicium fuit"
(Palavicino, *Austriaci Caesares*, 45–46; see also 93).

59. For Philip as the new Rudolf who accepts the Cross as his scepter, see Solorzano
Pereira, *Emblemata*, 82. This statement occurs in
the treatise on emblems in which Rudolf's vow
on the Cross is illustrated.

60. In the poem, the muse Urania prophesies that Philip will be taken into the Southern
Hemisphere, to the constellation of the Cross to
which he dedicated his life. Around him will be
the trophies of his battles for belief. Soon his
constellation will have a positive influence on
earth. For excerpts from the poem, see Hempel,
Philip II, 327. On Strasoldo, who was a member of
the Academia Veneta in the circle of Anguillara
and Tasso, see Giovanni Liruti, *Notizie delle vite e
opere scritte de' letterati del Friuli* (Venice, 1830), 4:93ff.

61. Dante had described a vision of Cato,
from whose features shone forth "the rays of the
four holy lights," the four stars which "never yet
were seen save by the first people" (*Purgatorio*, in
Le Opere, xxix, 130f.). Modern critics have sur-
mised that Dante had in mind the Southern

Cross belonging to the allegedly "unpeopled world behind the Sun," the Southern Hemisphere. For the identification of Dante's vision with the four stars over Eden, allegorically the four cardinal virtues, see Charles S. Singleton, *Journey to Beatrice*, Harvard University Dante Studies 2 (Cambridge, Mass., 1958), 159f. A seventeenth-century humanist at the court of the Spanish Hapsburgs identified this new constellation in the Antarctic polar region with the one described by Dante as the stars that had not been seen except by Adam and Eve. "De que como en profecia hablo el Dante, aun antes de nuestras navegaciones, diziendo, que avia el Polo Antartico se hallarian quatro en lugar de la cinosura. 'Io volsi a man destra, e posi mente. A l'altro Polo, e vidi quattro stelle, Non viste mai fuor che la prima gente'" (Solorzano Pereira, *Politica Indiana*, 33).

62. When the equator was crossed, in the early 1460s, the Southern Cross was revealed. It was first described by the Italian navigator Cadamosto, sailing under the Portuguese flag. Philip gained sovereignty of Portugal in 1580, and with the Portuguese possessions he became the first monarch in history to rule all four quarters of the globe. Since a new star was sought to replace the now-invisible North Star, the Southern Cross gradually became this beacon to mariners sailing in the Southern Hemisphere. On this discovery, see A. H. de Oliveira Marques, *History of Portugal* (New York, 1972), 1:270.

63. On the belief of the reappearance of the Cross at the Last Judgment, and on its relationship to the legend of the Last World Emperor, see W. Bousset, *The Anti-Christ Legend* (London, 1896), 232f.

CHAPTER 11

1. Lactantius identifies the Cross as the true sign of Jesus' blood, "signum . . . veri et divini sanguinis" (*Div. Inst.*, bk. 4, p. 26, cited in Daniélou, *Bible and the Liturgy*, 167 n. 5; see also Rohling, "Blood of Christ").

2. See Kantorowicz, *Laudes Regiae*, 8.

3. Valdesius, *Praerogativa Hispaniae*, 322, identifies Christ on the Cross as the image of the consecrated Host and draws from this the conclusion that the Spanish *Vexillium* is the consecrated *Corpus Domini*.

4. For this controversy, and for a brief discussion of the Hapsburg reaction, see Van der Osten Sacken, *San Lorenzo*, 86ff. For the issue of Christ's symbolic versus real presence, see the summary in "Eucharistie," *Lexikon für Theologie und Kirche* (Freiburg, 1959), 3:1142f. An earlier controversy regarding the real presence of Christ occurred in a Carolingian context. At the request of Charles the Bald, Paschasius Radbert composed a treatise in which the Flesh and Blood of Christ in the Eucharist were identified with that which He possessed while here on earth. From then onwards, this was the common belief. See Rohling, "Blood of Christ," 119f., and Rubin, *Corpus Christi*, 14ff.

5. A version of the legend was recorded by the Swiss minorite Johann von Winterthur, who was active in 1340. See *Chronica Iohannis Vitodurani*, MGH new series 3, ed. Friedrich Baethgen (Berlin, 1924), 29f.; this legend was endlessly repeated thereafter.

6. Palavicino, *Austriaci Caesares*, 43. The forest apparition of the Sacrament was deemed a bloodless martyrdom for Rudolf and, for example, in Didaco di Lequile, *Colossus Angelicus*, 188, Rudolf is called a second Saint Eustace. In 1302, with the intention of challenging secular associations to the Eucharist, Pope Urban VIII redefined the meaning of the *Corpus Mysticum* in the Bull *Unam Sanctum*. Originally designating the Sacrament of the Altar, Urban redefined the term *Corpus Mysticum* as the church, whose head was Christ and whose visible head was the vicar of Christ, the Roman Pontiff. See Kantorowicz, *King's Two Bodies*, 194ff.

7. Genesis 49:1ff.

8. This is recorded in Didaco di Lequile, *Colossus Angelicus*, 182ff.: "Iacob de filio suo Aser prophetico ore; eum benedicendo, protulit. Aser Pinguis est Panis tuus, & praebebit delicias regibus. . . . coniectandum est necessario oraculum illud singillatim Austriam Gentem respexisse, cui propterea Suum fecit Panem Vitae . . . Verum Pietas Eucharistica Austriaca . . . Quare dum Aser interpretetur Beatus, Austrio generi, Eucharistica Beatitate . . . decorato [locutum est]"

9. "Eo vel maximè quia Psalmographus cecinit: Beata gens, cuius est Dominus Deus eius, quem elegit in haereditatem sibi . . . Ergo Beata gens Austriaca" (ibid., 184). See the summary of the legend and its implications for the dynasty in

Vernulaei, *Virtutum*, 13ff. The book is dedicated to Spanish and Austrian members of the Hapsburg clan.

10. Vernulaei, *Virtutum*, 230: "Ut sit, illustris & omni pietate insignis Austriaca Gens haereditarium inde à Conditore suo Eucharistiae cultum-accepit."

11. According to Palavicino, *Austriaci Caesares*, 44, Rudolf followed the pattern of his ancestors, the Pierleoni and the Anicii. In having drunk piety with his mother's milk, he propagated eucharistic veneration in the world: "a parentum Anicianorum mammillis hanc Pietatum cum lactis dulcedine suaviter biberat." That ancestry is traced to Rudolf through the Burgundians.

12. For the recounting of Hapsburg eucharistic miracles, see, for example, Vernulaei, *Virtutum*, 12ff., and Palavicino, *Austriaci Caesares*, 43ff. Other examples are cited in the notes here and in Coreth, "Pietas Austriaca," 97ff. For later accounts of Hapsburg eucharistic devotion, see Combes, "Sainte Thérèse," 29ff.

13. The Hapsburgs were also kin to Clovis via a collateral link between Rudolf and the Burgundian royalty.

14. For the eucharistic meaning of baptism, see Daniélou, *Bible and the Liturgy*, 159, 163f.

15. See Kantorowicz, *Laudes Regiae*, 47, for the bishops' acclamation of Charlemagne as priest and king at a synod in Frankfurt in 794. He has shown that Pepin's anointment after the pattern of Israel's kings formed the cornerstone of the medieval king's divine right (57).

16. The image has been related to an eleventh-century text that describes Constantine consigning the relics of the Passion to Charlemagne. It forms the right panel of a triptych that included a central Crucifixion, now lost, and a left panel of Saint Helen (now in Brussels) and the Deposition and Ascent to Calvary on the interior panels. See Licia Collobi Ragghianti, ed., *Dipinti Fiamminghi in Italia 1420–1570* (Milan, 1980), 111f.

17. Pierre Aspeslag, *Chapel of the Holy Blood, Bruges* (Ostend, 1988), 1ff. The Shrine of the Holy Blood bears the crown and jewels of Charles the Bold and Mary of Burgundy, and the windows of the chapel that house it depict Emperor Charles V and his Burgundian ancestors.

18. On Saint Gudule as an ancestral saint, see chapter 8.

19. The miracle cited in Coreth, *Pietas Au-*striaca, 26, is repeatedly recorded. One instance occurs in Avancino, *Imperium Romano*, 379f.: "Cum venationis aestu per avia insequeretur feram, Eodem momento stetit in apice montis & mortis. Tam irremeabile videbatur illius iter, ac hujus. . . . Nisi ad Austriadum Orientem respexisset Maximilianus. Subiit animum Eucharistici epuli religio; Et quae Austriae fundavit solium, eandem servavit. Quo enim ascendere non poteráte homines, descenderunt Coelites Natali Stirpis pietate detracti. . . . Objectus est novo Eliae Panis Vitae. Et spes non dubia ambulandi in fortitudine cibi illius."

20. Palavicino, *Austriaci Caesares*, 92f.: "Prima aetas gemino prodigio è Coelo consecratur, summà & Maximiliani pietate . . . servatumque est . . . aestrum venationis, . . . nec pedem inde retrahere posset . . . ad divinum prorsus consilium confugit. Acciri iubet (audiri enim vox loquentis poterat) sacrum Mystam, qui sublime Eucharisticum nectar, delibandum saltem oculis, exhiberet . . . nutabat. . . . Accurrere è caelesti Aula' iubetur Angelus sospitator. . . . Hem quanto miraculo testatum videmus Eucharistiam Augustissimam Palladium esse Austriacae Domus, quae in extremis rerum articulis ad thaumaturgum Coeli Panem accurrens. . . . Nec mirum inde posteros Herõas Carolum, Philippos, & Ferdinandos."

21. See Leithe-Jasper and Distelberger, *Kunsthistorische Museum*, 29; also for the legendary inscription.

22. For this and related commissions, see De Bruyn, *Histoire*, 46ff.

23. This was observed by Michael Mezzatesta, who discusses the chapel, the windows, and the bronze effigies in relation to Hapsburg eucharistic veneration. See Mezzatesta, "Imperial Themes," 97ff. For a description of the windows see also De Bruyn, *Histoire*, 58–69.

24. See Coreth, *Pietas Austriaca*, 25ff.

25. "Numquam visa pompa major, ea ex Caesaris edicto. Moguntinus Archiepiscopus Sacris illo die operatus sub umbella Eucharistiam portabat" (Vernulaei, *Virtutum*, 26).

26. "& post Caesaris Principumque Nobiles Domestici cum cereis ardentibus omnes [sequebantur]. Fervebat pietate urbs tota, & tanti Imperatoris exemplo divini istius Sacramenti cultus in omnium animis cum amore crescebat" (Vernulaei, *Virtutum*, 26).

27. See Browe, *Textus*. The saint's life is related on p. 6ff.; Urban's Bull is quoted on p. 34. For the Mass of Bolsena of 1263—in which a host bled during the consecration of the mass—as a stimulus to Urban's action, see also Hirn, *Sacred Shrine*, 106ff.

28. See Hirn, *Sacred Shrine*, 113. On the exposition of the Eucharist and the forms of the monstrance, see Rubin, *Corpus Christi*, 288f.

29. Hirn, *Sacred Shrine*, 112.

30. Ibid., 111.

31. See Coreth, "Pietas Austriaca," 99.

32. The incident is recorded in Vernulaei, *Virtutum*, 26.

33. See Coreth, *Pietas Austriaca*, 31. On the Corpus Christi processions, see Karl Vossler, *Lope de Vega und sein Zeitalter* (Munich, 1932), 149–201. For examples of Corpus Christi veneration and miracles under Maximilian, Charles V, Ferdinand II, Philip II, and others, see Vernulaei, *Virtutum*, 23ff. For other examples of the Triumph of the Sacrament under Charles V and for their relationship to the Corpus Christi feast, see Habig-Bappert, *Eucharistie*, 58f. For related observances of eucharistic veneration, see Ludwig Pfandl, "Auto Sacramental," in *Lexicon für Theologie und Kirche* (Freiburg, 1965), 1:858. For a general discussion of Corpus Christi processions with a focus on England, see Rubin, *Corpus Christi*, 243ff.

34. On the dating of the earliest Auto Sacramental to Spain in 1467 during the reign of Ferdinand and Isabella, see Van der Osten Sacken, *San Lorenzo*, 110. For the dissemination of eucharistic doctrine in the Autos of Calderon, see Parker, *Allegorical Dramas*, 66f., and Brown and Elliott, *A Palace for a King*, 230. Coreth ("Pietas Austriaca," 94) links the development of sacramental drama to the pietistic literature of Justus Lipsius, which was disseminated to a larger audience by the works of his students, including Avancino and Vernulaei. On these authors, who also propagated the Hapsburg connection to the Cross, see also chapter 10.

35. On this see Scott, "Catafalques," 122, who quotes the contemporary work of Balthasar Porreno, *Dichos y Hechos di Filippo II*.

36. Sigüenza, *Fundación*, 594, describing the Holy of Holies: "ninguno se podía asentar en el Templo sino el Rey y el Sumo Sacerdote. . . . En este atrio exterior o grande hizo Salomón un pórtico . . . después de haber edificado su casa y palacio, como parece en el III de los Reyes."

37. I Kings 8:64; this passage refers to the dedication of the temple. In I Kings 9:25, we are told that "three times a year Solomon used to offer up burnt offerings and peace offerings upon the altar." For further references to the Solomonic tradition of the priest-king, see Van der Osten Sacken, *San Lorenzo*, 214f.

38. For the relationship of these roles to the concept of Adam as the image of God and the king of creatures, see Beskow, *Rex Gloriae*, 253f. See the recapitulation of this concept in Campanella in my chapter 9.

39. For Jesus as king and priest, see the discussion in Beskow, *Rex Gloriae*, 109f. Psalms 110:4: "Thou are a priest for ever after the Order of Melchizedek," was repeated for Christ. See also Hebrews 5:6 and Hebrews 4:14 which announces: "Since then we have a great high priest who has passed through the heavens, Jesus, the son of God." For His descent through Mary from the family of David, see Beskow, *Rex Gloriae*, 93f. For the theory that He must be descended from the tribes of both Judah and Levi in order to be both king and priest, see ibid., 110. For the parallelism between the offices of Christ and Adam, see ibid., 116. For the testimony of His Kingship over both the Jews and the Gentiles, see ibid., 97. For Jesus' names as indicative of his dual descent as formulated by Eusebius, in which Jesus is said to refer back to Joshua and Christ to Aaron, and for its later perpetuation, see ibid, 110. For Iraneus's demonstration of the relationship between Father and Son, from which he determines: "For this means that the Son, being God, receives from the Father, that is, from God, the throne of the everlasting kingdom, and the oil of anointing," see ibid., 116. For the tradition that Christ was anointed as king, priest, and prophet when the Spirit came upon him at the Baptism, see ibid, 118.

40. "Verum Christi Iesu Genealogia ab eius scriptoribus Mattheo & Luca. . . . Et sicut alii dixerunt Christi Genealogiam imperfectam esse duobus tribusue transcendentibus in linea gradibus sive personarum interpositionibus in ea factis, ut in typo primo aperuimus. Ità & hi tuae R.M. in Genealogia fecerunt. Ut Doctores sacri in Sancta Christi Genealogia continuationem exhibent; sic & nos quasuis interpositiones connectemur: intervalla omnia complebimus; ac per naturalem immediatam atq̃ legitimam successionem illā ducemus, ut modo tuae S.R.C.M. di-

rigo. Et sicut infinita sapientia ac S.C. Ecclesia Orthodoxa Christi Iesu humanam voluit patefacere generationem, ut convinceret ipsum esse illum, cui naturali atq́ haereditario iure conveniebat regale Davidiis sceptrum Iudaeorum Regis . . . & veritatis viam de S. tuae R.M. Genealogia docere, veluti ab illa id debeat germen pullulare, cuĺ Sceptrum, Imperium, ac Monarchia haereditario ac acquisito iure quoris dominio suis" (Sixto, *Genealogia*, 1–2). His demonstration of Philip's right to the unction by which God consecrated Clovis follows from this premise, see the text in chapter 10. It was further sustained for his son, Philip III, by Valdesius *Praerogativa Hispaniae*, 297f.

41. "Ex qua longi sanguinis & genealogiae descriptione colligitur, quod etiamsi attendatur lex Salica, qua foeminae in successione regni Francorum excluduntur, solumq; masculi succedunt, regnum Franciae ad Philippum III . . . pertinet iure successionis & primogeniturae recta masculina linea à masculo in masculum, cũ ex linea masculina Merovaei & Clodovaei descendat, itemque ex alia Pipini ab illis descendens directo" (Valdesius *Praerogativa Hispaniae*, 299). Refuting a pro-French declaration made to the Tridentine synod, Jacob Mendoza had already replied in 1546 that Francis I did not descend from Clovis and Charlemagne by the male line, but rather invalidly by the female line. He asserted therefore that the prerogatives bestowed by the ancient heritage belonged to the Hapsburg kings. As Clovis's legitimate heir, the lily shield that was bestowed from heaven was also proclaimed the sole property of the Spanish monarch: "Galliarum stemmatibus, licet concedere possimus è coelo demissa lilia, quod affirmare non audent boni auctores Galliae & investigatores antiquitatum, hoc stemma nõ quadrat Regibus hodernis Gallorum, qui non descendunt à Clodovaeo, cui lilia sunt concessa: sed ab Hugone Capeto & Philippo Valesio, & illa insignia sunt genuina & propria nostri Regis Philippi, qui à Clodovaeo recta linea derivatur . . ." (ibid., 306f.).

42. See ibid., 298ff.

43. For the conventionality of this designation in the Spanish tradition since the time of Isidore, who identified the king as *Sacerdos vel Pontificus*, see Borchardt, *German Antiquity*, 194. For the emperor as priest, see Sanserre, Jean Marie, "Eu-

sèbe," 139f. For the combining of the offices of priest and king in the seed of Jesse, the "two sticks" analogy in Ezekiel 37:15–28 affords a guide: "The word of the Lord came to me: Son of man, take a stick and write on it, For Judah . . . then . . . another stick and write upon it, For Joseph . . . and join them together into one stick . . . and tell the people . . . I will join with . . . the stick of Joseph . . . the stick of Judah. . . . Thus says the Lord God: Behold, I will take the people of Israel from the nations among which they have gone, and will gather them from all sides, and bring them to their own land; and I will make them one nation . . . of Israel; and one king shall be king over them all; and they shall be no longer . . . divided into two kingdoms . . . and I will be their God. . . . My servant David shall be king over them, and they shall all have one shepherd . . . and David my servant shall be their prince for ever. I will make a covenant of peace with them, and will set my sanctuary in the midst of them for evermore. Then the nations will know that I the Lord sanctify Israel."

44. For the quasi-sacerdotal powers of Constantine and Justinian, see Ladner, *Idea of Reform*, 124f. and n. 48. For the grounding of Hapsburg piety in a family tree that stretched to pious Aeneas through the Byzantine emperors and the saints of the early church, see Didaco de Lequile, who under the rubric "De Antiq. Orig. Austriacae Gentis Stemma VII, Ex Stirpe Aeneae, Juliorum Julianorum, Aniciorum, Perleonum, Frangipanum, Habsburgiorum" traces the roots of Hapsburg piety through these ancestors; the heritage is congealed in an emblem of Hapsburg eucharistic piety. See Didaco de Lequile, *Piisima . . . Domus Austriaca*, 201ff.

45. Sigüenza, *Fundación*, 495f.

46. For this interpretation see Panofsky, *Problems in Titian*, 73f.

47. See chapter 9. In the following century, Luca Giordano painted in the passage that led to the king's apartments an image of David observing the descent of the heavenly Jerusalem that was to be ushered in by his progeny, see Carr, "Luca Giordano," 278.

48. The references were perpetuated in later images. See ibid., 268, for the reflection of these works in Luca Giordano's lunette frescoes at the Escorial.

49. The tapestries were completed between 1625–28. For the commission, a description of

the tapestries, and of their reconstructed arrangement, see Scribner, *Triumph*, 16ff. For a discussion of the tapestries as a formal realization of Calderon's Auto Sacramentales, see Habig-Bappert, *Eucharistie*, 61f.

50. See Prudentius, vols. 1 and 2, *A Reply to the Address of Symmachus*, bk. 1, ll. 1ff., which refers to Theodosius's defeat of the pagan usurpers in 394.

51. See Scribner, *Triumph*, 93f., regarding this identification.

52. See ibid., 94. The members of the House of Austria include Ferdinand II, Philip IV, and their ancestors saints Leopold and Rudolf.

53. On the picture and its relationship to Philip II, see Sullivan "Propaganda," 243–59 and Carr, "Luca Giordano," 16f.

54. "Eucharistia. Anagramma Hic Austriae. Austriae etiam & Hic Genetrix, Munimen eius & inde moratur: Austrius hicque Pius nomen, & omen habet: Eucharistia. Anagramma Hec Austria. Hec Pietas aeterna, Hec Austria, ad astra reducens Quicquid in Austriacis Religionis erit. Eucharistia. Anagramma Cie Austria. Orcus, Sancte Panis, dum tantos provocat hostes, qui te conculcent, Austria Marte Cie. Primus Aser, qui in Gente Austriaca tanquam arma Gentilitia incruenta libamina Sacramenti Altaris constituit quique novo reverentiae paradigmate ingentia munera non dum aliis stirpibus concessa, magnae pietatis iure profudit, Rudolphus Habsburgicus Protoplastus, ac fundator eximius extitit" (Didaco di Lequile, *Colossus Angelicus*, 184–85). The author presents the formula in the context of the genealogical reconstruction that traces the Hapsburgs to Aeneas through the Anicio family, the Julio-Claudians, and so forth. The anagram is cited in Coreth, *Pietas Austriaca*, 29.

55. "Ita prima infantia Austriaci Imperii . . . ac nutrix lactari prius debuit mammillà Regum, nimirum Divinitate ipsá totà lactea in libo caelesti. Macte Rudolphe Heroes religisissime, instillabis e stirpe in Eucharistico succo Austriae familiae arbori augustissimae nobile alimentum, quo semper vivat, & floreat, ac triumphale antidotum adversus haeresim . . .

"Hoc verae Palladis, diviniae nimirum, genitae sapientiae palladio, Eucharisticum manna . . . arca. . . pietatis Haeres, & sanguinis, Austrii tui Gedeones. . . . Hoc demum est gentilitium magnae tuae gentis emblema . . . hic panis thaumaturgus patrator miraculorum qui orbem tuis

servabit; ac tuos tibi" (Palavicino, *Austriaci Caesares*, 44–46).

56. See Brown and Elliott, *A Palace for a King*, 230.

57. The villa was built by a nobleman, Adalbert of Sternberg, to serve as a hunting lodge for the emperor and his retinue. See Lubos Lancinger, Milan Pavlik, Pavel Preiss, and Ota Kukla, *Troja Château Prague*, trans. Stepan Kolar (Prague, n.d.), 6ff.

58. See Combes, "Sainte Thérèse," 28ff. In recalling the legends, Combes harks back to their recitation at the eucharistic congress held in Vienna in 1912.

59. Ibid., 30.

60. Ibid., 29ff.

CHAPTER 12

1. The emblem first appears in 1555 on a medal struck by Jacopo da Trezzo. See I. B. Supino, *Il medagliere mediceo nel R. Museo Nazionale di Firenze* (Florence, 1889), 141. For a prior discussion of Philip's solar imagery, see Tanner, "Titian," 9f.

2. Ruscelli, *Le Imprese illustri*, 14.f.: "Et che peró il Re autor di questa Impresa [intenda] . . . d'illustrare co'l santissimo lume di Dio questo nostro mondo pieno di tenebre co'l Motto, che si fa chiaramente intendere. . . . Et peró sapendosi, che molto spesso non solamente i Filosofi, ma ancora i Teologhi stessi sotto nome di Sole intendono Iddio . . . Tanto piú, che i Re stessi, in mano dé quali é risposto il cuor di esso Dio . . . con lo splendore suo . . . di allumarne ognuno . . . negli infideli . . . Dio stesso . . . infondendo . . . nella menta sua coi raggi del Sole, perche tale Imprese fosse, come un augurio, un oracolo, o un vaticino al mondo di tor via ogni falsa Eresia [e] vicinamenta . . . vedersi questa universale illustration del mondo con la conversion degli Infedeli all vera, catolica & santissima legge nostra." Four editions of Ruscelli's *Imprese* appeared in Venice in the second half of the sixteenth century.

3. Ibid, 15, also cited in Scott, "Catafalques," 128, and n. 98. Ruscelli's reference to Psalm 23 contributes an additional messianic note, for this Psalm announces the illumination by which the face of the Lord would be seen in its full glory.

4. See chapter 2.

5. Solorzano Pereira, *Emblemata*, 9ff.

6. For Apollo's importance in the *Iliad* and the *Aeneid*, see also Williams, *Aeneid*, 133f.

7. See Burton, *Pindar's Pythian Odes*, 159f. Apollonius Rhodius *Argonautica* I.1 begins with the invocation to Apollo. For Apollo's special importance as a protector of the Argonauts in the Alexandrian epic, see the citations in de la Ville de Mirmont, "Mythologie," 452, 458. In the Roman myth, Phoebus acts as the sailors' guide. In Valerius Flaccus (*Argonautica* I.5f.) Titus raises a temple to him, which resonates with references to Augustus's temple to Apollo that contained the Sibilline books. See ibid., 4 for the note that identifies Titus's temple with the Templum *Gentis Flaviae*.

8. Valerius Flaccus *Argonautica* V.415f.

9. See Philargyrius's commentary on Vergil cited in Vellay, *Les Légendes* I:283, n. 1.

10. See Gagé, *Apollon Romain*, 578. Nigidius's identification of the Penates with Apollo was widely disseminated through the account of Macrobius *Saturnalia* III.4. This identification survived to surface in the most famous Renaissance commentary on Vergil, that of Cristoforo Landino (*Disputationes Camuldulenses* [Venice, 1508], Giiir): "dii penates eadem dicent / quae dicturus esset Apollo. Multum iam praefecerunt dii penates: qui que obscurius Apollo significaverat: perspicue enodarunt: docentque in Italiam ad rerum divinarum cognotionem enavigandum esse."

11. For Nigidius as a source for the *Fourth Eclogue*, see Carcopino, *Virgile*, 56f., 72f., and the comments in Servius below.

12. *Virgil*, vol. 1, *Eclogue* IV.10: "iam regnat Apollo." Servius explains that this signifies the beginning of a Great Year when all the stars will return to the place they occupied at the beginning of the universe; then a new Golden Age will be born. "Solem ultimam [Cumana] voluit: novimus autem eundem esse Apollinem, unde dicit . . . tuus iam regnat Apolló dixit etiam, finitis omnibus saeculis rursus eadem innovari: quam rem etiam philosophi hac disputatione colligunt, dicentes, completo magno anno omnia sidera in ortus suos redire et ferri rursus eodem motu . . . Vergilius dicit reverti aurea saecula . . ." (Servii, *Grammatici*, 44f.). See also Carcopino, *Virgile*, 52, for Nigidius Figulus and other neo-Pythagorean sources who influence Vergil in this

interpretation. A prior Great Year was believed to have been initiated with Aeneas's founding of a new Troy in Rome; another with Romuleus's death in 721 B.C.

For a general discussion of the attribution of the last age to Apollo, see Carcopino, *Virgile*, 50f. For the interchangeability of the Great Year and the solar year, and for their millennial reverberations see Gagé, *Apollon Romain*, 520f.

13. Servius records the statement that Apollo signified Augustus, see n. 30.

14. See chapter 1. Aeneas summarizes Phoebus's help to the Trojans in *Aeneid* VI.56f.

15. This manuscript was offered for sale in 1581 to Cardinal Granvelle, who was purchasing for Philip II's library, but the book was bought by the Vatican. See Stevenson, *Miniature Decoration*, 12.

16. Iulius, the son of Aeneas and Lavinia, inherits his solar divinity from both his mother and father. Lavinia's solar ancestry is manifested in Vergil through the description of her father, Latinus, who "drives a four-horse car, twelve golden rays circling his gleaming brows, emblem of his ancestral Sun" (*Virgil, Aeneid* XII.161f.). On Latinus's solar ancestry, quadriga, and radial crown, see W. Warde Fowler, *The Death of Turnus* (New York, 1919), 58. For a further discussion, see Gagé, *Apollon Romain*, 610. This same heritage is inferred for Priam's royal house through Apollo's identification with the Trojan home gods and by Latinus's revelation that Latium's first settlers were named Laurentes after the laurel sacred to Apollo.

17. Antony's fall at Actium was prefigured on Aeneas's shield as the victory of Apollo over Dionysius (*Virgil, Aeneid* VII.675ff.).

18. Horace *Odes* I.11. 32f.

19. For Latium as the last of the lands inhabited by the gods, see *Virgil, Aeneid* VI.791–94. Latium too is the province of the solar god, and its eponymous ruler Latinus, his earthly counterpart. For Latium as the Trojans' original home, see chapter 1.

20. See Taylor, *Divinity*, 118f.

21. For a general discussion of this imperial concept, see Nock, "Emperor's Divine," 102ff.

22. Ovid *Metamorphosis* XV.865. See also Nock, "Emperor's Divine," 112f.

23. *Virgil, Aeneid* VI.69f.

24. See chapter 1. Servius notes that Augustus thus fulfills a promise that Aeneas made to

the Sibyl of Cumae. See the citation in Mayor, Fowler, Conway, *Virgil's Messianic Eclogue*, 102. The temple's cult statue was said to wear Octavian's features. See the discussion in Taylor, *Divinity*, 119ff., regarding Augustus's cult of Apollo which occupied a central place in the emperor's early religious reforms. For a discussion of the centrality of pietas for Augustus, especially in connection with the renewal of the Golden Age, see the citations in Gagé, *Apollon Romain*, 609.

25. In the *Fasti* III.420f., where Ovid celebrates Augustus's elevation to the pontificate, he refers to Augustus's familial relationship to Vesta and the Penates: "Over the eternal fire the divinity of Caesar, no less eternal, doth preside. . . . Ye gods of ancient Troy, ye worthiest prize to him who bore ye, ye whose weight did save Aeneas from the foe, a priest of the line of Aeneas handles your kindred divinities; Vesta, do thou guard his kindred head!"

26. For general discussions of Augustus's kinship to Apollo and for representations of the Julian gens in the likeness of Apollo, see Taylor, *Divinity*, 118f. See also Gagé, *Apollon Romain*, 616, for a general discussion of the topic, and 609, n. 2, for the image of Apollo which appeared at the altar at Carthage among the *Gens Iulia*. See also Ussani, *Studi*, 85 ff., for the cult of *Genius Augusti*, and for the foundation of this religious stature on their mythic and epic genealogy.

27. Suetonius records the legend that Apollo came to Augustus's mother Atia in the form of a serpent; Atia dreamed that the sun rose from her womb (*Suetonius*, vol. 1, *Lives of the Caesars*, bk. 2, chap. 94, pp. 265–66).

28. Suetonius reports a banquet honoring the Olympian gods in which Augustus came dressed as Apollo (ibid., bk. 2, chap. 70, p. 231). Apollo's cult statue in the Palatine Temple was reported to wear the features of Augustus.

29. For the notation that scholiasts of the *Fourth Eclogue* identify the *Regnum Apollonis* with Augustus's reign, see Taylor, *Divinity*, 119. For the concept that the secular games established in Apollo's honor in 17 B.C. initiated the New Age, see Gagé, *Apollon Romain*, 583 and 520f.

30. *Servii, Grammatici*, 46. He refers for this information to Nigidius Figulus: "Nigidius de diis lib. IV quidam deos et eorum genera temporibus et actatibus . . . Apollinis fore regnum . . . Augusti significari adfirmant ipsumque Augustum Apollinem." See also Taylor, *Divinity*, 119, 229, n. 27. These sources were known in the Renaissance. To cite one example: Claude Paradin (fl. mid–sixteenth century), *Devises héroïques et emblèmes* (Paris, 1622), 201, cites Pliny and Suetonius for Augustus's identification with Apollo.

31. See chapter 1. For other parallels between Augustus's astral identity and his devotion to Apollo, see Gagé, *Apollon Romain*, 595f.

32. Lucan, *The Civil War*, bks. 1–10, trans. J. D. Duff (Cambridge, 1957), bk. 1, ll. 53–59. On Nero's Apollonian identity, see L'Orange, *Apotheosis*, 61ff.

33. See Halsberghe, *Cult*, 152f. For an overview of solar imperial iconography from antiquity to the modern era, see the classic study by Kantorowicz, "*Oriens Augusti*."

34. On the solar chariot as an emblem of invincibility, see L'Orange, "Sol Invictus," 92f.

35. Drake, *In Praise of Constantine*, 21. "Vidisti enim, credo, Constantine, Apollinem tuum comitante victoria coronas tibi laureas offerentem quae tricennum singulae ferunt omen annorum." See also Gagé, *Apollon Romain*, 615, and Seston, *Vision païenne*, 382. According to one critic, this pagan vision was later transformed into the Christian sign of the Labarum, see notes to Drake, *In Praise of Constantine*, 73, and Gagé, *Apollon Romain*, 615, n. 2.

36. L'Orange ("Sol Invictus," 100f.) and Halsberghe (*Cult*, 167ff.) discuss the extraordinary heights attained by the cult of Deus Sol Invictus during the reign of Constantine. In the early part of his reign, Constantine declared that the power of Sol Invictus inspired him; later he took the place of Sol Invictus, invincible in the battle with darkness.

37. Drake, *In Praise of Constantine*, chap. 7, n. 13.

38. Ibid., chap. 3.

39. See chapter 5, n. 17. Among the many other examples are the images on the Arch of Constantine, where the emperor and sol are juxtaposed, and the statue of Constantine-Helios that was erected in Constantinople. For Constantine's monuments to Helios see Preger, "Konstantinos-Helios," 457f.; see ibid., 464f., for the association he established between Christ and Helios. For the continuation of the Byzantine emperor's solar identity, see Corippus *In Laudem Iustini Augusti Minoris* (London, 1927), 96ff.,

112ff., and the extensive critical commentary on these passages.

40. Macrobius *Saturnalia*, bk. I, chaps. 18, 19. Macrobius takes from Nigidius Figulus the identification of Apollo with the Penates, see Gagé, *Apollon Romain*, 579. Macrobius also coordinates the powers of the sun with the times of day, the seasons of the year, the parts of the body, and the ages of man. These connections are important to the concept of the emperor as the microcosmic god-man, as it appears, for example, in the *Anticlaudian* of Alain de Lille. Among the epithets Macrobius assigns to Apollo are "God with the Lamb's Fleece," "Guardian of Flocks," "Feeder of Sheep," and "Python Slayer" (Macrobius *Saturnalia*, bk. I, 17:43), some of which would later be assigned to Christ.

41. See Pierre Boyance, *Etudes sur le songe de Scipion* (Bordeaux, 1936): 18ff., which also discuss Apollo's lyre as the emblem of the harmony of the spheres he maintains, and to which he accords the harmony of the universe.

42. See Gagé, *Apollon Romain*, 678. The propriety of names was not lost on Philip II, who celebrated his namesake Philippus Arabus in his triumphal procession through the empire as heir-elect, see chapter 7.

43. See discussion in Halsberghe, *Cult*, 174.

44. See Drake, *In Praise of Constantine*, chap. 3, p. 87, n. 12. For the Christian adaptation of the charioteer image to represent the Quadriga Christi, on which the beasts represent the Evangelists, see Panofsky, *Problems in Titian*, 61f.

45. See Grabar, *Christian Iconography*, 117.

46. The designation *Sol Iustitiae* and *Oriens* formed the basis for the solar veneration of Christ; both designations are preserved in the *Roman Breviary*. For material summarizing this development, see Kantorowicz, "Dante's Two Suns," 217–31. The classic study of the subject is Dölger, *Sonne*. Here and in *Sol Salutis*, he provides an extensive discussion of the use of solar imagery in Greco-Roman and Byzantine cultures, among others.

47. For the solar metaphors which were coined for Christ and applied to the emperor, see Kantorowicz, "Dante's Two Suns," 229.

48. See Preger, "Konstantinos-Helios," 464, for Constantine's association with Christ-Helios. Eusebius develops Constantine's association with the sun, and Sunday is designated a day of religious observance. Constantine's rule is equated with the harmonious principles that regulate the planetary spheres. For these and other parallels in Eusebius *Life of Constantine* (I.6, II.4, III.4), see L'Orange, *Apotheosis*, 126f. He refers to Eusebius *Life of Constantine* (V.65, 72) for Constantine's evocation of the cosmic nature of this identity by his appearance with his twelve counselors in imitation of the sun's position in the zodiac. Constantine also borrowed from ecclesiastical language Christ's epithet *Sol Justi*.

49. See, for example, Kantorowicz, "Dante's Two Suns," 226ff., and Corippus In Laudem, esp. 130ff. and 160f.

50. For the combining of these feasts in Byzantium, see discussion in Tanner "Concordia," 13f.

51. For examples of this poetry, and the relation of these ceremonies to liturgical rites, see Kantorowicz, *Laudes Regiae*, 220f.

52. On this, see Bruce Eastwood and Hubert Martin, Jr., "Michael Italicus and Heliocentrism," *Greek, Roman, and Byzantine Studies* 27 (1986): 223–30. These authors discuss but disagree with the interpretation that a revival of Aristarchus of Samos's heliocentric theory inspired Italicus's panegyrics. However, they have not considered the argument from the point of view of imperial imagery that designated the emperor the center of the universe.

53. See Brennan, "Image of the Frankish Kings in the Poetry of Venantius Fortunatus," 3f., for the sources of his imagery in Corippus's panegyric of the Byzantine Emperor Justin II.

54. Einhard, "Karolus Magnus," ll. 44–45, 65ff., 13ff., cited in Godman, *Poetry*, 199: "Charlemagne's outstanding name is broadcast to the stars, look, the sun is now shining with beams of light—that is how David illumines the earth with the brilliance of his great love. There is however one point of difference between the two of them . . . the sun from time to time is covered with clouds and rainy weather . . . for twelve hours the sun is without its light, but Charlemagne continues to shine like an everlasting star . . . surpassing the sun." For the application of additional solar metaphors to Charlemagne, see Zwierlein, "Karolus Magnus–Alter Aeneas," 49f.

55. See Kantorowicz, "Dante's Two Suns," 221f., 227ff., and Kantorowicz, *King's Two Bodies*, 101f. He traces the source to the twelfth-century Byzantine court.

56. See Kantorowicz, *King's Two Bodies*, 101f.

57. See Kantorowicz, "Dante's Two Suns," 229f., for a discussion of the papacy's appropriation of the sun metaphor to itself in the eleventh century as part of a general trend to imperialize the papal office. Gregory VII established the sun and moon as respective symbols of church and empire; Dante changed the imagery to that of two suns to show that though their tasks are different, their powers are equal. Romanitas is a fundamental aspect of his concept; it was from Rome, he declared, that these two suns must shine. In the sixteenth-century decorations of the Vatican Palace, the papacy also used Apollonian and Trojan motifs, which may have been intended to support their bid for legitimacy as the heirs to Roman imperial sovereignty.

58. This processional chariot as well as Maximilian's Triumphal Arch were conceived of by the emperor himself in 1512; the woodcuts were produced in 1516–18. A fresco of this image, now destroyed, decorated the Nuremberg Town Hall; see Panofsky, *Life and Art*, 179. See further ibid., 181, regarding a drawing for Maximilian of 1518 and a woodcut of 1522, both of which bear the inscription *Roi Soleil*. A copy of Dürer's triumphal chariot was placed opposite Dürer's *Calumny of Apelles* in the Town Hall in Nuremberg. Since this juxtaposition cast Maximilian's solar identity in a judicial light, it stimulates reading Hapsburg connotations into Dürer's apocalyptic *Sun of Justice*. I have discussed this imagery in connection with Philip II: "Titian's Calumny, the Diana and Callisto for Philip II" (Paper delivered at the College Art Association Annual Meeting, New York, 1982). For the repetition of the rebus, "As the sun is in heaven, so is Caesar on earth," to apply to the assembly of Hapsburg emperors in Rubens's *Portico of the Emperors*, see Silver, "Paper Pageants," 302; see ibid., 296, for laurel symbolism in Maximilian's Triumphal Arch.

59. Cited in Scott, "Catafalques," 128.

60. Mattheus Hacus Samburgensis. Escorial MS a-IV-21. The conjunction of Jupiter and Venus in Philip's sun sign was interpreted by Samburgensis as symbolizing his supreme dominion of the empire. For a fuller discussion of Philip's astral iconography, see Taylor, "Architecture and Magic," 98f., and Tanner, "Titian," 153f.

61. For the development of heliocentrism in the Renaissance, see Heniger, "Pythagorean Cosmology," 35ff. He mentions that in 1576, Thomas Digges, a pupil of John Dee—who drew the horoscopes of Philip II and his wife Mary Tudor—published a diagram of the heliocentric system. It is interesting to note that Telesio dedicated his treatise on heliocentricity to the Hapsburg Emperor Rudolf II.

62. The passage is cited in Didaco di Lequile, *Colossus Angelicus*, 153. The image of Hercules took on added meaning for Philip due to Hercules' legendary founding of Spain.

63. This ironic transformation in which Spenser manipulates Philip's own image against him is established by Graziani, "Philip II's Imprese," 322–24. He notes a further expression of this identity (322) in John Upton's commentary on Spenser where he discusses the resemblances between the Souldan's grisly war chariot and the galleons of the 1588 Armada.

64. See Tanner, "Titian," 11f.

65. Ruscelli, *Le Imprese illustri*, 17ff. On the Byzantine identification of the imperial couple with the sun and moon, see discussion and bibliography in Kantorowicz, "Dante's Two Suns," 220 and n. 10f. The simultaneous appearance of these two heavenly bodies is an apocalyptic metaphor.

66. Ruscelli, *Le Imprese illustri*, 17ff.: "Regina aver co questa sua Impresa voluto mostra a se stessa, & altrui, ch'ella si truovi con la mente tanto elevata, & unita con Dio, che'l Cielo le venga ad esser tutto visibile, non per emisferio, & diviso, ma tutto intero, & così veda in esso tutti i suoi lumi in un tempo stesso, come di Cielo lo veggono i Beati."

67. See Jaynie Anderson, "Le Roi ne meurt jamais: Charles V's Obsequies in Italy," El Cardenal Albornoz y el Colegio de España (V) *Studia Albornotiana* (Bologna) 36 (1979): 385ff.

68. Ibid., 389f.

69. Corrado, *Descripción*, 192–93.

70. See Dölger, *Sol Salutis*, 157, for the use of this title in the Roman Breviary for the Christmas feast.

71. This discussion of the Saragossa catafalques is drawn from Scott, "Catafalques," 107ff.

72. Pitti, *Essequie*. The political significance of this solar imagery has been analyzed by Borsook, "Art and Politics."

73. Pitti, *Essequie*, 30. "Nec Occidet Ultra . . .

alludendo che si come il sole, ben che ad un emispero nuova & tramonti, non peró perde la luce, ma ad un'altro la trasporte . . ."

74. Ibid., 36–37.

75. "Come Apolo . . . tomando . . . forma humana . . . viva, pues . . . el Principe espanol, y todo el orbe súbdito de reciba, que el sol, sin que haya dios que lo estorbe come per ministerio, siempre algun reigno de su imperio." *Relación*, 106; see also 26.

76. See Brown and Elliott, *A Palace for a King*, 40.

77. Marciano, *Pompe Funebri*, 117: "Fu la propria sua impresa il sole sul carro nell' Oriente, col motto, Iam Illustrabit Omnia, reticenza [al] Apolline uccisore del Mostro delle Tenebre Pitone . . . simboleggiando il gran Monarcha, che saettó . . . con i Raggi della Religiosa Virtú il sozzo Pitone dell' empieta."

78. Caramuel Lobkowitz, *Philippus Prudens*, 1ff.

79. See chapter 9.

80. See Firpo, "Cité," 339.

81. Campanella, *Città*, xxviiff. The *City of the Sun* was written in 1602 in Naples, which was under Spanish dominion, rewritten in 1612, and published in 1623; it was reelaborated in 1636, see Firpo, "Cité," 327f. In the *Monarchia Messiae*, Campanella underwent a change in attitude and transferred the universal dignity to the pope, whom he designates as the supreme temporal and spiritual ruler.

82. The cube, the basis for all the proportions at the Escorial, is discussed in Juan de Herrera's (1530–97) *Discorso sobre la figura cubica*. See Alvarez Turienzo, *Escorial*, 170f. A large cube appears as the footstool of the Trinity in Luca Cambiaso's ceiling fresco at the Palace Church.

83. See Taylor, "Architecture and Magic," 99ff.

84. Cited in Alvarez Turienzo, *Escorial*, 122.

85. Ibid., 120; for other examples, see Hempel, *Philip II*, 84f.

86. See Brown and Elliott, *A Palace for a King*, 231.

87. Paraphrased from Sigüenza, *Fundación*, 403. The author claims credit for the iconography and notes that the library was begun by Pellegrino Tibaldi in 1592: "y la traza de las historias es mia." Philip is elsewhere associated with Joshua, for whom the sun also stands still, see Hempel, *Philip II*, 85.

88. "Las armas de esta tan insigne Monasterio son un laurel verde en campo de oro con unas parrillas de hierro ardiendo, la parte ancha hacia abajo y el laurel sobra unas llamas encendidas que llegan hasta las parrillas. Sobre el laurel una corona con una 'F': dorada en medio y a la mano derecha un rayo que hiere sobre el árbol, y a la izquierda otro, a la derecha un letrero que dice: Fulmina temnit. Este es, en suma, el argumento de lo que ahora se explicará por extenso" (Antonio Gracian, *Declaración de las armas de San Lorenzo el Real*, Escorial ms. &-II-1, cited in Alvarez Turienzo, *Escorial*, p. 169). For the emblems' intended placement on the Escorial's facade, see *El Escorial en la Biblioteca National*, 257f.

89. See Taylor, "Architecture and Magic," 99.

90. See Coreth, *Pietas Austriaca*, 21, and nn. 39, 40.

91. Palavicino, *Austriaci Caesares*, 93.

92. "Mitte timorem, Sol ille qui in coelo ardet, nihil incommodi potest illi afferre, qui hunc Solem Divinum adorat." The legend, which is recapitulated in Vernulaei, *Virtutum*, 29; Palavicino, *Austriaci Caesares*, 44, 197; Didaco di Lequile, *Colossus Angelicus*, 197, is cited in Coreth, *Pietas Austriaca*, 21. For the particularly eucharistic connotations communicated by Jesus' identification with the sun, and for the propagation of this iconography through the feast of Corpus Christi, see Firpo, "Cité" 536. See ibid., 537, regarding San Bernardino's dissemination of a solar motif for Christ's monogram.

93. Coreth, "Pietas Austriaca," 43.

94. On the development of the solar monstrance in the Counter-Reformation, see Noppenberger "Die eucharistische Monstranz," 29f. For examples of the solar monstrance within the Hapsburg sphere, see K. M. Swoboda, *Barock in Bohme* (Munich, 1964), 284f., and E. Hubala, *Die Kunst des 17C* (Berlin, 1970), fig. 390.

95. "Haec enim in famosissimo illo Urbis Capitolio. . . . De triumphi ritu apud Romanos . . . eo quia triumphans triplici iudio honorandus erat" (Didaco di Lequile, *Colossus Angelicus*, 107).

96. "At in presenti schemate congenitam cum tuo Genere, ac trino vultu exornatam Pietatem . . . nunc vidibit Maiestas tua. Quae cum ita sint . . . tale schemma pro Generis Austriaci fortunata, ac Divina Pietate, mediis coniugibus triumphante, Maiestati tuae prodio, quale dignum est, ut quamplurimis simulacris, quorum unum-

quodque sua sacramenta patefaceret, instar praecipuae memoriae, toti orbi perenniter derelinquendae, constaretur. Triumphasse olim, antiquioribus iam currentibus tempestatibus . . . Davidem . . . Iosephum . . . Mardocahem, etc. Historiae tradunt" (ibid., 106–7).

EPILOGUE

1. This interchangeability was expressed in Jacob Valdesius's *Praerogativa Hispaniae* for Philip III that celebrates the Spanish Hapsburgs as the legitimate heirs to the divine *oleum* with which God anointed Clovis. In developing the meaning of this inheritance, the author established the kinship between the Merovingians and Priam's royal house and the relationship between the Palladium, which fell to Troy from heaven to announce Priam's imperium, the divine shield, by which Numa cured his people from the plague, and the Lily shield, which God bestowed on Clovis: "reges oleo sancto coelitus demissio ungerentur, an id miraculum acciderit. . . . Clodovaeo . . . & ex eo Hispaniam" (Valdesius *Praerogativa*, 280f.). "Et cum Palladium in munitissima turri Troiana e coelo caderet, praenuntiatum fuit oraculo Apollonis, quod firmum Troianum Imperium foret . . . & ita Rex Franciae quia habet insigna a Deo omnium auctore & rege . . . (tres lilas / e coelo) . . . quae significationes habent. & celebrant Galli augurium, . . . e coelo scutum delapsum fuisse, ut tempore Numae Pompilii pestis immanissima cessavit scuto e coelo delapso, unde aruspices fortunatum eventum pronuntiarunt quod eo loco sedes Imperii colloranda erat. . . . lilia . . . illa insignia sunt genuina, & propria nostri Regis Philippi, qui a Clodoveo recta linea habet è coelo demissa . . . & ita crux Christi vexillum" (ibid., 302–3). In a seventeenth-century text dedicated to Philip IV, this interchangeability is given visual form: a seated figure that personifies Hapsburg Catholic piety tramples heresy with the aid of the Trojan Palladium, see Didaco di Lequile, *Rebus*, opp. p. 54. For Hapsburg knowledge of the cult and identity of Vesta and the Palladium, see Lipsius *De Vesta*, 1073ff.

2. See, for example, Palavicino, *Austriaci Caesares*, 44–45, who alternately calls "the Eucharist . . . this true Palladium of the Hapsburgs . . . this manna . . . this miraculous bread . . . that

nourishes the family tree . . . the emblem of the [Hapsburg] gens" ("manna dum arca vera," "panis thaumaturgus," "hoc verae Palladis," "tuae gentis emblema"). An accompanying anachronistic image shows Rudolf I wearing the collar of the Golden Fleece (ibid., 41).

3. Solorzano Pereira, *Emblemata*, 789.

4. Turning to distinguished voices of the past to explicate its meaning, the emblem's author identifies the *Aeneid* as the source of the inscription (ibid., 786ff.).

POSTSCRIPT

1. A movement is under way to rebuild the hanging gardens of Babylon—one of the Seven Wonders of the World—that were built more than two thousand five hundred years ago by King Nebuchadnezzar, who three times conquered Jerusalem and whose fabled empire prefigured the power and fame of Rome's. Based on ancient sketches, a replica of the ancient king's palace is under construction alongside the gardens, and eighty-foot brick walls rise around the space that used to be the ancient king's throne room. These monumental new projects were envisioned by Saddam Hussein. Efforts to link the new ruler and the Old Testament "king of kings" prevail, and he is popularly referred to as "the new Nebuchadnezzar." See John F. Burns "New Babylon Is Stalled by a Modern Upheaval," *New York Times*, 11 October 1990.

2. In Japan, site of the oldest hereditary monarchy in the world, this lore was recently brought to light on the occasion of Emperor Akihito's elevation to the Chrysanthemum Throne. The emperor—whose title is actually "Tenno" or Heavenly Sovereign, a name reflecting his traditional role as priest and king—sat on a canopied throne to receive world leaders and members of European royalty. Part of the preparations for the coronation included a ten-day ritual of food offerings, aimed at transforming the emperor into a "living god." The culminating rite in this "transformation" took place in the seclusion of a sacred shrine. The Shinto ritual is completely secret and may be guided by oral instructions that are passed from generation to generation, however the general outlines of the ceremony are known. The emperor, accompanied by a special coterie of priests enters a

specially built shrine, and passes to an inner
sanctum. There he partakes of the first fruits of
the season, after first making his offering to his
ancestors and to the deities of heaven and earth.
At last he reposes on a ceremonial bed to commune with his ancestor, the sun goddess. See
Steven R. Weisman, "Emperor's Ceremonial Bed
Still Keeps Its Secrets," *New York Times*, 9 October
1990.

3. "Sainthood Bid for Queen Isabella Stirs
Debate," *New York Times*, 28 December 1990.

4. Ibid.

5. Clyde Haberman, "Shades of Hapsburgs!
City Sees Splendid Future," *New York Times*, 25 October 1990.

6. Bill Keller, "Cult of the Last Czar Takes
Root in Russia," *New York Times*, 21 November
1990.

7. "Dust Off the Throne? Shine Up the
Crown? A Romanov Muses," *New York Times*, 30
August 1991.

8. "Romanov Heir Is Given Royal Russian
Funeral," *New Mexican*, 30 April 1992.

9. Ibid.

10. Harold Brooks-Baker, "Will Blue Blood
Succeed the Red Flag?" *New York Times*, 17 February 1990.

11. Ibid.

12. Roger Thurow, *Wall Street Journal*, 27
March 1991.

Select Bibliography

Abelard, Jacques. *Les Illustrations de Gaule et Singularitez de Troye de Jean Lemaire de Belges*. Geneva, 1976.

Adamietz, Joachim. "Zur Komposition der Argonautica des Valerius Flaccus." *Zetemata* 67 (1976): 1–128.

Alain de Lille. *Anticlaudianus*. Ed. R. Bossuat. Paris, 1955.

———. "The Anticlaudian of Alain de Lille." Trans. William Hafner Cornog. Ph.D. diss., University of Pennsylvania, 1935.

Alanus de Insulis. *Anticlaudianus*. Trans. James J. Sheridan. Medieval Sources in Translation, 14. Toronto, 1973.

Alvarez Turienzo, Saturnino. *El Escorial en las letras españolas*. Madrid, 1985.

Angeli, Giovanni. *L'Eneas e i primi romanzi volgari*. Milan, 1971.

Apollonius Rhodius. *The Argonautica*. Trans. R. C. Seaton. Loeb Classical Library. London, 1980.

Arias Montano, Benito. *Biblia Poliglota*. Vol. 8. Antwerp, 1572.

Ariosto, Ludovico. *Orlando Furioso*. Trans. William Stewart Ross. Indianapolis, 1968.

Avancino, Nicolao, S.J. *Imperium Romano Germanicum seu Elogia*. Vienna, 1663.

Barghahn, Barbara von. *Age of Gold, Age of Iron: Renaissance Spain and Symbols of Monarchy*. 2 vols. Lanham, Md., 1985.

Barker, Ernest, ed. and trans. *From Alexander to Constantine: Passages and Documents Illustrating the History of Social and Political Ideas, 336 B.C.–A.D. 337*. Lanham, Md., 1985.

Baron de Reiffenberg. *Histoire de l'ordre de la Toison d'or*. Brussels, 1830.

Bataillon, Marcel. "Plus oultre: La Cour découvre le nouveau monde." In *Les Fêtes de la Renaissance. II. Fêtes et cérémonies au temps de Charles Quint*. Paris, 1960, 13–27.

Baynes, Norman H. "Eusebius and the Christian Empire." In *Mélanges Bidez. Annuaire de l'Institut de Philologie et d'Histoire Orientales et Slavs*. Vol. 2. Brussels, 1934, 13–18.

Bayot, Alfonse. *La Légende de Troie à la cour de Bourgogne. Société d'émulation de Bruges. Mélanges I*. Bruges, 1908.

———. "Sur l'exemplaire des Grandes Chroniques offert par Guillaume Fillastre à Philippe le Bon." In *Mélanges Godefroid Kurth*. Paris, 1908, 183–90.

Beaune, Colette. "Saint Clovis: Histoire, religion royale et sentiment national en France à la fin du moyen âge." In *Le Métier d'historien au moyen âge. Etudes sur l'historiographie médiévale*. Paris, 1977, 139–56.

Beckwith, John. "Byzantine Influence on Art at the Court of Charlemagne." In *Karl der Grosse, Karolingische Kunst*, ed. Wolfgang Braunfels and

Hermann Schnitzler, vol. 3. Dusseldorf, 1965, 288–300.

Beer, Rudolf. "Die Galeere des Don Juan de Austria bei Lepanto." *Jahrbuch der kunsthistorischen Sammlungen der allerhöchsten Kaiserhauses* 15 (1894): 1–14.

Belting, Hans. "Die beiden Palastaulen Leos III im Lateran und die Enstehung einer päpstlichen Programmkunst." *Frühmittelalterliche Studien* 12 (1978): 55–83.

Benson, Robert L. "Political Renovatio: Two Models from Roman Antiquity." In *Renaissance and Renewal in the Twelfth Century*, ed. Robert L. Benson and Giles Constable. Cambridge, Mass., 1982, 339–86.

Bergmans, Paul. "Note sur la représentation du retable de l'agneau mystique dès Van Eyck à tableau vivant, à Gand en 1458." In *Fédération archéologique de Belgique: Annales du XXe congrès. Rapports et mémoires*, vol 2. Ghent, 1907, 1–36.

Bergweiler, Ulrike. *Die Allegorie im Werk von Jean Lemaire de Belges*. Geneva, 1976.

Beskow, Per. *Rex Gloriae, the Kingship of Christ in the Early Church*. Trans. Eric J. Sharpe. Uppsala, 1962.

Beumann, Helmut. "Nomen imperatoris— Studien zur Kaiser Idee Karls der Grossen." *Historische Zeitschrift* 185 (1958): 41ff.

———. *Die Ottonen*. Stuttgart, 1987.

Beye, Charles Rowan. *Epic and Romance in the Argonautica of Apollonius*. Carbondale, 1982.

Bloch, R. Howard. "Genealogy as a Medieval Mental Structure and Textual Form." In *Grundriss der romanischen Literaturen des Mittelalters*, vol. 11/1. *La Littérature historiographique des origines à 1500*, vol. 1: 135–56.

Bloch, Marc. *Feudal Society*. Trans. L. A. Manyon. Vol. 2. Chicago, 1961.

———. *Les Rois thaumaturges*. Publications de la faculté de lettres de l'Université de Strasbourg, vol. 19. Strasbourg, 1924.

Blunt, Anthony. "El Greco's 'Dream of Philip II': An Allegory of the Holy League." *Journal of the Warburg and Courtauld Institute* 3 (1939–40): 58–69.

Borchardt, Frank L. *German Antiquity in Renaissance Myth*. Baltimore, 1971.

Borsook, Eve. "Art and Politics at the Medici Court, III: Funeral Decor for Philip II of Spain." *Mitteilungen des kunsthistorischen Instituts in Florenz* (June 1969): 91–114.

Braudel, Ferdinand. *The Mediterranean and the Mediterranean World in the Age of Philip II*. Trans. Sian Reynolds. Vol. 2. New York, 1973.

Brennan, Brian. "The Image of the Frankish Kings in the Poetry of Venantius Fortunatus." *Journal of Medieval History* 10 (1984): 1–11.

Britnell, Jennifer. "Jean Lemaire de Belges and Prophecy." *Journal of the Warburg and Courtauld Institute* 42 (1979): 144–66.

Browe, Peter, S.J. *Textus Antiqui de Festo Corporis Christi. Opuscula et Textus Storiam Ecclesiae Eiusque Vitam Atque Doctrinam Illustrantia*. Series Liturgica. Monasterii, 1934.

Brown, Jonathan, and J. H. Elliott. *A Palace for a King: The Buen Retiro and the Court of Philip IV*. New Haven, 1980.

Buchheit, V. "Christliche Romideologie im Laurentius-Hymnus des Prudentius." In *Polychronion: Festschrift Franz Dölger zum 75. Geburtstag*, ed. Peter Wirth. Heidelberg, 1966, 121–44.

Buchner, Karl. *Vergil*. Brescia, 1963.

Buchthal, Hugo. *Historia Troiana: Studies in the History of Mediaeval Secular Illustration*. Studies of the Warburg Institute, vol. 32. London, 1971.

Burton, R. W .B. *Pindar's Pythian Odes: Essays in Interpretation*. Oxford, 1962.

Cairns, Francis. *Virgil's Augustan Epic*. Cambridge, 1989.

Calvete de Estrella, Juan Christóbal. *El felicíssimo viaje de'l muy alto y muy poderoso principe Don Felipe*. Madrid, 1930.

Cameron, Alan, *Claudian: Poetry and Propaganda at the Court of Honorius*. Oxford, 1970.

Campanella, Tommaso. *De Monarchia Hispanica*. Hardervici, 1640.

———. *La Città del Sole*. Ed. Edmondo Solmi. Modena, 1904.

———. *Monarchia di Spagna*. In *Opere*, trans. and ed. Alessandro d'Ancona, vol. 1. Torino, 1854.

Campo, Floria de. *Crónica general de España*. Medina del Campo, 1553.

Campos, F. J., and Fernandez de Sevilla. "Carta de fundación y dotación de San Lorenzo." In *Real monasterio de el Escorial*, Estudios en el IV centenario de la terminación del monasterio de San Lorenzo el Real de El Escorial. Madrid, 1984, 294–382.

Caramuel de Lobkowitz, Juan. *Philippus Prudens*. Antwerp, 1639.

Carcopino, J. *Virgile et le mystère de la IVe Eclogue*. Paris, 1943.

"Carmen de Exordio Gentis Francorum." In *Monumenta Germaniae Historia. Poetarum Latinorum Medii Aevi*, vol. 2, ed. Ernestus Dümmler. Berlin, 1884, 141–45.

Carr, Dawson. "Luca Giordano at the Escorial: The Frescoes for Charles II." Ph.D. diss., New York University, 1987.

Charles, Robert Henry. "Eschatology, the Doctrine of a Future Life in Israel." In *Judaism and Christianity: A Critical History*, ed. C. R. Henry. New York, 1953, 362–463.

Chiflet, I. Iacobo. *Vindiciae Hispanicae*. Antwerp, 1645.

Chueca Goitia, Fernando. *Casas reales en monasterios y conventos españoles*. Madrid, 1966.

Classen, Peter. "Res Gestae, Universal History, Apocalypse. Visions of Past and Future." In *Renaissance and Renewal in the Twelfth Century*, ed. Robert L. Benson and Giles Constable. Oxford, 1982.

Claudian. Trans. M. Platnauer. Vol 1. Loeb Classical Library. London, 1976.

Coleman, Christopher Bush. *Constantine the Great and Christianity*. Columbia University Studies in History, Economics and Public Law, no. 146. London, 1914.

Colonne, Guido delle. *The Destruction of Troy*. Trans. George A. Panton and David Donaldson. New York, 1969.

———. *Historia Destructionis Troiae*. Trans. M. E. Meek. Bloomington, 1974.

Columbo, Cristoforo. *Libro de las profecías*. Ed. C. de Lollis. Raccolta di documenti e studi pubblicata dalla R. commissione colombiana del quarto centenario dalla scoperta dell'America, pt. 1, vol. 2. Rome, 1894.

Columnis, Guido de. *Historia Destructionis Troiae*. Ed. N. E. Griffin. Cambridge, Mass., 1936.

Combes, André. "Sainte Thérèse de l'Enfant-Jésus et l'eucharistie." La Pensée Catholique. Vol. 50–51. Paris, 1957, 23–52.

Contile, Luca. *Ragionamento sopra la proprietà delle imprese*. Pavia, 1574.

Coreth, Anna. "Dynastisch-politische Ideen Kaiser Maximilian I." *Mitteilungen des Österreichischen Staatsarchivs*, 3. *Festschrift Leo Santifaller*. Vienna, 1950, 81–105.

———."Ein Wappenbuch Kaiser Maximilians I." *Mitteilungen des Österreichischen Staatsarchivs*, 2. Vienna, 1949, 291–303.

———. *Österreichische Geschichtsschreibung in der Barockzeit 1620–1740*. Veröffentlichungen der Kommission für Neuere Geschichte Österreichs, no. 37. Vienna, 1950.

———. "Pietas Austriaca. Wesen und Bedeutung habsburgischer Frömmigkeit in der Barockzeit." *Mitteilungen des Österreichischen Staatsarchivs*, 7. Vienna, 1954, 90–119.

———. *Pietas Austriaca*. Vienna, 1959.

Corrado, Francisco Gerónimo. *Descripción del túmulo (de) Felipe II*. Seville, 1869.

Creighton, M. *A History of the Papacy from the Great Schism to the Sack of Rome*, vol. 5. New York, 1897.

Daniélou, Jean. *The Bible and the Liturgy*. Notre Dame, Ind., 1956.

Dante. *Le Opere*. Ed. Michele Barbi. Florence, 1921.

Davidson, Bernice. "The Navigation d'Enea Tapestries Designed by Perino del Vaga for Andrea Doria." Art Bulletin 72, no. 1 (1990): 35–50.

De Bruyn, Abbé H. *Histoire de l'église de Sainte-Gudule*. Brussels, 1870.

de la Ville de Mirmont, H. "La Mythologie et les dieux dans les argonautiques et dans l'Enéide." Ph.D. diss., Paris, 1894.

De Vaux, Roland. "Le Roi d'Israël, Vassal de Yahvé." *Mélanges Eugène Tisserent*. Vol. 1. Rome, 1964, 119–33.

Delage, Emile. "Le Mythe des argonauts et la composition dans le IVe pythique." *Mélanges offerts à A. M. Desrousseaux*. Paris, 1937, 123-30.

Delatte, Louis. *Les Traités de la royauté d'Ecphante, Diotogéne et Sthénidas*. Bibliothèque de la faculté de philosophie et lettres, de l'Université de Liège, vol. 97. Paris, 1942.

della Corte, Francesco. "La 'Pronafonesi' della IV Egloga." Maia 34 (1982): 3–12.

Delmarcel, Guy. "Los Honores. Tapices I. Colecciones del Patrimonio Nacional." *Reales Sitios* 16, no. 62 (1979): 41–57.

Dempf, Alois. *Sacrum Imperium*. Reprinted Florence, 1988.

Deschaux, Robert. *Michault Taillevent*. Publications romanes et françaises, 132. Geneva, 1975.

Devisse, Jean. *Hincmar, archevêque de Reims, 845–882*. 3 vols. Geneva, 1975–76.

Dexel, Franz. "Des Prudentius Verhältnis zu Vergil." Ph.D. diss., Landshut, 1907.

Dictys. *The Trojan War*. Trans. R. M. Frazer, Jr. Bloomington, Ind., 1966.

Didaco di Lequile. *Colossus Angelicus*. Innsbruck, 1659.

———. *Piisima . . . Domus Austriaca.* Innsbruck, 1660.

———. *Rebus.* Innsbruck, 1660.

Dinkler, E. "Das Kreuz als Siegesreichen." *Zeitschrift für Theologie und Kirche* 62 (1965): 1ff.

Documentos para la historia del Monasterio de San Lorenzo el Real de El Escorial. Ed. Julian Zarco Cuevas. Madrid, 1985.

Dölger, Franz Joseph. *Die Sonne der Gerechtigkeit und der Schwarze.* Münster, 1918.

———. *Sol Salutis.* Munich, 1925.

Donati, Tiberi Claudi. *Interpretationes Vergilianae.* Ed. Henricus Georgii. Lipsiae, 1905.

Doutrepont, George. "Jason et Gédéon, patrons de la Toison d'or." *Mélanges Godefroid Kurth,* vol. 2. Liège, 1908, 191–208.

———. *Jean Lemaire de Belges et la Renaissance.* Académie royale de Belgique, Classe de lettres et de sciences moral et politiques, Mémoires, ser. D, vol. 32. Brussels, 1934.

Drake, Harold Allen. *In Praise of Constantine: A Historical Study and New Translation of Eusebius' Tricennial Orations.* University of California Publications, Classical Studies vol. 15. Berkeley, 1976.

Dürr, Emil. "Karl der Kühne und der Ursprung des habsburgisch-spanischen Imperiums." *Historische Zeitschrift* 113 (1913): 23–55.

Dynter, Edward de. *Chronique des Ducs de Brabant.* Trans. Jehan Wauquelin. Ed. P. F. X. DeRam. Brussels, 1854–60.

Einhard. *Vita Karoli Magni: The Life of Charlemagne.* Trans. Evelyn Scherabon Firchow and Edwin H. Zeydel. Coral Gables, Fla., 1972.

———. "Karolus Magnus et Leo Papa." In *Monumenta Germaniae Historia. Poetarum Latinorum Medii Aevi,* vol. 1, ed. Ernestus Dümmler. Berlin, 1880.

———. *Life of Charlemagne.* Trans. Samuel Epes Turner. Ann Arbor, 1960.

Eisler, William. "The Impact of the Emperor Charles V upon the Italian Visual Culture, 1529–33." In *Triumphal Celebrations and the Rituals of Statecraft,* ed. Barbara Wisch and Susan Scott Munshower. Papers in Art History from the Pennsylvania State University, vol. 6, pt. 1. University Park, Penn., 1990, 93–110.

Ekkehardi. *Uraugiensis chronica.* Ed. George Waitz. In *Monumenta Germaniae Historia. Scriptorum rerum Germanicarum,* vol. 6. Hannover, 1844.

El Escorial en la Biblioteca Nacional. Exhibition Catalogue. IV Centenario del Monasterio de el Escorial. Madrid, 1986.

Elliott, John H. *Spain and Its World, 1500–1700: Selected Essays.* New Haven, 1989.

Eusebius. *Ecclesiastical History.* Trans. Kirsopp Lake. 2 vols. Loeb Classical Library. London, 1953.

Fabre, Francesco José. *Descripción de las alegorias pintadas en las bovedas del real palacio de Madrid.* Madrid, 1829.

Faggin, Giuseppe. "Giangiorgio Trissino e l'Impero." In *Convegno di studi su Giangiorgio Trissino.* Vicenza, 1980.

Farina, Raffael. *L'impero e l'imperatore cristiano in Eusebio de Ceserea. La prima teologica politica del Cristianesimo.* Zurich, 1966.

Fernández de Oviedo y de Valdés, Gonzalo. *Catálogo real de Castilla.* 1532. Escorial Ms. Castellanos h.I.7.

Fichtenau, H. *The Carolingian Empire.* Oxford, 1967.

Fillastre, Guillaume. *Le Premier Volume de la Toison d'or.* 4 vols. Paris, 1517.

Firpo, Luigi. "La Cité idéale de Campanella et le culte de soleil." In *Le Soleil à la Renaissance.* Brussels, 1965.

Folz, R. *Le Couronnement impérial de Charlemagne.* Paris, 1964.

———. *L'idée d'Empire en occident du Ve au XIVe siècle.* Paris, 1953.

Fowler, W. Warde. *Aeneas at the Site of Rome.* New York, 1917.

Fredegarius. *Chronicarum Quae Dicuntur Fredegarii Scholastici.* In *Monumenta Germaniae Historia. Scriptorum rerum Merovingicarum,* ed. Bruno Krusch, vol. 2. Hannover, 1888.

Fuhrmann, Horst. *Germany in the High Middle Ages c. 1050–1200.* Trans. Timothy Reuter. Cambridge, Mass., 1987

Gagé, J. *Apollon Romain.* Bibliothèque des écoles françaises d'Athènes et de Rome, vol. 182. Paris, 1955.

Galinsky, C. Karl. *Aeneas, Sicily and Rome.* Princeton, 1969.

Ganshof, F. L. *The Carolingians and the Frankish Monarchy.* Trans. Janet Sondheimer. Ithaca, 1971.

Garibay, Esteban de. *Illustraciones genealogicas de los catolicos reyes de las Espanas.* Madrid, 1596; reprinted Madrid, 1974.

Gebwiler, Hieronymus. *Epitome Regii Hapsburgi.* Hannover, 1530.

———. *Libertas Germaniae.* Nuremberg, 1524.

Genealogie Ducum Brabantiae. Ed. Ioh. Heller. In *Mon-*

umenta Germaniae Historia. *Scriptorum rerum Germanicarum*, vol. 25.

Gnilka, Christian. *Studien zur Psychomachie des Prudentius*. Klassisch-Philologische Studien 27. Wiesbaden, 1963.

Godefridi Viterbiensis. *Speculum Regum; Pantheon*. In *Monumenta Germaniae Historia. Scriptorum rerum Germanicarum*, vol. 22, ed. G. H. Pertz. Hannover, 1872.

Godman, Peter, ed. *Poetry of the Carolingian Renaissance*. London, 1985.

———. *Poets and Emperors: Frankish Politics and Carolingian Poetry*. New York, 1987.

Goelzer, H. *Le Latin de Saint Avit, évêque de Vienne (450?–526?)*. Paris, 1909.

Gotho, Filippo. *Breve Raguaglio dell' Inventione, e feste de gloriosi Martiri*. Messina, 1591.

Grabar, André. *Christian Iconography. A Study of Its Origins*. Bollingen Series 35, no. 10. Princeton, 1961.

———. *L'Empereur dans l'art byzantin*. Strasburg, 1936.

Graf, Ernestus. "Ad Aureae Aetatis Fabulam Symbola." In *Leipziger Studien zur klassischen Philologie*, no. 8. Leipzig, 1885.

———. *Roma nella Memoria e Nelle Immaginazioni del Medio Evo*. 2 vols. Torino, 1882.

Grapheus, Cornelius. *La . . . triumphante entrée du . . . Prince Philipe*. Antwerp, 1550.

Grauert, Hermann. "Der deutschen Kaisersage." *Historisches Jahrbuch* 12 (1892): 100–143.

Graziani, René. "Philip II's Imprese and Spenser's Souldan." *Journal of the Warburg and Courtauld Institute* 27 (1964).

Gregory of Tours. *Historia Francorum*. In *Monumenta Germaniae Historia. Scriptorum rerum Merovingicarum*, vol. 1, ed. W. Arndt and B. Krusch. Hannover, 1885.

Griffin, Nathaniel Edward. *Dares and Dictys: An Introduction to the Study of Medieval Versions of the Story of Troy*. Baltimore, 1907.

Habig-Bappert, Inge. *Eucharistie im Spätbarock*. Münster, 1983.

Halsberghe, Gaston H. *The Cult of Sol Invictus*. Leiden, 1972.

Hammer, William. "The Concept of the New or Second Rome in the Middle Ages." *Speculum* 19 (1944): 50–62.

Harries, Jill. "Prudentius and Theodosius." *Latomus* 43 (1984): 69–84.

Hauck, Karl. "Der Missionsauftrag Christi und das Kaisertum Ludwigs des Frommen." In *Charlemagne's Heir: New Perspectives on the Reign of Louis the Pious (814–840)*, ed. Peter Godman and Roger Collins. Oxford, 1990, 275–96.

Hempel, Wido. *Philip II und der Escorial in der italienischen Literatur des Cinquecento*. Akademie der Wissenschaften und der Literatur. Abhandlungen der Geistes- und Sozialwissenschaftlichen Klasse, no. 8. Mainz. 1971.

Heniger, S. K., Jr. "Pythagorean Cosmology and the Triumph of Heliocentrism." In *La Soleil à la Renaissance*. Brussels, 1965.

Hermanni Athanenses. *Chronicon Colmariense*. MGHSS, vol. 17, ed. Georgius Heinricus Pertz. Hannover, 1861.

Hibernici Exulis. In *Monumenta Germaniae Historia. Poetarum Latinorum Medii Aevi*, vol. 1, ed. Ernestus Dümmler. Berlin, 1880.

Hirn, Yrjö. *The Sacred Shrine*. London, 1958.

Hispania-Austria. *I Re Cattolici, Massimiliano I e gli Inizi della Casa d'Austria in Spagna*. Exhibition Catalogue. Innsbruck and Milan, 1992.

Hoeflich, M. H. "Between Gothia and Romania: The Image of the King in the Poetry of Venantius Fortunatus." *Res Publica Literarum* 5 (1982): 123–36.

Homberger, Otto. *Die illustrierten Handschriften der Burgerbibliothek Bern*. Bern, 1962.

Hommel, Luc. *L'Histoire du noble ordre de la Toison d'or*. Brussels, 1947.

Horace. *The Odes and Epodes*. Trans. C. E. Bennett. Loeb Classical Library. London, 1962.

Hunterding, F., and F. Horsch. "Reconstruction of Old Master Paintings of King Willem II." *Simiolus* 19 (1989): 55–123.

Irenico, Francisco. *Germaniae*. Basel, 1520.

Jacquot, Jean, ed. *Les Fêtes de la Renaissance*. Vol. 2, *Fêtes cérémonies au temps de Charles Quint*. Paris, 1960.

Jarenbergh, Emile. "Fêtes données à Philippe le Bon et Isabelle de Portugal à Gand, en 1457." In *Annales de la Société royale des Beaux-Arts et de Hératiers* 12 (1863–72): 1–36.

Joly, A. *Benoit de Sainte-More et le Roman de Troie*. Paris, 1871.

Junquera de Vega, Paulina, and Concha Herrero Carretero, eds. *Catálogo de tapices del patrimonio nacional*. Vol. 1, *Siglo XVI*. Madrid, 1986.

Kampers, Franz. *Die deutsche Kaiseridee in Prophetie und Sage*. Munich, 1896.

———. "Kaiserprophetien und Kaiser Sagen in Mittelalter." *Historische Abhandlungen* 8 (1895): 49ff.

Kantorowicz, Ernst. "Dante's Two Suns." *Semitic and Oriental Studies*, University of California Publications in Semitic Philology, no. 11 (1951): 217–31.

———. *Frederick the Second, 1194–1250*. Trans. E. O. Lorimer. New York, 1931.

———. *The King's Two Bodies*. Princeton, 1957.

———. *Laudes Regiae: A Study in Liturgical Acclamations and Mediaeval Ruler Worship*. Berkeley, 1958.

———. "Oriens Augusti—Lever du Roi." *Dumbarton Oaks Papers* 17 (1963): 117–77.

Katznellenbogen, Adolf. *Allegories of the Virtues and Vices in Mediaeval Art*. New York, 1964.

Kervyn de Lettenhove, H. *La Toison d'or: Notes sur l'institution et l'histoire de l'ordre depuis l'année 1429 jusqu'à 1559*. Brussels, 1907.

Klerk, Jan de. *Les Gestes des Ducs de Brabant*. Brussels, 1839.

Knight, W. F. Jackson. *Vergil's Troy*. Oxford, 1932.

Kubler, George. *Building the Escorial*. Princeton, 1982.

Kurth, Godefroid. *Clovis*. Tours, 1896.

———. *Histoire poétique des Mérovingiens*. Reprinted Geneva, 1968.

Kurze, Dietrich. *Johannes Lichtenberger: Eine Studie zur Geschichte der Prophetie und Astrologie*. Historische Studien, vol. 379. Lubeck, 1960.

———. "Prophecy and History." *Journal of the Warburg and Courtauld Institute* 21 (1958): 63–85.

Ladner, Gerhardt B. *The Idea of Reform: Its Impact on Christian Thought and Action in the Age of the Fathers*. New York, 1959; rev. ed., 1967.

Lammers, Walther. "Ein karolingisches Bildprogramm in der Aula Regia von Ingelheim." *Festschrift für H. Heimpel zum 70. Geburtstag*. Göttingen, 1972, 226–89.

LaMonte, John H. *Feudal Monarchy in the Latin Kingdom of Jerusalem, 1100–1291*. Medieval Academy of America Monographs, no. 4. Cambridge, Mass., 1932.

Laschitzer, Simon. "Die Genealogie des Kaisers Maximilian I." *Jahrbuch der kunsthistorischen Sammlungen der allerhöchsten Kaiserhauses* 7 (1888): 1–200.

———. "Die Heiligen aus der Sipp-, Mag- und Schwägeschaft des Kaisers Maximilian I." *Jahrbuch der kunsthistorischen Sammlungen des aller-* höchsten Kaiserhauses 4 (1885): 70–288, and 5 (1886): 117–262.

Lefèvre, Eckard. "Das Pröoemium der Argonautica, des Valerius Flaccus." Akademie der Wissenschaften und der Literatur, no. 6. 1971.

Lefèvre, Raoul. *L'Histoire de Jason*. Ed. Gert Pinkernell. Frankfurt, 1971.

———. *The Recuyell of the Historyes of Troye*. Trans. H. Oskar Sommer. London, 1894.

Leithe-Jasper, Manfred, and Rudolf Distelberger. *The Kunsthistorische Museum Vienna: The Treasury and the Collection of Sculpture and Decorative Arts*. London, 1982.

Lemaire de Belges, Jean. *Les Illustrations de Gaule et Singularitez de Troye*. Paris, 1512.

Lenkeith, Nancy. *Dante and the Legend of Rome*. The Warburg Institute, Medieval and Renaissance Studies, Supplement II. London, 1952.

Leto, Giulio Pomponio. *Romanae Historiae Compendium*, Ms. Vat. Lat. 10936.

Lhotsky, Alfons. "Apis Colonna." *Mitteilungen des Institut für Geschichtsforschung und Archivwissenschaft in Wien*, 55 (1944): 171–245.

Lipsius, Justus. *De Cruce*. Antwerp, 1594.

———. *De Vesta et Vestalibus Syntagma*. Antwerp, 1603.

———. *Opera Omnia*. Louvain, 1596.

L'Orange, H. P. *Apotheosis in Ancient Portraiture*. New Rochelle, N.Y., 1982.

———. "Sol Invictus Imperator. Ein Beitrag zur Apotheose." *Symbolae Osloenses* 14 (1935): 86–114.

Lottin, O. "Le Traité de Alain de Lille sur les vertus, les vices et les dons du Saint-Esprit." *Medieval Studies* 12 (1950): 20–56.

Lovejoy, A. O., and George Boas. *A Documentary History of Primitivism and Related Ideas in Antiquity*. Baltimore, 1935.

McGinn, Bernard. *Visions of the End*. New York, 1979.

Macrobius. *Commentary on the Dream of Scipio*. Trans. William Harris Stahl. New York, 1966.

Macrobius. *Commentarii in Somnium Scipionis; Saturnalia*. Ed. James Willis. 2 vols. Leipzig, 1963.

Mal Lara, Juan de. *Descripción de la Galera Real*. Reprint of manuscript, Biblioteca Colombina B.4a, 445–41. Seville, 1876.

Male, Emile. *L'Art religieux de la fin du Moyen Age en France*. Paris, 1908.

Manilius. *Astronomica*. Trans. G. P. Goold. Loeb Classical Library. London, 1977.

Marciano, Marcello. *Pompe Funebri dell' Universo nella morte di Filippo IV*. Naples, 1666.

Mareno, Pietro. *Compendio della Stirpe di Carlo Magno et Carlo V*. Venice, 1545.

Marignola, Johannes de. *Kronika Marignolova*. Fontes Rerum Bohemicarum, vol. 3. Prague, 1882.

Matsche, Franz. *Die Kunst im Dienst der Staatsidee Kaiser Karls VI*. 2 vols. Berlin, N.Y., 1981.

Mayor, Joseph B., W. Warde Fowler, and R. S. Conway. *Virgil's Messianic Eclogue*. London, 1907.

Meier, Christel, ed. "Die Rezeption des Anticlaudianus Alans von Lille in Textkommentierung und Illustration." *Text und Bild*. Weisbaden, 1980.

Memoridas de Fray Juan de San Geronimo. Colección de documentos inéditos para la historia de Espana. Ed D. Miguel Salvà and D. Pedro Sainz de Baranda. Vol. 7. Madrid, 1845.

Meyer, Paul. "Les Premières Compilations françaises d'histoire ancienne." *Romania* 14 (1895): 1–81.

Mezzatesta, Michael. "Imperial Themes in the Art of Leone Leoni." Ph.D. diss., New York University, 1980.

Molinet, Jean. *Chroniques*. Ed. George Doutrepont and Omer Jodogne. 3 vols. Académie royale de Belgique. Brussels, 1935–37.

Mommsen, Theodore E. "Aponius and Orosius." In *Late Classical and Mediaeval Studies in Honor of Albert Mathias Friend, Jr.* Princeton, 1955.

Monod, Gabriel. *Etudes critiques sur le source d'histoire mérovingienne: Recueil de travaux originaux ou traduits relatifs aux sciences historiques*. Vol. 8. Paris, 1872.

Moore, E., ed. *Tutte le opere di Dante*. 4th ed. Oxford, 1963.

Müllerus, C., ed. *Fragmenta Historicorum Graecorum*. Vol. 2. Paris, 1848.

Mütherich, Florentine. "Book Illumination at the Court of Louis the Pious." In *Charlemagne's Heir: New Perspectives on the Reign of Louis the Pious (814–840)*, ed. Peter Godman and Roger Collins. Oxford, 1990, 593–604.

Neuwirth, Joseph. *Der Bildercyklus des Luxemburger Stammbaumes aus Karlstein*. Forschungen zur Kunstgeschichte Böhmens. Gesellschaft zur Förderung Deutscher Wissenschaft, Kunst und Literatur in Böhmen. Vol. 2. Prague, 1897.

Nigellus, Ermoldus. *In honorem Hludowici; Ad Pippinum Regum II* In Monumenta Germaniae Historia. Poetarum Latinorum Medii Aevi, vol. 2, pt. 1, ed. Ernestus Dümmler. Berlin, 1884.

Nisard, M. Charles. *Juste Lipse, Joseph Scaliger et Isaac Casaubon*. Paris, 1852.

Nock, Arthur Darby. "The Emperor's Divine Comes." *Journal of Roman Studies* 37 (1947): 102–16.

Noppenberger, Fran X. "Die eucharistische Monstranz des Barockzeitalters." Ph.D. diss., Munich, 1958.

Norden, Karl. *On Vergil and Ennius*. Berlin, 1915.
———. *Die Geburt des Kindes*. Leipzig, 1924.

Ocampo, Floriando. *Cronica general de Espana*. Medina del Campo, 1553.

Ortiz, Antonio Domínguez, Concha Herrero Carretero, and José A. Godoy. *Resplendence of the Spanish Monarchy, Renaissance Tapestries and Armor from the Patrimonio Nacional*. New York, 1991.

Ottonis Episcopi Frisingensis. *Chronica sive Historia de duabus Civitatibus*. In Monumenta Germaniae Historia. Scriptorum rerum Germanicarum, ed. Adolfus Hofmeister. Hannover, 1912.

Ovid. *Fasti*. Trans. J. G. Frazer. Loeb Classical Library. London, 1967.

Owen, D. D. R., trans. *The Legend of Roland*. London, 1973.

Pacelli, Vincenzo. "Il 'Monogramma' Bernardiano: Origine, diffusione e sviluppo." In *S. Bernardino da Siena predicatore e pellegrino*. Atti del Convegno Nazionale di Studi Bernardiani. Messina, 1985, 253–60.

Palavicino, Hortensio. *Austriaci Caesares*. Mediolani, 1649.

Palmer, Anne-Marie. *Prudentius on the Martyrs*. Oxford, 1989.

Panofsky, Erwin. *Early Netherlandish Painting*. 2 vols. Cambridge, Mass., 1964.
———. *The Life and Art of Albrecht Dürer*. Princeton, 1971.
———. *Problems in Titian, Mostly Iconographic*. New York, 1969.

Parker, Alexander A. *The Allegorical Dramas of Calderón: An Introduction to the Auto-Sacramentales*. Oxford, 1943.

Peterson, Erik. "Christus als Imperator." In *Theo-

logische Traktate. Munich, 1951, 151–64.

Pindar. *The Odes of Pindar.* Trans. Sir J. E. Sandys. Loeb Classical Library. London, 1978.

Pitti, Vincenzo. *Essequie della Sacra real Maesta Re de Spagna D. Filippo II . . . celebrata da D. Ferdinando Medici, Gran Duca di Toscana nella città di Firenze.* Florence, 1598.

Pontano, Iovanni. *Carminum.* Basel, 1531.

Poupardin, René. "L'Onction impériale." *Le Moyen-Age,* ser. 2, vol. 9 (1905): 113–26.

Preger, Theodor. "Konstantinos-Helios." *Hermes* 36, no. 4 (1901): 457–69.

Prudentius. Trans. H. J. Thomson. 2 vols. Loeb Classical Library. Cambridge, 1969, 1974.

Redlich, Oswald. "Rudolf von Habsburg in der volkstümlichen Überlieferung." *Jahrbuch des Vereines für Landeskunde von Niederösterreich* (1918): 1–11.

Reeves, Marjorie. *The Influence of Prophecy in the Later Middle Ages: A Study in Joachimism.* Oxford, 1969.

———. *Joachim of Fiore and the Prophetic Future.* New York, 1977.

Regel, Georgius. *De Vergilio Poetarum Imitator Testimonia.* Göttingen, 1907.

Rekers, B. *Benitos Arias Montano.* London, 1972.

Relación de lo que ha sucedido in la cuidad de Valladolid (en el) Felicísimo Nacimiento del Príncipe Don Felipe. Valladolid, 1605; reprinted Valladolid, 1916.

Reydellet, Mark. *La Royauté dans la littérature latine, de Sidoine Apollinaire à Isidore de Seville.* Bibliothèque des écoles françaises d'Athènes et de Rome, vol. 243. Rome, 1981.

Ripa, Cesare. *Iconologia.* Padua, 1611.

Rohling, Joseph Henry. "The Blood of Christ in Christian Latin Literature before the Year 1000." Ph.D. diss., Catholic University, 1932.

Roo, Gerard de. *Annales Rerum Belli Domique ab Austriacis Habsburgicae Gentis.* Innsbruck, 1592.

Rosenthal, Earl E. *The Cathedral of Granada.* Princeton, 1961.

———. "Die 'Reichskrone,' die 'Wiener Krone' und die 'Krone Karls des Grossen' um 1520." *Jahrbuch der kunsthistorischen Sammlungen in Wien* 66 (1970): 7–48.

———. "The Invention of the Columnar Device of Emperor Charles V at the Court of Burgundy in Flanders in 1516." *Journal of the Warburg and Courtauld Institute* 36 (1973): 198–230.

———. "Plus Ultra: Non Plus Ultra, and the Columnar Device of Emperor Charles V." *Journal of the Warburg and Courtauld Institute* 34 (1971): 204–28.

Roth, K. L. "Die Trojansage der Franken." (Pfeiffer's) *Germania* 1 (1856): 34–52.

Roux, R. *Le Problème des Argonautes.* Paris, 1949.

Rubin, Miri. *Corpus Christi: The Eucharist in Late Medieval Culture.* Cambridge, 1991.

Rubio, L. "El Monasterio de San Lorenzo El Real." In *Real Monasterio de el Escorial.* Madrid, 1984: 223–93.

Ruscelli, Girolamo. *Le Imprese illustri.* Venice, 1566.

Salvatore, A. *Studi Prudenziani.* Naples, 1950.

Sanchez y Escribano, F. *Juan de Mal Lara, su vida y sus obras.* New York, 1941.

Sanserre, Jean Marie. "Eusèbe de Césarée et le 'Césaropapisme.'" *Byzantion* 42 (1972): 131–95.

Santos, Francisco de los. *Descripción del Real Monasterio de San Lorenzo de El Escorial.* Trans. George Thompson. London, 1760 (originally published Madrid, 1657).

Saxl, Fritz. "Veritas Filia Temporis." In *Philosophy and History: Essays Presented to Ernst Cassirer.* Oxford, 1936, 200ff.

Schardius, Simon. *De Iurisdictione, Autoritate et Praeeminentia Imperiali.* Basel, 1566.

Schedel, Hartmann. *Liber Chronicarum.* Nuremberg, 1493.

Scheicher, Elizabeth. "Heraldica y Origen de la Nobleza de los Austrias en la Biblioteca Escorial." Trans. Julia Hernandez Sans. *Reales Sitios* 17, no. 103 (1990): 49–56.

Schellhase, Kenneth C. *Tacitus in Renaissance Political Thought.* Chicago, 1976.

Schneider, Karen. "Der 'Trojanische Krieg' in späten Mittelalter: Deutsche Trojaromane des 15. Jahrhunderts." *Philologische Studien und Quellen,* vol. 40. Berlin, 1968.

Scholz, Bernhard Walter, with Barbara Rogers, trans. *Carolingian Chronicles.* Ann Arbor, 1970.

Schramm, Percy Ernst. *Die deutschen Kaiser und Könige in Bildern ihrer Zeit 751–1190.* Munich, 1983.

———. *Herrschaftszeichen und Staatsymbolik: Beiträge zu ihrer Geschichte vom dritten bis zum sechzehnten Jahrhundert.* In *Monumenta Germaniae Historia. Scriptorum rerum Germanicarum,* vol. 12. 3 vols. Stuttgart, 1954–56.

———. *Kaiser, Rom und Renovatio.* Studien der Bibliothek Warburg, vol. 17. 2 vols. Leipzig, 1929.

———. "'Mitherrschaft im Himmel': Ein Topos des Herrscherkults in christlicher Einkleidung." In *Polychronion: Festschrift Franz Dölger zum*

75. Geburtstag, ed. Peter Wirth. Heidelberg, 1966, 480–85.

———. Sphaira, Globus, Reichsapfel. Stuttgart, 1958.

Schulte, Alois. Kaiser Maximilian I als Kandidat für den päpstlichen Stuhl 1511. Leipzig, 1906.

Scott, John Beldon. "The Catafalques of Philip II in Saragossa." Studies in Iconography 5 (1979): 107–34.

Scribner, Charles, III. The Triumph of the Eucharist: Tapestries Designed by Rubens. Ann Arbor, 1982.

Sears, Elizabeth. "Louis the Pious as Miles Christi." In Charlemagne's Heir, ed. Peter Godman and Roger Collins. Oxford, 1990.

Sedulius Scotus. "Carmina." In Monumenta Germaniae Historia. Poetarum Latinorum Medii Aevi, vol. 3, Ludovicus Traube. Berlin, 1896, 151f.

Segal, Charles. Pindar's Mythmaking: The Fourth Pythian Ode. Princeton, 1986.

Seibt, Ferdinand. Karl IV. Munich, 1979.

Seifried, Ioanne. Arbor Aniciana. Vienna, 1613.

Servii. Grammatici Qui Feruntur in Vergilii Bucolica et Georgica. Ed. George Thilo. Leipzig, 1927.

Seston, William. "La Vision païenne de 310 et les origines du chrisme constantinien." In Mélanges Franz Cumont. Annuaire de l'Institut de Philologie et d'Histoire Orientales et Slavs. Vol. 4. Brussels, 1936, 373–95.

Shaffer, Ellen. The Nuremberg Chronicle. Los Angeles, 1950.

Shapiro, Meyer. "The Joshua Roll in Byzantine History." In Late Antique, Early Christian and Mediaeval Art. New York, 1979, 48–66.

Sigüenza, Fray Jose de. La Fundación del Monasterio de el Escorial por Felipe II. Reprinted Madrid, 1927.

Silver, Larry. "Paper Pageants: The Triumphs of Emperor Maximilian I." In Triumphal Celebrations and the Rituals of Statecraft, ed. Barbara Wisch and Susan Scott Munshower. Papers in Art History from the Pennsylvania State University, vol. 6, pt. 1. University Park, Penn., 1990, 292–331.

Silvestris, Bernard. The Cosmographia. Trans. Winthrop Wetherbee. New York, 1973.

Sixto, F. Francisco. Genealogia Gloriosissimae Prosapiae Austriadis Ab ad Adamo ad Philippum. Naples, 1573.

Smith, Macklin. Prudentius' Psychomachia: A Reexamination. Princeton, 1976.

Snell, Bruno "L'Arcadia: Scoperta di un paesaggio spirituale." In La cultura greca e le origini del pensiero europeo. Trans. Vera degli Alberti. Torino, 1951.

Solorzano Pereira, Juan de. Emblemata. Madrid, 1653.

———. Politica Indiana. Madrid, 1647; reprinted Madrid, 1948.

Steger, Hugo. David Rex et Propheta. Erlanger Beiträge zur Sprach und Kunstwissenschaft, no. 6. Nuremberg, 1961.

Steppe, J. K. "Vlaams Tapijtwerk van de 16e de eeuw in Spaans Koninklijk bezit." In Miscellanea Jozef Duverger, vol. 2. Ghent, 1968, 719–65.

Stettiner, R. Die illustrierten Prudentiushandschriften, 2 vols. Berlin, 1895, 1905.

Stevenson, Thomas B. Miniature Decoration in the Vatican Virgil. Tübingen, 1983.

Strong, Roy. Splendour at Court: Renaissance Spectacle and the Theatre of Power. London, 1973.

Suetonius. Trans. J. C. Rolfe. 2 vols. Loeb Classical Library. London, 1957.

Sullivan, Edward J. "Propaganda and Politics in the Sagrada Forma." Art Bulletin 57 (1985): 243–59.

Taeger, Fritz. Charisma: Studien zur Geschichte des antiken Herrscherkultes. Vol. 2. Stuttgart, 1960.

Tanner, Marie. "Chance and Coincidence in Titian's Diana and Actaeon," Art Bulletin 56, no. 3 (1974): 535–50.

———. "Concordia in Piero della Francesca's Baptism of Christ." Art Quarterly 35, no. 1 (1972): 1–21.

———. "Titian: The Poesie for Philip II." Ph.D. diss. New York University, Institute of Fine Arts, 1976.

Taylor, Lily Ross. The Divinity of the Roman Emperor. Philological Monographs of the American Philological Association, no. 1. Middletown, Conn., 1931.

Taylor, Rene. "Architecture and Magic: Considerations on the Idea of the Escorial." In Essays in the History of Architecture Presented to Rudolf Wittkower, vol. 2. New York, 1967, 81–109.

———. "El Padre Villalpando y sus ideas estéticas." Anales y boletín de la Academia de bellas artes de San Fernando, no. 2. Madrid, 1952.

Terlinden, Victor. "Coup d'oeil sur l'histoire de l'ordre illustre de la Toison d'or." In La Toison d'or: Cinq siècles d'art et d'histoire. Musée communal des Beaux-Arts, Bruges, 1962, 19–33.

———. "Das goldene Vliess." In Festschrift für Otto von Habsburg zum 50. Geburtstag. Vienna, 1965.

Tessier, G. Le Baptême de Clovis. Paris, 1964.

Tormo y Monzó, Elias, and Francisco J. Sanchez

Canton. *Los tápices de la casa del rey N.S.: Notas para el catálogo y para la historia de la colección y de la fabrica.* Madrid, 1919.

Tourneur, Victor. "Les Origines de l'ordre de la Toison d'or et la symbolique des insignes de celui-ci." *Bulletin de la classe des lettres et des sciences morales et politiques, Académie royale de Belgique,* 5th ser., 42. Brussels, 1956, 300–323.

Triumph der Eucharistie. Tapestry Exhibition. Cologne, 1954–55.

Ussani, Vincenzo, Jr. *Studi su Valerio Flacco.* Rome, 1955.

Valdesius, Jacobus. *Praerogativa Hispaniae.* Ed. princ., Granada, 1602; reprinted Frankfurt, 1626.

Valerius Flaccus. *Argonautica.* Trans. J. H. Mozley. Loeb Classical Library. London, 1972.

Van den Bergen-Pantens, Christiane. "Guerre de Troie et héraldique imaginaire." *Revue belge d'archéologie et d'histoire de l'art* 52 (1983): 3–21.

Van der Osten Sacken, Cornelia. *San Lorenzo il Real de el Escorial, studia iconologica,* Münchener Universitätschriften, Fachbereich Geschichts- und Kunstwissenschaften, no. 1. Munich, 1979.

Vellay, Charles. *Les Légendes du cycle troyen.* 2 vols. Monaco, 1957.

Vernulaei, Nicolai. *Virtutum Augustissimae Gentis Austriacae.* Louvain, 1640.

Vest, Eugene B. "Prudentius in the Middle Ages," Ph.D. diss., Harvard University, 1932.

———. "The Psychomachia of Prudentius." M.A. thesis. Northwestern University, 1929.

Villalpando, Ioannes Baptista. *In Ezechielem Explanationes.* 3 vols. Rome, 1596.

Virgil. Trans. H. Rushton Fairclough. 2 vols. Loeb Classical Library. London, 1950, 1978.

Wallach, Luitpold. *Alcuin and Charlemagne: Studies in Carolingian History and Literature.* Cornell Studies in Classical Philology, no. 32. Ithaca, 1959.

Warburg, Aby. "Divinazione antica pagana in testi ed immagini de'l eta di Lutero." In *La Rinascita del paganesimo antico,* trans. Emma Cantimore. Florence, 1980.

Watson, A. *The Early Iconography of the Tree of Jesse.* London, 1934.

Weber, Annemarie. "Der österreichische Orden vom Goldenen Vliess: Geschichte und Problem." Ph.D. diss., Bonn University, 1971.

Weitzmann, Kurt. *The Joshua Roll: A Work of the Macedonian Renaissance.* Studies in Manuscript Illumination, no. 3. Princeton, 1948.

Williams, R. D. *The Aeneid.* London, 1987.

Wion, Arnoldo. *Lignum Vitae ad Philippum II Hispaniarum.* 2 vols. Venice, 1595.

Woodruff, Helen. "The Illustrated Manuscripts of Prudentius." *Art Studies* 7 (1929): 33–79.

Wright, David H., ed. *Vergilius Vaticanus.* Graz, 1984.

Yates, Frances A. *Astraea: The Imperial Theme in the Sixteenth Century.* London, 1975.

Zanker, Paul. *The Power of Images in the Age of Augustus.* Trans. Alan Shapiro. Jerome Lectures, no. 16. Ann Arbor, 1990.

Zeller, Gaston. "Les Rois de France, candidats à l'empire: Essai sur l'idéologie impériale en France." *Revue Historique* 173 (1934): 237–311, 497–534.

Zwierlein, Otto. "Karolus Magnus–Alter Aeneas." In *Literatur und Sprache im Europäischen Mittelalter: Festschrift für Karl Langosch zum 70. Geburtstag,* ed. A. Onnerfors, J. Rathofer, F. Wagner. Darmstadt, 1973, 44–52.

Index

Aachen, 41, 44, 80, 171, 210, 262n. 24, 271n. 27, 275n. 105
Aaron, 29, 78, 80, 171, 258nn. 29–31, 264n. 45, 293n. 38
Abraham, 47, 60, 76, 118, 218, 261
Achilles, 16, 187, 148
Actium, battle of, 14–15, 19, 28, 149, 227–28, 256n. 50
Adam, 45–97 passim, 123, 143, 158, 178, 182, 195, 198, 206, 217, 243, 271n. 31, 272n. 41, 286n. 5, 301n. 61., 303n. 38
Adso, *Letter on the Antichrist*, 121, 282n. 16
Aeneas, 16, 24–26, 30–31, 34–89 passim, 100, 107, 109, 115, 118–21, 126, 145, 250, 271n. 23, 281n. 8; ancestral cult, 15, 68; ancestor of Christian emperors, 2, 50, 69–71, 76, 80, 93, 145, 178, 193, 202, 257n. 5, 270n. 15, 272nn. 39, 45, 274n. 84, 275n. 95, 276nn. 110, 122, 127, 277n. 134, 278n. 145, 279n. 167, 280n. 176, 298n. 32, 299n. 41, 305n. 54; ancestor of Augustus, 2, 13–14, 19, 21, 68–69; ancestry, divine, 11, 13, 56, 69, 254n. 4, 255n. 12; and Apollo, 11, 13, 15; apotheosis, 16; in Christian

eschatology, 34, 69, 121–22; founds New Troy in Italy, 6, 11–17, 19, 48–49, 54–55, 73–97 passim, 149, 195, 227, 254nn. 2, 4, 6, 7, 256n. 41, 268n. 13; as king, 15, 254nn. 2, 4, 255n. 33; model for Christian emperors, 1, 41–42, 88, 113, 137–38, 198; and Penates, 11, 13–15, 17, 254nn. 9, 10, 254nn. 9, 10, 307n. 25, 269n. 5; piety, 15, 25–26, 42, 47, 69, 198, 202, 228, 254n. 2, 255n. 17, 256n. 51; as priest, 15, 21, 255n. 33, 307n. 25; and prophecy, 13, 15–16, 19; shield, 14, 19, 265n. 81, 270n. 9, 306n. 17; universal domain, 14
Aeneas at Carthage, 12, 13, 41–43
Aeneas Sacrificing, 15, 16, 21
Aeneas with Anchises, Ascanius, and the Palladium, 13, 14
Alain de Lille, *Anticlaudian*, 45–52, 54, 60, 66, 264n. 46, 266n. 95, 269n. 27, 282n. 23
Alcuin, 42, 71, 81, 186, 263n. 33, 266nn. 88, 94, 281n. 186
Alecto, 15, 48, 258n. 11
Alexander the Great, 72–89 passim, 116, 134, 163, 255n. 35, 260n. 51, 271n. 26

Alexander VI, Pope, 100, 274n. 90
Alfonso I, of Naples, 289n. 36
Americas, 4, 7–8, 109, 127–57 passim, 168, 181, 206, 215, 223–33 passim, 251, 292n. 22
Anastasius, Emperor, 37, 75
Anchises (father of Aeneas), 13, 15, 68, 70, 72, 85, 126, 255n. 12, 270n. 19, 274n. 84
Anchises (Frankish ruler), 70–71, 81, 98, 270n. 19, 274n. 84
Anchises, 95, 97–98
Andrew (Saint), 151, 288n. 25
Anicio gens, 191, 192, 195, 198, 208, 297nn. 24, 26–31, 299n. 44
Anne of Austria, 245
Annius of Viterbo, 88, 274nn. 90–91
Annointing of David, 38, 38
Ansibert, 71, 98, 277
Antenor, 73, 89, 97
Antichrist, 120–21, 123–24, 128, 179, 181, 257n. 3, 281n. 9, 282n. 22, 283n. 36, 285n. 28
Antony, Mark, 14–15, 228, 306n. 17
Apianus, Peter, 235
Apollo, 11–18 passim, 70, 118, 145, 148, 161, 178, 223, 227–48 passim, 306–10, 307nn.

Apollo (*continued*)
32–34, 308nn. 40–41; and
Aeneas, 227–28, 306nn. 14,
16; and Argonauts, 227,
306nn. 7–8; and Augustus,
227–30, 256n. 54, 306nn. 17,
24, 307nn. 24–31; and Charlemagne, 233, 308n. 54; and
Charles V, 233–35; and
Clovis, 233, 308n. 53; and
Constantine, 230–32, 307nn.
35–39, 307n. 39, 308n. 48;
and the Escorial, 243–45; in
Fourth Eclogue, 223, 225, 227,
306nn. 11–12; and Frederick
II, 233; in Homer, 306n. 6;
and Jesus, 225, 231–32, 245–
47, 308nn. 44, 46–48; 310nn.
92, 94; and the Last World
Emperor, 231; and Maxi-
milian I, 233, 308n. 58; and
the Penates, 227, 306nn. 10,
16, 308n. 40; and Philip II,
223, 235–48, 308n. 42,
309nn. 61–62; and Saint
Lawrence, 245; and the
Spanish Hapsburgs, 239–40,
243; and Tommaso Cam-
panella, 243, 245
Apollonian Quadriga, 229, *229*
Apollonius Rhodius, *Argonautica*, 148, 253, 255, 286–
87
Apotheosis of Otto I, 83, *83*
Ara Pacis, 15–16, 21–22
Arcadius, 45, 78, 265n. 54
Argo, 5–9, 17–18, 145–59 passim, 250, 253n. 4, 256n. 39,
268n. 19, 287n. 21
Argonauts, 6–9, 17–32 passim,
53–58, 103, 148–50, 152, 154,
156–58, 227, 256n. 48
Argonauts Destroy Troy, 55, *55*
Arianism, 37–38, 185–86, 260n.
58, 261n. 4, 262n. 16
Aries the Ram, 17, 147–51, 154,
157, 161, 255, 268nn. 2, 10–
11, 14–17, 286–87, 288nn.
23, 30; and Aeneas, 149; and
Augustus, 149, 287n. 11; and
Burgundian-Hapsburg dy-
nasty, 154–61; and the Cru-
sades, 150, 287n. 17; and
Fourth Eclogue, 148; and
Golden Fleece, 147–50; and
Lamb of God, 149–52, 157,
287nn. 15, 16

Ariosto, Lodovico, *Orlando Furioso*, 116, 157, 289
Arma Christi, 34
Armada, 237, 309n. 63
Arnulf, Saint, 71
Ascanius (Iulus), 13–14, 55,
137, 256n. 55
Assaracus, 13, 255
Asser, 208, 221, 301n. 8, 305n.
55
Astraea, 31–32, 46, 66, 90, 93,
113, 137, 223, 259n. 41, 276n.
119
Atlas, 139
Augustus, 1, 29, 31, 41, 113,
118, 142–78 passim, 225,
230, 257n. 62, 281n. 8, 282n.
21, 294n. 56; Aeneas's descendant, 14–15, 19, 21, 29,
68–69, 121, 256n. 55, 269n.
3, 270n. 9; ancestor cult, 19,
21, 67–68, 255n. 19, 256n.
56, 269nn. 3–4; and Apollo,
19, 227–30, 256n. 54, 257n.
61, 306n. 24, 307nn. 24–31;
apotheosis, 21, 31, 68, 171–
74, 229, 257n. 64, 269n. 3;
and Christianity, 23–24, 28,
32, 34, 54, 90, 257n. 2,
260nn. 46, 62, 277n. 125; divine ancestry and divinity,
14, 19, 21, 256nn. 52, 56,
257n. 64, 286n. 1, 307n. 27;
emperor, 19, 21–22, 28, 54,
67–70, 93, 149, 256n. 44,
257n. 58; Peace of Brindisi,
21, 28; and the Penates, 14,
19, 21, 174, 229, 256n. 51,
257n. 61, 269n. 5, 307n. 25;
piety, 21, 256n. 54, 269n. 5,
295n. 2, 307n. 24; as priest,
21, 68, 257n. 59; and prophecy, 21; universal dominion,
19; and Vergil, 19–20, 227,
256nn. 44–45
Augustus, 21, *22*
Augustus of Primaporta, 20, 21,
28
Augustus with the Sibyl, 225, *226*,
227
Aurelian, Emperor, 230
*Austriacae Gentis Stemma ex Stirpe
Aeneae Trojani*, 201, *202*
Auto Sacramentales, 215, 221,
303n. 34, 304n. 49
Avancini, Nicholas, *The Triumph
of Piety*, 202

Aventine, Mount, 100
Aventinus, Johann, 103
Avit, 37, 75, 262, 270
Aytinger, Wolfgang, 126, 283n.
40

Baldwin, 151, 196–97, 210
Baptism of Christ, 38, *38*
Baptism of Clovis, 91, *92*
Basilica of San Lorenzo, View
of High Altar, *173*
Bassus family, 193, 195
Battle of Jericho, 77, *78*
Battle of Lepanto, 8–9, *8–9*
Bebel, Heinrich, 103, 276n. 145
Beck, Leonhard, 107, 208
Begga, 71, 98, 109, 275n. 105,
277n. 132
Begga, 96, *97–98*
Benoit de Sainte Maure, 54–56,
267n. 10
Benzo of Alba, 122
Berosus the Chaldean, 54, 57,
59, 87–88, 113, 267nn. 7–8,
268n. 17, 274nn. 91, 93,
278nn. 147, 151, 279n. 155,
280n. 177, 298n. 41
Bible. See New Testament; Old
Testament
Bible of Charles the Bald, 80
Blichilde, 71, 98, 268n. 24,
277n. 131
Blichilde and Ansibert, 95, *97–98*
Boaz (Boz), 76, 107, 167, 289n.
37, 291nn. 17–18
Bonasone, Giulio, *Neptune
Calming the Tempest*, 115, *116*
Boniface VIII, 275
Brandt, Sebastian, 124, 279n.
167, 282n. 14
Breu, Jorg: *Aeneas Founds the Ro-
man Empire*, ii–iii, *iv*; *The Proph-
ecy of Daniel*, 144, *145*
Brigid (Saint), 123–24, 126, 128
Brindisi, Peace of, 21, 28
Buen Retiro, 244
Burgkmaier, Hans: *Charlemagne*,
109, *111*; *Clovis*, 109, *110*,
185; *Hector*, 103, *105*; *Saint
Rudolf*, 208, *209*
Burgundy, house of, 98, 100,
103, 109, 115, 124–46 pas-
sim, 150–59, 181–82, 191–
212 passim, 268nn. 20–21,
24, 277n. 134, 278n. 139
Byzantium, 5, 34, 37–38, 42–
45, 49, 68–70, 72, 75, 77–78,

80–100 passim, 107, 109,
121–51 passim, 165, 186–97
passim, 217, 231–33, 237,
252, 270n. 8

Calderón, Pedro, 221, 300n. 50,
303n. 34, 305n. 49
Calvete de Estrella, 134
Cambrai, Peace treaties, 59,
118, 142, 157, 268n. 23
Campanella, Tommaso: City of
the Sun, 243, 245, 310n. 81;
Monarchy of Spain, 145, 178–
79, 181, 243, 294n. 61, 295n.
75
Capet, Hugh, 52, 87, 91
Carl Franz Josef, Emperor,
269n. 2
Carolinginas, 36, 39, 41–44, 52,
70–73, 75–76, 80–82, 85, 87,
91, 97–98, 103, 109, 141, 149,
186, 193, 211, 233, 270n. 8,
274n. 84, 275n. 107, 282n.
16, 296n. 15
Cassiodorus, History of the Goths,
36, 297n. 29
Castille house of, 109, 127, 133,
141, 154, 251
Catálogo real de Castilla, 113
Celtis, Conrad, 103
Charlemagne, 36, 45, 49, 52,
57, 82, 97–98, 100, 103, 109,
111, 115–16, 118, 121, 124,
128, 151, 212, 261n. 2,
262nn. 21, 27, 266nn. 89–91,
270n. 7, 271nn. 20, 22, 273n.
63, 275n. 104, 276nn. 229,
123; Alexander the Great,
kinship with, 72, 271n. 26;
Byzantine ancestry, 72–73,
82, 90, 100, 151, 186, 271n.
27, 273n. 71, 275n. 96, 296n.
14; Clovis: assimilation to,
42; kinship with, 262n. 28;
cult of the Eucharist, 210; as
emperor, 39, 42–44, 68–73,
75, 87, 90, 97, 171; as God's
anointed, 42, 261n. 11, 263n.
34, 302n. 15; Jesus, assimilation to, 44; legends of, 42–
44, 127, 264n. 44, 277n. 134;
as microcosmic man, 49,
282n. 15; as New Aeneas,
41–42, 71, 262n. 27; as New
Constantine, 82, 186, 197,
271n. 27; Old Testament patriarchs, 43, 80–81, 263n. 34,

266n. 91, 273n. 55, 275n. 97;
piety, 42, 262, 266n. 90; as
priest-king, 42, 80, 210,
263nn. 35–36, 302n. 15;
relics of the Passion, 42,
263nn. 34, 44, 273n. 58,
302n. 16; as saint, 42, 68, 87;
solar iconography, 233,
308n. 54; Trojan ancestry,
41–42, 70–73, 75, 80, 89–90,
271nn. 24, 27, 274n. 84,
275n. 207, 276n. 122; Vision
of the Cross, 296nn. 12–13
Charlemagne, 96, 97–98
Charlemagne to the Hapsburgs, 103,
104
Charles (duke of Lotharingia
and Brabant), 91, 98
Charles the Bald, Emperor, 71,
80, 301n. 4
Charles the Bold, 154, 302n. 17
Charles II (king of Spain), 159,
161, 221
Charles IV, Emperor, 93, 97–98
Charles IV, 96, 97–98
Charles V, Emperor, 5, 59, 66,
102, 145, 170, 280nn. 168–
84, 281nn. 186–87, 285n. 27,
302n. 17; apotheosis, 231;
and Augustus, 113, 116,
280nn. 174–75; Byzantine
imperial title, 109, 280n. 168;
as emperor, 7, 109, 113, 115–
18, 126–28, 138–39, 141,
143, 167; Eucharist, veneration of, 212, 214–15, 246,
302nn. 25–26, 303n. 33;
Greek ancestry, 116–17;
Hebraic ancestry, 113, 118;
Jerusalem, title to, 109, 280n.
168, 284n. 45; Last World
Emperor, 126–28, 130, 179;
Los Honores Tapestries, 60–66,
117–18, 268n. 26; monastic
retirement of, 130, 146;
mythic genealogy, 115–18,
280nn. 177–79; as New Ae-
neas, 113, 289n. 43; as New
Charlemagne, 116, 128,
289n. 43; as New Jason,
289n. 42; and Order of the
Golden Fleece, 155–57,
288nn. 33–34, 289nn. 35–44;
and Philip II (son), 7, 131,
133–34, 138–39, 141, 143,
235, 284n. 1; Roman ancestry of, 113, 116–18; solar ico-

nography of, 233, 235–37,
246; Trojan ancestry of, 60,
107, 113, 115–17; as universal monarch, 109–13, 155,
233, 235; vassals, 115–17,
280nn. 178–84; veneration
of the Holy Cross, 191
Charles VI, Emperor, 292n. 23
Chateau-Cambrensis, treaty of,
142
Chaucer, Geoffrey, 268n. 12,
286n. 5, 287n. 17
Childebert, 78
Christ. See Jesus Christ
Christ as Emperor, 43, 44
Christ as the Solar Charioteer,
231, 232
Christianity: adaptation of pagan myths, 1–3, 6–9, 22–23,
27–34, 52–60, 69–70, 87–88,
103, 107, 118, 143, 145, 149,
151, 171, 175, 178, 223; Eucharist, 170, 175, 181, 207–
22, 246, 248; and Golden
Fleece legend, 149–52, 156;
Holy Cross, 183–207; mili-
tancy of, 5, 7–9, 158, 202,
204; as Roman state religion,
23–34, 120–21, 162, 183–84,
204, 231; Second Coming,
24, 29–31, 34, 90, 120–21,
123–24, 150–52, 171, 181–
82; solar iconography, 223,
230–33, 235–40, 243–46,
248
Christus Imperator, 35, 35
Claudia, 176, 178
Claudian, In Rufinum, 45, 193,
264–65n. 54
Clement of Alexandria, 231
Cleopatra, 15
Clothilde, 36
Clovis, 95, 97–98
Coecke van Aelst, Pieter: Philip
between Ascanius and Servius Tullius, 136, 137; Philip and the
Olympian Gods, 136, 137; Philip
II and Charles V, 134, 135
Coello, Claudio, The Adoration of
the Sagrada Forma, 220, 221
Columbus, Christopher, 4, 7–
8, 127, 154, 168, 179, 251,
284nn. 46–47, 50, 292n. 22,
Lettera Rarissima, 127–28
Columns of Hercules, 7, 113,
155–56, 288n. 34, 289nn. 35–
40

Concord, Concordia, 16, 28, 46, 48, 255n. 32, 258n. 23
Concordia Rejoices at the Return of the Roman Standards, 29, 29
Conrad II, Emperor, 274n. 82
Conrad III, Emperor, 84–85
Constantine (the Great), 4, 81–82, 87, 100, 118, 120, 124, 162, 198, 259–60, 296n. 16, 298nn. 37, 40, 299n. 44, 300nn. 52, 54, 270n. 7; Aeneas's descendant, 193, 298n. 32; and Apollo, 70, 230–31, 270n. 17, 307nn. 35–39; as emperor, 31–34, 37–38, 42, 68–70; founder of new Troy, 70, 193, 195, 270n. 17; and *Fourth Eclogue*, 32; German ancestry, 100; Holy Cross, vision and veneration of, 183–86, 188, 190–91, 193, 197, 202, 204, 295n. 3, 296nn. 12, 19; Jesus, compared with, 31, 34, 259n. 38, 260nn. 52, 55, 58; Old Testament patriarchs, compared with, 77–78; piety of, 295n. 2; as priest, 34, 260n. 55, 304n. 44; as saint, 68; Trojan ancestry, 193, 270n. 15; and the Trojan legend, 31, 270n. 17; universal sovereignty of, 31, 70
Constantine, 31, 32
Constantine II, 251
Constantine XI, 252
Constantine, Donation of, 273n. 55, 275n. 103
Constantinople, 5, 8–9, 41, 78, 81, 118, 124, 143, 151, 191, 197, 210, 230, 252, 253n. 6, 270nn. 16–17
Copernicus, Nicolaus, *De Revolutionibus Orbium Caelestium*, 236
Coronation of David, 38, 38
Corpus Christi, Feast of, 207, 214–15, 218, 246, 303nn. 27, 28, 33
Correggio (Antonio Allegri), *The Martyrdom of the Four Saints*, 191, *192*, 193
Cort, Cornelius, 178
Council of Nicaea, 134
Coxie, Michael, 180
Crispus, 259
Croesus, 47

Cross. *See* Holy Cross
Cross Bay Reliquary, 40, 41
Crown of the Holy Roman Emperor, 83, 84
Crusades, 2, 6–7, 25, 42–43, 45, 56–58, 78, 90, 122, 141, 150–58 passim, 188
Cumaean Sibyl, 6, 11, 15, 18–19, 120–22, 223, 225, 227
Cyrus, 81, 179

Daniel, 24, 120, 145, 151, 257, 282n. 15
Dante Alighieri, 233, 276nn. 110–20, 277n. 126, 301n. 61; *De Monarchia*, 92–93, 113; *Paradiso*, 93
Dardanus, 11, 13–14, 69–70, 72, 93, 97–98, 115, 198, 254, 270n. 14, 298n. 32, 299n. 41
Dardanus, 94, 97–98, 254n. 4, 255n. 12, 270n. 14
Dares the Phrygian, 267nn. 3, 10, 272n. 44, 299n. 41; *De Excidio Troiae Historia*, 53, 76, 195
David, 26–27, 30–31, 37–38, 49–50, 76–78, 80–81, 83, 90, 93, 118, 130, 134, 163, 217, 258n. 31, 272n. 46, 273nn. 55, 58
de los Santos, Francisco (Fray), 167
De Maisse, 170
Decius, 262
Dictys the Cretan, 267nn. 3–4; *Ephemerii Belli Troiani*, 53, 195, 299n. 41
Didaco di Lequile, *Piisima . . . Domus Austriaca*, 198, *199–201; Rebus*, 207
Diocletian, 120, 262
Dionysius the Areopagite, 244–45
Divine Wisdom tapestry, 60, 61
Doda, 71
Donatus, 266n. 94, 270n. 9
Doria, Andrea, 156
Dungal, 71, 266
Dürer, Albrecht, 235, 253n. 4; *Apocalypse*, 126; *Charlemagne*, 100, *101; Maximilian I*, 124, *125*, 283n. 38; *Maximilian I's Triumphal Car*, 233, *234*, 235; *Triumphal Arch of Maximilian I, 106*, 107
Dynter, Edward de, 277n. 134

Eden, 24, 29, 48, 60, 118–19, 143, 149, 154, 178, 206
Einhard, 71, 233, 262nn. 26–27; *Life of Charlemagne*, 39, 41, 87, 97
Ekkehard of Aura, 85, 282n. 17
Eleanor of Aquitaine, 55
Eleanor of Portugal, 296
Eleanor of Toledo, 280
Eleanora Gonzaga, 115
Elijah, 211, 218
Elizabeth I (queen of England), 237
Erasmus, Desiderius, 253, 278n. 150
Ermoldus Nigellus, 71; *In Honorem Hludowici*, 81
Erythrean Sibyl, 130
Eschatology. *See* Last World Emperor
Escorial, 134, 143, 162–82, 214–15, 218, 221, 243–45, 290nn. 1–10, 293nn. 40–41; and Battle of San Quentin, 162; effigies at, 170, 214, 218, 292nn. 31–22, 302n. 23; as heavenly Jerusalem, 169–71, 181, 292nn. 25–29; as imperial edifice, 163–64, 170–75, 293n. 43; and Saint Lawrence, 162–63, 293nn. 46–50, 310n. 88; solar imagery at, 178, 243–45, 310n. 88; as Solomon's Temple, 143, 164–69, 215, 291nn. 12, 14–20, 292n. 25
Este, Alfonso d', 116, 280n. 184, 289n. 43
Este, house of, 115–16, 156
Eucharist, 170, 175, 181, 207–22, 246, 248, 293nn. 41, 45, 301n. 4, 302n. 14, 303nn. 28, 33, 305n. 54, 311n. 2. *See also* Corpus Christi, feast of
Eucharistic Chariot, 246, 247
Eusebius, 31, 33, 231, 259nn. 38, 44, 260n. 48, 271n. 17; *Chronographia*, 54, 87, 93, 267n. 8, 272n. 40, 285n. 10
Eustace (Saint), 301n. 6
Eutichio, 191, 193
Evander, 254n. 7
Eve, 206
Eyck, Jan van: *Annunciation*, 151; *Ghent Altarpiece, 152–53, 153*
Ezekiel, 123, 130, 169–70, 175, 292n. 25, 293n. 47

Ferdinand (brother of Charles V), 133, 138, 143
Ferdinand (cardinal-infant), 159
Ferdinand II, Emperor, 7, 109, 127, 141, 154, 300n. 52
Ferdinand III, 198
Fernandez, Sebastian: *Courtyard of the Kings*, 164, *166*; *Solomon*, 164, *166*
Fillastre, Giullaume, 150–51, 268n.19, 288nn. 20–23
Flavia, 191
Flavian dynasty, 255n. 35, 257n. 6, 269n. 3, 286n. 4, 296n. 14, 299n. 41, 306n. 7
Flight of Aeneas, 91, *92*
Florence, 115, 117
Flotner, Peter: *Tuisco to Charlemagne*, *72, 73*
Fortunatus, Venantius, 75, 78, 272n. 38
Fortune, 47–48, 60, 66, 265nn. 74, 76
Fortune tapestry, 60, *63, 66*
Foundation of Paris, 91, *92*
Four World Monarchies, 24, 47, 66, 76, 81, 92, 113, 120, 145, 150, 178, 181, 243, 273n. 66, 282n. 15
Francis I (king of France), 109, 156–57, 298n. 40, 304n. 41
Francisco de los Santos, 167
Franco, 73, 76
Frangipani family, 193
Franks, 36–52, 54, 59, 70–73, 75–76, 85, 87, 89–91, 93, 98, 107, 121, 147, 158, 185–86, 188, 233, 272nn. 39, 45, 274n. 84, 275n. 93
Franz I, Emperor, 269n. 2
Franz Josef (emperor of Austria), 252
Fredegarius, 75–76, 267n. 3, 271n. 26, 272nn. 41, 44–45, 273n. 66
Frederick I (Barbarossa), 42, 85, 87, 89–90, 188, 265
Frederick I, 187, *188*
Frederick II, Emperor, 56, 90–92, 122–23, 150, 233, 268n. 15, 275n. 99, 282n. 22, 283nn. 25–28, 33, 300n. 52
Frederick III, Emperor, 100, 124, 286n. 44, 296n. 13
Fulmina Temnit, *244, 245*
Fury, 13, 113, 258n. 11

"Gamaleón," 123
Garibay, Esteban de, 142–43, 196
Gattinara, Mercurino, 113
Gebwiler, Hieronymous, 103; *Epitome Regii Hapsburghi*, 103, *105*, 278n. 147
Gerard de Roo: *Annales Rerum Belli Domique ab Austriacis Habsburgicae*, 98, *99*, 100
Gerberga, 91, 98, 277n. 133
Gerberga and Lambert, *96*, 97–98
Ghibellines, 91
Gideon, 8
Gigantomachia, 116, 256n. 57, 264n. 54, 280n. 182
Giordano, Luca, 304nn. 47–48; *Allegory of the Golden Fleece*, 159, *160–61*, 161; *Indus*, 240, *240*
Giuliana of Liege, 214–15, 303n. 27
Godfrey of Bouillon, 127, 284n. 45
Godfried of Viterbo, 275nn. 95–97, 276n. 124, 282n. 19; *Speculum Regum*, 73, 89–90
Golden Fleece, 5–8, 17–19, 21, 24–25, 53–58, 66, 76, 137, 148–54, 156–59, 161, 227, 256n. 41, 257n. 6, 258n. 19, 259n. 40; and Aries, 147–50, 157; and Mystical Lamb, 58, 149–50; and Philip the Good, 57–59; and Titus, 56, 149. *See also* Order of the Golden Fleece
Goletta, battle of, 118, 156, 191, 289n. 42
Gomarra, 285n. 27
Gonzaga, Federigo, 116, 280n. 183
Gonzaga, house of, 115–16, 156
Goths, 36
Gracchae, 14
Gracian, Antonio, *Declaración de las Armas de San Lorenzo el Real*, 245
Granada, Luis de, 300
Great Interregnum, 90–91, 123–24
Great Schism, 91, 126
Greco, El (Domenikos Theotokopoulos), *The Dream of Philip II*, *203*, 204
Greece: ancestry for Christian

monarchs, 88–89, 103, 107, 116–17, 279nn. 157–58; destruction of Troy by, 6, 11, 13, 16–18, 53, 89, 120–21
Gregory of Tours, 37, 75, 185, 261n. 3, 272n. 43, 295n. 7
Gregory I, 37
Gregory VII, 309n. 57
Gregory IX, 90–91
Gregory XIII, 158, 237
Grunpeck, Joseph, *Prognosticum*, 124
Gudule (Saint), 211, 275n. 105
Guelphs, 91, 117, 124
Guido delle Colonne, 267nn. 11–12, 268nn. 13–16; *Historia Destructionis Troiae*, 55–58, 88, 149–50
Gutenberg, Johannes, 119

Hadrian of Castello, 100
Hadrian I, 186
Hapsburg dynasty, 98–100, 118, 175, 197, 249–50, 252, 305n. 52; Aeneas, descent from, 299n. 41, 305n. 54; Byzantine ancestry, 297nn. 30–31, 299n. 41; Clovis, descent from, 297n. 30, 304n. 41, 311n. 1; Constantine, descent from, 299n. 41; Constantinian imagery, 188–91, 202, 204, 299n. 49; Eucharist, miracles and veneration, 207–8, 215, 217–18, 221–22, 246, 248, 293n. 45, 300n. 50, 301n. 8, 302nn. 10, 12, 302n. 20, 305nn. 54, 55, 57–58; as God's anointed, 311n. 1; Hebraic ancestry, 100, 118, 164, 168, 170, 198, 268n. 24; hereditary concept of imperium, 134–35; Holy Cross, veneration of, 183, 188, 190–91, 193, 198, 202, 204, 298n. 39, 300nn. 49. 58; Jesus, consanguinity with, 207; Last World Emperor legend, 124, 145, 283n. 40; Order of the Golden Fleece, 154–59, 161; piety, 183, 202, 207–8, 218, 295n. 3, 301n. 8, 302nn. 10–11, 304n. 44, 305n. 54, 310nn. 95–96; Roman ancestry, 98, 100, 118; solar iconography, 225, 233, 237, 239–40, 246, 248; Trojan an-

Hapsburg dynasty (continued)
  cestry, 1, 4–5, 8–9, 60, 100,
  118, 198, 202, 268n. 24,
  278nn. 135–36; universal
  sovereignty, ambitions for,
  139, 141–42, 146, 165, 183,
  191, 208, 299n. 42
Hapsburg, Otto von, 252
Heavenly Jerusalem. See Jerusa-
  lem, New (Heavenly)
Hector, 16, 46, 66, 71, 73, 103,
  107, 116, 134, 137, 198, 254n.
  9, 255n. 33
Hector's Son, Franco, and His Trojan
  Kin, 73, 74, 75
Heere, Lucas de, Philip II as So-
  lomon, 167, 169
Helena (Saint), 118, 193, 202,
  273n. 74
Heliocentrism, 232, 235, 243,
  308n. 52, 309n. 61
Henry II (Hold Roman em-
  peror), 84
Henry II, 84, 85
Henry II (king of England), 55,
  265n. 59, 267n. 10
Henry II (king of France), 142,
  162, 170
Henry III, 143
Henry IV, 122
Henry VI, 89
Henry VII, Emperor, 91–93,
  98, 113, 233, 276nn. 109–10,
  119–20
Heraclius, 72, 82, 90, 196–97,
  298n. 38
Heraclius, 196, 197
Hercules, 139, 149, 155, 198,
  236, 240
Herrera, Juan de, 165, 243–44,
  310n. 83
Hezekiah, 83, 245
Hibernicus, Exul, 263n. 27,
  266n. 94, 271n. 20
Hincmar of Reims, 71, 261n. 8,
  273n. 54; Life of Saint Remi, 37
History of Aeneas, 137, 138
Hohenstaufen dynasty, 56, 77,
  85, 87–98, 103, 122–23, 188,
  233, 274n. 88, 275n. 97,
  282n. 19, 296n. 16
Holy Cross, 183–207, 295nn.
  3–4, 296nn. 17–19, 297n. 28,
  299n. 47, 301nn. 63, 1, 2
Holy Grail, 210, 212
Holy League, 8–9, 158, 204

Holy Sepulchre, 7, 25, 42, 44,
  56–57, 121, 127, 150, 154,
  181–82, 294n. 59, 295n. 77
Homer, 80, 88; Iliad, 11, 15–17,
  53, 227, 254nn. 1–2; Odyssey,
  11, 254n. 1
Homeric hymns, 229
Honor tapestry, 66
Honores, Los (tapestries), 60, 61–
  66, 66, 117
Honorius, 34, 45, 184, 259n.
  37, 264n. 52, 265n. 54
Honorius, 184, 185
Horace, 256nn. 54, 57, 264–
  65n. 54
Hortolà, 179, 181
House of Austria. See Hapsburg
  dynasty
Hunibald, 75, 103
Huys, Pieter, Reconstruction of So-
  lomon's Temple, 167, 168
Hyginus, 253

Iam Illustrabit Omnia, 223, 224,
  225, 305nn. 1–2, 310n. 77
Iasius, 11
In Hoc Signo Vinces, 184, 202,
  204, 299n. 49, 300n. 54
Indies, 285n. 27
Infamy tapestry, 64, 66, 118
Innocent III, 45, 275
Innocent IV, 91
Inquisition, 131
Interior of the Holy of Holies, 170,
  172
Irenicus, Franciscus, 103; Ger-
  maniae, 103–4
Iron Age, 15, 24, 26, 48
Isaac, 179
Isabel de Valois, 142, 237
Isabella (daughter of Philip II),
  143, 158, 218
Isabella (queen of Spain), 7,
  109, 127, 141, 154, 251
Isabella of Portugal, 287
Isabelle (wife of Frederick II),
  90
Isaiah, 127, 225
Isidore of Seville, 263n. 35
Islam, 5, 7–9, 70, 121, 152, 179,
  186, 240, 243
Iulus (Ascanius), 13–14, 55,
  137, 306n. 16
Ivan III, 252
Ivan IV, 252

Jachim, 167, 289n. 37, 291nn.
  17–18
Jacob, 47, 97, 208, 221, 277,
  301n. 8
James, 42, 127
Janus, 19, 59–60, 87–89, 103,
  113, 142, 198, 274n. 93
Japhet, 179
Jason, 5–6, 8, 17, 53, 55, 58, 66,
  76, 115, 137, 147, 149, 156,
  227, 287n. 12, 289n. 42
Jason Arriving at Troy, 56, 57, 58
Jason Capturing the Golden Fleece,
  55, 56
Jerusalem, 4–5, 9, 121, 143,
  162; Christian monarchs of,
  90, 107–27 passim, 141, 151,
  181, 197, 238; crusades to recapture, 7, 78, 90, 122, 127,
  142, 150, 152; destruction by
  Pompey, 54; destruction of
  Temple by Titus, 6, 24–25,
  56, 58, 149; founding of, 93;
  in legends of Charlemagne,
  44; New (Heavenly), 29–30,
  34, 127, 153, 169–71, 174–79,
  181–82, 218, 225, 258n. 29,
  259nn. 32–33, 274n. 82,
  292nn. 25–29, 295n. 75,
  304n. 47; Solomon's Temple
  of, 127, 163–65, 167, 169,
  171, 179, 181, 215, 244, 289n.
  37, 291n. 14, 284n. 50, 285n.
  28, 291nn. 12, 14–20
Jesse, 80, 100, 107, 134, 152,
  164, 212, 245, 304n. 43
Jesuits, 300nn. 50, 54
Jesus Christ, 2, 36–38, 45–88
  passim, 103, 127, 135, 141,
  169–70, 178, 193, 195, 197–
  98, 210, 217; and Aeneas,
  30–31, 88; ancestry of, 30,
  37, 76–97 passim, 107, 179,
  198, 217, 262n. 15, 299n. 45,
  303nn. 39–40; baptism, 37–
  38, 210, 261nn. 9–10, 285n.
  10, 303n. 39; birth during
  reign of Augustus, 22–24, 54,
  69–70, 88, 90; Charlemagne's
  identification with, 42–44,
  80; Clovis's identification
  with, 36–38; and Eucharist,
  207, 210, 214–15, 218, 246,
  248; Fourth Eclogue, saviour of,
  32–34, 277n. 125; as imperial
  model, 43, 52; as king, as

emperor, 28–29, 34–35, 195, 258n. 31, 259n. 33, 260n. 62, 261nn. 9–10, 12, 285nn. 9–11; in military context, 34, 43, 184, 260n. 59, 265n. 55, 266n. 93; monogram, 184, 197, 204, 207, 295n. 3, 300nn. 54, 55; as priest and king, 29, 78, 97, 210, 217, 258n. 31, 260n. 59, 277n. 126, 293n. 38, 294n. 59, 303n. 39; and Roman law, 93; Second Coming, 24, 29–31, 34, 90, 120–21, 123–24, 150–52, 171, 181–82, 281n. 4; solar iconography of, 31, 225, 231–33, 248
Joachim of Fiore, 123–24, 179, 282nn. 23–24, 283n. 25
John (Saint), 42, 120, 127, 149, 151–52, 170, 181, 292n. 28
John of Luxembourg, 93, 275nn. 104–8
John the Fearless, 287n. 18
John I (duke of Brabant), 91
Jordanes, Getia, 36
Joseph (husband of Mary), 47, 78, 97, 262
Joseph (son of Jacob), 60, 118
Joseph of Arimathea, 210
Josephus, 54, 87
Joshua, 78
Joshua Roll, 77–78
Juan of Austria, 5
Juana (daughter of Ferdinand and Isabella), 154, 214
Judah, 198, 277
Judiasm, 37, 47, 120, 181; ancestry for Christian monarchs, 76–78, 80–81, 83, 85, 87–89, 97–98, 100–18 passim, 134, 163, 171, 198, 217, 275n. 97, 278nn. 150–52, 279nn. 154–56, 159, 280n. 177; destruction of Temple, 6, 24–25, 56, 58, 149; mixture with pagan and Christian myths, 2–3, 7–8, 23, 33–34, 54, 59–60, 67, 143, 145, 175, 218, 225; Solomonic motifs in the Escorial, 163, 165, 167–71, 181
Judith, 47
Julian the Apostate, 297n. 28
Julio-Claudian dynasty, 19, 69, 230, 255n. 35, 256n. 55,

257n. 64, 269nn. 3, 5, 270n. 9, 278n. 135, 294n. 54, 299n. 46
Julius Caesar, 13, 14, 19, 47, 66, 68, 116, 164, 255n. 19, 256n. 56, 269n. 3, 291n. 10
Julius II (Pope), 101, 107, 126, 275
Juno, 107, 150
Jupiter (Jove), 5, 13, 16–19, 21, 69, 97–98, 116, 139–63 passim, 204, 254n. 4, 267n. 4, 297n. 23
Jupiter, 94, 97–98
Justice tapestry, 66
Justinian, Emperor, 118, 193, 260, 262, 297n. 29, 304n. 44

Karlstein, 97
King David, 77, 78
Klerk, Jan de, 276n. 109
Klingenburg, Heinrich von, 278–79
Knight Confronting Vices, 49–50, 51

Labarum, 184, 184, 197, 207
Lactantius, 31, 120, 259n. 40, 301n. 1
Lambert, 91, 98
Laomedon, 17, 53, 76
Last Supper, 44, 210, 212
Last Supper, 212, 213
Last World Emperor, 120–24, 126–28, 130, 138, 145–46, 179, 181, 191, 231, 281nn. 9–12, 282–83
Latinus, 80, 171, 258n. 30, 293n. 38, 306nn. 16, 19
Laurentians, 246
Lavinia, 16, 138, 227, 255
Lawrence (Saint), 162, 164, 259n. 32, 291n. 8, 293nn. 46–50, 310n. 88; as Augustus, 176, 178; Ezekiel, parallels with, 175; and Heavenly Jerusalem, 175–76; as priest, 175, 178; solar imagery of, 178, 245; and Troy, 176, 178
Lazius, Wolfgang, 103, 278n. 148
Lefèvre, Raoul, Recuyell of the Histories of Troye, 58–59, 268nn. 20–21, 288n. 34
Lemaire, Jean (de Belges), 268nn. 22–25, 284n. 55; Con-

cord of the Human Race, 142; Illustrations de Gaul et Singularitez de Troye, 59–60, 128, 142
Leo III, 39, 41–42, 296
Leoni, Leone, Charles V Dominating Fury, 112, 113, 280n. 175
Leoni, Pompeo: Hapsburg Effigies in the Escorial, 170, 172–73; Philip II, 131, 132, 146
Leopold I, 222
Lepanto, battle of, 8–9, 158, 204
Leto, Pomponios, 270n. 15, 299n. 41
Levi, 277
Libra, 16, 21, 255n. 30, 257n. 62, 287n. 74
Lichtenberger, Johann, 283nn. 36, 40; Prognosticatio, 124
Lipsius, Justus, 295n. 3, 297n. 23, 298n. 39, 300n. 49, 303n. 34; De Cruce, 196–97, 202
Liutgard, 84
Lobkowitz, Juan Caramuel de, 164; Philippus Prudens, 240, 243
Longinus, 263n. 34
Louis of Hungary, 214
Louis the Pious, 49, 81, 134, 186, 188, 266n. 93, 273n. 64
Louis the Pious, 186, 187, 188
Louis IV, 282n. 16
Louis VII, 274n. 87
Louis IX (Saint), 91
Louis XII, 100, 142
Louis XIV, 245
Lucan, 230
Lupold of Babenberg, 93, 97, 276nn. 122–24
Luxemburg, house of, 91, 93, 98
Luxuria and Sobrietas, 27, 28

Macrobius, Ambrosius: Dream of Scipio, 230–31, 235–36, 264; Saturnalia, 230, 308n. 40
Magellan, Ferdinand, 8
Magnus, 47
Mal Lara, Juan de, 253nn. 2–4, 286n. 2
Malachi, 231
Manilius, 149, 286nn. 1, 5, 288n. 23
Marc Antony, 306n. 17
Marcus Aurelius, 113
Mareno, Pietro, Compendio della Stirpe di Carlo Magno et Carlo V, 113, 115

Margaret (daughter of Charles V), 280n. 179
Margaret (daughter of John I of Brabant), 91, 98
Margaret (regent of the Netherlands), 59, 142, 210, 268n. 23, 284n. 55
Maria Theresa, 222, 245
Mariana, Juan de, 298
Marignola, Johan, Chronicon, 94–96, 97–98, 277nn. 125–27
Marius, Gaius, 47
Marliano, Luigi, Columns of Hercules, 155, 155, 156
Mars, 13
Martin V, 126
Mary (sister of Charles V), 133, 214, 294n. 69
Mary, Virgin, 31–32, 42, 46, 60, 78, 97, 118, 142, 151, 225, 259n. 41
Mary of Burgundy, 98, 100, 124, 154, 208, 214
Mary of Hungary, 294n. 69
Mary of Portugal, 139, 214
Mary Tudor, 139, 141–42, 309n. 61
Maurus, Hrabanus, 186–87, 266n. 93
Maxentius, 31, 162, 183–84, 202
Maximilian I, Emperor, 98, 100–103, 107, 109, 117, 142, 154, 214, 278nn. 139–40, 296n. 2; as new Elijah, 211–12, 302nn. 19–20; and cult of the Eucharist, 208, 211–12; as Last World Emperor, 124, 126, 191, 283nn. 34–42, 44; mythic genealogy, 101–9, 212, 278nn. 139, 141, 144–52, 279nn. 153–67; as "New Constantine," 190–91, 283n. 34; papal aspirations, 100–101, 107, 278nn. 142–43; as priest-king, 101, 107; solar iconography of, 233, 236, 309n. 58
Maximilian I, Emperor, 100–101, 102, 103
Maximilian II, Emperor, 98, 133, 143, 277n. 130
Medici family, 115, 156, 280n. 179
Melchizedek, 78, 118, 218, 243
Melek-el-Kamel, 90

Mendoza, Jacob, 298n. 40, 304n. 41
Mennel, Jacob, 103, 279; Fürstliche Chronik, 103, 107; Linea Hebreorum/Linea Grecorum/Linea Latinorum, 107, 108, 109
Meroveus, 98, 272n. 36
Merovingians, 36–39, 75, 77–78, 80–81, 85, 97–98, 109, 141, 185–86, 193, 211, 233, 272n. 38
Microcosmic man, 24, 45, 49, 231, 264n. 51, 265n. 55, 282n. 15, 288n. 23
Miles Christi, 43, 43
Milvian Bridge, battle of, 31, 34, 37, 184, 207
Mohammed, 66
Monegro, Juan Bautista: Courtyard of the Kings, 164, 166; Saint Lawrence, 174, 175; Solomon, 164, 166
Montao, Benito Arias, Biblia Poliglota, 167, 168, 290n. 1, 291n. 12, 293n. 40, 298n. 35
Moses, 29, 34, 47, 93, 118, 130, 163, 165, 179, 218
Muhlberg, battle of, 113, 118, 128, 133
Murillo, Bartolomé Esteban, Fray Julian's Vision of the Ascension of the Soul of Philip II, 205, 206

Napoleon Bonaparte, 154–55, 269n. 2, 288n. 32
Naucler, Johannes, 103, 279n. 150
Nebuchadnezzar, 24, 150, 179, 311
Neptune, 17
Nero, 69, 230, 265n. 59, 270n. 10, 307n. 32
New Jerusalem, 29–30, 34, 127, 153, 169–71, 174–79, 181–82, 218, 225, 258n. 29, 259nn. 32–33, 274n. 82, 292nn. 25–29, 35, 295n. 75, 304n. 47
New Man, 46–49, 60, 66
New Testament, 24, 31, 54, 68, 78, 81, 120, 170
New Troy, 6, 13–14, 16, 21, 54, 60, 119, 148, 193, 195, 227
New World. See Americas
Nicaea, council of, 134
Nicholas II, 252

Nigidius Figulus, 227, 306nn. 10–11, 307n. 30, 308n. 40
Ninus, 81, 89
Noah, 59–60, 73, 76, 87–89, 97–98, 103, 107, 113, 118, 120, 142, 165, 179, 195, 198, 243
Noah, 94, 97–98
Noah/Janus, 103, 105
Nobility tapestry, 60, 62, 118
Norman Anonymous, 83
Numa, 175, 311n. 1
Nuremberg Chronicle, 73, 272n. 33

Octavian. See Augustus
Old Testament, 3, 8, 24, 29, 31, 33, 37, 43, 47, 54, 59–60, 67–68, 76–78, 80–81, 83, 85, 87–88, 97, 134, 141, 146, 168–70, 208, 217, 221, 261n. 13, 274n. 82
Olybria family, 193
Order of the Golden Fleece, 4, 7, 57–59, 115, 141, 146–59, 161, 211, 223, 235, 250, 268n. 18, 287n. 18, 288–89, 290n. 49
Origen, 23–24, 33, 169, 292n. 26
Orley, Bernard van: Charlemagne Depositing the Holy Grail, 210, 210; Charles V Accompanied by His Patron St. Charlemagne, 212, 213; The Conversion of Emperor Constantine, 190, 191
Orosius, Paulus, 113, 138
Osiris, 103, 198, 278n. 152
Otto of Freising, 89, 274nn. 92–93, 282n. 19
Otto the Saxon, 282
Otto I, 82–84, 121, 171, 274n. 77, 282n. 16
Otto II, 82, 273n. 73
Otto III, 82
Ottocar, 190
Ottomans. See Turks
Ottonian dynasty, 82–85, 97, 103, 188, 274nn. 76–82
Ottonian Family Tree, 84, 86, 87
Ovid, 228; Fasti, 230, 254n. 9, 255n. 32, 273n. 63, 286n. 1

Paleologus, Andreas, 109, 299n. 42
Palladium, 55, 70, 175, 178,

195, 197, 212, 221, 254n. 10, 270nn. 16–17, 271n. 32, 298n. 32, 302n. 20, 305n. 54, 311nn. 1–2

Pallas, 26

Pannemaker, William: *Adoration of the Lamb*, 181, *182; Moses Directs the Construction of the Ark of the Covenant*, 179, *180; Noah Constructs the Ark*, 179, *180*

Papacy, 90–91, 274nn. 86, 88, 275n. 103, 282n. 20, 283nn. 25–26, 309n. 57

Paracelsus, 283n. 36

Parcere Subiectis, 14, 42, 81, 250, 263n. 30, 311n. 4

"Parcere Subiectis," 250, *250*

Paris (city), 91

Paris (Trojan prince), 53

Parousia, 121, 171, 206

Paul (Saint), 93, 120, 292n. 26

Paul the Deacon, 42, 70

Pavia, battle of, 119

Pax Augusta, 21–22, 33

Penates, 11–15, 17, 19, 21, 68, 149, 174, 176, 178, 227, 229, 249, 254nn. 9–10, 269n. 5

Penates Appear to Aeneas in a Dream, 11, *12*

Perino del Vaga (Pietro Bonaccorsi), *Neptune Calming the Tempest*, 115, *116*

Perleoni family, 193

Perret, Pedro: *Ground Plan of the Escorial*, 164, *165; View of the Escorial*, 163, *164*

Peter (Saint), 40–41

Peter Gives the Vexillium to Charlemagne, *40*, 41, 186

Peutinger, Conrad, 103, 278n. 151

Phaeton, 237

Pharamund, 98

Phoebus. See Apollo

Philip the Fair, 126, 138, 154, 214, 283n. 42

Philip the Good of Burgundy, 6–7, 57–58, 98, 100, 138, 146–47, 150–53, 156, 210–12, 214, 268n. 20, 277n. 134, 287n. 18, 288nn. 20, 23, 29, 34

Philip the Good Attends the Baptism of Clovis, 147, *147*

Philip of Macedon, 134, 138

Philip II, 131–45, 284–86, 293n. 41, 294n. 59, 295n. 75–76, 298n. 40, 300n. 60, 301n. 62; as absolute monarch, 4, 131, 133, 245; Aeneas, descent from, 299n. 41; as Aeneas, 137–38, 145, 204; ancestor cult, 143, 170, 218; apotheosis, 159, 206; Argonautic imagery of, 5, 8–9, 145, 158–59, 250, 286n. 2; as new Asser, 221; Battle of St. Quentin, 162; Byzantine ancestry of, 191, 193–97, 297nn. 30–31; Byzantine title and claims to sovereignty, 141, 151, 197; and Campanella, 178–79; Charlemagne, descent from, 151, 158; and Charles V, 7, 131, 133–34, 138–39, 141, 143, 235, 284n. 1; Clovis, descent from, 297n. 30, 304n. 41, 311n. 1; Constantine, descent from, 299n. 41; as new Constantine, 204; and the Escorial, 162–82; Eucharist, cult of, 175, 215, 217–18, 221–22, 246, 248; Four continents, ruler of, 139; Fourth *Eclogue*, 222, 285n. 13; funerary rites, 181–82, 204, 237–38; as God's anointed, 158, 217, 304nn. 40–41, 311n. 1; Holy Cross, veneration of, 183, 191, 193, 195–98, 202, 204, 206; as imperial ruler, 5, 7–9, 128, 131–35, 137–39, 141–43, 145–46, 170, 214, 218, 299n. 42; Jerusalem, title to, 141; Jesus, assimilation to, 82–83, 181–82; as Last World Emperor, 138, 145–46, 181; marriages, 139, 141–42; mythic genealogy, 158; Old Testament ancestors, 134, 198, 217; Order of the Golden Fleece, 157–59, 161; piety, 202; as priest king, 141, 143, 181, 217–18; relics, 217, 290n. 46; Roman imperial ancestry, 137, 163, 196–97; as new Rudolf, 221, 300n. 59; solar iconography of, 145, 222–23, 225, 235–40, 243–46, 248, 305nn. 1–3,

309nn. 60–66, 71–73, 310nn. 75, 77, 87, 92; as Solomon, 134, 143, 145, 162, 167–68, 215, 285n. 9, 290nn. 4, 6, 291nn. 14, 21, 292n. 23; syncretistic genealogy, 298n. 41; Trojan ancestry, 137, 141, 198; as universal monarch, 143, 162, 197–98

Philip II, 236, *236*

Philip II in Armor as the Rising Sun, 240, *241*

Philip II Rules the Four Continents, 139, *140*, 141

Philip III, 193, 197, 296n. 12

Philip IV, 159, 222, 239–40, 244, 246

Philippus Arabus, Emperor, 138, 231, 308n. 42

Phineas, 47

Phrixus, 5, 17, 66, 147, 150, 249, 255n. 36, 286nn. 2–3

Pindar, *Pythian Ode IV*, 6, 17, 153, 155, 255n. 35, 256n. 38, 286nn. 2–3

Pippin of Aquitaine, 71, 270n. 23

Pippin the Younger, 71, 81

Placido, 191, 193

Plato, 148, 264

Pompey, 54, 227

Pontano, Giovanni, 253n. 4, 279n. 167; *Urania*, 154

Porfyrius, 186

Potence of the Order of the Golden Fleece, 155, *156*

Prague, 93, 97, 171, 222

Presentation of Christ, 38, *38*

Priam, 11, 15, 18, 31, 53, 60, 66, 71, 89, 91, 98, 103, 122, 134, 149, 158, 198, 249, 267n. 4, 311n. 1

Priam, *95*, 97–98

Priam the Younger, 73, 76, 271n. 26, 275nn. 106–7

Probus, 262

Probus family, 193

Prometheus, 60

Prospectus Genealogicus, 198, *199*

Prudentius, 257n. 8, 258nn. 20, 31, 259n. 35, 273n. 62, 293n. 38, 294n. 51, 58, 293n. 43; and the *Aeneid*, 25–27, 30, 257n. 9, 258nn. 11, 19, 259nn. 32, 36; *Apotheosis (The Divinity of Christ)*, 34, 121,

Prudentius (continued)
257n. 5; and Augustan
themes, 28–29, 258n. 26;
Contra Orationem Symmachi,
184, 259n. 36, 270nn. 11–12,
281n. 12, 294n. 52, 297n. 28;
Crowns of Martyrdom, 175–76,
293nn. 46–50, 294nn. 51–52,
54–55, 57–58; *Psychomachia*,
25–31, 34, 43, 45, 48–49, 51–
52, 54, 69, 171, 193, 257n. 9,
258nn. 10–11, 14, 19, 26, 28–
31, 259nn. 32–33, 263n. 41,
264nn. 45, 48, 266n. 94,
292nn. 29; and Theodosius,
25, 31, 34, 257n. 8, 259nn.
36–38
Pseudo-Methodius, 121, 126,
128, 282n. 14

Quellinus, Erasmus, *Philip-
Apollo*, 242, 243
Querini family, 294n. 58

Raphael (Raffaello Sanzio), *Fire
in the Borgo*, 126
Regensburg, battle of, 186
Regnum Apollonis, 229–31
Remi, 158, 185–86
Remus, 66, 175
Res Gestae, 21
Ripa, Cesare, 287n. 16
Riti, Biagio, *Poemi Scritti in Lode
de la Sacra Real Fabrica de lo Escuriale*, 162
Romano, Giulio, *Fall of the Giants*, 116, *117*
Romanov, house of, 252
Rome, 36, 41, 45–46, 59, 75–
76, 81, 93, 113, 119, 249–50;
ancestry for Christian monarchs, 67–71, 75–76, 82, 87–
90, 92–93, 97–98, 100, 103,
107, 113, 116–18, 137, 143,
163, 171; under Augustus,
19, 21–22, 28, 119; Christian
historic destiny, 31, 34–35,
69, 171, 254n. 8, 257n. 3,
259n. 36, 260n. 48, 270nn.
11–12, 276n. 112, 277n. 134,
286n. 4, 281nn. 1, 2, 6, 9, 12,
283n. 36, 285n. 28, 286n. 4,
294nn. 51, 53; Christianity as
state religion, 23–34, 120–
21, 162, 183–84, 204, 231;
under Constantine, 31–34,
37; imperial ideology, 2, 13–
14, 19, 21, 60; laws, 93, 233,

276n. 115; medieval and renaissance views of, 53–55,
60, 66, 73; motifs in the Escorial, 170–71, 174–76, 178;
myths and legends of, 1, 11,
56, 66; as New Jerusalem, 30;
as New Troy, 6, 13–14, 16,
18, 21, 54, 227; as papal seat,
4, 39, 41, 126; prophecy of
future greatness, 13–16, 68–
69, 81, 93, 254n. 8; restoration of empire, 119–22, 126–
27; sacked by Charles V, 128;
sun god myths, 225, 227–31;
Trojan past, 1–2, 6, 11, 13–
19, 21, 48–49, 53–55, 60, 76,
93, 149
Romulus, 13–14, 66, 69, 71,
175–76, 259n. 32, 262n. 27,
271n. 22
Romulus Augustus, 36
Rubens, Peter Paul: *Eucharistic
Saints*, 220, 221; *The Triumph of
the Eucharist over Pagan Sacrifice*,
218, 219; *The Victory of Eucharistic Truth over Heresy*, 218, 219
Rudolf I, Emperor, 98–100,
124, 158, 183, 188, 202, 206,
215, 218, 246, 277n. 135; Eucharistic miracle, 208, 222,
301nn. 5–6, 8–9; Hebrew
and Roman heritages, 100; as
New Asser, 208, 301n. 8,
305n. 55; Vision of the
Cross, 190, 204, 296nn. 17–
19, 300n. 58
*Rudolf Leads the Priest Bearing the
Eucharist*, 208, 209
Rudolf and the Scepter of the Cross,
188, 190
Rudolf II, Emperor, 309n. 61
Rufinus, 45, 265n. 54
Ruscelli, Girolamo, 223, 225

Saint Quentin, battle of, 142,
162
Salian dynasty, 84, 91, 122
Samburgensis, Mattheus
Hacus, 235
Samuel, 37, 118
Sanudo, Marino, 101
Saracens, 186, 188
Sarcophagus of Junius Bassus, 195,
195
Saturn, 14–15, 24, 32, 48–98
passim, 103, 148, 223, 254–56
Saturn, *94*, 97–98

Saul, 78
Saxons, 78, 82–85, 89, 91, 122
Schaufelein, Hans, *Triumphal
Chariot of Charles V*, 233, *234*,
235
Schedel, Hartmann, 73
Scipio, 14, 116
Scribonia, 256
Second Coming, 24, 29–31, 34,
90, 120–21, 123–24, 150–52,
171, 181–82
Sedulius Scotus, 81
Seifried, Ioanne, *Arbor Aniciana*,
193, 195, 198
Sem, 179, 198, 243
Servius, 286n. 7, 306nn. 12–13,
24, 307n. 30
Servius Tullius, 137, 229
Seven Virtues tapestry, 60
Shakespeare, William, 268n. 12
Sheba, 168
Sibylline Oracles, 119–22, 128,
228–29, 243, 281n. 8
Sicamber, 73, 85, 158
Siege of Jerusalem by Titus, 58, *58*
Sigismund, Emperor, 98, 283n.
32, 287n. 18
Sigüenza, Father José, 162, 165,
167, 169–70, 215, 217, 245,
310n. 87
Silvestris, Bernard, 264n. 51,
265n. 55, 266n. 87
Silvius Tullus, 14, 66
Simon of Cyrene, 191
Sixto, Francisco, 158, 198, 217
Solomon, 30, 49, 78, 81, 83,
127–55 passim, 163–71, 181,
215, 244, 285n. 9, 291nn. 14,
21, 292nn. 23, 35, 303nn. 36–
37
Southern Cross, 206, 300nn.
60–61, 301n. 62
Spain, 178–79, 182, 197, 202,
207, 284n. 50, 285n. 28,
294n. 59, 299n. 47
Spenser, Edmund: *The Faerie
Queene*, 237
Stabius, Johann, 103, 278–79
Stilicho, 264nn. 52, 54
Strasoldo, Giovanni, 174, 206,
300n. 60
Strigel, Bernard, *Calvary Altar-
piece*, *189*, 191
Suetonius, 41, 174, 282n. 21,
307nn. 27–28
Suleiman the Magnificent, 5
Sulla, Lucius Cornelius, 47

Sun King. *See* Apollo
Sylvester, 38, 185
Symmachi family, 193

Tacitus, Cornelius, 72–73, 88, 271n. 29, 274n. 91, 278n. 151
Tau, 197
Telephorus, 283
Telesio, Bernardino, 243, 309n. 61
Tellus, 195
Teophane, 82
Tertullian, 120
Terzi, Francisco, 236
Teucer, 13
Theodolf, 266n. 94
Theodoric the Great, 36, 261n. 2
Theodosius, 25, 31, 34, 49, 69, 78, 81–82, 120, 176, 178, 184, 218, 259n. 36, 262n. 21, 270n. 7, 281n. 11, 295n. 4, 297n. 28, 305n. 50
Theodulf, 266
Three Baptisms: Christ, Constantine, and Clovis, 38, *39* 186
Throne of Grace, 211, *211*
Tibaldi, Pellegrino, 294n. 58, 310n. 87
Tiberius, 269n. 3
Tiburtine Sibyl, 33, 54, 121
Tiepolo, Giovanni Battista, 141; *Triumph of Spain*, 239–40
Tiphys, 18, 148, 157
Titian (Tiziano Vecelli), 145; *Allegory of Lepanto*, *216*, 217; *Charles V at Muhlberg*, 113, *114*, 128, 217; *Gloria*, 128, *129*, 130, 135, 284n. 60, 285n. 11; *Saint Lawrence*, 176, *177*, 178
Titus, 6, 24–25, 56, 58, 134, 149, 255n. 35, 257n. 6, 296n. 14, 306n. 7
Titus Returns to Rome in Triumph with the Jewish Temple Spoils, 24–25, *25*
Tobias, 47
Toledo, Juan Bautista de, 290n. 3, 291n. 12
Tournai, 276n. 107
Trajan, 118
Tree of Jesse, 78, *79*, 80, 100, 273n. 53
Trent, council of, 179
Trezzo, Jacopo da, *Sic Erat in Fatis*, 162, *163*
Tribeta, 89
Tridentine Council, 207

Trier (Trèves), 82, 89, 171, 230
Trissino, Giangiorgio, *Italia Liberata dai Goti*, 118, 281n. 187
Triumph of the Church Militans, 202
Trojan War, 91, 92
Tros, 255
Troy, 9, 45–46, 119, 193, 249–50; ancestry for Christian monarchs, 67–73, 75–77, 80, 83, 85, 88–89, 91–93, 97–98, 100–17 passim, 137–49 passim, 171, 198, 202, 267n. 10, 270n. 15, 271nn. 19–20, 24, 26, 272nn. 39, 43, 45, 274nn. 78, 84, 93, 275nn. 95, 97, 105, 106; destruction by Argonauts, 6, 17, 53, 55, 148, 227; destruction by Greeks, 6, 11, 13, 16–18, 53, 89, 120–21, 148; as Frankish settlement, 72–73, 76, 89, 97; myths and legends of, 1, 6, 19, 31, 51–60, 66, 122, 145, 149–50, 176, 178, 267nn. 2–6, 268nn. 12, 23, 272nn. 41, 43; as Roman past, 1–2, 6, 11, 13–19, 21, 48–49, 53–55, 60; Rome as New Troy, 6, 13–14, 16, 21, 54, 60, 119, 148, 193, 195; sun god myths, 225, 227
Tudor, house of, 139, 141–42
Tuisco, 72–73, 88, 115
Tunis, battle of, 118, 191
Turks, 5, 7–9, 57, 90, 118–38 passim, 141–42, 145, 150–58 passim, 179, 181, 191, 204–36 passim, 243
Turnus, 15–16, 25–26, 107, 255n. 27, 256n. 57, 258n. 11, 258n. 15, 278n. 152
Turpin, 264
Twin Towered Domus Anicia, 198, *200*
Typhis, 46

Ulysses, 11, 46, *55*, 254
Universal Chronicle, 33, 54, 76, 85, 89, 267nn. 5–7, 272n. 40, 274n. 92, 275n. 97
Universal Monarch, 109, 113, 155, 197–98, 233, 235
Urban IV, 215
Urban VIII, 301n. 6

Valdesius, Jacobus, *Prerogative Hispaniae*, 197
Valerius Flaccus, Gaius, *Argonautica*, 17–18, 24–25, 56, 58,

253, 255, 256n. 40, 257n. 6, 286nn. 3–4
Valois, house of, 142–43, 237
Varosino, Giovanni, 237
Vatican Virgil, 11, 12, 13, 41–42, 227, 306n. 15
Venus, 13, 15, 21, 55, 255
Vergil, 113, 266n. 94, 276nn. 112, 120, 286n. 7, 287n. 8; *Aeneid*, 1, 6, 11, 13–17, 19, 21–23, 25–26, 28, 30–31, 34, 41–42, 45–46, 48, 51–52, 55, 58, 60, 68–69, 71, 81, 93, 109, 137, 157, 193, 204, 227; *Fourth Eclogue*, 6–7, 18–19, 21, 24, 32, 90, 92–93, 137, 148, 152, 159, 222–23, 225, 227, 229, 231, 250, 255n. 28, 256n. 48, 259n. 41, 273nn. 63–64, 279n. 167, 286n. 7, 287n. 10, 294n. 51; *Georgics*, 230
Veritas Filia Temporis, 141, 218, 285n. 22
Vernulaeus, 202
Vespasian, 134, 255n. 35, 257n. 6
Vesta, 68, 176, 178, 254n. 10, 256n. 51, 257n. 59, 269n. 5, 298n. 32
Vijd, Jodocus, 153
Villalpando, Juan Bautista, 170, 172
Virtues, 25, 31, 266nn. 85, 90, 92, 95, 269n. 27, 301n. 61; as components of Christ, 45; as components of the ruler, 48–51, 60, 61, 259n. 38, 264n. 48, 274n. 83; Roman state, as symbols of, 26–27, 264n. 48; as soldiers, 25–29, 264nn. 48–49; syncretistic ancestry, 27, 29; and Trojan legend, 25–27, 29–31. *See also* Prudentius, *Psychomachia*
Virtues Build the Heavenly Jerusalem, 30, *30*
Virtues Triumphant, 49, *50*
Vittorino, 191, 193
Vivian Bible, 42

West/East imperial supremacy, 6, 11, 16, 18, 42, 45, 178, 297n. 23, 298n. 36. *See also* Four World Monarchies
Wierix, Ian, Reconstruction of Solomon's Temple, 167, *168*
Wion, Arnoldo: *Lignum Vitae*, 193, *194*, 198